Fugitives from Justice

Sergeant J.B. Gillett, Texas Ranger in 1879.
Photo from 1921 edition of *Six Years with the Texas Rangers*.

Fugitives from Justice

The Notebook of Texas Ranger Sergeant James B. Gillett

introduction by
Michael D. Morrison

STATE HOUSE PRESS
Austin, Texas
1997

Library of Congress Cataloging-in-Publication Data

Gillett, James B., 1856-1937.
Fugitives from justice / the notebook of Texas Ranger
Sergeant James B. Gillett ; with an introduction by
Michael D. Morrison.
p. cm.
Includes index.
ISBN 1-880510-37-5 (alk. paper)
ISBN 1-880510-39-1 (deluxe ed. alk. paper)
ISBN 10880510-38-3 (pbk. : alk. paper)
1. Fugitives from justice—Texas—Directories.
2. Criminals—Texas—Biography.
I. Title

HV6786.G55 1996
364.1'025'764—dc20   95-40117

Printed in the United States of America

cover design by David Timmons

STATE HOUSE PRESS
P.O. Box 15247
Austin, Texas 78761

Table of Contents

Foreword   vii

List of Fugitives from Justice
   Alphabetical listing by county   3-153
   Counties not in alphabetical order:
      Bee   153
      Bowie   154
      Brazos   156
      Eastland   159
      Grayson   160
      Kimble   162
      Mason   162
      Raines   162
      San Augustine   164
      San Patricio   165
      Shackelford   167
      Travis   168
   Rewards Offered by the Governor   173-179
   Index to *List of Fugitives*   180-227

Gillett's Notebook   229
   Index to Gillett's Notebook   273

List of Illustrations
   Gillett on horseback in 1879   frontispiece
   Gillett's rifles   xi
   Gillett's belt knife   xii
   Gold Marshal's badge presented in 1882   228
   Gillett in 1925   230
   Miscellany found in the Notebook:
      Wanted poster, James F. Collins   264
      Railroad pass   265
      Calling cards   266
      Wanted and Reward announcements   267-271
      Telegram, Clay Drye wanted notice   272

Foreword

The citizens of Texas and Waco will celebrate two remarkable anniversaries in 1998 — the 175th anniversary of the creation of the Texas Rangers and the 30th anniversary of the Texas Ranger Hall of Fame and Museum. In anticipation of these events, the people of Waco and State House Press are pleased to make available this reprint of the copy of the rare 1878 *List of Fugitives from Justice* that once belonged to frontier Texas Ranger James B. Gillett.

The Texas Rangers are the oldest state law enforcement agency in the nation, existing before the state of Texas or even the Republic of Texas. Stephen F. Austin could not have imagined that the ten man "ranging company" he created in 1823 would evolve into one of the best known law enforcement agencies in the world — or that its history would span nearly two centuries.

The first ragtag companies of Texas Rangers guarded settlements in the Mexican province of Tejas from Indian attack. Rangers died at the Alamo defending the freedom and rights of Anglo and Hispanic settlers after dictator Santa Anna set aside the Mexican constitution. In the 1870s and 1880s they brought law to the roughest frontier settlements. During the Roaring Twenties they patrolled early oil field boom towns and fought bootleggers. The Great Depression saw them hunting down criminals like Bonnie and Clyde. Modern Rangers now perform duties unheard of a century ago, such as investigating white collar crime and waging a high tech war on drugs. However, like their predecessors, they continue to pursue cattle thieves, rescue kidnap victims, and hunt murderers. Like the Rangers who fought at the Alamo, some have given their lives in performance of their duty. Whether employing horse and saddle or laptop computer, the men and women who serve as Texas Rangers are living symbols of the heritage of Texas and the ideals of Texans. Popular television programs, PBS documentaries and novels are testimony to the enduring legend of the Texas Rangers.

Since 1968, the City of Waco has honored this heritage and service by supporting an educational institution dedicated to this unique law enforcement organization — the Texas Ranger Hall of Fame and Museum. Its mission is to tell the story of the Texas Rangers and to serve as the principal repository for Texas Ranger memorabilia and archives. As the institution approaches the 30th anniversary of its founding, the Hall of Fame and Museum prepares for a third century of Texas Ranger history by planning new exhibits, educational programs and publications.

The publication of this book helps to preserve a fascinating era of frontier history, when Texas Rangers were the law in vast areas of Texas. This book came to the Texas Ranger Hall of Fame and Museum through the generosity and interest of Mr. J. K. Colquitt of San Angelo, Texas. In the spring of 1992, Colquitt approached former Hall of Fame Curator Tom Burks about a "Texas Rangers list of outlaws" in his possession. It had been the property of his grandfather, the well known 19th Century Texas Ranger James B. Gillett. The book was described as a small volume, bound in black leather, and containing pencil and ink notations in Gillett's own hand. Burks immediately recognized the importance of the book — a very early edition of the highly sought after "Black Book" of fugitives issued to Texas Rangers between the 1870s and 1900 that served as a blanket arrest warrant. He also knew the importance of James B. Gillett to Texas Ranger history. Mr. Colquitt hoped to find a home for the book in a public institution rather than a private collection. Negotiations were undertaken by the city administration of Waco through Curator Burks and the book was acquired for the Texas Ranger Hall of Fame and Museum. It is one of two known copies of the 1878 edition, the earliest edition now known to exist, but other editions are known to have been printed in 1882, 1889, an addendum in 1891, in 1896 and in 1900.

The story of its original owner is as interesting as the book. James Buchanan Gillett was born in Austin, Texas, in 1856. His father, James S. Gillett, had been a Quartermaster for the Texas Rangers and Adjutant General of Texas under Sam Houston. The young Gillett was undoubtedly raised on tales of the Texas Rangers.

James Gillett, the younger, enlisted as a Texas Ranger at age eighteen with Captain D.W. Roberts' company in Menard County. In August of 1875, the new recruit acquitted himself well in a running fight between the Rangers and a Lipan Apache raiding party on the South Concho River. In January of 1878 Corporal Gillett commanded a squad of Rangers in pursuit of murderer Dick Dublin, and after a prolonged scout the Rangers located his camp. Dublin ran into the brush as they approached but Gillett fired at and killed him. It was about this time that Gillett was issued his copy of the 1878 fugitive book.

In the summer of 1879 recently promoted Sergeant Gillett was transferred to George W. Baylor's company which was sent to El Paso County. Local peace officers had proven inadequate to cope with criminals who congregated along the border and a plea to the governor brought in the Rangers. The *List of Fugitives* undoubtedly went with Gillett to El Paso in his saddlebags. The Rangers "swept" the area questioning travelers, checking the "Black Book " for names and descriptions, and arresting wanted men.

In 1881 Gillett left the Ranger service for a short stint as a well paid express guard for the Santa Fe Railroad. Shortly thereafter he became City Marshal of El Paso and protected grateful residents until 1885. In later life he served other counties as sheriff, but eventually he became a rancher. He founded the famous 06 Ranch near Alpine, managed the huge Estado Land and Cattle Company, and finally moved to the 30,000 acre Barrel Spring Ranch where he was to live for the remainder of his life. He died at Marfa, Texas, in 1937.

Gillett chronicled his life in his autobiography *Six Years with the Texas Rangers* privately printed by Von Boeckmann-Jones

Company Publishers of Austin in 1921 and republished by Yale University Press in 1925. His copy of the *Fugitives List* was passed down to his daughter and then to his grandson Mr. Colquitt.

The 1878 *Fugitives List* contains several additional items of historical interest. Gillett inserted lined note pages with his descriptions of desperados such as Sam Bass and his gang. Interleaved between the pages were two of Gillett's calling cards and several postcard-sized circulars containing the names, descriptions and photographs of other wanted men.

Mr. Colquitt donated several other items when he delivered the book to the Texas Ranger Hall of Fame and Museum. One of the artifacts, almost equal to the book in importance, was a gold City Marshal's badge presented to Gillett by the grateful citizens of El Paso. It is internationally known as one of the premier examples of a frontier law enforcement badge and is described in the book *Triggernometry*.

Leafing through the pages of the *Fugitives List* we can understand not only how far law enforcement has come in the last century, but how many challenges remain the same.

For the Citizens of Waco
and the Texas Ranger Hall of Fame and Museum

Michael D. Morrison, Mayor
City of Waco, Texas

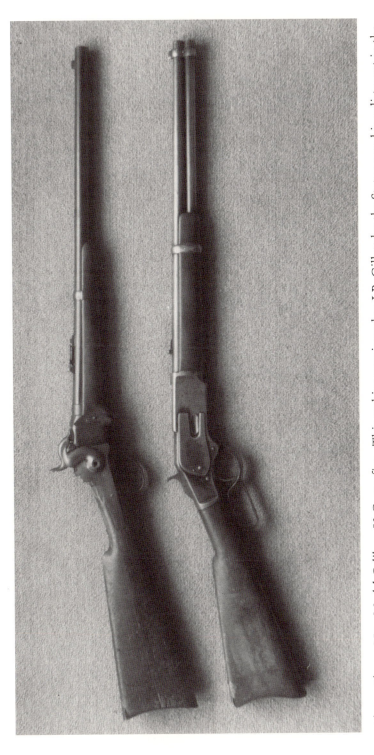

Above: Sharps New Model Caliber .50 Centerfire. This carbine was issued to J.B. Gillett by the State upon his enlistment in the Rangers on June 1, 1875. Below: Model 1873 Winchester Carbine bought by J.B. Gillett and used by him in many encounters with bandits, Apaches and raiders from Mexico. Gillett paid $40.00 for it—a month's pay. Photo courtesy of the Texas Ranger Hall of Fame and Museum.

J.B. Gillett's belt knife, made by Manhatten Cutlery Co., Sheffield. While Gillett's Ranger Company was cooperating with Joaquin Terrazas' force against Victorio's band of Apaches, a Mexican soldier stole it from him. Terrazas later sent it back to him with the message that "the thief wouldn't steal any more knives." Photo courtesy of the Texas Ranger Hall of Fame and Museum.

I.
List of Fugitives

A LIST

OF

FUGITIVES FROM JUSTICE

———————— ◆ ————————

ADJUTANT GENERAL'S OFFICE, STATE OF TEXAS,⎫
AUSTIN, January 1, 1878 ⎭

I CERTIFY that the following List of Fugitives from Justice is compiled from official record, received from the several counties, and now on file in my office.

WM. STEELE,

ADJUTANT GENERAL

Page 124

LIST OF FUGITIVES FROM JUSTICE.
1876 ——— 1876

FROM RECORDS IN THE ADJUTANT-GENERAL'S OFFICE

ATASCOSA COUNTY.

Lane, Samuel—Murder; committed December 3, 1868; indicted March 9, same year.

Garcer, Albert—Theft of a gelding; committed August 10, 1870 indicted November 22, same year. Dark, heavy set Mexican, about forty years of age.

Rosas, Santiago—Theft of an ox, value $20; committed July 10, 1870 indicted November, same year. Mexican.

Cruz, Narcio—Theft of a horse, June 25, 1871; indicted September same year. Small dark Mexican.

Hernandez, Saferino—Theft of an ox, value $20; committed October 1, 1872; indicted January 8, 1873. Tolerably tall, dark Mexican.

Haskel, Allen—Bigamy; committed July 24, 1868, May 20, 1871; indicted January 9, 1873. Fair complexion; red hair, blue eyes; about 5 feet 6 inches, and about 45 years old.

Mancho, Santiago—Murder; committed May 5, 1873; indicted November 5, same year. Small, tolerably fair Mexican, about 30 or 35 year old.

Vasquez, Polonio—Theft of a hog; committed March 2, 1872; indicted September 5, same year.

Garza, Carpio, and Garza (whose Christian name is unknown)—Theft of a mare (two indictments); committed June 10, 1874; indicted July 8, same year.

Williams, Harry—Theft of a mare; committed January 5, 1874; indicted July 8, same year. Fair complexion, blue eyes, sandy hair; about 5 feet 10 or 11 inches high; about 40 years old.

Hampton, John—Assault with intent to murder (4 indictments); committed January 14, 1874; indicted July 12, same year. About 6 feet high, 25 or 30 years old, fair complexion, reddish or sandy hair.

Trevinio, Juan—Theft of a beef steer; committed January 9, 1874; indicted July 10, same year.

Stidham, Wm., jr.—Theft of neat cattle; committed May 15, 1874; indicted July 11, same year.

Rogers, Lewis; Houston, Jack; and Laymon (whose Christian name is unknown)—Theft of a hog; committed September 20, 1874; indicted September 24, same year.   Transient characters.

Vice, E. M., alias Major Vice—Murder; 20 years old, 6 feet high, slim, stoop shoulders, light complexion and hair, grey eyes, great boaster.

Slaughter John H.—Theft; indicted September 9, 1876; 32 years old, 5 feet 6 inches high, black hair and eyes, dark complexion.   Probably about Fort Concho.

Gatlin, James—Theft; indicted September 9, 1876; dark complexion, medium height, dark hair and eyes.

Goins, Reuben—Theft; indicted January, 1877; 32 years old, dark hair and eyes, dark sandy beard, 5 feet 8 inches high, part Indian.

Elgo, J. R., alias Ogle—Theft; indicted September 1877; 26 years old, 5 feet 11 inches high, light complexion and hair, parents live 8 miles above Waco.

James, J. T.—Swindling; 55 years old; 6 feet high, red face, sandy hair and beard, slightly grey, red eyes, talkative; about Fort Mason.

Lemon, Savino; and Achone, Pamphilio—Theft.

Ainsley, Wm.—Aiding prisoner to escape; stout built, red complexion, 5 feet 10 inches high.

Gomez, Abarista—Theft.

Cantoon, Ramon—Theft.

Schoonover, Frank.

Williams, Joe.

Scawts, August, and Taylor, James—Theft; indicted September, 1876.

Lopez, Dionicio—Theft of a gelding; committed May 5, 1875; indicted June 10, 1875.   Mexican.

Garcia, Luciano—Theft of neat cattle; committed May 5, 1875; indicted June 10, same year.   Mexican.

Shafer, Henry—Theft of timber, value $20; committed October 5, 1875; indicted October 13, same year.   Dark complexion, dark hair and black eyes, about 37 years of age, and about 5 feet 9 inches high, is a German.

Reynolds, John—Theft from a house; committed September 3, 1875; indicted October 13, same year.   About 24 years old, fair complexion, gray eyes, about 5 feet ten inches high.

Domingo, Murro—Assault with intent to commit rape; committed July 15, 1875; indicted October 14, same year. Short, heavy Mexican, 35 years of age.

Garza, Refugio—Theft of a hog; committed December 21, 1875; indicted February 10, 1876.   Mexican.

Miller, Alsey—Theft of hogs; committed December 27, 1875; indicted February 10, 1876.

Alcorta, Severo—Assault with intent to murder; committed December 28, 1875; indicted February 10, 1876.

Martin, Gamboa—Theft of six head of cattle; committed February 1, 1876; indicted February 11, same year.

Martinez, Juan—Theft.

Cornet, Joe—Theft.

Fulton, Clay—Embezzlement.

Casinova, Santano—Theft; indicted September 17, 1877.

Fernandez, Casinova—Theft; indicted September 18, 1877.

Vager, Pedro—Attempt to kill; indicted September 18, 1877.

Coy, Cecilio Hernandez—Theft; indicted September 18, 1877.

Silvar, Antonio—Theft of cattle; indicted September 16, 1877.

Elgo, J. R.—Theft of hogs; indicted September 6, 1877.
Brown, John—Assault to kill; indicted September 8, 1877.
Orosco, Ramon—Theft of cattle; September 8, 1877.

ARANSAS COUNTY.

Wittington, John—Murder; committed September 21, 1869; indicted February, 1870.

Connelly, Michael—Theft; committed September 10, 1870; indicted October, 1870.

Spicer, C. C.—Murder; committed April 14, 1871; indicted May, 1871.

Murphy, Patrick—Theft; committed August 8, 1871; indicted February, 1872.

Marshal, Gabriel—Perjury; committed August 2, 1872; indicted October, 1872; colored, 6 feet high, 30 or 35 years of age.

Rowland, Monroe—Murder; committed July 28, 1873; indicted October, 1873; 23 years, spare built, dark complexion, 5 feet 10 inches, black hair.

Mason, Edward—Burglary; committed February 6, 1873; indicted October, same year; spare built, 5 feet 10, dark hair, 23 years.

McFarland, Scotty—Theft; committed September 28, 1874; indicted October, same year.

Weaver, Edward—Swindling; committed October 17, 1874; indicted February, 1875; spare built, 5 feet 10 inches, brown hair, 25 years.

Gleason, John—Assault with intent to kill and murder; committed June 13, 1875; indicted October, same year; stout built, light hair, 180 pounds, 35 years, florid complexion.

Humphries, Wm.—Theft and burglary; date not stated in the indictment; indicted February, 1876; negro, heavy built, stammers.

Thompson, Wm. (Bill)—Murder; June 1, 1868; indicted Oct., 1872.

BLANCO COUNTY.

Nichols, Geo.—Theft of cattle; indicted September 8, 1876; about 35 years old, 5 feet 9 inches high, heavy set, round built, auburn hair, florid complexion; supposed to be in Wilson or Atascosa county.

Ratliff, Wm.—Theft of hogs; indicted September, 1876; about 32 years of age, 5 feet 9 inches high, spare built, light hair, blue eyes.

Ratliff, James—Theft of cow; indicted September, 1876, 5 feet 6 inches high, will weigh about 158 pounds, light complexion, blue eyes.

Ratliff, Geo.—Theft of cattle; indicted September, 1876; rather heavy build, florid complexion, blue eyes.

Ratliff, Joseph—Theft of cattle; indicted September, 1876; is between 50 and 60 years of age, weighs 175 pounds, very broad shoulders, 5 feet 10 inches high, hair very gray, rather talkative, is the father of William, James and George Ratliff; all in Nueces county.

Headspeth, Wm.—Theft of mare; indicted March, 1877; about 5 feet 7 inches high, 26 years old, well made, round face, small brown eyes, hair brown; *gone to Black Hills.*

Ballard, Andrew J.—Theft of mule; indicted September, 1876; about 5 feet 10 inches in height, weighs about 160 pounds, dark complexion, dark hair, stands straight.

Gibson, Wm.—Theft of cattle; was convicted March, 1876; sentence 2 years in the penitentiary, escaped on way to penitentiary; about 20 years old, 5 feet 6 inches high, light complexion, hair inclined to curl, will weigh about 150 pounds; was in Coleman and adjoining counties when last heard from; is still in the cattle business.

Hoover, Wm.—Murder; was convicted of murder in the first degree in March, 1877, and punishment assessed at 99 years in the penitentiary; escaped before sentence. Is about 23 years old, 5 feet 8 inches high, heavy set, light gray eyes, with a nervous, wild expression, dark hair, wears little or no whiskers, will weigh about 160 pounds. Has a very ugly scar, perhaps a bullet wound, on the wrist of his left arm; was in Coleman county when last heard from.

Goff, Wm.—Theft of mare; indicted September, 1876, is about 32 years old, sallow complexion, dark hair and eyes, will weigh about 160 pounds.

Ruff, John—Theft of cattle; indicted October, 1874.

Bundick, Chas.—Theft of hogs; indicted September, 1876. About 5 feet 7 inches high, spare built, will weigh about 140 pounds, dark complected, black eyes, dark hair, usually wears moustache, is about 27 years old.

Tyner, Mart.—Assault with intent to murder; indicted March, 1877. About 25 years old, 5 feet 8 inches in height, light complexion, whiskers sandy, gray eyes, was convicted of theft in Bexar about June, 1877, and escaped from the penitentiary a short time after, is perhaps in Wilson county, has a father there.

Pope, Lem.—Theft of hogs; indicted September, 1877; negro, about 45 years old.

BOSQUE COUNTY.

Cox, Solomon—Murder; committed 1868; indicted 1875.

Fulkenson, Wm., and Jones, Jeff.—Murder; committed 1870; indicted 1875.

Wood, L. E.—Assault with intent to murder; committed 1875; indicted 1875.

Whittley, Jasper—Assault with intent to murder; committed 1875; indicted 1875.

Overstreet, W. P.—Murder; committed 1875; indicted 1875.

Howard, M. D.—Murder; committed 1873; indicted 1874.

Galbreath, M. H. (alias "Bud")—Murder; committed 1874; indicted 1874; about 23 or 25 years old; about 5 feet 7 or 8 inches high, weighs about 135 or 140, small feet, about number 5 or 6 shoe; light blue eyes, auburn hair, inclined to curl, small head, face and nose; hair grows down on the forehead near the eye brows.

Harvick, Nicholas (alias "Dock")—Murder; committed 1870; indicted 1870; is 5 feet 10 or 11 inches, spare made, 150 pounds, swarthy complexion, gray eyes, 40 years old, getting gray, upper lip sharp, one front tooth projects like a tusk: supposed to be in San Saba county. Went into a church house in this county, shot and killed an old man and his son, about five years old, on Sunday morning.

Brady, P. W.—Murder; committed 1875; indicted 1875; Irishman; about 5 feet 4 inches high, weighs about 130, blue eyes, between 40 and 50 years old, very gray, broad forehead, small nose, turns to one side, generally goes shaved smooth.

Slade, Sam.—Murder ; committed 1875 ; indicted 1875.

Heusen, Albert—Murder; committed 1874; indicted 1874; about 24 or 25 years old, light complexion, blue eyes, about 5 feet 8 inches high, slender, weight 140 or 145, thin visage.

Heusen, Henry—Murder; committed 1874; indicted 1874 ; about 23 or 25 years old, light complexion, blue eyes, 5 feet 8 inches high, slender, weight 135 or 140.

Foster, Wm.—Murder ; committed 1875 ; indicted 1875 ; supposed to be at Abbotts, in Jack or Young counties ; Abbott lives in the Keechie Valley. His father lives in Bosque county. Reward of $200.

McCurry, Richard—Theft ; committed 1875 ; indicted 1875 ; fair complexion, blue eyes (crossed), about 5 feet 7 inches high, weight about 140.

Kyrkendall, Jos.—Murder ; committed 1875 ; indicted 1875 ; light complexion, red hair, blue eyes, freckled face, Roman nose, about 5 feet 8 inches high ; supposed to range in Lamar county. and Indian Nation ; description given in proclamation. Reward of $200.

BURLESON COUNTY.

Allen, Noah—Murder ; indicted August, 1875.

Burton, ——— —Assault with intent to murder ; indicted April, 1871.

Brown, Harris—Theft of hogs ; indicted October, 1876 ; white, 20 years old, 5 feet 4 inches, dark complexion.

Cook, E. T.—Murder ; indicted December, 1872 ; a white man, nothing further known.

Collins, Monroe—Theft of cattle ; indicted October, 1876.

Franklin, Burrel—Theft of a hog ; indicted October, 1876 ; negro.

Gorman, John—Murder ; indicted December, 1872 ; white, lives in Coryell county, near Hamilton line.

Green, ——— —Theft ; indicted April, 1876 ; white, low, heavy set, dark, lives in Brazos county.

Hobbs, Joseph—Two charges, theft of a horse, two cases ; indicted April, 1873 ; boy, 18 or 20, light complexion, blue eyes, 5 feet 4 inches, lives in Wilson county.

Joiner, J. W.—Murder ; indicted September, 1869.

Jones, Carter—Theft of gelding ; indicted October, 1876.

Kay, George—Murder ; indicted December, 1870 ; 5 feet 8 or 9 inches, 33 or 34 years, light complexion, sandy hair, blue eyes.

King, Alfred—Murder ; indicted August, 1873 ; negro.

Knight, Clinton G.—Assault to murder ; indicted April, 1875 ; 6 feet, dark complexion, curly hair, blue or gray eyes. Last heard from at Texarkana, Bowie county, or Arkansas.

Lindsly, John—Assault to murder ; indicted October, 1868 ; supposed to be dead.

Logan, Matthew—Murder ; indicted March, 1869 ; lives in Milam county, near line of Falls.

Lackey, Hugh L.—Murder ; indicted August, 1873 ; low, heavy set, blue eyes, light hair.

Lewis, Morris—Theft of a mare ; indicted April, 1875.

May, Taylor—Theft of a beef steer ; indicted December, 1870 ; white, 5 feet 6 inches, dark complexion.

Mitchell, Benjamin—Arson and assault to murder, two cases ; indicted April and August, 1871 ; negro, supposed to be in Washington county,

Morgan, —— —Theft of yearling; indicted April, 1874.

Morgan, Thomas—Theft of gelding; indicted October, 1874; 5 feet 8 or 9 inches, weighs 175 pounds, black hair and eyes, Brown county.

McCulloch, Green—Theft of a cow, two cases; indicted April, 1875; white, supposed to live in Milam county.

Pucket, Richard T.—Murder; indicted December, 1873; white, 5 feet 6 inches, dark hair and eyes. In Williamson county, Circleville.

Pucket, Bud—Theft of gelding; indicted December, 1873; supposed to be in Bell or Williamson county.

Richardson, William—Assault to murder; indicted April, 1874.

Stevenson, Albert—Murder; indicted September, 1869; yellow negro, 35 years old, blue eyes, 5 feet 10 inches, thought to be on the Rio Grande river.

Scrofford, —— —Theft of yearling; indicted April, 1874.

Scott, Jack—Theft of yearling; indicted April 1874.

Salter, Geo. W.—Theft of a hog; indicted April, 1875.

Smith, alias Webb, Charles—Theft of two geldings; indicted December, 1875.

Stewart, Edmond—Burglary and theft; indicted April, 1876; negro, 6 feet high, thought to be in Grimes county.

Teaff, Jesse L.—Assault to murder, first charge; selling mortgaged property, second charge; indicted December 1870; 3 indictments, 6 feet high, light complexion, dark hair. In Bell county.

Tabor, William—Murder; indicted November, 1872; 5 feet 6 inches, light complexion, light hair, blue eyes, bald, 170 or 180 pounds.

Turney, Thomas—Murder; indicted August, 1873; 5 feet 6 inches, 25 years old, blue eyes, dark hair, red whiskers, Cooke county.

White, Thomas—Murder; indicted March, 1869; in Tennessee, at or near Nashville.

Woodruff, William—Theft; indicted December, 1870; white, 35 years, 5 feet 6 inches, dark complexion.

Wood, George—Murder; indicted December, 1870.

Walter, Judge—Murder; indicted December, 1870.

Willett, N. F.—Murder; indicted December, 1872.

Willett, E. T.—Murder; indicted December, 1872.

Wilson, Jerry—Theft of a hog; indicted October, 1876; negro, lives in Washington county.

Osteen, Ben.—Accessory to a felony; indicted March, 1877; white, 23 or 24 years of age, low, heavy set, black hair and eyes. In Williamson county, near Florence.

COLORADO COUNTY.

McDowell, James—Bigamy; about 5 feet 10 inches high, 32 years old, dark complexion, with black hair and eyes.

Lewis, Bill—Theft of a gelding; darkey, small and black.

Robinson, H. T.—Theft of a gelding.

Perry, Alonzo—Murder.

Sanders, Alexander—Theft of a mare.

Williams, D.—Theft of a gelding.

Jackson, John—Theft of two beef steers.

Abbott, James C.—Swindling; white.

Miller, Chancy—Theft of a gelding; darkey, 6 feet high, weighs 200 pounds, 28 years old, and badly pock-marked.

Brown, J. Wesley—Murder; darkey.

Williams, Ervin—Assault with intent to murder, 2 cases.

Bolin, Alick—Theft of cattle; darkey.

Faweet, Wm.—Burglary; mulatto.

Bloodgood, Martin—Swindling; white, 5 feet 9 inches high, spare made, weight 140 pounds.

Todd, John—Murder; darkey.

Holden, Henry—Theft of hogs; darkey.

Kalb, Allen—Theft of a cow; white, 6 feet high, 50 years old, weighs 150 pounds, spare built, black eyes, 2 cases.

Hill, Alick—Murder; darkey.

Graves, Henry—Theft of a colt.

McCoy, John—Theft of a mare.

Powell, E. N.—Theft of a work ox.

Kirk, John—Theft of a gelding; white, 6 feet 8 inches high, 27 years old, dark complexion, weighs 140 pounds.

Rhodes, Ennis—Theft of a bale of cotton ; darkey.

Beeman, A. L.—Embezzlement; white, 6 feet high, 28 years old, sandy whiskers, dark hair, and one cock-eye.

Adkins, Ed.—Murder ; darkey.

Harbert, John—Assault with intent to murder; yellow, 5 feet 8 inches high, 30 years old.

Banks, Charles—Theft of gelding; darkey.

Connor, Tom—Kidnapping; white.

Phule, H.—Theft of a note; German.

Escontreas, Peter—Theft of a horse ; Mexican.

Kyle, Bur—Theft of a heifer; darkey.

Stockman, Chas.—Theft of a cow ; white, red hair, 25 years old, 5 feet 10 inches high, heavy set.

Gray, Malcom—Assault with intent to kill and murder; 2 cases; white, 6 feet high, spare made, 30 years old, dark complexion.

Roly, James—Rape ; white.

Byars, Cass—Assault with intent to murder; white, 5 feet 11 inches high, 26 years old, spare made, dark complexion, very straight.

Buel, D. A.—Assault with intent to murder ; white, 30 years old, 5 feet 10 inches high, dark complexion.

Rola, James—Theft of two mules and ambulance; white.

Terrill, James—Swindling; white.

Williams, John, alias Gillmore—Theft of a jackass ; darkey.

Turner, Sim—Rape ; darkey.

Berry, John—Forgery; mulatto.

Butterworth, Walter—Theft of a cow.

Eafron, George—Assault with intent to murder.

Shoemake, Calvin—Theft of cows; white; 2 cases; 45 years old, 5 feet 10 inches high, weight 180 pounds, dark complexion.

Townsend, Beth—Theft of cows ; white, 5 feet 10 inches high, 30 years old.

Howard, B. A.—False swearing.

Crane, L. P.—Seriously threatening to take the life of a human being ; white.

Reed, Luke—Theft of property over the value of $20; black, 45 years old, 5 feet 8 inches high.

Smothers, Henry—Seriously threatening to take the life of a human being ; darkey ; 2 cases.

Rivers, Harry—Theft of two geldings; white, fine looking and sharp.
Foster, Adam—Theft of a mare.
Boil, Chas.—Burglary; white.
Schmidt, John—Theft of property over the value of $20; white.
Reese, Sam—Theft of property under the value of $20.

CALDWELL COUNTY.

Mackey, Jack—Theft from a house; committed January 28, 1875; indicted September 13, same year; negro, 5 feet 8 or 9 inches high, weighs 170 pounds, 40 years old.
Hunt, Roan—Assault with intent to murder; committed July 10, 1875; indicted September 13, same year; negro.
Strickland, Jos. W.—Theft from a house; committed January 1, 1875; indicted September 13, same year; is 5 feet 10 inches high, weighs 135 pounds, 30 years old, florid complexion; is near Columbus.
Wilson, Wm.—Assault with intent to murder; committed June 1, 1875; indicted September 15, same year; white.
Butler, Gabe—Murder; committed September 25, 1875; indicted January 12, 1876; dark complexion, 6 feet high, 28 years old, spare built; is in Alabama.
Patrick, Andrew—Murder; committed September 25, 1875; indicted January 12, 1876; mulatto, 5 feet 9 inches high, 23 years old, scar across one cheek.
Green, —— ——Murder; committed September 25, 1875; indicted January 12, 1876; white.
Taylor, Balsel—Theft from a house; committed October 5, 1875; indicted April 12, 1876; is 5 feet 9 inches high, weighs 150 pound, 25 years old.
Lot, Jack—Theft of neat cattle; committed April 10, 1876; indicted April 14, same year; three indictments filed same day; white.
Mitchell, Jack, alias Jack Mathews—Theft from a heuse; committed April 1, 1876; indicted April 15, same year; negro.
Barrington, Manly—Theft of hogs; committed February 1, 1876; indicted April 15, same year; is 5 feet 8 inches high, weighs 125 pounds, 37 years old, red hair.
West, Augustus—Threat to seriously injure a human being; committed August 7, 1875; indicted April 15, 1876.
Whitley, Henderson—Threat to seriously injure a human being; committed August 7, 1875; indicted April 15, 1876.
Malone, Geo.—Threat to seriously injure a human being; committed August 7, 1875; indicted April 15, 1876.
Hall, John W.—Assault with intent to murder; committed October 30, 1874; indicted April 15, 1876; is 6 feet high, weighs 150 pounds, 50 years old; is in Nevada or California.
Kinsey, Noah—Murder; committed December 5, 1873; indicted January 10, 1874; white.
Burns, Cook—Theft of neat cattle; committed August 4, 1873; indicted January 10, 1874; white.
Person, Rolan—Theft of hogs; committed January 19, 1873; indicted January 10, 1874; is black, 5 feet 9 inches in height, weighs 150 pounds, 35 years old, pigeon-toed, almost identical in appearance with Henry Elmore.

McGee, Robert—Assault to kill; June 23, 1876; indicted October 2, 1876; white, 35 years old, 5 feet 11 inches, slender, fair complexion.

Haynes, Alvin—Theft of neat cattle; committed December 16, 1873; indicted January 10, 1874; white, 5 feet 10 inches high, weighs 165 pounds, is 35 years old.

Tucker, Sim—Murder; committed May 10, 1873; indicted January 15, 1874; mulatto, 5 feet 11 inches high, weighs 175 pounds, 45 years old, convicted and escaped from jail.

Elmore, Henry—Murder; committed May 10, 1873; indicted January 15, 1874; black, 5 feet 9 inches high, weighs 150 pounds, 35 years old, prominent front teeth; said to be in Austin; convicted and escaped from jail.

Priest, Dock—Theft of a hog; committed April 30, 1873; indicted January 15, 1874; white, 6 feet high, weighs 140 pounds, 40 years old.

Vaughan, William—Theft of neat cattle; committed August 10, 1873; indicted January 15, 1874; white.

Jennings, Thomas—Murder; committed May 10, 1873; indicted April 18, 1874; white, 5 feet 9 inches high, weighs 160 pounds, 33 years old, dark complexion.

Priest, M. W.—Theft of a gelding; committed August 23, 1874; indicted September 14, same year; white, 6 feet high weighs 140 pounds, 40 years old.

Doran, Thomas—Theft of a gelding; committed August 23, 1874; indicted September 14, same year; white, 5 feet 10 inches high, weighs 160 pounds, 35 years old, light complexion.

Reed, James—Robbery; committed August 18, 1874; indicted September 19, 1874; Irish, 5 feet 7 inches high, weighs 150 pounds, 45 years old.

Tomlinson, Wm.—Theft of hogs; committed November 10, 1874; indicted January 9, 1875; white, 5 feet 10 inches high, weighs 145 or 150 pounds, 55 years old, gray head and bread, runs from DeWitt county to Live Oak county.

Ingram, Thomas—Assault with intent to murder; committed December 10, 1874; indicted Junaury 9, 1875; white.

Washington, Frank—Assault with intent to murder; committed September 29, 1874; indicted January 9, 1875; black, 6 feet high, weighs 175 pounds, 21 years old.

Gatewood, P. M.—Theft of neat cattle; committed December 5, 1874; indicted January 12, 1875; white, 6 feet high, weighs 165 pounds, 35 years old.

Johnson, James—Murder; committed April 5, 1875; indicted April 17, 1875; white, 5 feet 10 inches high, weighs 150 pounds, 55 years old.

Foley, Patrick H.—Assault with intent to murder; committed February 17, 1875; indicted April 17, same year; Irish, 6 feet high, weighs 175 pounds, 35 years old, blue eyes, fair complexion, light hair and whiskers; supposed to be about Houston or Galveston.

Hynes, Jube—Theft from a house; committed December 23, 1874; indicted April 17, 1875; black, 5 feet 8 inches high, weighs 150 pounds, 55 years old.

Edwards, Allen—Theft from a house; committed February 24, 1875; indicted April 17, same year; black, 5 feet high, weigh 90 pounds, 15 years old.

Hisaw, Green—Theft of hogs; committed December 10, 1874; indicted April 17, 1875; black, six feet high, weighs 150 pounds, 40 years old, scars on his breast, bald on top of his head; supposed near Columbus.

Burleson, Ike—Theft of a gelding; committed April 4, 1875; indicted April 17, same year; negro, 5 feet 6 inches high, weighs 135 pounds, 21 years old, on Colorado below Bastrop.

Bishop, Thos.—Theft of 3000 rails; committed January 1, 1875; indicted April 20, same year; white, 5 feet 10 inches high, weighs 150 pounds, 38 years old.

Harris, Jim—Theft of a gelding; committed June 25, 1875; indicted September 9, same year.

Hodge, Ben—Theft from a house; committed August 2, 1875; indicted September 9, same year.

Bateman, Bell—Murder; committed May 10, 1867; indicted June 4, 1867; 6 feet high, weighs 130 pounds, 35 years old, spare built, fair skin, reported killed.

Blalock, Thaddeus—Murder; committed March 10, 1867; indicted June 4, same year, 6 feet high, weighs 150 pounds, 40 years old.

Currier, Richard—Murder; committed May 10, 1876; indicted June 4; same year.

Sullivan, James M.—Murder; committed May 10, 1865; indicted May 27, same year; 5 feet 6 inches high, weighs 140 pounds, 33 years old, red complexion, red hair and beard, supposed to live in San Augustine or Nacogdoches county.

Quatlebum, Jas.—Theft of cattle; committed October 15, 1875; indicted January 11, 1876; white.

Montgomery, Lucinda—Murder; committed May 1, 1868; indicted June 1, same year; black.

Henson, Adam—Murder; committed November 5, 1868; indicted December 5, 1868; 5 feet 6 inches high, weighs 165 pounds, 30 years old; white.

McKean, Joseph—Murder; committed February 24, 1869; indicted April 30, same year; is 5 feet 7 inches high, weighs 120 pounds, about 40 years old, blue eyes, light hair, face badly powder-burnt, was confined in Lunatic Asylum; white.

Ridout, Horace—Murder; committed November 7, 1868; indicted December 8, 1869; is 6 feet high, weighs 175 pounds, 30 years old, supposed to be in Alabama or Mississippi.

Kirksey, Peter—Murder; committed May 28, 1870; indicted June 3, same year; is black, 6 feet high.

Moore, Coley—Theft from a house; committed October 1, 1869; indicted June 3, 1870.

Whitington, John—Theft of a colt; committed July 1, 1870; indicted December 29, same year; 3 indictments; reported hung at Fort Gibson.

Schoonover, Isaac—Theft from a house; committed April 18, 1871; indicted same day; is 6 feet high, weighs 150 pounds, 50 years old, lives in the neighborhood of Fort Mason.

Randle, Henry—Assault with intent to murder; committed July 20, 1871; indicted August 22, same year; white.

Howard, Ben—Theft of neat cattle; committed December 25, 1870; indicted August 24, 1871; negro, short, heavy set; reported dead, 5 feet 10 inches high, 45 years.

Whitis, Rhodes—Theft of neat cattle; committed August 8, 1871; indicted August 24, same year; negro, spare built, 5 feet, 7 or 8 inches high, weighs 130 pounds, 23 years old.

West, Richard—Arson; committed August 28, 1871; indicted same day.

Holmes, Sci.—Theft from a house; committed September 15, 1871; indicted January 5, 1872.

Hart, Zan.—Theft of a mule; committed October 1, 1871; indicted January 6, 1872; light complexion, 5 feet 9 inches high, weighs 140 pounds, 30 years old; supposed to be in Chihuahua.

Smith, George—Theft of hogs; committed December 4, 1872; indicted January 8, 1873; light mulatto (nearly white), freckled, 5 feet 7 inches high, weighs 140 pounds, 22 years old; is on the Colorado river, in Fayette or Colorado county.

Harper, Granison—Theft of a mare; committed August 10, 1873; indicted January 6, 1874; copper-colored negro, 6 feet high, weighs 140 pounds, 21 years old; calls himself Jim Harper, and lives near Flatonia.

Ellis, James—Assault to kill; committed December 19, 1876; indicted October 7, 1877: white, 22 years old, 5 feet 9 inches.

Foreman, Thomas—Theft; committed February 13, 1877; indicted September 25, 1877; white, 25 years, medium height, dark hair.

Petty, Theodore—Theft of hogs; indicted September, 1875; forfeited bond September 28, 1877; old man, small, gray hair, probably in Mason or Llano.

CHAMBERS COUNTY.

Haywood, Chas.—Swindling; indicted January, 1872; 5 feet 10 inches high, bald-headed, light brown hair, light complexion, large prominent nose, gray eyes, 155 pounds, upper front teeth out, 45 years old, hails from Buffalo, N. Y.

Vosberg, Theodore—Swindling; indicted January, 1872; about 5 feet 4 inches, light complexion, gray eyes, light hair, heavy moustache, 33 years, put on a good deal of style in talking.

Church, Rollin—Swindling; indicted January, 1872; about 5 feet 8 inches, black hair and eyes, moustache and whiskers *a la Burnside*, 150 pounds, 45 years, generally elegantly dressed; last heard from in Waco.

Private reward of $50.00 offered for each.

COMAL COUNTY.

Lane, Jack...Murder; committed November 27, 1870; indicted January 18, 1871. Is about 25 years old, 5 feet 6 inches high, small stature, black hair.

Stein, John...Rape; committed August 5, 1872; indicted October 8, same year, 35 years old, slender build, German, moustache and beard.

Branch, Ike...Theft of mare; committed December 14, 1872; indicted February 5, 1873, negro.

Davis, Tom...Theft of gelding; committed October 15, 1872, indicted February 5, 1873, negro, 30 years old.

Harris, Lewis...Theft of oxen; committed March 15, 1872; indicted February 6, 1873.

Magoffin, John...Theft of mare; committed September 1, 1871; indicted February 6, 1873; yellow negro, 27 years old, medium size.

Darby, Harmon...Theft of mare; committed December 14, 1872; indicted February 6, 1873; negro.

Lee, Bill...Theft of mare; committed December 21, 1873; indicted February 5, 1874; negro, 25 years old, medium size.

Ramsey, Rave, and Harris, Anderson...Theft of neat cattle; committed October 15, 1875; indicted February 10, 1876; both young negroes.

Ramirez, Alex...Murder; committed September 10, 1875; indicted October 6, 1875; young Mexican, small size, light complexion.

Meyer, Paul...Theft of hogs; committed October 20, 1874; indicted September 20, 1877; German, 22 years old, medium size, small beard.

COMANCHE COUNTY.

Knowles, A. J...Assault with intent to kill and murder; committed January 12, 1871; indicted March 31, same year.

Hogue, George...Murder; committed April 6, 1872; indicted May 17, 1872.

Northcut, Wm....Murder; committed September 20, 1872; indicted November 15, same year; 22 years, 5 feet 10 inches, dark complexion, black eyes and hair.

Raddatz, Frank...Assault with intent to kill and murder; committed July 1, 1872; indicted November 15, same year; is 5 feet 10 inches high, spare made, thin visage, German extraction, about 25 years old.

Anderson, Felix....Assault with intent to kill and murder; committed January 1, 1872; indicted February 16, same year.

Wood, Wm....Assault with intent to kill and murder; committed May 23, 1871; indicted August 10, same year.

Barney, Wm. (alias Barney Williams)...Theft of a gelding; committed August 1, 1871; indicted November, 1873.

Mackey, A. J....Murder; committed April 27, 1874; indicted May 13, same year; is about 5 feet 8 inches high, spare made, rather light complexion, quick spoken, is known as Nat Makey.

Ward, Harmon....Murder; committed August 14, 1875; indicted October 30, same year.

Watkins, Joe...Theft from a dwelling house; committed July 31, 1875; indicted October 30, same year.

McAfee, Barney....Theft of one mare; committed April 10, 1875; indicted May 29, 1875; Irishman; about 45 or 50 years old, 5 feet 9 inches high.

Roch, Ed....Theft of cattle; committed August 23, 1877; indicted September 28, 1877; 28 or 30 years old, 5 feet 8 inches high, light complexion, light hair, blue eyes.

Redden, Wm....Robbery; committed January 10, 1876; indicted March 2, 1876.

Johnson, J. C....Theft of hogs; committed November 10, 1876; indicted April 20, 1876.

Story, C. W., and Dickison, Wm....Theft of two mares; committed August 1, 1876; indicted September 26, 1876.

Thompson, Charles...Assault with intent to kill and murder; committed July 26, 1876; indicted September 26, 1876; 20 years old, fair complexion, brown hair, about 5 feet 7 inches high.

Tyre, Neil...Assault with intent to kill and murder; committed July 26, 1876; indicted September 26, 1876, 23 years old, dark complexion, dark hair and eyes, 5 feet 7 inches high, face badly scarred by burn.

White, Shad...Theft of cattle; committed March 1, 1877; indicted March 30, 1877.

King, S. R...Aiding prisoner to escape; committed March 9, 1877; indicted March 30, 1877.

Huff, Branch...Assault with intent to kill and murder; committed September 8, 1877; indicted September 28, 1877.

Sharp, Richard...Burglary; committed April 10, 1877; indicted September 28, 1877.

Alsop, A. M...Assault with intent to rape; committed April 3, 1877; indicted September 28, 1877; about 5 feet 8 inches high, sandy complexion, 28 years old, blue eyes.

Bailey, D., and James...Murder; committed May 10, 1877; indicted September 28, 1877.

Mayfield, Harry...Theft of a gelding; committed May 15, 1877; indicted September 28, 1877.

CORYELL COUNTY.

Dublin, Richard...Murder; indicted April 1873; supposed to be in Kimble county. *Killed by James B. Gill*

Raby, James R...Charged with an attempt to kill and murder, and burglary and embezzlement; he is an ex-sheriff of this county, and left here with a large amount of tax money; is about 50 years old, red face, hair gray, well educated and of good address; indicted September, 1876.

Raby, Guy...Indicted September, 1876; same charges as above; he is about 21 years old, no beard, light complexion and hair, weighs about 150 pounds, large ears; is said to be on the clear fork of the Brazos with Oglesby's cattle herd; is son of J. R. Raby.

Williams, Marion...Theft of cattle; indicted January, 1874.

Hall, Andrew...Threatening to take life.

Hall, Frank...Aggravated assault.

Boyd, G. W...Murder.

Vines, Wm...Murder; indicted April, 1873.

Freeland, Isaac...Murder; indicted March, 1876.

Rooch, Daniel...Murder; indicted April, 1867.

Taylor, Geo. W...Assault with intent to murder; indicted March, 1869.

May, S...Theft of a gelding; indicted March, 1869.

Taylor, Geo. W...Murder; indicted April 3, 1869.

Simms, Dick...Theft of a cow; indicted April 3, 1869.

Jenkins, Wm...Murder; indicted October, 1869.

Jeffries, Wm...Robbery; indicted October, 1869.

Westfall, Samuel...Assault with intent to murder; indicted October, 1869.

Jeffries, Sam...Murder; indicted October, 1869.

Harris, Artemus...Murder; indicted October, 1869.

Bell, Wm., Scott Williams and Eli McGuire...Theft of a gelding; indicted July, 1871.

Bryant, John...Theft of $40 from a house; indicted July, 1871.

Watson, Dave R...Theft of a gelding.

Jenkins, N. A...Theft from a house: indicted July, 1871.

Wilson, Geo. I...Murder; indicted November, 1871.

Crow, Pinkney...Theft of a steer; indicted November, 1870.

McCallister, D. B.

Reeder, Ham...Theft of a steer; indicted April, 1872.

Riley, James...Theft of a mare; indicted October 31, 1872.

Oliver, A. D...Assault with intent to murder; indicted October 31, 1872.

Terry, James...Theft of a steer; indicted October 31, 1872.

Hamby, E. M., and Carodine, John...Swindling; indicted July, 1871.

Patterson, James...Assault with intent to murder; indicted January, 1872.

Williams, Frank, and Williams, Robert...Theft of a cow; indicted January, 1872.

Brown, Noah...Theft of cow; indicted January, 1874.

Fisher, King...Theft of a gelding; indicted October, 1872.

Autrey, Robert...Arson; indicted January, 1874.

Swanner, Joel...Theft from a house; indicted October, 1873.

Barney, Wm...Theft of a mare; indicted October, 1873.

Borders, J. G...Murder; indicted April, 1874.

Bass, Jordan...Assault with intent to murder; indicted April, 1874.

Gillam, Wm., and Lewis, Joel...Assault with intent to murder; indicted April, 1874.

Ross, E. H...Assault with intent to murder; indicted April, 1874.

Momkin, Peter...Assault with intent to murder; indicted January, 1874.

Woody, Wiley...Theft from a house, indicted January, 1873.

Thompson, Thomas...Theft of a cow; indicted January, 1874.

Pruitt, Wm., and Muckelroy, Ben...January term, 1874.

Ashlin, John, and Kelley, Abe...Theft of a bull; indicted October, 1874.

Bailey, D...Assault with intent to murder; indicted October, 1874.

Hill, Philip...Theft of a Winchester rifle, value of $30.00.

Hardwick, C. T...Theft of a mule; indicted October, 1875.

Henderson, H. A...Murder; indicted September, 1876.

Wilson, W. A...Assault with intent to murder; indicted September, 1877.

Taylor, John...Theft of a mare; indicted September, 1877.

Waters, Wm...Theft of a gelding; indicted September, 1877.

Balch, A. W...Assault with intent to murder; indicted September, 1877.

Cox, James...Assault with intent to murder; indicted March, 1877.

Shaver, B. F...Assault with intent to murder; indicted March, 1877.

Pope, Henry...Assault with intent to murder; indicted March, 1877.

McQuillen, C...Forgery; indicted March, 1877.

Manning, Wm...Assault with intent to murder; indicted March, 1877.

Pinkston, Thomas...Theft of cattle; indicted March 1877.

Montgomery, R. M...Theft of gelding; indicted March, 1877.

DEWITT COUNTY.

May, Henry B...Forgery; indicted August 13, 1876.

Beck, Webb...Theft of a gelding; indicted December 9, 1875; negro boy 17 or 18 years old, black, under medium size, supposed to be out west, escaped from jail.

Reyes, Damian...Murder; indicted December 13, 1875; Mexican, under medium size, about 25 years old, dark complexion, speaks English fluently, was raised in DeWitt county, is on the Rio Grande with a gang of desperadoes.

Demonett, Michael...Theft of a gelding; indicted April 10, 1876; is of French parentage, about 24 years old, dark complexion, medium height, last heard from was in Harris county.

Brossell, J. W...Threat to take human life; indicted April 11, 1876; is a physician, 5 feet 10 or 11 inches high, weighs 130 or 140 pounds, dark complexion, black hair and eyes, of gentlemanly appearance and address, about 30 years old, black moustache and beard.

Neal, Calloway...Theft of a mare; indicted April 11, 1876; mulatto.

Kerlicks, John...Murder; indicted February 4, 1874; was a youth when offense was committed, of Polish or German parentage, is supposed to be in Houston, as he has relatives there in the railroad office; 2 indictments.

Murray, York...Theft of a gelding; indicted September 27, 1871; negro.

Robinson, Witz...Assault to murder; indicted April 4, 1873; mulatto, medium size, slight stoop in shoulders, eyes large, was formerly owned by B. M. Odom, of the Raymond House, and is supposed to be in Austin.

Sanchez, Francisco...Theft of two geldings; indicteted December 4, 1872. Mexican.

Odom, Oliver...Assault to murder; indicted April 8, 1874.

Harris, Will...Assault to murder; indicted April 8, 1874; is about 30 years old, light complexion, medium size, light hair, blue or gray eyes.

Butler, Wm. H...Theft of a gelding; indicted April 9, 1874; is about 25 years old, black eyes and hair, dark complexion, tall and slender, is said to be in the Houston jail.

Stratton, Chas...Murder; indicted April 9, 1874; light hair and blue eyes, large mouth, small size, slender, 25 years old, lives in Matagorda or Brazoria county.

Steen, Peter...Theft of a gelding; indicted April 11, 1874.

Tuton, Oliver...Theft from a house; indicted August 10, 1874; light hair, blue or gray eye—one eye out—large mouth, medium size, looks down when spoken to, about 26 years old, has a forbidding countenance.

Day, Alf...Assault to murder; indicted August 15, 1874; is about 20 years old, light complexion, small size, no beard, looks like a youth, eyes very large, mouth large.

Horrett, Voll...Theft of mare; indicted December 9, 1874; red complexion, blue eyes, 23 years old, hair light, is a German, lived in Medina county, medium size.

Williams, G W...Assault to murder; indicted December 10, 1874; is about 23 years old, tall, of good address, eyes light gray or blue, hair light, is from Kentucky, last heard from was in Luling, carpenter by trade, is apt to be drinking.

Davis, Burrell...Rape; indicted April 9, 1875; negro, medium size, 30 years old, quick spoken, large eyes, has been convicted and sentenced to be hanged, escaped from jail, is very black.

Hollan, Jerry...Assault to murder, indicted April 10, 1875; is a mulatto.

Morrow, Aleck...Theft of a mare; indicted August 9, 1875; dark complexion, eyes and hair, 26 years old.

Roberts, Buck...Theft of mare; indicted August 10, 1875; is small, 22 years old, light complexion, blue eyes, slender.

Jackson, John...Theft of a gelding; indicted August 11, 1875; white.

Puffpower, Chas...Theft of a colt; indicted August 13, 1875; German.

Humphreys, Wm...Defacing brand; indicted December, 1876; 20 years old, white, under medium size, is out West, beyond San Antonio.

Milam, Chas., and Riley, Bob...Theft of goods and chattels; indicted December, 1876; both negroes.

Ferguson, Dock...Theft of mare; indicted December, 1876; medium size, dark complexion, black eyes, Roman nose, 35 years old.

Mills, Jesse...Theft of cow; indicted June, 1877; is a negro, medium size, 30 years old.

Sherral, Joe...Rape; indicted June, 1877; negro.

2

Wilkerson, Chas...Theft of gelding; indicted June, 1877; white.

Clifford, Wesley...Assault to murder; indicted June, 1877; mulatto, medium size, 30 years old, good looking and intelligent.

Cox, Joe...Burglary; indicted June, 1877; white, medium size, fair complexion; 30 years old, face scarred and disfigured from a burn or scald, eyes blue or gray.

ELLIS COUNTY.

Barnes, J. S...Theft of cattle; committed January, 1873; indicted September, 1873; large, heavy set, dark complexion, 25 or 30 years old.

Ainsworth, Levin...Murder; indictment in Dallas county; indicted September, 1873; 5 feet 10 or 11 inches high, slender, light hair, restless blue eyes, an incessant smoker.

Dickson, Ed...Assault to murder; committed October, 1873; indicted January, 1874; negro, about 6 feet high, about 27 years old, very black.

Turner, Isaiah...Theft of cattle; committed November, 1873; indicted January, 1874; very low, and heavy set, blue eyes, very close together and deeply set.

Henderson, Charles...Theft of cattle; committed April, 1874; indicted May, 1874; about 5 feet 9 inches high, light hair, one eye white, and a bad scar on one cheek, looks as if burnt, about 28 years old.

Henderson, J. A...Theft of cattle; committed April, 1874; indicted May, 1874; light hair and blue eyes, weighs about 165 pounds; these two are noted thieves.

Turner, Dick...Driving steer from range; committed July, 1872; indicted May, 1873; light hair and grey eyes (cock-eyed), about 26 years old, 5 feet 7 inches, weighs 140 pounds.

Estes, — ...Theft of cattle; committed May, 1875; indicted May, 1875; rather cuffy, square built, blue eyes, light hair, weighs 165 pounds.

Powers, L M...Theft of cattle; committed May, 1875; indicted May, 1875; about 6 feet 2 inches high, slender, raw-boned, blue eyes and light hair, about 33 or 34 years old.

Parker, Wesley...Theft of mare; committed August, 1874; indicted September, 1874; light complexion, blue eyes, about 5 feet 6 inches high, and weighs about 140.

Smith, Thomas...Theft; committed December, 1875; indicted January, 1876; negro, about 5 feet 11 inches high, weighs about 150 pounds, and about 25 years old; his hair grows down to his eyes.

Phelp, T. W...Assault to murder; committed December, 1875; indicted January, 1876; about 6 feet 2 inches high, weighs about 220 pounds, light sandy hair, red whiskers and blue eyes, and large white upper teeth, which he shows most of the time.

Gober, James...rescuing prisoner; committed May, 1875; indicted January, 1876; about 5 feet 7 inches high, grey eyes and grey hair, between 60 and 65 years old, smokes incessantly, and weighs about 160 or 180 pounds.

McKinley, L. L...Rescuing prisoner; committed May, 1875; indicted January, 1876; about 6 feet high, weighs about 180 pounds, black hair and black eyes, limps in his walk, and big-toe off of one foot.

Brandon, John...Rescuing prisoner; committed May, 1875; indicted January, 1876; about 40 years old, 5 feet 9 inches high, and dark complexion.

Weldon, John...Rescuing prisoner; committed May, 1875; indicted January, 1876; between 25 and 30 years old, weighs about 165 pounds, about 5 feet 10 inches high, black hair, fair skin, and blue eyes, rather large.

O'Connor, John...Perjury; committed June, 1874; indicted November, 1876; large Irishman, about 5 feet 11 inches high, weighs about 200 pounds, sandy hair, almost red, sandy moustache, blue eyes, about 40 years old.

Knowles, R. E...Theft of gelding; committed May 1875; indicted September, 1875; a large, light-haired, blue-eyed, sandy-whiskered Welchman, speaks rather broken, talks a good deal on Scripture.

Goode, Milton...Assault with intent to murder; committed August, 1875; indicted September, 1875; small man, with blue eyes, and light complexion.

Harrell, Wm...Forgery; committed June 1875; indicted September, 1875.

Herring, Owen...Assault with intent to murder; committed September, 1876; indicted November, 1876; about 5 feet 11 inches high, sandy moustache and blue eyes, weighs about 135, and about 28 years old.

Saunders, Charles...Theft of cattle; committed October, 1873; indicted January, 1874; about 5 feet 10 inches high, light hair and blue eyes, about 25 years old, and rather fair.

Page, H. H...Theft of mare; committed April, 1873; indicted September, 1873.

Wright, Thomas...Murder; committed October, 1871; indicted January, 1872; about 5 feet 10 inches high, broad shoulders and heavy-set, quick, restless gray eyes, red sandy hair, and coarse, heavy whiskers and moustache, supposed to be in Arkansas, on White river, ferrying.

Squires, Joseph...Theft of gelding; committed June, 1872; indicted September, 1872; light hair, gray eyes, was a boy when indicted.

Wright, Wiley, Jr...Murder; committed October, 1871; indicted May, 1872; slender and tall, about 6 feet and 2 inches high, blue eyes and light hair, and about 25 years old.

Page, W. H...Theft of mare; committed April, 1873; indicted September, 1873; a smooth face, light hair, blue eyes, very tall, 6 feet 2 or 3 inches, 26 or 27 years old.

Potts, Bill...Theft of gelding; committed April, 1872; indicted May, 1872.

Tam, Silas...Assault with intent to murder; committed October, 1865; indicted, December, 1865.

Hurst, W. H...Theft of cattle; committed October, 1865; indicted December, 1865.

Morrison, — ...Assault with intent to murder; committed October, 1865; indicted December, 1865.

Mills, Milford...Theft of cattle; committed October, 1865; indicted March, 1866.

Beaty, John...Theft of $40; committed January, 1866; indicted March, 1866.

Bushby, James...Theft of $40; committed January, 1866; indicted March, 1866.

Brown, Thomas...Theft of $25; committed October, 1865; indicted March, 1866.

Cross, A. J...Theft of cattle; committed June, 1866; indicted September, 1866.

Sims, Dan...Assault with intent to murder; committed February, 1877; indicted May, 1877; negro.

Morris, Wm...Theft of cattle; committed May, 1877; indicted May 1877.

Hodge, H. J...Assault with intent to murder; committed May, 1877 indicted May, 1877.

Hines, Ben...Theft of hog; committed April, 1877; indicted May 1877; large negro, black, very tall, and weighs about 200 pounds; is around Waco occasionally.

ERATH COUNTY.

Pew, Wade...Murder; committed August, 1875; indicted November, same year; negro.

Sneed, Elijah...Theft; committed April, 1875; indicted June, same year; about 30 years old, light complexion, tall, and slim built.

Tinsley, Homer...Assault to murder; committed December, 1874; indicted June, 1875; heavy built, 5 feet 9 or 10 inches high, dark curly hair, florid complexion weighs about 180 pounds, and is about 30 years old; supposed to be in Colorado.

Sisk, H...Taking into possession live stock with intent to defraud; committed May, 1875; indicted June, same year.

Foster, R...Taking into possession live stock with intent to defraud; committed May, 1875; indicted June, same year.

Lanford, A. M...Theft of hogs; committed December, 1874; indicted June, 1875; 40 years, heavy built, near sighted.

Leonard, Wm...Taking possession of live stock with intent to defraud; committed February, 1875; indicted June, same year; tall in person, and of very dark complexion; supposed to be in Eastern Texas; 45 years old.

Thornton, Batty...Murder; committed May, 1875; indicted June, same year; about 25 years old, 5 feet 7 or 8 inches high, light complexion, dark brown hair, blue eyes, and weighs about 140 pounds. In Mississippi.

Rodgers, John...Theft of mules; committed April, 1875; indicted June, same year; about 22 years old, and rather heavy built; likely be found at his father's house in Burnet county.

Duncan, W. B...Theft of cattle; committed February, 1875; indicted June, same year; heavy built, dark complexion, and about 50 years old; nearly always has a pipe in his mouth; supposed to be at Clarksville, Arkansas.

Gass, Sam, and Gass, Mary...Kidnapping; committed 1876; indicted December, same year; Sam Gass is about 31 years old, light complexion, sandy beard, weighs 140 pounds, spare built; Mary, his wife, 21 years, slim, and medium height.

White, Thos...Theft of horses; indicted June, 1875.

Hurrier, Joseph...Theft of a hog; committed December, 1874; indicted March, 1875; German. Resides in Dallas.

Cork, B. B...Theft of a hog; committed December, 1874; indicted March, 1875; Irishman. Resided in Dallas.

Jackson, W. R...Assault to murder; committed January, 1875; indicted March, same year; about 27 years old, and rather heavy built; lives in Fannin county.

Burnett, James...Assault to murder; committed January, 1875; indicted March, same year.

Middleton, John, Jr...Driving cattle not his own, with intent to defraud; committed June, 1874; indicted November, same year; about 35 years old, and of dark complexion; lived in Hood county.

Whitworth, E. R...Altering marks and brands with intent to defraud; committed March, 1873; indicted November, same year; tall, spare made, dark complexion, and black hair and eyes, 35 years old.

Stockton, Porter...Assault to murder; committed February, 1871; indicted April, same year; about 5 feet 8 inches high, weighs about 140 pounds, light complexion, light hair, sandy moustache, and 25 or 26 years old.

Armstrong, G. W...Assault to murder; indicted May, 1872.

Furguson, Nick...Assault to murder; indicted May, 1872.

Summerville, M. W...Murder; committed December, 1873; indicted February, 1874; near 6 feet high, dark complexion, black hair and eyes, and about 40 years old; supposed to be in Mississippi.

Hughes, Jos. H...Theft of one head of cattle; committed August, 1873, indicted November, same year.

Edwards, Joe ..Murder; committed September, 1872; indicted November, same year; about 6 feet high, about 36 years old, spare built, dark hair and complexion, and weighs about 140 or 150 pounds.

Woods, A. J...Theft of cow; committed December, 1870; indicted April, 1871.

Gibbs, John A...Murder; committed February, 1868; indicted April, 1871; about 5 five feet 10 inches high, dark complexion, about 50 years old, and weighs about 150 pounds.

Francis, James...Theft of cattle; committed August, 1873; indicted November, same year; about 5 feet 10 or 11 inches high, light complexion, light hair, about 35 years old, and weighs perhaps 150 pounds.

Powers, Asa...Theft of a cow; committed March, 1872; indicted May, same year; about 5 feet 10 inches high, light complexion and hair, perhaps 26 or 27 years old, and weighs probably 150 pounds; supposed to be in Colorado.

Coates, James...Theft of a cow; committed October, 1872; indicted November, same year.

Weston, John...Theft of an ox; committed September, 1872; indicted November, same year.

Fade, Willis...Theft of yearling; indicted November, 1872.

Salmon, George...Robbery, indicted May, 1872.

Elliott, J. M...Theft of a steer; indicted November, 1872.

Hill, Richard...Theft of cattle; indicted November, 1873.

McClusky, N. T...Incest; committed, 1876; indicted December, same year; near 60 years old; fled the county in company with his daughter, his paramour.

Wilson, G. W...Theft of horse; committed 1876; indicted December, same year; about 30 years old; fled to Kentucky, and has been demanded by our Governor.

Sagister, D. W...Kidnapping; committed 1876; indicted December, same year; about 36 years old, heavy build, light beard, 5 feet 9 inches high, weighs about 180 lbs; in southwestern part of the State.

Wright, A. L...Theft of cattle; committed 1876, indicted December, same year.

Ledbetter, Lewis...Indicted December, 1876.

Shelby, J. J...Murder; committed October, 1875; indicted December, same year; about 28 years old; heavy build, 5 feet 8 inches high, light complexion, blue eyes, weighs about 150 lbs.; very affable; went, likely, to Missouri.

Morrison, George...Assault with intent to murder; committed January, 1871; indicted May, same year; about 40 years old, sandy beard, 5 feet 10 inches high; in Colorado.

Isbell, John...Murder; committed November, 1875; indicted December, same year; about 26 years old.

Majors, Riley—Incest; committed 1876; indicted December, same year; about 45 years old, medium size, sandy beard.

Berry, Chas. P...Theft of hog; committed 1876; indicted July, same year; about 23 years old, 5 feet 7 inches high, dark hair, no beard; likely in Arkansas or the city of Dallas.

Adams, Frank, Laman, Dan, and Corley, John...Theft of cattle; committed 1876; indicted July, same year.

Beggers, Robert...Driving cattle from range with intent to defraud; committed 1874; indicted March, 1875; about 27 years old, heavy build, 6 feet 11 inches high, no beard, full face, weighs about 175 lbs.

Lasier, Jack...Assault with intent to murder; committed December, 1874; indicted February, 1875; about 6 feet high; 38 years old, spare build, red hair and beard, and a carpenter by trade.

FRANKLIN COUNTY.

Easley, Hardy H...Theft; committed September 25, 1876; indicted November 1876; about 28 years of age, 5 feet 10 inches high, fair complexion, light hair; supposed to be in Arkansas, near Texarkana.

Head, Lorenzo...Theft; committed September, 1876; indicted November, 1876.

Hall, Thomas...Accessory to murder; committed March 30, 1877; indicted November 2, 1877.

Frazier, James...Theft; committed September 30, 1877; indicted November 2, 1877; about 25 years old, 6 feet high.

Wade, Howard (colored)...Theft; committed August 15, 1876; indicted November 2, 1877; about 21 years old, six feet high.

FREESTONE COUNTY.

Brown, Elisha...Murder; indicted August 12, 1865; white.

Pierce, David...Murder; indicted March 7, 1867; white.

Maddox, James...Assault with intent to murder; indicted March 11, 1869.

Watley, Wat...Murder; indicted September 14, 1869; white.

Jones, James...Murder; indicted September 12, 1870; white.

Mayhor, John...Murder; indicted September 12, 1870; white.

Smith, S. S....Theft of cattle; indicted December 4, 1870; white.

Harris, John...Intent to murder; indicted December 21, 1870; white.

Fains, Thos. R...Selling mortgaged property; indicted December 13, 1870; white; in Walker county.

Bond, George...Intent to murder; indicted April 12, 1871; white.

Melton, John...Murder, indicted April 14, 1871; white.

Childers, Jas...Theft of cattle; indicted April 21, 1871; four indictments; in Van Zandt county.

Childers, Charles...Theft of cattle; indicted April 21, 1871; three indictments; in Van Zandt county.

Mitchell, Jack...Theft of a gelding; indicted August 13, 1872; white.

Furlow, Miles...Theft of a plow; indicted August 21, 1872; negro.

Weaver, Ezekiel...Murder; indicted August 21, 1872.

Weaver, Wesley...Murder; indicted August 21, 1872.

Adams, David...Intent to murder; indicted December 11, 1872; white.

Granbery, Oscar...Murder; indicted December 11, 1872; white; in Brown or Comanche county.

Johnson, R. C...Intent to murder; indicted December 17, 1872; white.

Dennis, Ludd...Theft of cattle; indicted December 17, 1872; white.

Williams, Spencer...Theft of a cow; indicted April 16, 1873; white.

Jackson, Daniel...Theft of a cow; indicted April 16, 1874; negro.

Pruitt, Geo...Intent to murder; indicted April 16, 1873; white.

Cunningham, Leige...Theft of cattle; indicted August, 1873; negro.

Shelton John...Theft of a cow; indicted August, 1873; white.

Thompson, E. J...Intent to murder; indicted December 10, 1873; white.

Moseley, W. J...Swindling; indicted December 12, 1873; white.

Canisse, James...Theft of a horse; indicted December 18, 1873; white.

Jackson, Seof...Theft of a mare; indicted December 18, 1873; is also indicted for intent to murder; negro.

Jackson, Geo...Theft of a gelding; indicted August 11, 1874; white; in Bandera county.

Jones, John...Theft of a plow; indicted August 15, 1874; negro.

Holder, Amos...Theft from a house; indicted August 15, 1874; negro.

Brown, Gabe...Attempt to commit rape; indicted August 1874; negro.

Abney, Jerry...Theft of hogs; indicted August 19, 1874; negro.

Steene, Phillips...Theft of hogs; indicted December 17, 1874; negro.

Walker, Bailey...Theft from a house; indicted December 17, 1874; negro.

Pricel, J. H...Perjury; indicted December 23, 1874; white; has a ranche on line of Boerne and Comanche counties.

Andings, Wm...Theft of cattle; indicted December 23, 1874; white.

Lindsey, George...Theft of cattle; indicted September 14, 1869; negro.

Pettet, J. W...Perjury; indicted April 10, 1875; white.

Graham, J. F...Murder; indicted April 18, 1875; white.

Burleson, M. P...Burning a house; indicted April 10, 1875; white.

Kalb, John...Theft of hogs; indicted April 10, 1875; white.

Bryan, Jerry...Theft of hogs; indicted August 11, 1875; three indictments; white.

Bryan, Reuben...Theft of hogs; indicted August 11, 1875; three indictments; white.

Oliver, Dun...Theft of cattle; indicted August 19, 1875; white.

Roan, Allen...Assault to rape; indicted August 23, 1875; white.

McElroy, J. J... Theft of cattle; indicted August 23, 1875; white.

Harper, Henry...Theft of a hog; indicted December 23, 1875; negro.

Miles, Thomas...Murder; indicted April, 1876; white; last seen in Tom Green county.

Abney, Jerry...Theft of hogs; indicted August, 1874; negro.

Chambless, George...Assault with intent to kill; indicted October 4, 1877; white.

Davis, Sam...Assault to rape; indicted December 11, 1872; white.

Lamar, Raphael...Assault to kill; indicted September 14, 1869; white.

Mitchell, Jack...Theft of gelding; indicted August 13, 1872; white.

McCollum, Thomas...Assault to kill; indicted December 23, 1874; white; last seen in Hill county.

Pool, Ben...Assault to kill; indicted April 16, 1873; white.

Sanders, Lafayette and James...Theft of steer; indicted December.11, 1872; white, last seen in Van Zandt county.

Tatum, Anderson, alias John Brown, alias John Read...Assault to kill; indicted October 7, 1876; negro.

Williams, Henry...Altering marks; indicted December 20, 1875.

Waters, Pole...Theft from house; indicted December 1875; white.

GOLIAD COUNTY.

Halbert, J. M...Theft; said to be in Caldwell county.

Olgin, E...Rape, murder and abduction; 3 cases; indicted August, 1869; Mexican; may be in Bexar or Nueces county.

Innman, Eli....Theft of a mare; somewhere in Northern Texas.

Perkins, Roder....Assault with intent to murder; indicted February, 1871; dark skin—a little negro blood; probably in Southwestern Texas.

Gilcrease, Charles...Assault with intent to murder; indicted June, 1871.

Fulcrod, Charles...Theft from house; negro.

Rice, Elias...Theft of a gelding; he lives in Atascosa county

Winslow, Thomas...Offering to bribe a witness, etc.; 2 cases; he stays in Wilson or Gonzales county.

Orta, Antonio, and Garza, Martina...False imprisonment; both Mexicans; in Mexico.

Hill, J. T., and Warmack, R. H...Producing abortion; Hill is a physian, red complexion, 5 feet 8 or 10 inches high; they live in Madison county, or somewhere near the line of that county.

McDaniel, Jake...Theft of a gelding; negro; probably in Wilson county.

Lunsford, Bud....Assault with intent to murder; indicted February, 1874.

McCarty, William...Theft of a calf; probably in Nueces county.

Douglas, Hill...Theft from a house; a negro boy 21 years of age or more.

Allen, Geo....Theft; 2 or three cases; boy, 20 years of age, small and dark complexion, a *terrible* liar.

Williams, Wm...Theft; he is in Wilson county, probably with Thos. Winslow.

Gill, Samuel...Theft of a hog.

Russell, Wm...Murder; indicted October, 1875; this man is a blacksmith, lame in one leg, lives in Williamson county.

Brooking, W. H...Theft; several cases; is dark complexioned man, black eyes, about 24 years of age, and 5 feet 8 or 10 inches high; probably in the Indian nation.

Hughes, Wm. F...Theft; several cases; medium size, light hair and light complexion, 21 or 22 years old, about 5 feet 6 or 8 inches high.

Ferguson, Lark....Robbery; dark skin; about 5 feet 10 or 11 inches high.

Martin, John H...Theft of cattle, etc.; a tall, fine looking man, light complexion and blue eyes, about 28 or 30 years of age.

HAMILTON COUNTY.

Hughett, James...Theft of cattle; indicted February 7, 1874; 26 years old, 5 feet 9 inches high, light hair and beard, fair complexion and blue eyes.

Deaton, J. M....Theft; indicted February 7, 1874; 5 feet 10 inches high, 160 lbs., black hair, dark complexion, 25 years old.

Deaton George...Theft; indicted May 9, 1874; 23 years old, 140 lbs., spare made, fair complexion and auburn hair.

Kirkland, Aaron. ..Theft; indicted May 9, 1874; 24 years old, 5 feet 9 inches high, 135 lbs., freckled face, dark complexion, black hair.

Highshaw, James...Theft; indicted February 20, 1875; 24 years old, 135 lbs., fair complexion and sandy hair.

Vanwinkle, Sam...Murder; indicted May 21, 1875; 18 years old.

Furgison, Ault...Murder; indicted September 20, 1876; 25 years old. 145 lbs., 5 feet 10 inches high, dark complexion, sandy hair, and considerably specked with smallpox.

Inins, Joel....Theft; indicted September 21, 1876; 30 years old, red complexion, light hair, and below ordinary size.

Hughes, J. W. W...Murder; indicted October, 1874; 30 years old, 6 feet high, 160 lbs., fair complexion, light hair, one stiff finger; was sentenced to the penitentiary for fifteen years; escaped before reaching his destination.

Lambert, Miles...Theft; indicted February 7, 1874.

Andrews, Felix...Theft; indicted October 22, 1874.

Jordan, John....Theft; indicted February 20, 1875.

Brock, John...Assault with intent to kill; indicted February 20, 1875.

Cunningham, F. M...Theft; indicted May 17, 1875.

Underwood, Nathan...Theft; indicted May 21, 1875.

Myers, Milton....Theft; indicted May 21, 1875.

Stinett, G. W...Theft; indicted October 23, 1875.

Bell, L. S....Theft; indicted September 21, 1876.

HAYS COUNTY.

Henderson, James...Murder; indicted November 5, 1869; committed May 25, 1869; about 35 years old, weighs about 160 pounds, about 5 feet 11 inches high, has blue eyes, and dark hair and whiskers.

St. Charles, Elbert...Murder; committed January 6, 1868; indicted November 22, 1870; negro, is about 50 years of age, 5 feet 9 inches high, when last heard from was in Brazos county.

Woods, Frank...Theft of a mare and colt; committed June 1, 1871; indicted November 17, 1871; negro, about 6 feet in height.

Driskill, Tilman...Murder; committed August, 1871; indicted November 17, 1871; weight about 180 pounds, 5 feet 10 inches high, 30 years old, blue eyes and dark hair, is a stock driver.

Morales, Valentine...Murder; indicted November 10, 1874.

Chapman, John G...Murder: committed November 26, 1874; indicted March 25, 1875; about 37 years old, dark hair and eyes, little gray, but uses dye on hair and whiskers.

Johnson, F. E...Passing a forged instrument of writing and swindling; indicted August 4, 1875; is about 22 years old, weighs about 160 pounds, light hair and blue eyes, good looking.

Tickereno, Evan...Theft of neat cattle; indicted April 3, 1876; is about 50 years old, weighs about 150 pounds, has gray hair and whiskers, and black eyes, is a Mexican.

Rector, Joseph...Assault with intent to rape; committed March 10, 1876; indicted April 1, 1876; is a mulatto, weighs about 180 pounds, 5 feet 8 inches high, good looking, resembles a Mexican.

Halford, Jerry...Theft of a horse and gelding; committed January 7, 1876; indicted April 1, 1876.

Eastham, Claude...Theft of a gelding; committed June 15, 1876; indicted September 12, 1876; is about 20 years of age, light blue eyes, light hair, without beard, when last heard from was in Louisiana.

Shafercater, August....Theft of cattle; committed August 8, 1875; indicted September 14, 1876; is about 23 years of age, weighs about 140 pounds, light hair, beardless, is a German, but speaks good English.

Nichols, Dan...Theft of hogs; committed November 30, 1875; indicted September 14, 1876; is about 25 years old, light hair and whiskers, weighs about 200 pounds, about 5 feet 9 inches high.

Condray, Wm. and L. C...Theft of cattle; committed January 1, 1876; indicted March 15, 1877; L. C. is about 60 years of age, bald-headed, with gray hair and beard, weighs about 145 pounds, has blue eyes; Wm. is about 22 years of age, light hair and blue eyes, weighs about 170 pounds.

Wise, P. H...Theft of cattle; committed February 15, 1877; indicted March 15, 1877; is about 25 years of age, dark hair and eyes, weighs 140 pounds, about 5 feet 6 or 8 inches high, indicted in Hood county in the name of *Henry* Wise.

Moore, Columbus...Bigamy; committed December 20, 1876; indicted March 16, 1877; about 27 years of age, is a blacksmith by trade; last heard of was in Robertson county.

Holland, Ellen...Bigamy; committed December 20, 1876; indicted March 16, 1877; is living with Columbus Moore as his wife; is about 25 years of age.

Hill, T. L...Theft of two geldings and theft of two mules; indicted September 15, 1877.

Anderson, John...Theft of two beef steers; indicted September 12, 1877.

Stephenson, Wm...Theft of two geldings; indicted September 12, 1877.

Martin, D...Theft of a beef steer; indicted September 12, 1877.

HILL COUNTY.

Barton, George...Theft of gelding; offense committed June, 1873; about 35 years old, fair complexion, light hair and blue eyes, and is about 5 feet 11 inches high.

Morris, A. J...Assault to murder; committed October, 1873.

Harrington, Dell....Theft of cow; offense committed 1873.

McMeans, T. E....Assault to kill; offense committed October, 1873; is 40 years old, 5 feet 10 inches high, slender build, light complexion, light hair and whiskers, and blue eyes.

Monroe, James...Theft of a gelding; offense committed October, 1873.

Fileds, J. L...Theft of mare; offense committed February, 1874; about 6 feet high, fair complexion, black hair, blue eyes, and is about 30 years old.

Bateman, Henry...Theft of heifer; committed February, 1875.

Allison, Neal...Theft of cows; committed 1872; about 6 feet high, dark hair and blue eyes, and is 28 or 30 years old. Last heard of in Williamson county.

Davis, Ben...Assault to murder; committed March, 1873; about 5 feet 10 or 11 inches high, swarthy complexion, light or sandy hair and whiskers, blue eyes, and has a scar on his nose.

Wilson, James...Theft of hogs.

Green, William...Theft of yearling; offense committed June, 1872. About 22 years old, heavy build, fair complexion, light hair, blue eyes, and about 5 feet 8 inches high.

Murphy, Tom...Theft of cow; committed 1874. About 5 feet 8 inches high, swarthy complexion, light hair, blue eyes, and about 25 years old.

McKee, S. W...Murder; committed December, 1872.

Hancock, John...Theft of bell; committed September, 1874. About 5 feet 8 inches high, sandy hair, fair complexion, blue eyes, and is 25 or 30 years old.

Pinley, Jesse....Theft of bell; committed September, 1874. About 6 feet high, rather dark complexion, and dark hair and eyes.

Brown, James...Theft of yearling; committed 1874.

Morgan, A. C...Murder; committed August, 1874. About 30 years old, 6 feet high, heavy build, grey eyes, dark hair, and rather light complexion.

Evans, Bud....Theft of mule; committed 1875. About 5 feet 8 inches high, fair complexion, light hair, blue eyes, and about 35 years old.

Filley, Frank....Assault to murder.

Burton, Sam...Assault to murder. About 5 feet 10 inches high, about 38 years old, heavy build, light hair, blue eyes, has a small scar on upper lip, talks a great deal, and gets drunk whenever he can get whisky.

Richey, James...Theft of gelding.

James, J. W...Theft of mare. About 45 years old, sandy hair, light complexion, blue eyes, 6 feet high, talks a great deal, and is a considerable trader.

Prichard, Wm...Assault to murder.

Barker, James...Theft of steer. About 5 feet 10 inches high, swarthy complexion, blue eyes, heavy build, and about 45 years old.

White, W. A...Murder; about 5 feet 11 inches high, light complexion, blue eyes, slender build, one front tooth out and is about 35 or 40 years old.

Wilson, Henry...Theft of bacon; committed February, 1875; about 6 feet high, dark complexion, dark hair and eyes and about 25 years old.

Estus, James...Theft of an ox; committed September, 1874.

Blythe, Calvin...Obtaining money under false pretenses; about 6 feet high, black hair and black eyes.

Scott, Samuel...Theft of a gelding; committed 1876.

Parker, Pink...Theft of cow; committed 1876; about 5 feet 8 inches high and 35 years old; mulatto.

Tallent, F. M...Perjury; committed September, 1874; about 5 feet high, 25 or 30 years old, dark hair, blue eyes, and fair complexion.

Hardin, John...Murder; he is the notorious desperado, John Wesley Hardin.

Taylor, John...Theft of mule; about 23 years old, 5 feet 11 inches high, light hair and eyes.

Glenn, David...Theft of a steer; about 20 years old, dark complexion, and dark eyes.

Herring, R. F...Theft of horses; about 30 years old, about 5 feet 10 inches high, fair complexion, light hair, blue eyes, and talks but little.

Ross, S. P...Murder; about 60 years old; last heard of in California.

Bell, A. D...Theft; about 35 years old, 6 feet high, fair complexion, and light hair.

Stutts, Samuel...Murder.

Rowell, John...Assault to rape.

Bennett, W. H...Murder; about 55 or 60 years old, 5 feet 10 inches high, dark complexion, dark hair and whiskers—whiskers turning gray, and slightly hump-shouldered; last heard of in Bell county.

Johnson, J. R...Theft.

Anderson, C. B...Theft; about 5 feet 8 inches high, about 40 years old, heavy build, weighs about 160 pounds, brown hair, swarthy complexion, and large blue eyes.

Bell, James...Theft; about 40 years old, about 5 feet 10 inches high, black hair, blue eyes, swarthy complexion, very talkative, and drinks whisky to excess.

Bevens, Allen...Theft of a horse.

McKissick, A. H...Theft of mules; in penitentiary at Little Rock, Ark.

Ivey, G. W...Theft of mare.

Dunlap, Robert...Theft of mares.

Pain, Wm...Assault to kill.

Walters, Thomas...Theft of mare.

Yeager, Frank...Theft of a steer; offense committed October, 1871.

Oliver, Henry...Theft of a mare; is a low, heavy-set, copper-colored negro, about 25 years old.

Glenn, Wm...Theft of cattle; offense committed January, 1873; about 45 years old, about 5 feet 10 inches high, heavy-set, dark complexion, dark hair, gray eyes, and will weigh 175 or 180 pounds.

Glenn, James...Theft of cattle; offense committed January 21, 1873; about 35 years old, 5 feet 10 inches high, light complexion, gray eyes and dark hair.

McInch, C. P...Theft of yearling; offense committed March, 1873; about 50 years old, 5 feet 10 inches high, heavy-set, dark complexion, black hair and blue eyes.

Smith, Thos. W...Theft of cow; offense committed January, 1873.

Collins, Eli...Fraudulently disposing of mortgaged property; offense committed September, 1872; about 45 years old, about 6 feet high, dark complexion, black hair and eyes, spare build, stands erect, and has one hand crippled; last heard of in Gonzales county.

Smith, R. T...Theft of steer; committed June, 1873.

McKinney, Joe...Theft of yearling; committed April, 1873; about 25 years old, 6 feet high, spare build, light hair, blue eyes, and fair complexion.

Herring, J. W...Burglary; offense committed May, 1873.

Hays, Wm...Theft of steer; committed June 12, 1875; indicted May, 1876; is about 27 years old, 5 feet 8 inches high, fair complexion, light hair and light blue eyes.

Duncan, Milton...Assault with intent to murder; committed March 28, 1876; indicted May, 1876; is about 24 years old, fair complexion, dark hair, about 5 feet 8 inches high and round faced.

Greer, Nat...Theft of mare; committed June 12, 1875; indicted February, 1876.

Parker, Pink, F. M. C...Theft of cow; committed Nov. 15, 1875; indicted February, 1876; is about 6 feet high, copper color, 35 years old.

Blythe, Calvin...Obtaining money under false pretense; committed September 26, 1876; indicted October, 1875.

Scott, Samuel...Theft of gelding; committed December 15, 1875; indicted February 1876; is about 25 years old, 5 feet 7 inches high, light complexion, blue eyes and brown hair.

Burdett, Lewis—Theft of gelding; committed May 10, 1875; indicted October, 1875; is heavy set, medium height, and of rather dark complexion, hair ditto, talkative and boastful, with a desire to be conspicuous, and weighs about 170 or 180 pounds.

Gregory, William...Theft of horse; committed June 5, 1876; indicted November, 1876.

Stevens, Miles—Aiding in the escape of prisoners; committed August 14, 1876; indicted November, 1876; is about 20 or 21 years old, about 5 feet 8 or 9 inches high, fair complexion, light hair, blue eyes and moves awkwardly.

Vanzant, Baxter...Theft of mare; committed April 23, 1876; indicted May, 1876.

Cotner, H. C...Theft of mare; committed April 23, 1876; indicted May, 1876.

Picard, Nathan...Theft of overcoat; committed January 10, 1876; indicted November term, 1876.

Woods, Wm. E....Assalt with intent to murder; committed March 15, 1875; indicted November term, 1876; is about 5 feet 10 inches high, 28 years old, dark complexion, dark hair and eyes.

Laurance, J...Theft of yearling; committed October 7, 1874; indicted October term, 1874.

McLain, C. P...Theft of gelding; committed June 7, 1875; indicted June, 1875; is about 5 feet 10 inches high, light complexion, blue eyes, dark hair, about 25 or 26 years old; escaped after having been convicted and before sentence was passed.

Myers, D. T...Assault with intent to murder; committed March 10, 1875; indicted June, 1875.

Wilson, Henry...Theft of bacon; committed February 28, 1875; indicted June 1875; is about 5 feet 10 inches high, dark complexion, dark eyes and black hair, 28 years old.

Wheeler, Fernande...Theft of oxen; committed September 1, 1874; indicted February 1875; is about 6 feet high, dark complexion, dark eyes and black hair, is about 45 years old.

Powers G. H. and Estus, Jo...Theft of cattle; committed May 7, 1875; indicted June, 1875; Jo. Estus is about 5 feet 8 inches high, light complexion, blue eyes, dark hair, rather heavy set; Powers' description unknown; several indictments against each of them for same offense.

Woods, Ella...Seduction; committed April 10, 1876; indicted June, 1877.

JOHNSON COUNTY.

Lang, Joseph—Theft; committed September, 1871; indicted December, same year; is 6 feet high, has a sallow complexion, and weighs 160 pounds, 35 years old.

Williams, Jas.—Theft; committed June, 1872; indicted August, same year.

Haynes, George—Burglary; committed July, 1872; indicted August, same year.

Jones, J. E.—Theft; indicted August, 1872; is about 5 feet 6 inches high, and has a fair complexion.

Waters, Bill J.—Murder; committed December, 1872; indicted December, same year; is 6 feet high, and weighs 180 pounds; negro.

Smith, Wm.—Theft; committed December, 1872; indicted December, same year; is 5 feet 9 inches high, and weighs 160 pounds; negro.

Hollace, Thos.—Theft; committed December, 1872; indicted December, same year.

Bryant, John—Theft; committed March, 1873; indicted April, same year; is 5 feet 9 inches high, has a fair complexion, and is 29 years old.

Powers, Thos.—Theft; indicted August, 1873.

Hinton, J. C.—Theft; committed July, 1874; indicted August, same year.

Fisher, W. F.—Theft; committed July, 1874; indicted August, same year.

Walker, D. N.—Assault to murder; committed August, 1874; indicted August, same year; is 5 feet 8 inches high, and has black hair; last heard of in Mason county.

Haskey, Boss, or Hurkey—Theft; committed August, 1874; indicted August, same year.

Futhey, G. W.—Illegal marriage; committed June, 1874; indicted August, same year.

Harrison, J. D.—Theft; committed June, 1874; indicted August, same year; is 5 feet 9 inches high, has a fair complexion and light hair.

Walker, Nels—Theft; committed June, 1874; indicted August, same year; negro.

Sandy, Harrison—Theft; committed July, 1874; indicted August, same year.

Duke, Kit—Theft; committed July, 1874; indicted August, same year; is 5 feet 7 inches high, and his complexion is fair.

Franks, Jno.—Theft; committed June, 1874; indicted August, same year.

Austin, Jas.—Theft; committed June, 1874; indicted August, same year; is 5 feet 9 inches high, has a light complexion, sandy hair, and weighs 145 pounds.

McClendon, Z. A.—Theft; committed January, 1874; indicted August, same year; is 6 feet high, has a florid complexion and blue eyes.

Gatewood, P. M., alias John—Swindling; committed June, 1874; indicted August, same year; is 6 feet high, has a fair complexion, light hair, is quick spoken, and walks very erect.

Trussell, J.—Theft; committed May, 1874; indicted August, same year.

Jordon, T. W.—Theft; committed May, 1874; indicted August, same year.

Patrick, E.—Theft; committed June, 1874; indicted August, same year.

Hall, D. N.—Assault to murder; committed April, 1875; indicted April, same year; is 6 feet high, has a fair complexion and light hair.

Parker, Lafayette—Assault to murder; committed January, 1875; indicted April, same year; is 5 feet 10 inches high, has light hair and a fair complexion.

Shadrick, R. M.—Theft; committed June, 1875; indicted April, same year.

Mills, Geo.—Theft; committed January, 1875; indicted April, same year; is 5 feet 9 inches high, and weighs 165 or 170 pounds.

Mahaffey, Henry—Theft; committed August, 1875; indicted April same year.

Bledsoe, Sol.—Murder; committed December, 1875; indicted January, 1876; is 5 feet 10 inches high, has dark hair, fair complexion, blue eyes, and weighs 160 pounds.

Roberts, John—Theft; committed August, 1875; indicted August, 1876; is 5 feet 10 inches high, has a florid complexion and black hair.

Robinson, Winchester—Assault to murder; committed November, 1876; indicted December, 1876.

Coffee, Shadrick—Theft; committed October, 1876; indicted December, 1876; negro.

Braziel, Bob.—Assault to kill; committed November, 1876; indicted December, 1876; said to be in Comanche county.

Watson, Shelt.—Assault to kill; committed November, 1876; indicted December, 1876; said to be in Comanche county.

Baker, John—Assault to kill; committed November, 1876; indicted December, 1876; said to be in Comanche county; report has it that the three above named are all together.

Whitsitt, James—Theft; committed May, 1876; indicted December, 1876; fair complexion.

Morris, Bob.—Theft; committed June, 1876; indicted December, 1876.

Fuller, A. J.—Theft; committed June, 1876; indicted December, 1876.

Johnson, John W.—Assault to kill; committed June, 1877; indicted June, 1877; 6 feet high, fair complexion, slender build.

Blair, Doc.—Assault to kill; committed June, 1877; indicted June, 1877; boy, 17 years old, fair.

Cregg, Ben.—Theft; committed June, 1877; indicted June, 1877.

Haley, James; and Patton, J. R.—Cattle stealing.

HOOD COUNTY.

Cornelius, William—Theft of cattle; indicted November, 1873; light hair and eyes, 40 years old, weighs 150 pounds, 5 feet 10 inches high.

Mitchell, Wm.—Murder; indicted March, 1874; dark eyes and hair, 24 years old.

Graves, Mit—Murder; indicted March, 1874; dark hair and blue eyes, a little cross-eyed, 25 years old, heavy build.

Faucett, William—Assault to murder; indicted July, 1874; six feet high, dark hair and eyes, and 27 or 28 years old.

Middleton, John—Theft of horse (three cases); indicted July, 1874; five feet 10 inches, heavy set, dark hair and eyes, about 35 years old, and talks loud.

Smith, Jack—Theft from house; indicted November, 1874; about 5 feet 6 inches high, black hair and eyes; and says he is half Cherokee.

Nelson, Geo.—Assault to murder; indicted December, 1874; 27 years old, 5 feet 10 inches, heavy set.

Mathews, Joe.—Assault to murder; indicted December, 1874; young, light complexion, and small.

Welchell, Edward.—Theft of cattle (2 cases), December, 1874; Dutchman.

Wise, Henry—Theft from house; indicted April, 1875; five feet 6 inches high, dark hair and dark eyes, 25 years old.

Logan, Wm.—Theft of cattle; indicted April, 1875; about 70 years old, light hair and complexion.

White, W. W.—Attempt to bribe; indicted April, 1875; dark hair and eyes, between 30 and 40 years old, medium size.

Bassett, Jack—Theft of cattle; indicted August, 1875.

Bassett, Reuben—Theft of cattle; indicted August, 1875.

Airy, Thos.—Murder; indicted June, 1876; about 18 years old, rather tall, and dark complexion.

Warren, Morey—Theft of horse, June, 1874; indicted November, 1874.

Watts, Thos.—Theft of hogs.

Covington, W. B.—Theft of cattle, August 6, 1876; indicted November, 1876; blue eyes, auburn hair, 25 years old, weighs 160 pounds, 5 feet 11 inches high.

Ethel, Chas., alias Thos. Smith—Theft of horse; indicted November, 1876; 25 years old, blue eyes, light complexion, 5 feet 10 inches high.

JEFFERSON COUNTY.

Stephenson, Warren...Murder; committed in 1875; indicted April, 1876. About 5 feet 10 inches high, weighs 200 lbs., florid complexion, light hair and thin blue eyes, rather slow in his movements, 50 years old. Was heard of at Rockport, Aransas county, in 1876; probably in that or adjoining counties now.

Garner, Wesley...Arson; committed May, 1877; indicted July, 1877. About 5 feet 10 inches high, weighs 180 lbs., dark, swarthy complexion, dark hair and eyes, slow spoken, heavy voice, wears no beard, heavy features, about 55 years old. Was reported to be in Austin, Texas, in July and August last, driving a dray.

KINNEY COUNTY.

Smith, Sam...Arson; indicted May, 1875. Negro; one arm off.

Sovereign, P. C...Theft of mules; indicted December, 1874.

More, Benj...Theft of mules; indicted December, 1874.

Young, John...Assault to murder; indicted May, 1875. Negro, heavy set.

Remson, Charles...Assault to murder; indicted May, 1875. One leg off.

Henry, Wm....Assault to murder; indicted May, 1875.

Lewis, James—Murder; indicted May, 1875. Negro, tall, slim and a lean face.

Hamilton, Robert—Theft of geldings; indicted September, 1875. Is about 25 years old, tall and slim.

Sierra, Jose—Theft of gelding; indicted September, 1875. Mexican, light complexion, 26 years old.

Burns, Pink—Theft of gelding; indicted September, 1875.

Wheat, J. C.—Murder; indicted May, 1876; 52 years old, tall, sandy complexion.

Lavin, Mamuel—Theft from a house; indicted August, 1874.

Jones, J. S.—Obtaining money under false pretenses; indicted August, 1874.

Ramorez, Santiago.—Theft of gelding; indicted August, 1874. Mexican.

Harrison, Henry.—Theft of gun; indicted April, 1873. Was a United States soldier at time of indictment.

Weaver, Ed.—Theft of gelding; indicted April, 1873.
Miranda, Simon.—Murder; indicted April, 1873.
Adrienne, Chas.—Obtaining money under false pretenses; indicted December, 1873.
Andrada, Julian.—Theft of gelding; indicted August, 1874.
Moore, John.—Theft of watch; indicted December, 1874.
Nelson, Fred.—Assault to kill; indicted December, 1874. Mulatto.
Nanez, Domasio.—Theft from house; indicted January, 1876.
Almares, Jesus.—Theft; indicted May, 1876.
Woesner, Henry.—Murder; indicted November, 1876. Medium size, red complexion, 30 years old, heavy set, bald head.
Villaloras, Antonio.—Theft of cow; indicted November, 1876.
Warrior, Scott.—Theft of gelding; indicted November, 1876. Negro.
Doran, Thomas—Assault to kill; indicted November, 1876.
Staggs, John.—Theft of mare; indicted November, 1876. Tall, young.
Griner, Dallas.—Theft of gelding; indicted November, 1876. Negro.
Brunson, John.—Theft of cattle; indicted May, 1877.
Hall, Caleb.—Theft of cattle; indicted May, 1877.

AUSTIN COUNTY.

Lilly, Richard—Assault with intent to murder.
Pitts, Lee—Murder.
Hunt, Henry—Murder.
Green, A. A.—Theft.
Middleton, Austin—Murder.
Henson, Jack—Murder.
Deggs, Richard—Theft.
Murphy, E. M.—Murder.
Hodge, Hamilton—Murder.
Whatley, Ben—Murder.
Scurry, Polk—Murder.
Osborne, Rufus—Murder.
Goode, Wm.—Assault with intent to murder.
Sims, Isam—Theft.
Deggs, Prince—Theft.
Willis, Edward—Theft.
Byers, Alec.—Theft.
Gage, John, alias Steve Snelling—Theft.
Matthews, Alfred—Theft.
Gilbreath, Wm.—Theft.
Gilbreath, Wm.—Serious threats to take life.
Simpson, W. I.—Assault with intent to murder.
Johnson, Henry—Rape.
Sherman, Cene—Theft.
Jackson, Wm.—Murder.
Wallnetzek, Thomas—Theft.
Clay, Robert—Murder.
Renz, August—Theft.
Stevens, Wiley—Theft.
Norris, C.—Assault with intent to murder.
Armstrong, Stephen—Theft.
Jones, Schen—Assault with intent to murder.
3

Jones, Sehen—Forgery.
Dibble, Dan—Theft.
Francis, Morris—Theft.
Ward, Mason—Theft.
Groce, Ellison—Theft.
Davis, Alec.—Murder.
Butler, Oliver—Assault with intent to murder.
Willis, James—Theft.
Key, Pinkney—Assault with intent to murder.
Giles, Eastland—Assault with intent to rape.
McMahan. John—Murder.
Delano, Oll.—Murder.
Davis, Dood—Murder.
Davis, Dock—Murder.

ANDERSON COUNTY.

Grimes, Sya—Murder; committed 1867; indicted 1867; large yellow negro, a blacksmith; heard of in Austin.

Hammel, Robt.—Murder; committed 1867; indicted 1867.

Atkinson, Robt.—Murder; committed 1867; indicted 1867.

Lacy, Irvin—Murder; committed 1870; indicted 1870; large negro, black, weighs nearly 200 pounds.

Willett, Nathan—Murder; committed 1871; indicted 1871.

Grun, Bird—Theft of hogs; committed 1873; indicted 1873.

Griffin, Moses—Theft of hogs; committed 1873; indicted 1873.

Freeman, Foster—Murder; committed 1873; iudicted 1873; small man, slender, blue eyes; broke jail.

Simpson, J. W.—Burglary; committed 1873; indicted 1873; about 50 years old.

Hoffman, H.—Assault to murder; committed 1873; indicted 1873; German; about 30 years old, light hair, blue eyes; is thought to be west of San Antonio.

Arnold, Isaac—Assault to murder; committed 1873; indicted 1873.

Sanders, Chas.—Assault to murder; committed 1873; indicted 1873.

Brooks, N. S.—Theft; committed 1874; indicted 1874; about 50 years old, blue eyes and gray hair; in north and northwest Texas.

Shannon, F. M.—Theft; committed 1875; indicted 1875; had a brother in San Antonio.

Stanford, Jno.—Theft; committed 1875; indicted 1875.

Paston, J. H.—Offering a bribe; committed 1876; indicted 1876; small man, about 50 years old, gray eyes; from Trinity county.

Johnson, J. M.—Offering a bribe; committed 1876; indicted 1876; slender man, about 30 years old, blue eyes.

Williams, Elbert—Murder; committed 1876; indicted 1876; negro.

Healy, J. H.—Theft; committed 1876; indicted 1876; about 50 years old, blue eyes, quick spoken; Irish.

Donnell, Jno.—Theft; committed 1876; indicted 1876; negro.

Dickum, Jno.—Theft; committed 1876; indicted 1876; blue eyes, about 25 years old, slender.

Saunders, J. W.—Embezzlement; committed 1877; indicted 1877.

Langlois, P. L.—Theft; committed 1877; indicted 1877; slender, about 30 years old, black hair and eyes, sallow complexion.

Horn, Pink—Rape; committed 1877; indicted 1877; dark or sallow complexion, about 19 years old.

BANDERA COUNTY.

Moore, Wm.—Theft of a mare; change of venue from Gillespie county; indictment filed.

Myrick, Wm., Sr.—Murder; indicted 1870; is about 5 feet 8 or 9 inches high, about 50 years old, hair red, eyes yellowish gray, complexion red.

Myrick, Wm., Jr.—Assault with intent to murder; indicted January, 1874; is about 30 years old, sandy hair, gray eyes, about 5 feet 8 inches high.

Leakez, J. M.—Theft of a heifer; indicted September, 1876; is about 6 feet high, sandy hair, light blue eyes, florid complexion.

Brown, Geo. C.—Theft of a gelding; indicted March, 1877; is about 26 years old, about 5 feet 7 inches high, light complexion, inclined to freckle, auburn hair, brownish gray eyes, has remarkably small feet, and weighs about 130 pounds.

Elliot, John—Burglary; indicted September, 1877; is about 17 years old, complexion light, hair very light, 5 feet 6 or 7 inches high, weighs about 125 or 130 pounds.

Tores, Mogan—Theft of a gelding; Mexican; indicted September, 1876; is about 25 or 30 years old, about 5 feet 6 inches high, spare build, copper color, hair and eyes black; broke jail about last August.

Stokes, Z. P.—Theft of a cow; indicted September 27, 1876; is about 6 feet 2 or 3 inches high, a little stoop-shouldered, black hair, very dark brown or black eyes, about 31 years old, voice very coarse and harsh, a regular gambler.

Reed, Oscar—Theft of a beef; indicted September 27, 1876.

BURNET COUNTY.

Owen, P. C.—Theft of a gelding; committed August 31, 1870; indicted December 1, same year.

Barnes, Thomas—Theft of beef steers of value of $80; committed November 1, 1870; indicted December 3, same year.

Carver, George, Sr., and Carver, George, Jr.—Murder of George Mosely and James Sharp; committed February 1, 1870; indicted December 3, 1870; both supposed to be hung.

Yerger, E. M.—Unlawful marriage; committed November 9, 1869; indicted April 5, 1871; is about 6 feet 2 inches in height, about 34 or 35 years of age, dark hair and brown eyes; fair complexion, well educated, school teacher by profession and strong taste for phrenology; when last heard from was in Colorado; peculiar appearance of the eyes.

Andrews, J. J.—Theft of gelding; committed July 1, 1871; indicted April 8, same year; negro, black, about 24 years old, large hands and feet, curly hair and thick lips, about 5 feet 9 inches high, and heavy set.

Grindstaff, John—Murder; committed December 1, 1870; indicted April 11, 1871; heavy set, about 5 feet 8 inches high, light complexion, yellowish eyes, light hair, about 35 years old, weight about 180 pounds.

Jackson, Antona—Assault with intent to murder; committed April 23, 1871; indicted August 9, 1871; negro, copper-colored, about 5 feet 8 or 9 inches high, about 30 years of age, spare build, weight about 160 pounds.

Queen, Jenison—Theft of gelding; indicted August 11, 1871; white man; when last heard from was in San Saba county.

Queen, John—Theft of gelding; indicted August 11, 1871; white man; when last heard from was in San Saba county.

Turner, Manly—Defacing brand on stock with intent to defraud; committed November 25, 1870; indicted August 13, 1871; about 5 feet 7 inches high, 28 years old, light complexion and hair, gray eyes, heavy set, weighs about 165 pounds, rather good looking and plays cards; when last heard from, two months ago, was at Houston, Texas.

Hudgens, Harrison—Theft of neat cattle over $20 in value; committed December 9, 1871; indicted December 14, 1871; about 26 years of age, 5 feet 7½ inches high, dark complexion, dark hair and eyes, weighs 165 pounds, heavy set; when last heard from was in Bandera county, Texas, about three years ago.

Parker, James—Murder; committed February 1, 1872; indicted April 3, same year; Irishman, about 28 or 29 years old, 5 feet 8½ inches high; weighs about 160 pounds, dark complexion and hair, and black eyes; when last heard from was in Colorado.

Perkins, William—Murder; committed August 11, 1872; indicted September, same year; the murder was committed in Lampasas county; Englishman, about 35 years old, about 5 feet 6 inches high, weighs 135 or 140 pounds, dark complexion, black hair and eyes, physician by profession, and a particular friend of James P. Newcomb, late of Austin.

Barton, Al.—Theft of neat cattle; committed March 25; indicted April 12, same year; 26 or 27 years old, 5 feet 10½ inches high, weight 175 pounds; light complexion and hair, gray eyes; when last heard from was in Colorado.

Thompson, Bud; Hart, Charley, alias Clarke, Charley—Theft of gelding in each case; committed April 1, 1874; indicted August 8, same year; Hart is about 26 years old, dark hair and eyes, about 5 feet 10 inches high, weighs about 140 pounds; lived in Hunt county, and was under conviction for murder in Collin county, but had made his escape pending an appeal; claimed to be a nephew of Judge Hardin Hart, of Waco, Texas; when Hart left had a recent shot-gun wound through the knee-joint, and supposed to be lame. Bud Thompson is 5 feet 8 or 9 inches high, a heavy brutal countenance, light complexion, hair and eyes, heavy build, about 25 or 26 years old, and weighs some 175 pounds.

Stinnett, Clay; Caven, Edward; Caven, Wm. T.—Murder; committed September 1, 1873; indicted August 8, 1874. Clay Stinnett is about 28 years of age, about 5 feet 4 inches high, dark complexion and hair and black eyes, weighs about 130 pounds, and has a small patch of white beard on the left jaw about the size of a half dollar; when last heard from was in the State of Alabama. Edward Caven is about 24 years of age, 5 feet 11 inches high, slender form, weighs about 160 pounds, brown hair, blue eyes and regular features, wears a brown moustache, and travels from Burnet county to the Rio Grande, frequently in Kimble, Mason and Gillespie counties. Wm. T. Caven is about 22 years of age, near 6 feet high, weighs some 200 pounds, dark complexion, black hair, brown eyes, no beard, has youthful but homely features; ranges through the counties of San Saba, Mason, Gillespie, and to the Rio Grande. Ed. Caven above mentioned is one of the men recently captured by Capt. McNelly with King Fisher on the Rio Grande.

Shufler, John—Forgery; committed November 22, 1874; indicted

December 5, same year; when last heard from, about 18 months ago, he was in Mason county, Texas.

Stuart, John—Theft of neat cattle ; committed July 15, 1874 ; indicted December 5, same year ; about 28 years old, weighs about 165 pounds, 5 feet 10 inches high, dark complexion, tolerably heavy brown beard, dark eyes and hair ; his range is in Coryell, Coleman and San Saba counties.

Brown, James—Theft of neat cattle ; committed August 1, 1874 ; indicted December 5, same year ; about 21 years old, no beard, dark complexion, light hair, brown eyes, round face, about 5 feet 7 inches high, weighs 165 pounds ; ranges from Burnet to Bandera county.

McKeen, J. B.—Theft of neat cattle ; committed November 16, 1874 ; indicted December 5, same year ; about 40 or 45 years old, 5 feet 5 inches high, heavy set, heavy bearded man, weighs some 145 or 150 pounds, regular features and heavy moustache.

Smart, John, Sr.—Murder ; committed January 25, 1875 ; indicted March 30, same year ; about 45 or 50 years old, 5 feet 9 inches high, grayish hair and whiskers, resides in Cabinal Canon, Bandera county, Texas ; the Governor has offered a reward of $250 for his apprehension.

Sneed, Berry—Murder ; committed January 25, 1875 ; indicted March 30, same year ; resides in Cabinal Canon, in Bandera county, Texas ; the Governor has offered $250 reward for his apprehension.

Farris, Charlie—Theft of hog ; committed May 25, 1875 ; indicted August 7, same year.

Farris, Henry—Theft of hog ; committed May 25, 1875 ; indicted August 7, same year.

McCormick, Lum—Theft of hog ; committed May 25, 1875 ; indicted August 7, same year.

Daniels, William—Theft of mare ; committed July 10, 1875 ; indicted August 7, same year.

Freeman, George—Theft of gelding ; committed February 1, 1875 ; indicted April 1, same year.

Word (Christian name unknown)—Theft of gelding ; committed February 1, 1875 ; indicted April 1, same year. Is about 5 feet 8 inches high, dark complexion, full face, dark eyes and dark hair, round head, weighs 170 lbs., about 24 or 25 years old.

Walker (Christian name unknown)—Theft of gelding ; committed February 1, 1875 ; indicted April 1, same year. Is about 5 feet 10½ inches high, dark complexion, dark hair and eyes, dish face, 22 or 23 years old, weighs 165 or 170 lbs., stoop shoulders, leans forward when walking, prominent chin. Last heard from was in Kansas.

Moore, Buck—Theft of neat cattle ; committed January 15, 1875 ; indicted April 5, same year. Is about 25 years old, 5 feet 8 inches high, dark complexion, dark hair and eyes, weighs 150 lbs., formerly resided in Fayette county, Texas.

Wyrick, James, alias "Slim Jim"—Theft of neat cattle ; committed January 15, 1875 ; indicted April 5, same year. Is about 27 years old, 6 feet high, weighs 180 pounds, dark complexion, black hair and eyes, heavy countenance, and of taciturn disposition. When last heard from was near Fort Worth.

Mason, James P.—Theft of neat cattle ; committed January 15, 1875 ; indicted April 5, same year. Is 25 years old, 5 feet 8 inches high, weighs 170 lbs., light complexion, light hair, grey eyes and light moustache. Since this indictment he has murdered Rans Moore, of Kimble county, on the head of the Llano river. $1000 is offered by the widow. He formerly lived in Walker county, Texas, and was in that county when last heard from.

Huddleston, —— —Theft of neat cattle; committed January 15, 1875; indicted April 5, same year. Is about 45 years old, weighs about 145 lbs., 5 feet 8 inches high, light complexion, bushy grayish whiskers. Lived on Onion creek, Travis county, 9 miles from Austin.

Wilder, ——, alias Bill Ridgeway—Theft of neat cattle; committed January 15, 1875; indicted April 5, same year. Is about 27 years old, 5 feet 10½ inches high, light complexion, light hair and dark grey eyes, weighs 175 lbs. Is step-son of Huddleston, above mentioned, and lived with him on Onion creek, Travis county, at the time the indictment was found.

Clarke, Wm.—Robbery; committed March 1, 1875; indicted April 5, same year. Is 27 years old, 5 feet 8 inches high, light complexion, yellowish hair, light moustache, yellow eyes, weighs 160 pounds. Is a widower, with two children.

Sheffield, Wm.—Assault with intent to murder; committed March 22, 1875; indicted April 5, same year.

Eldridge, Bud—Theft of a hog; committed December 27, 1874; indicted April 5, 1876. Is about 18 years old, about 5 feet 6 inches high, grey eyes, light complexion and hair. When last heard from was living on the Cibolo, in Bexar county, with his father, Peter Eldridge.

Bailey, Mort.—Theft of neat cattle; committed July 1, 1874; indicted April 5, 1873.

Wright, Bud—Swindling; committed March 10, 1875; indicted April 6, 1876.

Myrick, Wm.—Murder; committed January 22, 1875; indicted April 6, same year. Is 25 or 26 years old, 5 feet 8 inches high, dark complexion and hair, brown eyes, and weighs 165 lbs. His range is in Bandera county; has a brother living there.

Wilcoxen, Hugh—Theft from a house; committed July 11, 1875; indicted August 3, same year. Age 22 or 23 years, 5 feet 6 inches high, light complexion, dark eyes, thin chin whiskers, light brown hair, and weighs 125 lbs. Is a native of Missouri.

Storrs, Wm.—Theft of neat cattle; committed July 1, 1875; indicted August 6, same year. Age 40 years, 5 feet 8 inches high, sandy hair some grey, something peculiar about one of his eyes, either blind or gotched.

Atwood, Wm.—Murder; committed August 15, 1875; indicted February 4, 1876. Age, 21 or 22 years, light complexion, blue eyes, light brown hair, 5 feet 7½ inches high, and weighs about 150 lbs.

Dale, Miny—Unlawful marriage; committed December 2, 1875; indicted February 4, 1876. Aged 40 years, negro, black as ink, 5 feet 9 inches high, weighs 155 lbs, preaches sometimes. Last heard from was at Bagdad, Williamson county, Texas.

Baird, John—Theft of a mule; committed December 15, 1875; indicted February 4, 1876. Aged 30 years, light complexion and hair grey, almond shaped eyes, weighs 150 lbs. Reward for this man offered by the Governor for the murder of Dan Huster, of Mason countty. When last heard from he was living in Bexar county, west of San Antonio.

Whittington, T. W.—Theft of a mule; committed December 15, 1875; indicted February 4, 1876.

Tatum, Bud—Theft of neat cattle; committed January 28, 1876 indicted February 4, same year. Negro.

Shaver, George—Theft of gelding; committed June 2, 1876; indicted June 20, same year. Resides near Corn Hill, Williamson county, with his father.

Olney, Joseph—Theft of hogs; committed November 15, 1875; indicted February 4, 1876. Is 25 years old, 5 feet 6½ inches high, light complexion, light hair and blue eyes. Ranges from Burnet county to Bandera.

Brown, W. P.—Murder of John Calvert, committed February 16, 1876; indicted June 21, 1876; 28 years old, 5 feet 11 inches high, dark complexion, black, crossed-eyes, awkward shape, weighs about 175 pounds.

Moore, Jake—Theft of a gelding; committed June 5, 1875; indicted June 22, 1875; negro, about 22 years of age, rather slender form; was sent to the penitentiary from Bosque county in 1876.

Gibson, Felix—Theft of a gelding; committed May 1, 1876; indicted June 22, 1876.

Jones, Sam—Theft of a gelding; committed February 23, 1876; indicted October 11, 1876; about 23 years old, weighs about 165 pounds, 5 feet 6 or 7 inches high, thin red beard, grey eyes, plays the fiddle; formerly lived in DeWitt county, Texas.

Taylor, A. T.—Seriously threatening to take life; committed October 6, 1876; indicted October 11, 1876; about 28 years of age, 5 feet 7 or 8 inches high, weighs about 160 pounds, brown hair.

Campbell, George—Theft of a steer, October, 1876; indicted April, 1877; is about 24 years old, 5 feet 6 or 7 inches high, light complexion, brown hair; when last heard from was near Williams' ranche in Brown county.

Fezelle, Balus J.—Theft of a cow; committed March 15, 1876; indicted October 14, 1876.

Olney, Joseph—Murder of Deputy Sheriff Martin; committed September 1876; 7, indicted October 14, 1876; is 25 years old, 5 feet 6½ inches high, light complexion, light hair and blue eyes; ranges from Burnet county to Bandera county.

Conroy, alias Ross—Robbery; committed September 24, 1876; indicted October 16, 1876.

Campbell, W. E.—Swindling; committed August 15, 1874; indicted October 16, 1876; about 35 years old, 5 feet 7 or 8 inches high, weighs about 150 pounds, brown hair and reddish brown beard, blue eyes; is a stock trader, and when last heard from was in the Indian Territory.

Vineyard, Joseph—Theft of a cow; committed September 15, 1876; indicted April 14, 1877.

Smith, William—Theft of a cow; committed January 26, 1877; indicted April 14, 1877; is about 22 years old, light complexion, heavy set, weighs 160 pounds, and is about 5 feet 7 inches high, very little beard.

Caffal, Thomas—Theft of neat cattle; committed May 15, 1877; indicted October 13, 1877; is about thirty years of age, 5 feet 8 inches high, brown hair, is dissipated in his habits; lives in Gonzales county; is a stockman, and is well known at Rockdale, in Milam county.

Cruz,—— —Assault with intent to murder; committed June 1, 1877; indicted October, 1877; he is a Mexican.

Tinker, William—Theft of neat cattle; committed April 20, 1877; indicted Otober 13, 1877; lives in Lampasas county; is a stockman.

BRAZORIA COUNTY.

Brown, Natt.—Murder; committed March 31,1866; indicted October, 1866; negro.

Powell, George—Murder; committed April 3, 1869; indicted November, 1869; negro.

Johnson, Ben. F.—Murder; committed November 9, 1869; indicted November, 1869; negro.

Spencer, Mat.—Murder; indicted January 9, 1871; negro.

Higgins, Cris. C.—Theft of hogs; indicted January 22, 1874.

Williams, Alexander—Theft of cattle; indicted October 8, 1874.

Scull, Riley—Assault with intent to kill; indicted October 31, 1874.

Edwards, Geo.—Assault with intent to commit rape; indicted October 31, 1874.

Bar-Santee, Edward—Assault with intent to murder; indicted October 15, 1874.

Brown, Ben.—Theft of cattle; indicted May 11, 1875.

Glover, Augustus—Murder; indicted January 9, 1871; white.

Adderson, Mike—Theft; indicted October 8, 1875; negro.

Coward, Richard M.—Theft; indicted October 24, 1876; white.

Bonner, Augustus—Theft; indicted April 21, 1877; negro.

Stewart, Andrew—Theft; indicted April 21, 1877; negro.

BASTROP COUNTY.

Rosanky, Herman—Murder; committed July 3, 1867; indicted December 16, same year.

Petty, George—Murder; committed February 1, 1868; indicted June 16, 1868.

Weaver, James—Murder; committed March 15, 1868; indicted June 16, same year.

Mayfield, Thomas—Assault with intent to kill and murder; committed November 29, 1868; indicted February 16, 1869.

Nolen, Dallas—Theft of a horse; committed April 16, 1869; indicted May 11, same year.

Lock, Adam—Theft of a mare; committed November 4, 1869; indicted December 18, same year,

Curtis, Joseph—Murder; committed June 1, 1869; indicted December 20, same year.

O'Conner, Arthur—Theft from a house; committed August 20, 1870; indicted December 1, same year.

Hall, David J.—Theft of a mare; committed September 20, 1870; indicted December 1, same year.

Jones, Lisbon—Burglary; committed September 13, 1870; indicted December 1, same year.

Barker, Joseph—Murder; committed July 11, 1870; indicted December 2, same year.

Morris, Bob.—Murder; committed December 17, 1869; indicted December 6, 1870.

Davis, E. L.—Murder, committed December 17, 1869; indicted December 6, 1870.

Parason, Bill—Murder; committed July 6,.1870; indicted December 8, 1870.

Smith, Russell—Kidnapping; committed November 25, 1869; indicted December 8, 1870.

Partilla, Elya—Murder; committed February 11, 1870; indicted December 9, same year.

Johnson, Jeff.—Theft of a gelding; committed October 1, 1870; indicted December 8, same year,

Stallings, Jeptha—Murder; committed March 5, 1870; indicted December 8, same year.

Walters, M. P.—Murder; committed March 20, 1871; indicted March 21, same year.

Hanley, Fred—Assault to kill and murder; committed October 5, 1870; indicted December 8, same year.

Hall, John—Murder; committed December 30, 1870.

Gordon, Jeff.—Theft from a house; committed June 10, 1871; indicted July 28, same year.

Crayton, Bob.—Theft of gelding; committed March 1, 1871; indicted July 28, 1871.

Ellis, Jack—Theft of gelding; committed April 23, 1871; indicted July 28, same year.

Whittington, John—Theft of a gelding; committed April 10, 1871; indicted August 1, same year.

Borra (col.)—Murder; committed July 8, 1871; indicted August 1, same year.

Simpson, James—Murder; committed October 4, 1871; indicted December 6, same year.

Hazel, James—Murder; committed October 4, 1871; indicted December 6, same year.

Davis, Blucher—Theft of a steer; committed September 13, 1871; indicted December 7, same year.

Bird, W. H.—Assault to kill and murder; committed December 10, 1871; indicted March 29, 1872.

Boese, Henry—Swindling; committed November 15, 1871; indicted in two cases April 20, 1872; is about 5 feet 6 inches high, light red hair, blue eyes, about 50 years old, a German, and was once surveyor of this county.

Coulson, Bart.—Theft of a filly; committed June 1, 1872; indicted July 26, same year; is about 5 feet 4 or 5 inches high, light hair, face freckled, about 23 or 24 years old, talks very much.

Lee, Isaac—Assault to kill and murder; committed June 1, 1872; indicted July 26, same year.

Irvin, Bill—Assault to kill and murder; committed July 4, 1872; indicted July 26, same year.

Lawhon, P. A.—Theft of a mare; committed April 11, 1872; indicted July 30, same year.

Glasscock, Wm.—Theft of a mare mule; committed June 1, 1872; indicted July 30, same year.

Yoe, Gus.—Assault to kill and murder; committed November 4, 1872; indicted November 29, same year.

Gould, Ed. Uriah—Theft of a stallion; committed August 10, 1872; indicted November 30, same year; is about 5 feet 6 inches high, weighs 150 pounds, light brown hair, 22 or 23 years of age, has once been arrested and was a short time since in Kerr county.

Thompson, T. G.—Theft of tobacco; committed February 1, 1872; also indicted for embezzlement.

Ridgeway, Wm. H.—Murder; committed November 3, 1872; indicted December 3, same year; is about 6 feet high, dark hair and eyes, well formed and erect, very plain and positive in his speech, about 40 years old.

Pierson, Tom.—Assault to kill and murder, two indictments; committed December 25, 1872; indicted March 20, 1873; indicted for murder committed June 23, 1873; indicted August 1, same year.

Holt, Thomas—Assault to kill and murder; committed January 9, 1873; indicted March 27, same year.

Jones, Adolph—Murder; committed March 20, 1873; indicted March 31, same year; negro, big and black.

Perkins, Chas.—Murder; committed April 1, 1868; indicted March 31, 1873.

Hoffman, Bonny—Assault to kill and murder; committed July 3, 1873; indicted August 1, same year.

Hoffman, Geo.—Assault to kill and murder; committed July 3, 1873; indicted August 1, same year.

Verdry, Geo. P.—Theft from a house; committed May 31, 1873; indicted August 1, same year.

· Jackson, John—Theft of a gelding; committed May 2, 1873; indicted August 2, same year.

Speed, W. W.—Theft of cow; committed November 15, 1873; indicted November 28, same year.

Speed, G. W.—Theft of cow; committed November 15, 1873; indicted November 28, same year.

Wilson, Joseph—Theft of a cow; committed November 15, 1873; indicted November 28, same year.

Smith, Jim—Theft from a house; committed September 10, 1873; indicted November 28, same year.

Fowler, Dock—Theft of a beef steer; committed August 15, 1873; indicted November 28, same year; negro.

Calhoun, W. E.—Murder; committed October 24, 1873; indicted November 28, 1873.

Moore, Buck—Theft of neat cattle; committed October 1, 1873; indicted December 6, same year.

White, Dan—Theft of a mare; committed September 12, 1873; indicted December 6, same year.

Sears, Geo. W.—Assault to kill and murder; committed June 13, 1873; indicted December 6, same year.

Griffin, Lee—Theft of neat cattle; committed November 1, 1873; indicted December 6, same year; is about 5 feet 10 inches high, thin visage, freckled face, light red hair, about 20 years old.

Eisenbach, John—Theft of a cow; committed March 15, 1873; indicted December 6, same year.

Fuller, James—Theft of a cow; indictments of stealing calf 1, cattle 2; committed in 1874; indicted in 1874.

Arnold, Mose—Murder; committed January, 1873; indicted March 27, 1874.

Ball, Thomas—Theft of hogs; committed December 5, 1873; indicted March 27, 1874.

Ayers, Thomas—Assault to kill and murder; committed January 23, 1874; indicted March 27, same year.

Williams, Bill—Theft of a mule; committed November 1, 1873; indicted March 28, 1874.

Gorman, Dr. S.—Assault to kill and murder; committed February 10, 1874; indicted March 28, same year; medium height, bald-headed, about 60 years old.

Null, Thomas—Theft of a calf; committed February 28, 1874; indicted March 28, same year; is about 5 feet 11 inches high, light sandy hair and beard, about 30 years old.

Williams, Bull (alias Dudley Hill)—Assault to kill and murder; committed January 21, 1874; indicted March 31, same year.

Preistley, Geo.—Theft from a house; committed June 20, 1874; indicted July 31, same year.

Trubey, Wm. M.—Theft of money; committed May 1, 1874; indicted August 4, same year.

Alsop, Joe (alias Drew Alsop)—Unlawfully and fraudulently selling an estray; committed May 1, 1874; indicted August 1, same year.

Williams, Ish—Theft of a pony; committed August 12, 1874; indicted November 30, same year.

Powers, Jas. H.—Theft of a bull calf; committed April 1, 1874; indicted December 1, same year.

Power, Wm. M.—Theft of a calf; committed April 1, 1874; indicted December 1, same year.

Whittington, Park—Theft of a hog; committed November 1, 1874; indicted December 3, same year.

Clanton, James—Theft of a cow; committed December 3, 1874; indicted December 3, same year.

Talley, Nathan—Assault to kill and murder; committed November 3, 1874; indicted December 3, same year.

McCarthey, Jeff.—Theft of seed cotton; committed August 20, 1874; indicted December 3, same year.

Ramsey, E.—Theft of ox; committed February 1, 1875; indicted March 30, same year.

Williams, Scott—Theft of a black hog; committed July 6, 1875; indicted July 31, same year.

Power, Wm. M.—Theft of a dun gelding; committed July 11, 1875; indicted July 31, same year.

Clark, Louis (alias Whiten)—Theft of a sorrel mare; committed June 1, 1875; indicted August 1, same year.

Rector, Tobe (alias Oliver)—Theft from a house; committed August 2, 1875; indicted August 6, same year.

Shelton, M. L.—Swindling; committed April 17, 1875; indicted August 6, same year; is 5 feet 4 or 5 inches high, dark complexion, light hair, about 30 years old.

White, Louis—Theft of bay mare; committed June 8, 1875; indicted August 6, 1875.

Carruthers, Henry—Murder; committed September 9, 1875; indicted November 27, same year; is about 25 years old, about 5 feet 8 inches high, weighs 140 or 150 pounds, rather dark complexion, dark hair and eyebrows, dark hazel eyes, has a quick, flashing eye, talks tolerably fast and earnest.

Gardner, Wm.—Assault to kill and murder; committed September 21, 1875; indicted November 21, same year.

Dock (a freedman)—Theft of a hog; committed October, 1875; indicted December 1, same year.

Glasscock, John—Assault to kill and murder; committed September 1, 1875; indicted December 20, 1875.

Waggonner, J. L., Waggonner, Wm., Gentry, F. M.—Theft of beef; committed October 4, 1875 ; indicted December 20, same year.

Coulson, Nelson (a freedman)—Assault to kill and murder ; committed in Travis county, November 20, 1875; indicted December 3, same year.

Race, Bloz—Theft of a mare and gelding; committed November 16, 1875 ; indicted December 3, same year.

O'Neal, Wiley—Theft of a mare ; committed October 10, 1875; indicted December 3, same year.

Commus, James—Theft of a gelding; committed January 16, 1876 ; indicted April 26, same year.

Johnson, John—Theft of a gelding ; committed Jan. 6, 1876 ; indicted April 26, same year.

Jackson, A. J.—Theft of cow; committed November 15, 1875; indicted April 26, 1876.

Johnson, John—Theft of a sorrel gelding; committed January 5, 1876 ; indicted April 26, same year.

Sims, Dock—Theft of a bay mare; committed April 13, 1876; indicted April 27, same year.

Potts, John—Theft of gelding; committed February 25, 1875 ; indicted April 29, same year.

Gage, Geo.—Theft of a colt; committed April 1, 1875 ; indicted April 29, 1876.

Nolen, Wm.—Theft of gelding; committed February 1, 1876 ; indicted April 29, same year; is about 5 feet 8 inches high, weighs 150 pounds, light hair, about 20 years old, defective eyes.

Moore, App.—Assault with intent to kill ; committed February 18, 1876 ; indicted April 29, same year.

Robinson, Thomas—Murder; indicted April 25, 1877 ; negro.

Peterson, William—Murder; indicted April 25, 1877 ; negro.

Squirrelhunter, Sam—Murder; indicted April 25, 1877 ; he professes to be a fortune-teller, cuts cards and uses coffee grounds.

Nicholson, Sam—Rape ; indicted April 25, 1877.

Gentry, Chas.—Rape ; indicted October 20, 1877.

Gradington, Richard—Murder; indicted October 22, 1877.

Shelton, Freeman—Murder ; indicted October 22, 1877.

Lee, John—Assault with intent to kill; indicted October 22, 1877.

Junkins, Jo.—Assault to kill; indicted October 23, 1877.

Rawles, S. A. (three indictments)—Theft of cow; indicted October 23, 1876 ; is about 6 feet high, slender build, dark hair and eyes, sharp features, about 25 years old.

Burlin, Calhoun—Jointly indicted with Rawles.

Robinson, Geo.—Forgery ; indicted April 18, 1877.

Meek, Louis D.—Murder ; indicted April 20, 1877.

Spears, Everett—Murder; indicted April 20, 1877.

Branton, Ben—Theft of cow ; indicted April 20, 1877.

Standifer Lem—Theft of a cow ; indicted April 20, 1877.

Ward, Henry T.—Bigamy ; indicted April 20, 1877.

Potts, Haywood—Theft of a gun ; indicted April 23, 1877 ; is about 5 feet 10 inches high, light hair and eyes, rather heavy build, about 24 years old.

Gould, Jake—Theft of a mare ; indicted April 23, 1877.

Olive, Robt.—Kidnapping ; indicted April 23, 1877.

COLEMAN COUNTY.

Redden, Thomas...Theft of cattle; indicted April, 1877; is about 5 feet 8 inches high, and weighs about 150 pounds, fair complexion and light moustache, about 23 years old.

Gerdner, Mike...Theft of cattle; indicted April, 1877; about 5 feet 7 or 8 inches high, weighs about 140 pounds, fair complexion, light brown hair, 28 or 30 years old.

Carter, G. V...Assault with intent to murder; indicted April, 1877.

Drout, old man...Theft of a hog; indicted April, 1877.

Elston, Charles...Assault with intent to murder; indicted April, 1877.

Lehpart, Dave...Assault with intent to murder; indicted April, 1877.

Shelley, Malley...Assault with intent to murder; indicted April, 1877.

Shelley, Stephen...Theft of cattle; indicted April, 1877.

Nichols, Sage...Theft of cattle; indicted April, 1877.

Clark, P. J...Forgery and also swindling; indicted October, 1877; escaped from Brown county jail; about 5 feet 10 or 11 inches high, weighs about 160 pounds, fair complexion, about 40 years old, hair getting gray, has been shot in one of his hands so as to deform it.

CALHOUN COUNTY.

Romero, Louis...Murder; committed July 20, 1866; indicted November 21, same year.

Clarke, ——...Murder; committed August 31, 1866; indicted February 8, 1867.

Mangle, ——...Murder; committed February 9, 1867; indicted February 8, 1868.

Lane, R. P...Assault with intent to murder; committed December 10, 1868; indicted February 9, 1869.

Williams, Sidney...Burglary; committed December 23, 1870; indicted February 10, 1871.

Harris, Wesley...Assault with intent to murder; committed May 7, 1870; indicted October 8, same year; negro.

Fast, Frank, alias Ferris...Theft of cattle; committed April 10, 1875; indicted May 7, same year; negro.

Irvine, Joe...Assault with intent to murder; committed April 16, 1875; indicted May 8, same year.

Anderson, Jim...Theft of cattle; negro.

Richard, Jno...Assault to murder; white.

Jackson, Wm...Maiming; negro.

CAMP COUNTY.

Lester, Lovelace...Assault to kill and murder; committed August 20, 1874; indicted October 21, same year; is a mulatto, about 23 years old, 5 feet 9 or 10 inches high, weighs 150 to 160 pounds.

Tulkington, Henry...Assault to kill and murder; committed March 15, 1873; indicted October 22, 1874; is black, 6 feet high, spare made, 24 to 26 years old, and will weigh about 150 pounds.

Botton, Rufus...Theft; committed January 7, 1875; indicted April

16, same year; is black, heavy set, about 30 years old, thick heavy lips, weighs 175 pounds, 5 feet 8 or 9 inches high.

Staton, Ned...Theft; committed December 7, 1874; indicted August 11, 1875; copper-colored, about 30 years old, 5 feet 10 inches high, one eyeball enlarged, will weigh 150 pounds.

Phifer, Jack...Incest; committed November 7, 1873; indicted August 14, 1875.

Davis, George...Rape; offense committed July 25, 1875; indicted August 14, same year; is black, 5 feet 10 inches high, 30 or 33 years old, weighs 150 to 168 pounds.

Williams, Wm...Theft; committed December 1, 1875; indicted December 16, same year; is 22 years old, 5 feet 8 inches high, fair complexion, blue eyes, sandy hair, will weigh about 135 or 140 pounds.

Little, J. D...Illegal voting; committed February 15, 1876; indicted April 14, same year; has fair complexion, blue eyes, light hair, about 48 years old, weighs 175 or 180 pounds.

Williams, Thomas...Bigamy; indicted April, 1876.

Dickson, Alfred...Perjury; indicted November 11, 1876.

Simmons, Prince...Assault to murder; indicted November 11, 1876.

Longmire, Leroy...Threat to take life; indicted November 10, 1876.

Campbell, G. W...Swindling; indicted November 11, 1876.

Isham, Joe...Unlawful marriage; indicted August 17, 1877.

Knighton, K. M...Theft; indicted April 13, 1877.

Pitts, Robert...Threat to take life; indicted Aug. 13, 1877.

Parker, Keinchern T...Theft; indicted November 9, 1877.

Garrett, Enoch—Theft; indicted November 9, 1877.

Boyd, Richard...Theft and altering mark; indicted November, 1877.

CHEROKEE COUNTY.

Wood, Thompson...Murder; committed February 10, 1865; indicted March, 1865; about 5 feet 9 inches high, weighs about 200 pounds, dark complexion, and about 55 years of age; said to live on Flat Lake, 9 miles from Minden, La.

Alexander, Wm...Murder; indicted March, 1866.

Hoffman, C. W...Assault to murder; committed July 10, 1866; indicted September, 1866.

Killough, Charles (negro)...Assault to murder; indicted August, 1868; said to be at Marshall, Texas, or Shreveport, La.

Land, Wm...Theft of a horse; committed February 15, 1869; indicted February, 1869; is about 26 or 28 years old, 5 feet 10 inches high, sallow complexion, dark hair, blue eyes, and supposed to weigh 150 pounds.

Mallard, E. W...Theft of mule; indicted August, 1869; about 25 years of age, light complexion, light hair, blue eyes, and about 5 feet 8 inches high.

Whitesides, James...Assault to murder; indicted February, 1870.

Duncan, James...Murder; committed December 10, 1868; indicted December, 1870.

Weaver, George...Murder; committed May 10, 1873; indicted July, 1873.

Broughton, Charles...Theft from a house; committed July 10, 1873; indicted November, 1873.

Agnew, Lewis H...Assault to murder; committed May 10, 1868; indicted July, 1874; about 45 years old, fair complexion, light hair, blue eyes, stoop-shouldered, somewhat gray, about 5 feet 10 inches high, and weighs about 175 pounds; in Mississippi.

Crunk, Wm...Assault to murder; committed March 10, 1874; indicted July, 1874; low stature, dark complexion, black hair and eyes, about 5 feet 8 inches high, and weighs about 150 pounds.

Winters, John S...Assault to murder; committed June 19, 1875; indicted July, 1875; about 6 feet high, weighs about 180 pounds, light complexion, light hair, blue eyes, and about 35 years old.

Wiley, Albert...Assault to murder; committed June 19, 1875; indicted July, 1875.

Maroney, D. R. C...Assault to commit rape; committed June 29, 1875; indicted July, 1875.

Brittain, Wm. P...Assault to murder; committed January 24, 1876; indicted January, same year; about 24 years old, 5 feet 8 inches high, dark hair, yellowish blue eyes, rather fair complexion, slender built, weighs about 130 pounds, has a scar on one temple—probably the right—and wears No. 4 or 5 boots.

Priestly, Wm...Murder; committed March, 1873; indicted July, 1873; sallow complexion, dark hair; blue eyes, crippled in one hand, about 40 years old, 6 feet high, and weighs about 135 pounds; probably in Mississippi.

Clayton, Ed...Theft of hogs in March, 1875; indicted July, 1875; two cases.

Walker, Charles...Theft (felony); committed January, 1874; indicted July, 1874; about 5 feet 8 inches high, weighs about 130 pounds, light complexion, light hair, blue eyes, and about 24 years old.

Daniels, John...Assault to murder; committed December, 1869; indicted December, 1870; dark hair, blue eyes, about 30 years old, and 5 feet 10 inches high.

Brownlee, Henry...Assault to murder; committed December, 1868; indicted July, 1869; fair complexion, light hair, and blue eyes; thought to be in the Indian Nation.

Slaughter, C. A...Swindling; committed April 5, 1871; indicted July same year; about 5 feet 9 inches high, dark hair, black eyes, black whiskers, 45 years of age, and weighs 130 pounds.

Rountree, Ellen...Murder; committed October, 1864; indicted March, 1872.

Sexton, Samuel...Assault to murder; committed August 20, 1872; indicted November, same year.

Martin, Smallard...Assault to murder; indicted July, 1873; thought to be dead.

Atkins, Ira B...Swindling; committed May, 1872; indicted November, 1873; fair complexion, light hair, and blue eyes.

Dial, Wm...Seduction; committed June, 1872; indicted November, 1873; florid complexion, red hair, about 5 feet 10 inches high, weighs about 150 pounds, and is about 38 years old.

Goodwin, Wm. T...Swindling; committed November, 1873; indicted July, 1874; two causes; fair complexion, light hair, blue eyes, about 5 feet 11 inches high, and weighs about 150 pounds.

McCrimmon, Lot...Theft of hog; committed August, 1874; indicted November, same year; freedman; about 32 years old, 6 feet high, and weighs about 140 pounds.

Walters, Henry...Assault to murder; committed July, 1875; indicted July, same year.

Wilkins, John D...Theft of hogs; committed January, 1875; indicted July, same year; about 24 years old, 5 feet 10 inches high, light hair, blue eyes, round face, and weighs about 140 pounds.

Florence, Robert...Theft of mule; committed 1875; indicted October, 1876; dark complexion, black hair and eyes, is about 26 years of age, and weighs about 150 to 160 pounds, rather heavy build, about 5 feet 10 inches high; doubtful.

Kendrick, Samuel...Assault to murder; committed 1876; indicted October 14, 1876; dark complexion, light hair, hazel eyes, and about 25 years of age, heavy set, weighs about 160 pounds, about 5 feet 10 inches high.

Thomas, Alfred...Two cases; theft of hogs and assault to murder; theft committed 1877; assault to murder committed February, 1877; indicted March, 1877; negro.

Holloway, W. M...Theft of an estray horse; committed January, 1877; indicted March, 1877; about 5 feet 9 inches high, one leg a little shorter than the other, dark complexion, about 37 years of age, weighs about 140 pounds.

CLAY COUNTY.

Barrington, James...Murder; committed May, 1873; indicted April, 1874; about 26 years old, 5 feet 11 inches high, rather slender built, feminine appearance, light hair, large blue eyes, and walks very erect; forfeited bond.

Blanton, John D...Assault to murder; indicted April, 1874; about 37 years old, 5 feet 7 inches high, light complexion, light hair, blue or gray eyes, and weighs about 160 pounds.

Brown, John...Assault to murder; indicted April, 1875; about 27 years old, about 5 feet 9 inches high, weighs about 165 pounds, dark complexion, and black and rather bushy hair, drinks considerably, and rather boisterous.

Stevens, John...Wilfully permitting John Wilson (charged with murder) to escape from custody; indicted August, 1875; about 35 years old, 5 feet 11 inches high, rather stoop-shouldered, freckled faced, light hair and fair complexion; one eye crossed.

Newsom, W. H...Wilfully permitting John Wilson (charged with murder) to escape from custody; indicted August, 1875; about 30 years of age, 5 feet 7½ inches high, fair complexion, light hair and blue eyes.

Whaley, W. H...Assault to murder; indicted December, 1875; about 27 years old, 6 feet high, weighs about 165 pounds, rather loose and clumsy build, fair complexion, light hair, red beard and large blue eyes; at San Antonio when last heard of; has a wife and two children.

Dodd, James...Theft of horses; indicted December, 1875.

Freeman, Bill...Theft of horses; indicted December, 1875.

Nichols, James...Rape; indicted April, 1876; about 22 years old, 5 feet 8 inches high, fair complexion, blue eyes and dark hair; last heard of in Williamson county.

Standifer, Mack...Assault to murder; indicted April, 1876; about 24 years old, about 5 feet 8 inches high, heavy, square build, light complexion, large pale blue eyes, light curly hair, and weighs about 160 pounds, handsome, loud, coarse voice; parents live in Lampasas county.

Cox, Roland...Assault to murder and forcibly breaking jail; two cases; indicted April, 1876; about 22 years old, about 5 feet 7 inches high, light blue eyes, brown hair, and weighs about 140 pounds; likely to be found with Mack Standifer.

Shaver, G. W....Rape; committed February, 1876; indicted April, 1876.

Zoozier, Ed....Murder; committed May, 1873; indicted April, 1874.

Burdell, Dr....Theft; indicted May, 1876. Was last heard of practicing medicine in Johnson county.

Wiley, Wm....Assault to kill; indicted May, 1877. Age, 27 years, red complexion, brown eyes, black hair.

Simmons, F. J....Assault to kill; indicted May, 1877. Age, 25 or 26 years, light complexion, blue eyes, dark curly hair, weighs 140 lbs.

Sullivan, Dick, alias Dick Hill—Burglary; indicted May, 1877. Age, 26 years, light hair, fair complexion, very broad and high forehead.

Hardie, Mit...Assault to kill; indicted October, 1877. Age, 25 years, 5 feet 7 inches high, light complexion, has a scar diagonally across his nose.

Martin, Sell...Assault to kill; indicted October, 1877. Age, 25 years, 5 feet 6 inches high, light complexion.

COLLIN COUNTY.

Bird, James...Assault to murder; committed August, 1866; is about 33 years old, 5 feet 10 inches high, hair dark; supposed to be in Comanche or adjoining counties.

Amberg, Jas...Robbery; committed March, 1867.

Flournoy, W. B...Theft; committed August, 1866.

Wash, David...Assault to murder; committed August, 1866.

Little, Jas...Theft; committed March, 1877.

Little, David...Theft; committed March, 1867.

Blythe, Lemuel...Theft; committed March, 1867.

Setser, Sam...Theft; committed March 1867.

Young, Jas...Murder; committed September, 1867.

Davis, Eli...Assault to murder; committed September, 1867.

Lindsay, Lewis...Assault to murder; committed September, 1867; is about 34 years old, light complexion, short, heavy set; is out west.

Collins, John...Theft; committed September, 1867.

Prewitt, Lewellyn...Theft; committed March, 1867.

Duncan, Jas...Theft; committed March, 1868; is about 32 or 33 years old, 5 feet 11 inches high, low, black hair and eyes; now in Northern Missouri.

Penick, Taylor...Theft; committed March, 1868.

Wilson, Charles...Forgery; committed March, 1868.

Duncan, S. L....Theft; committed April, 1868.

Smith, T. Y....Theft; committed September, 1868.

Warrenberg, Geo...Theft; committed April, 1868.

Miller, Albert...Theft; committed September, 1868.

Bacon, Sam...Theft; committed April, 1868.

Elder, Turner...Theft; committed April, 1868.

Sanders, B. F...Murder; committed March, 1869.

Smith, August...Theft; committed July, 1871.

McNab, John...Theft; committed November, 1870.

4

McNab, Jasper...Theft; committed November, 1870.

Brinlee, David...Murder; supposed to be in Bosque or Johnson counties or thereabout.

Elliott, Alfred...Theft; committed November, 1870.

Bishop, —— ...Theft; committed November, 1870.

Hamilton, M. M...Swindling; committed March, 1871.

Fuell, Com...Assault to murder; committed March, 1871; now in Mo.

Doggett, John...Theft; committed March, 1871.

Green, John...Swindling; committed July, 1871; is in Arkansas.

Judd, F. R...Theft; committed November, 1871.

Kennedy, John...Theft; committed November, 1871.

Boren, Jack...Theft; committed March, 1869; supposed to be in Williamson or adjacent counties.

Lipscomb, O. C...Selling mortgaged property; committed February, '75; in Kentucky; 5 feet 10 inches high, brown hair and whiskers, blue eyes, slender and stoop-shouldered.

Irving, Anthony...Theft; committed June, '75.

Smoot, Hice...Theft; committed June, '74; black, 25 years old, heavy set.

Barton, W. R...Theft; committed October, '74; 35 years old or more, curly black hair; drives cattle to Missouri.

Wilson, Isaac...Theft; committed October, '74.

Williams, Thos...Theft; committed February, '75.

Mackey, Mace...Theft; committed February, '75.

Irving, Anthony—Theft; committed June, '75.

Hunt, Wm...Theft; committed October, '75.

Connelly, Ben...Murder; committed October, '75; is about 28 years old, 5 feet 5½ inches high, well formed, brown hair, blue eyes, speaks slowly, a school teacher.

Boren, Robt...Theft; committed March, '69.

Blalock, Jas...Theft; committed November, '70; 50 years old, brown hair, rather heavy built, blue eyes.

Rike, Henry...Murder; committed November, '70.

Cole, F. P...Murder; committed November '70; is about 36 years old, dark skin, black hair and eyes, weighs 170 pounds.

Cobston, Thos...Theft; committed March, '71.

Cobston, Hence...Theft; committed March, '71.

Henry, Chas....Perjury; committed July, '71; is about 30 years old, 5 feet 10½ inches high, brown hair, large mouth and square shoulders.

Frost, Wm...Murder; committed July, '71.

Dearing, B. F...Theft; committed November, '71.

Stokes, Lane....Theft; committed November, '71.

Washington, Jack...Theft; committed November, '71.

Kiggin, John...Theft; committed March, '72.

Scott, W. M...Theft; committed March, '72.

Bean, Henry...Theft; committed July, '72.

Ford, John...Theft; committed November, '72.

Hawkins, Theme...Theft; committed November, '72.

Johnson, G. B...Swindling; committed October, '73.

McMarlin, Howard....Assault to murder; committed March, '73; supposed to be in Arkansas.

Jennings, W. S...Seduction; committed March, '73.

Hill, Chas...Aiding prisoners to escape; committed October, '73; black eyes and hair, small man, about 26 years old; last heard of was at Fort Worth; one indictment for theft.

Cartwright, J. J...Assault to murder; committed November, '72; blue eyes, dark hair, Roman nose, 28 years old.

Bounds, Joseph...Assault to murder; committed July, '73; is about 25 years old, 5 feet 10 inches high, full faced, high forehead, blue eyes, light hair and complexion.

Campbell, Floyd...Theft; committed February, '74; has dark hair, heavy eyelids, light eyes, about 28 years old; supposed to be in the Indian Territory.

Robinson, Dick...Seduction; committed June, '74.

Jones, Z. T...Murder; committed October, '74; is about 23 years old, 5 feet 10 or 11 inches high, light complexion, retiring manners.

Deer, Drew...Murder; committed, 1875; about 25 or 30 years of age, light complexion and hair, 5 feet 9 or 10 inches high.

Houston, Jno...Theft; committed, 1875.

Starks, W. J., alias Tescubee, June...Theft; committed, 1875; about 22 or 25 years of age, 5 feet 8 inches high, light hair and complexion, blue or gray eyes, slender.

Weldon, T. A...Assault with intent to murder; committed, 1875.

Coyle, M. S...Theft; committed, 1876; about 22 years of age, 5 feet 10 or 11 inches high, light hair and tanned light complexion, heavy set.

Weldon, Joseph...Murder; committed, 1876; about 45 years of age, sandy or red hair and complexion, about 5 feet 8 or 9 inches high, heavy set; lately Southwest.

Neill, H. K...Incest; committed, 1876.

Omstead, Israel W...Theft; committed, 1876; about 40 years of age, brown hair, 5 feet 10 or 11 inches high, heavy brown whiskers, blue or gray eyes; talkative.

Feagle, Wm...Embezzlement; committed, 1876; about 25 or 30 years of age, dark hair, light complexion, 5 feet 11 inches high, slender, polished and educated, once a clerk in Charleston, S. C.; last heard of in Ellis county.

Lee, Knox...Embezzlement; committed, 1876; about 30 years of age, 5 feet 11 inches high, light complexion, dark hair, smooth face or thin whiskers, lawyer.

Green, Jas...Assault to murder; committed, 1877.

Hicks, David...Theft; committed, 1877.

Ross, George...Embezzlement; committed, 1877.

McGreror, J. D...Embezzlement; committed, 1877.

Stewart, Wm...Forgery; committed, 1877.

Anderson, Wm...Assault to murder; committed, 1877.

Abernathy, John...Assault to murder; committed, 1877; about 20 or 25 years of age.

Polk, Thos...Forgery; committed, 1875, about 20 or 25 years of age.

GONZALES COUNTY.

Pressnal, A. K.—Murder; committed April 17, 1865; indicted October 12, same year.

Baltzell, Wm.—Murder; committed September 8, 1867; indicted October 17, same year. Is about 6 feet high, fair complexion, auburn hair, blue eyes, weighs about 175 pounds, 38 or 40 years old.

Jones, Jack—Murder; committed December 20, 1866; indicted October 18, 1872; negro.

Brady, Hut—Murder; committed February 10, 1868; indicted April 10, same year.   And indicted for assault with intent to murder, October 20, 1870.

Bean, Russell—Assault with intent to murder; committed December 3, 1867; indicted April 16, 1868.   Is about 5 feet 9 or 10 inches high, heavy set, florid complexion, black hair, one eye out, other one blue, 48 or 50 years old.   Also, indicted for assault to murder, October 25, 1870. Indicted for murder, October 24, 1871.

Woodley, Henry—Grand larceny; indictment lost; indicted January 1868; negro.

Mills, Thomas—Theft; indictment missing; indicted Fall term, 1869.

Darden, John—Theft; two indictments; committed June 10, 1869; indicted October 21, same year.

Coulter, Charles—Theft; two indictments; committed June 10, 1869; indicted October 21, same year.

Jolley, Logan—Theft; committed April 10, 1870; indicted April 21, same year.

Jolley, Logan—Theft; committed April 10, 1870; indicted April 21, same year.

Dikes, Lewis—Theft; committed January 30, 1868; indicted April 22, 1870.

Key, James—Theft; committed August 10, 1869; indicted April 22, 1870.

Wyatt, Gus—Theft; committed April 1, 1860; indicted April 22, same year; negro.

Russell, Thos.—Assault to murder; committed July 1, 1870; indicted October 25, same year.

Johnson, Wm.—Assault with intent to murder; committed July 1, '70; indicted October 25, same year.

Miller, Lewis—Theft; committed October 22, '70; indicted October 27, same year; negro.

Russell, Thos.—Theft; committed October 24, '70; indicted October 27, same year.

Brown, Sam.—Assault to murder; committed October 25, '70; indicted October 27, same year.

Dorris, Miles—Theft; committed October 1, '70; indicted October 28, same year.

Chambers, John—Theft; committed February 18, '71; indicted, February 21, same year.

Bobo, Young—Theft; committed February 18, '71; indicted February 21, same year.   Also, theft; committed February 20, '71; indicted February 21, same year.

Chambers, John—Theft; committed February 18, '71; indicted February 22, same year.

Halford, Nathaniel—Murder; committed May 19, '71; indicted June 22, same year.

Chambers, John—Theft from a house; committed January 10, '71; indicted June 22, same year.

Cottingham, Thos.—Theft; committed May 8, '71; indicted June 22, same year.

Cooley, Richard—Pettit larceny; committed June 15, '71; indicted June 24, same year.

Cooley, Richard—Grand larceny; committed October 15, '70; indicted indicted June 24, '71.

Harrison, Austin—Theft; committed July 2, '71; indicted October 20, same year; negro.

Anderson, Richmond—Murder; committed February 1, '71; indicted October 24, same year.

White, T. D. O.—Accomplice to murder; committed July 15, '71; indicted October 24, same year.

Halford, Nathaniel—Murder; committed May 19, '71; indicted Octo-25, same year.

Lamkin, Crump, alias Tecumseh—Assault to murder; committed October 16, 71; indicted October 25, same year; negro.

McMickle, Columbus—Theft; committed February 17, '72; indicted February 26, same year.

Anderson, Bob, alias Bob Walker—Assault to murder; committed August 20, '72; indicted October 8, same year.

Welch, Mike...Theft; committed February 1, 1872, indicted October 10, same year.

Franklin, T. J...Murder; committed September 1, 1872; indicted October 10, same year.

Houston, Geo...Theft from house; committed March 4, 1872; indicted October 12, same year.

Washburne, T. H., alias Frank Warner...Theft from house; commit-March 4, 1872; indicted October 12, same year.

Rudder, Sam...Assault with intent to murder; committed May 17, 1872; indicted October 15, same year.

Thompson, Wm., alias Paschal Pugio...Theft from house; committed June 1, '72; indicted October 16, same year.

Roberts, Jacob...Theft; committed January 17, '73; indicted February 7, same year.

Sutton, Frank...Assault to murder; committed December 25, '72; indicted February 7, '73.

Davidson, John...Theft; committed January 1, '73; indicted February 12, same year; three cases.

Holmes, J. F...Theft; committed January 1, '73; indicted February 12, same year; three cases.

Dadvidson, John...Theft; committed September 19, '72; indicted February 12, '73.

Holmes, Thos...Theft; committed January 1, '73; indicted February 12, same year; two indictments.

Irvin, Gus...Assault with intent to murder; committed October 1, '73; indicted October 10, same year.

Robinson, John...Assault with intent to murder; committed November 10, '72; indicted October 10, '73.

Brimsbury, Jas...Assault with intent to murder; committed May 10, '73; indicted October 13, same year.

Walker, Isaiah...Murder; committed February 24, '73; indicted October 16, same year; a very tall, large negro, copper colored, 40 years old.

Roberts, Jas...Theft; committed December 3, '73; indicted February 7, '74.

Royalls, Shonae...Murder; committed December, '73; indicted February 7, '74.

Noble, Dick...Theft; committed January 5, '73; indicted February 11, '74; negro, very black, very large navel, lives in Guadalupe county.

Mathis, Peter...Theft; committed October 10, '73; indicted February 11, '74.

Wilson, Henry...Theft; committed November 3, '73; indicted February 11, '74.

Bunton, Fred, alias Jack Davis...Assault with intent to murder; committed July 9, '73; indicted May 7, '74.

Hart, Jos...Murder; committed March 7, '74; indicted May 14, '74; slender built, about 30 years old, light complexion.

Leagan, Morris...Rape; committed September 13, 1874; indicted Oct. 3, same year.

West, John C...Theft of steer; committed November 1, 1873; indicted October 6, 1874.

Haynes, Peter...Theft of gelding; committed October 10, 1873; indicted October 14, 1874.

Smith, Cap...Theft of cow; committed April 10, 1874; indicted October 12, same year.

Crenshaw, Nick...Theft of cattle; committed April 5, 1874; indicted October 12, same year.

McCall, Sam (alias Sam Kindred)...Assault to murder; committed May 23, 1874; indicted October 12, same year.

Goodin, John D. and Autizer, Wm....Murder; committed August 10, 1874; indicted October 14, same year.

Anderson, Andrew...Murder; committed September 14, 1874; indicted October 14, same year.

Smith, Bill...Theft of cattle; committed April 1, '74; indicted February 2, '75.

White, Bill...Theft of gelding; committed December 2, '74; indicted February 2, '75.

Houston, Thomas (alias Exline)...Theft of gelding; committed July 24, '73; indicted February 2, '75; in the Penitentiary or escaped.

Alex (a freedman)...Assault to murder; committed December 5, '74; indicted February 4, '75.

White, Arch...Murder; committed January 1, '75; indicted February 4, same year.

McCallum, George.. Assault to murder; committed January 1, '75; indicted May 7, same year.

Franklin, W. Rhett...Assault to murder; committed January 10, '75; indicted May 7, same year.

Spriggs, Daniel...Theft of gelding; committed September 10, 1873; indicted May 7, 1875.

Monroe, George...Threat to take life; committed May 1, 1875; indicted May 7, same year.

Johnson, Ben., alias Sam...Theft of hogs; committed March 10, 1875; indicted May 7, same year.

Harris, Geo...Theft of mare; committed April 10, 1875; indicted May 7, same year.

Herndon, Jas. T...Theft of cattle; committed May 1, 1875, indicted May 7, same year.

Wright, Wm...Assault to murder; committed April 10, 1875; indicted May 11, same year.

Garcia, Antonio...Theft of calf; committed March 10, 1875; indicted September 30, same year.

Fones, Joseph...Theft of sow; committed January 25, 1875; indicted September 30, same year.

Bowden, Chas...Assault to murder; committed September 1, 1875; indicted October, same year.

Evans, David...Assault to murder; committed July 18, 1875; indicted September 30, same year.

McKinnon, Jno...Theft of neat cattle; committed August 10, '75; indicted October 5, same year.

Trafton, Robt...Swindling; committed August 1, '75; indicted October 8, same year.

McBride, A. Hilliard...Theft of cattle; committed November 10, '74; indicted October 8, '75.

McCarty, W. P...Assault to murder; committed September 26, '75; indicted October 8, same year.

Giddings, Verastus...Theft of colt; committed March 1, '74; indicted October 8, same year. This man has escaped from penitentiary.

White, Miles (C.)...Theft of gelding; committed July 10, '75; indicted January 29, '76.

Cochran, Buck...Assault to murder; committed December 24, '75; indicted February 1, '76.

Clemons, Frank...Theft of hogs; committed January 1, '76; indicted February 5, same year.

Callison, Thos.; Day, Alfred; Allen, ——...Robbery; committed January 22, '76; indicted February 5, same year.

Reid, Ruffian...Assault to murder; committed December 10, '75; indicted February 5, '76.

Stewart, Allen; Neal, Wesley, alias Neal, Calloway...Theft of two geldings; committed November 11, '75; indicted February 5, '76; colored.

Davis, Samuel...Theft of hog; committed December 1, '74; indicted October 16, '76.

Love, James...Theft of yearling; committed August 1, '76; indicted October 11, same year.

Montgomery, Robt...Theft of cattle; committed May 1, '76; indicted October 16, same year.

Franks, Bud...Assault to murder; committed September 1, 1876; indicted October 16, same year.

Montgomery, Robt...Theft of cattle; committed September 1, 1876; indicted October 16, same year.

Phillips, Gage...Theft of cattle; committed August 1, 1876; indicted October 16, same year.

Hilliard, Elias...Threat to take human life; committed January 4, 1876; indicted October 17, same year.

Hedrick, Geo. W...Theft of oxen; committed July 20, 1876; indicted April 6, 1877.

Peak, Wm...Theft of cattle; committed November 1, 1876; indicted April 9, 1877.

Ivey, Ben...Theft of gelding; committed January 1, 1874; indicted April 11, 1877; escaped from penitentiary.

Johnson, Chas. D....Theft of money and goods; committed July 1, 1876; indicted April 11, 1877.

Kinney, Jno. D....Assault to murder; committed December 26, 1876; indicted April 6, 1877.

McCracken, Lycurgus...Theft of filly; committed January 1, 1877; indicted October 6, same year.

Rogers, Wm., and Robinson, L. C...Theft of a calf; committed August 20, 1877; indicted October 6, same year.

Carroll, Lewis (alias James, Henry)...Murder; committed May 1, 1877; indicted October 6, same year.

Stratton, Richard...Murder; committed February 24, 1873; indicted October 9, 1877.

Stratton, Richard...Assault to murder; committed February 24, 1873; indicted October 9, 1877.

Clements, Manning...Murder; committed July 25, 1872; indicted October 10, 1877.

GILLESPIE COUNTY.

Paul, William...Murder; indicted November 21, '65.

Banta, Jacob...Murder; indicted November 21, '65.

Gibson, Samuel...Murder; indicted November 21, '65.

Gibson, Robert...Murder; indicted November 21, '65.

Hanes, Wm...Murder; indicted November 21, '65.

Benson, Jehu...Murder; indicted November 21, '65.

Cadwel, John...Murder; indicted November 21, '65.

Glenn, Jas...Murder; indicted November 21, '65.

Glenn, James...Murder; indicted November 21, '65.

Burnham, Wm...Murder; indicted November 21, '65.

Vaughn, Jesse...Murder; indicted November 21, '65.

DeRusk, Samuel...Murder; indicted November 21, '65.

Neal, M. L...Murder; indicted November 21, '65.

Kent, ——...Murder; indicted November 21, '65.

Freeland, ——...Murder; indicted November 21, '65.

Vickers, ——...Murder; indicted November 21, 65.

Doss, Samuel...Murder; indicted March 18, '65; supposed to be in New Mexico or Colorado Territory.

Deveraux, Julius...Assault to kill; indicted May 14, '68.

Waldrip, James B...Theft of hogs; indicted March 15, '72.

Waldrip, Ben.; Hutchinson, Geo.; Berry, Silas; Berry, Wm. Bait... Theft of hogs; indicted July 15, '75.

Birkley, M...Theft; indicted November 16, '75.

Bockley, C. R...Theft; indicted November 16, '75.

Riley, James, of Blanco county...Theft of gelding; indicted March 19, '74; had once been arrested and gave bond, which was forfeited.

Walker, James...Assault to murder; indicted July 17, '73.

Colbath, Ambrose...Murder; indicted July 20, '75; of Blanco county.

Kirchner, Johan...Incest; indicted October 28, '76; about 30 years old, weighs 150 pounds, sandy hair, light complexion, of Gillespie.

Seiter, Henriette...Incest; indicted October 28, '76.

GRIMES COUNTY.

Barton, Jerry...Murder; committed August, '66; indicted November, same year; negro.

Ballenger, V...Theft of horse; committed April, '68; indicted June, same year; murder committed January, '70; indicted October, same year.

Chatham, W. L...Embezzlement; committed November, '67; indicted June, '68; crippled and goes on crutches.

Williams, Felix...Murder; committed August, '67; indicted June, '68.

Sapp, Wm...Murder; committed April, 68; indicted December, same year.

Thomas, W. S...Embezzlement (two cases); committed October, '69; indicted December, same year.

Jones, Hamp...Theft of horse; committed August, '70; indicted October, same year; negro.

Brown, Sawney...Theft from house (two cases); committed September, '70; indicted October, same year; negro.

Dawson, Moses...Bigamy; committed March '69; indicted February, '71; negro.

Walker, Daniel...Assault to murder; committed September, '71; indicted October, same year; negro.

Boller, Caleb...Assault to murder; committed October, '71; indicted October, same year.

Shannon, Isaac...Theft from house; committed June, '70; indicted October, '71; negro.

Bartlett, J. D...Theft from house; committed October, '71; indicted October, same year.

Lewis, Taylor...Assault to murder; committed October, '71; indicted February, '72.

McLane, Silas...Theft from house; committed May, '72; indicted same year; negro.

Young, Moses, alias McIntosh...Theft of gelding; indicted June, 1872; negro.

Thayor, C. H...Swindling; committed October, '71; indicted June, '72.

Jones, Charles...Theft of ox; committed May, '71; indicted June, '72; negro.

Williams Charles...Theft of a mare; committed May, '72; indicted October, same year; Theft of gelding (three cases); committed May, '72; indicted October, same year; negro.

Garrett, Thos...Assault to murder; committed September, '72; in-indicted October, same year.

Tabb, Jacob...Theft from house; committed August, '72; indicted October, same year; negro.

Wilson, Mat...Murder; committed October, '72; indicted October same year; negro.

Greer, Stephen...Murder; committed October, '72; indicted October, same year; negro.

Pugh, Wm...Murder; committed October, '72; indicted October, same year; negro.

Miller, Henry...Theft from house; committed December, '72; indicted February, '73; negro.

Hadley, Barney...Theft of heifer; committed October, '72; indicted February, '73; negro.

Harn, S. M...Assault to murder; committed March, '73; indicted June, same year. Theft of horse; committed May, '73; indicted June, same year.

Garrett, J. D...Murder; committed July, '72; indicted June, '73.

Roco, Matilda...Murder; committed July, '72; indicted June, '73.

Raby, J. W...Murder; committed February, '73; indicted June, same year.

Venters, Thos...Assault to rape (two cases); committed June '73; indicted June, same year; negro.

Dillinger, L. D...Bigamy; committed June '71; indicted October, '73.

Norwood, Henry...Theft from house; committed June '73; indicted October same year; negro.

Felder, Stephen...Assault to murder; committed October, '73; indicted October, same year; negro.

Wafford, Walter...Theft of horse; committed September, '73; indicted October, same year.

Miller, John...Theft of gelding; committed January, '74; indicted February, same year.

Davis, D. C...Swindling; committed August, '73; indicted June, '74;

Vines, Jackson...Swindling; committed August, '73; indicted June '74.

Page, George...Assault to murder; committed July, '74; indicted October, same year.

Murphy, Bob....Theft from house (two cases); committed February, '74; indicted October, same year; negro.

Jackson, John...Theft of mare; committed June, '74; indicted October, same year; negro.

Cobine, W H...Theft from house; committed August, '74; indicted October, same year.

Vines, Washington...Swindling; committed August, '73; indicted October, '74.

Langford, Jas...Theft of a hog; committed January, '75; indicted February, same year.

Alexander, Peter, alias Andrew Reed...Theft from house; committed December, '74; indicted February, '75.

Vance, Joseph...Murder; committed November, '74; indicted February, '75.

Taylor, Gabe...Theft of bull yearling; committed December, '74; indicted February, '75; negro.

Hightower, Simon...Theft of hog; committed December, '74; indicted February, '75; negro.

Lemuel, Eli...Theft from house; committed September, '74; indicted February, '75; negro.

Sims, Sophia...Murder; committed April, '75; indicted June, same year; negress.

Bowdon, W. W...Theft from house; committed March, '75; indicted June, same year.

Tubbs, John...Theft of hog; committed October, '74; indicted June, '75; negro.

Whitehead, O. C...Murder; committed September, '75; indicted October, same year.

Warren, Jas...Murder; committed September, '75; indicted October, same year.

St. Cloud, V. E...Murder; committed September, '75; indicted October, same year.

Nash, John...Assault to murder; committed October, '75; indicted February, '76.

Brown, Samuel...Theft of hog; committed October, '75; indicted February, '76; negro.

Jackson, Ike...Assault to murder; committed January, '76; indicted February, same year; negro.

Hardy, Wm...Theft from house; committed December, '76; indicted February, same year.

Howard, Sam...Swindling; committed December, '75; indicted February, '76; negro.

Lee, Kaufman...Theft; committed January, '76; indicted February, same year.

Johnson, Willis...Theft of yearling; committed August, '75; indicted May, '76; negro.

Fairfax, Israel...Robbery; committed April, '76; indicted May, same year; assault to murder; committed April, '76; indicted May, same year; negro.

Nale, Richard...Assault to murder; two cases; committed April, '76; indicted May, same year.

Sally, Jerry...Theft of cattle; committed February, '76; indicted May, same year; negro.

Banks, Jas...Murder; committed October, '75; indicted February, '76; negro.

Gregg, Harmon...Murder; committed August, '76; indicted November, '76.

Johnson, Morris...Theft of hog; committed December, '76; indicted May, '77; negro.

Jones, Pat...Theft of filly; committed September, '75; indicted October, '75; negro.

Mitchell, Daniel...Assault to kill; committed July, '76; indicted November, '76; negro.

May, Alex...Murder; committed November, '76; indicted February, '77.

Marion, Geo...Murder; committed September, '76; indicted November, '76.

Nevells, Reuben...Theft of gelding; committed October, '76; indicted November, '76.

Neeley, Wm...Theft of heifer; committed December, '75; indicted November, '76.

Neeley, Henry...Seduction; committed June, '76; indicted November, '76.

Robertson, Joseph....Theft of gelding; committed October, '76; indicted November, 76.

Rhodes, D. R...Swindling; committed April, '77; indicted May, '77.

Rice, Worley....Theft of cattle; committed April, 77; indicted May, '77.

Smith, Geo...Attempt to rape; committed November, '76; indicted November, same year; negro.

Sneed, Nelson...Assault to kill; committed March, '77; indicted May, '77; negro.

Thomas, John...Assault to kill; committed September, '76; indicted November, '76; negro.

Thomas, Gilbert...Perjury; committed February, '77; indicted May, '77; negro.

Walter, Wm...Theft; committed March, '76; indicted May, 76.

HUNT COUNTY.

Brooks, W. W...Murder; indicted March 22, 1867.

Hays, R. H...Murder; indicted February 28, 1871.

Lehew, Cicero...Murder; indicted June 28, 1871.

Voyles, Oscar...Murder; indicted July 22, 1875.

Wortham, Thomas...Assault to murder; indicted October, 20, 1871.

Durham, Harry...Assault to murder; indicted March 7, 1873.

Hill, Wm...Asault to murder; indicted October 17, 1874.

Nolan, J. J...Assault to murder; indicted January 8, 1877.

Brady, John...Assault to murder; indicted March 18, 1876.

Brady, Lundy...Assault to murder; indicted March 18, 1876.
Williams, John...Assault to murder; indicted July 9, 1875.
Wilkins, Isaac...Incest; indicted October 25, 1871.
Riley, Elizabeth...Incest; indicted October 25, 1871.
Nowell, Isaac ..Adultery; indicted July 4, 1872.
Finley, Nancy...Adultery; indicted March 7, 1872.
Cowan, Jack...Assault to rape; indicted March 12, 1873.
Beard, Moses....Aiding prisoners to escape; indicted July 19, 1876.
Gibson, R. B...Swindling; indicted July 3, 1872.
Foster, Ed...Threat to take life; indicted March 7, 1873.
Hopkins, Thomas...Assault to rob; indicted October 13, 1874.
Mitchell, John....Assault to murder; indicted January 25, 1877.
Lovejoy, Wm., alias Braden, Wm...Assault to murder; indicted Jnauary 11, 1877.
Strickland, Amos...Theft of animals; indicted February 22, 1871.
Fields, Wm...Theft of animals; indicted October 25, 1871.
Meyers, Shelton....Theft of animals; indicted March 7, 1872.
Taylor, George and Benjamin....Theft of animals; indicted March 1, 1873.
Pickett, Andrew....Theft of animals; indicted October 8, 1874.
McDaniel, John...Theft of animals; indicted July 9, 1875; four cases.
Mitchell, C. R....Theft of animals; indicted July 9, 1875.
Swift, Pat. H...Theft of animals; indicted October 17, 1874.
Coy, Wm...Theft of animals; indicted July 13, 1875.
Sullivan, Bud....Theft of animals; indicted July 22, 1875.
Cooper, James...Theft of animals; indicted July 22, 1875.
Brady, Nas; and Dill, Lum...Theft of animals; indicted July 7, 1876.
Green, A. J...Theft of animals; indicted July 13, 1876.
Hendrix, John...Theft of animals; indicted July 19, 1876.
Parkhill, James...Perjury; indicted July 22, 1875.
Thayer, Wm. T...Theft of cattle; indicted January 25, 1877.

JACKSON COUNTY.

Parsons, Jeff...Murder; committed March, 1869; indicted November, 1869; mulatto, 28 or 29 years old.
Martin, John...Murder; committed March, 1870; indicted October, 1870; Irishman.
Loomis, Warner...Manslaughter; 25 or 26 years old, about 5 feet 10 inches high; white.
Ford, Henry....Murder; about 22 years old, 5 feet 10 inches high; negro.
Atkisson, Thos..–Theft of beef steer; about 24 years old, 5 feet 9 or 10 inches high; white.
Young, Bob...Theft of a hog; committed December, 1874; indicted February, 1875; negro, stout build; last heard of in Victoria county.
Nichols, J. A....Attempting to pass counterfeit money; white, about 25 years old, at least 6 feet high.

JACK COUNTY.

McMillan, M...Murder; indicted June, 1874; is 6 feet high, weighs 155 pounds, light complexion, black hair, blue eyes, 35 years old, and is slightly pock-marked.

Simpson, Thomas...Murder; indicted June, 1874.

Halsell, Jennie...Theft from house; indicted June 1874; negress.

Burns, T. J...Murder; indicted June, 1874; is 5 feet 6 inches high, weighs 130 pounds, light or sallow complexion, dark hair, blue eyes (weak and downcast) and 20 years old.

Cantwell, Robt...Assault to murder; indicted June 1874; is 5 feet 4 inches high, weighs 125 pounds, has fair complexion, black hair, blue eyes, and is 20 years old.

Drummond, Chas...Theft of cattle; indicted June, 1874; is 6 feet 1 inch high, weighs 165 pounds, has a sallow complexion, light hair, pale blue eyes, and is 35 years old.

Nix, Newton...Swindling; indicted June, 1874; is 6 feet 1 inch high, weighs 150 pounds, has a fair complexion, black hair, blue eyes, and is 45 years old. In Kansas.

Baldwin, Wm...Theft of cattle; indicted June, 1874; is 5 feet 8 inches high, weighs 160 pounds, has a sandy complexion, red hair, blue eyes, and is 40 years old.

Jones, Elmira...Perjury; indicted October, 1874; negress.

Pruitt, John...Theft of cattle; indicted February, 1875; is 5 feet 8 inches high, weighs 140 pounds, has a dark complexion, black hair, black eyes, and is 30 years old.

Gibson, J. A...Assault to murder; indicted February, 1875; is 6 feet 2 inches high, and weighs 180 pounds.

Lanley, Moses...Theft of cattle (two cases); indicted February, 1875; is 5 feet 11 inches high, weighs 180 pounds, has a fair complexion, black hair, black eyes, and is 38 years old.

Brady...Theft of cattle; indicted February, 1876.

King...Theft of cattle...indicted February, 1876.

Faulkner, Billy...Assault to murder; indicted February, 1875.

Gibbons, J. W...Theft of cattle (two cases); indicted February, 1875; is 5 feet 6 inches high, weighs 160 pounds, has a fair complexion, black hair, blue eyes, and is 22 years old.

Fondren, John...Murder; indicted February, 1875; is 5 feet 4 inches high, weighs 120 pounds, has a fair complexion, black hair, blue eyes, and is 18 years old.

Standifer, James...Theft of cattle; indicted October, 1875; is 6 feet high, weighs 160 pounds, has a fair complexion, black hair, black eyes, and is 22 years old.

Standifer, Calvin...Theft of cattle; indicted October, 1875; is 5 feet 8 inches high, weighs 160 pounds, has a fair complexion, red hair, blue eyes, and is 25 years old.

Sherman, Willard...Theft of cow; indicted June, 1876; is 5 feet 10 inches high, weighs 155 pounds, has a fair complexion, black hair, blue eyes, and is 22 years old.

Waldrup, Monroe...Theft of horses; indicted March, 1876; is 5 feet 10 inches high, weighs 145 pounds, has a light complexion, light hair, blue eyes, and is 22 years old.

Stover, W. E...Theft; indicted June 30, 1875; is 6 feet high, weighs 200 pounds, has a fair complexion, dark hair, blue eyes, and is 33 years old.

Adams, John...Assault to murder; indicted October 28, 1876; is 5 feet 10 inches high; weighs 140 pounds, has a fair complexion, light curly hair, blue eyes, and is 23 years old.

Ruble, F. M—Theft; indicted May 10, 1877; is 6 feet high, weighs 140 pounds, has a dark complexion, black hair, blue eyes, and is 27 years old.

Wilson, J. H...Murder; indicted November 6, 1877; is 5 feet 10 inches high, weighs 130 pounds, has a fair complexion, black hair, blue eyes, and is 33 years old.

Morris, Jake...Assault to murder; indicted November 7, 1877; is 5 feet 10 inches high, has a sandy complexion, light and sandy hair, blue eyes, and is 24 years old, weighs 140 pounds.

Mullins, Z...Assault to murder; indicted November 7, 1877.

KARNES COUNTY.

Pinson, George...Murder; committed December 25, 1866; indicted November, 1867. Weighs 140 lbs., 5 feet 10 inches high, 36 years of age, light complexion.

Wright, John S...Assault to murder; committed February 19, 1867; indicted November, same year.

Oneal, Jack...Theft; committed April 1, 1870; indicted November, same year. Weighs 160 lbs., 5 feet 10 inches high, 40 years old, dark complexion, black eyes and hair.

Hickman, Charles...Theft; committed December 20, 1870; indicted March, 1871. Weighs 150 lbs., 6 feet high, 40 years old, light complexion, grey eyes.

Lovelace, Thomas...Theft; committed April 1, 1870; indicted March, 1871.

De Board, Wm...Murder; committed January 1, 1868; indicted July, 1871. Weighs 130 lbs., 5 feet 5 inches high, light complexion, blue eyes, is 40 years old.

Collins, John...Assault to murder; committed April 10, 1870; indicted March term, same year.

Ethridge, Wm...Assault to murder; committed November 1, 1873; indicted November, same year. Weighs 140 lbs., 5 feet 9 inches high, 35 years old.

Robberson, Eugene...Forgery; committed May 9, 1874; indicted July, same year.

Murray, John...Assault to murder; committed July 12, 1875; indicted July, same year. Weighs 170 lbs., 6 feet high, 30 years old, dark complexion, black eyes and hair.

Ward, Jno...Perjury; committed March 2. 1875; indicted November, same year.

Phillips, Gage...Five cases; theft and assault to murder; committed in all the cases in 1876; indicted same year. Weighs 160 lbs., 6 feet high, 27 years old, dark complexion, black hair and eyes.

Smith, Sidney...Murder; committed March 10, 1876; indicted March, same year.

Lusk, S. B...Forgery; committed June 1, 1874; indicted March, 1876.

Greenwood, John...Theft; committed July 17, 1873. Weighs about 150 lbs., 6 feet high.

Hues, Robert...Murder; committed March 8, 1877; indicted same year.

Gintz, John...Rape; committed March 8, 1877; indicted same year.

Baily, Mat...Forgery; committed March 10, 1877; indicted same year.

Phillips, Bill...Theft; committed March 10, 1877; indicted same year.

Callison, J. C...Theft; committed March 10, 1877; indicted same year.

Collins, Joe...Assault; committed March 10, 1877; indicted same year.

Boba, John...Theft; committed March 11, 1875.

KENDALL COUNTY.

Good, Isham J...Theft of cattle; committed February, 1873; indicted April, 1875. Is 30 years old, has a fair complexion, is 5 feet 9 inches high, and has light hair. Last heard of in Coleman county.

Hamilton, Robt...Forgery; committed October, 1875; indicted December, same year. Is 28 years old, has a fair complexion, is 5 feet 9 inches high, and has light hair.

Langston, Herbert...Theft of gelding; committed October, 1870; indicted December, 1871. Theft of mare; committed March, 1871; indicted December, same year. Is 35 years old, has a fair complexion, is 6 feet 2 inches high, and has light hair. Last heard of in Atascosa county.

McClure, James...Theft of mare; committed July, 1873; indicted August, same year. Is 55 years old, has a dark complexion, is 6 feet 2 inches high, and has gray beard and gray hair.

Sneed, Berry...Assault to murder; committed July, 1875; indicted August, same year. Is 32 years old, has a fair complexion, is 6 feet high, and has brown beard and hair. Last heard of in Burnet county.

Tatsch, August...Theft of cattle. Supposed to be in Mason county.

Hoag, Martin...Theft of bacon.

LIMESTONE COUNTY.

Cotton, Mitch...Murder; indicted June 22, 1872.

Rhodes, Henry...Theft of mule; indicted June 11, 1873; negro; average size, copper-colored, talkative, talks loud, slightly dish-faced.

Stevens, Ben, alias Ben Smith...Theft; indicted June 14, 1873.

Trammel, Wood...Murder; indicted October 17, 1873; negro; nearly black, heavy set, weighs 180, 5 feet 8 inches high, 35 years old, does not talk much but rather loud, full face.

Jeffries, Preston...Theft of cow; indicted October 17, 1873.

Mills, Tom...Murder; indicted October 23, 1873.

Cox, Green...Assault with intent to murder; indicted October, 1873.

Clendenan, Benjamin...Murder; indicted October, 1873; medium size, rather heavy set, round shoulders, freckles on face, brown eyes and hair, talks little, rather slow, 28 years old; supposed to be in Montague county.

Adams, Jno...Theft of yearling; indicted October, 1873; negro.

VonCannon, Geo...Assault with intent to murder; indicted, February, 1872; white; about 28 years old, dandy in appearance, is a dancing-master; was last seen, four months ago, in San Antonio.

Thompson, James M...Murder; indicted June, 1874; medium size, light complexion, light beard, eyes and hair light, face rather sharp, 25 years old, quick spoken, round shoulders.

Goodman, Wm., alias J. M. Goodman...Assault with intent to murder; indicted June, 1874.

Marshall, Ambrose...Theft of two oxen, indicted June, 1874; negro.

Jacobs, Bass...Assault with intent to murder; indicted June, 1874; negro.

Hall, Wm. N...Theft of cow; indicted June, 1874; an accomplice to willful burning, June, 1874; assault with intent to murder, October, 1874.

Taylor, Titus...Theft of cow; indicted June, 1874; negro; black, low, heavy set, 35 years old, rather crabbed spoken, talks little, scar on left breast, and two scars on back just in lower part of left shoulder, long; made with knife by surgeon.

Medlock, Jerry...Arson; indicted June, 1874; negro; very black, quick spoken, slender, 5 feet 10 inches high, 40 years old.

George, W. R. and Cary...Murder; indicted October, 1874; white.

Anderson, Doc...Assault with intent to murder; indicted October, 1874.

Kuttner, J...Theft; indicted February, 1876.

Bonesteele, Burglary; indicted September, 1876; white; 21 years old.

Hood, Willie...Murder; indicted September, 1876.

Cornelius, A. C...Murder; indicted September 7, 1876.

Pevyhouse, A....Theft; indicted September, 1876; spare made, 5 feet 8 inches high, light skin, light hair, thin beard, reddish, sandy colored and rather scaly face, does not talk much, uneducated.

O'Neil, Reuben; O'Neil, James; Cravy, Ike...Arson; indicted September, 1876; Reuben O'Neil, aged 50 years, hair getting gray, face very red, drinks a good deal, eyes gray, 6 feet high, lively, talkative. The other two are young men; James is a son of Reuben O'Neil; they are all together out west, and are well armed and will be hard to arrest.

Thompson, Frank and Simon...Murder; indicted March, 1877; Simon 5 feet 8 inches high, 28 year old, skin fair, eyes blue, hair auburn, little beard, sharp features, can't write. Frank has dark hair, 5 feet 10 inches high, dark eyes, looks up from under his eye-brows, little hump-shouldered, not very talkative, somewhat of country appearance.

Smith, Preston...Assault with intent to murder; indicted March, 1877.

Perry, B. M...Theft; indicted March, 1877.

Fielder, Jno...Theft; indicted March, 1877; hair rather black, eyes dark, 18 years old, heavy eye-brows, heavy set, not very talkative, dark skin, talks long and easy, has scar on one thigh; supposed to be in Parker county.

Sherod, Nolly...Swindling; indicted October, 1874; average size, stoop-shoulders, little bow-legged, fair skin, blue eyes, light hair, rather talkative.

Preston, Richard, alias Preston, Dick....Incest and rape; indicted October, 1874; negro, nearly black, 5 feet 10 inches high, heavy set, very thick lips, rather talkative and boastful, especially of his property.

Wynn, Charley...Murder; indicted October, 1874.

Pelham, H. B...Theft of merchandise; indicted February, 1875; average size, heavy set, gray eyes, light hair, 35 years old, somewhat bald, coarse features; supposed to be in the Northern States.

Callens, Adolphus...Murder; indicted February, 1875; this man has one hand off; is supposed to be in the western counties.

Caldwell, Samuel...Theft of a bale of cotton; indicted February, 1875.

Thrift, Wm...Theft of a beef steer; indicted February, 1876; white, 5½ feet high, dark complexion, hair and eyes dark, 24 years old, talks quick, slight brogue, rather talkative, great trader.

Jones, Benj...Assault with intent to murder; indicted June, 1875; light hair and eyes, spare made, 20 years old.

Peeples, George...Theft of two oxen; indicted June, 1875.

Wilcox, Henry, and O'Brien, Johnny...Burglary; indicted June, 1875; former very bald-headed, gray eyes, hair light, speaks sharp, very full forehead, intelligent looking, average size; latter, small, dark hair and eyes, quick spoken, talkative, 35 years old; both Northern men.

Trammel, Sim...Assault with intent to murder; indicted June, 1875.
Jackson, Ceaf...Theft of a gelding; indicted June, 1875.
Potter, Ben...Theft of a beef; indicted June, 1876.
Full er, Miles...Assault with intent to murder; average size, 26 years old, dark hair and dark skin, hazel eyes, don't talk much, heavy eyebrow, keeps his eyes down.
Pulley, W. L...Theft; indicted June, 1875; 30 years old, average size, light blue eyes, auburn hair, insipid or apathetic countenance, slight nasal voice, passes himself off for a preacher, is a Mason; went from here to Louisiana, but may be now in the West.
Cooper, E. C...Theft of a beef; indicted June, 1875.
Bluitt, Isaac...Theft of a hog; indicted October, 1875.
Lea, Harris...Theft of a calf; indicted October, 1875.

LAMAR COUNTY.

Bell, John...Murder.
Conelias, Thos...Killing hogs of another.
McCarty, Joseph...Forgery.
Baker, R. L...Abortion and murder.
Wade, Nancy...Infanticide.
Vess, Louis...Assault to murder.
Tubbs, John...Assault to murder.
Burton, Harvey...Murder.
Daughtery, E. C...Murder.
Heifler, Augustus...Murder.
Hicks, Harvey...Murder.
Carico, W. B...Murder.
Jenkins, A. M...Murder.
Smith, Samuel...Assault to kill; committed June, 1865; indicted October, same year.
Terry, A. N...Theft (two cases); committed April, 1865; indicted October, same year.
Widener, Mary J., alias Mary J. Anderson...Theft.
Robinson, Ally...Theft; committed September, 1866; indicted October, same year.
Turner, Jno. F...Assault to kill; committed April, 1866; indicted October, 1869.
Harmon, Thos. N. B...Assault to kill.
Winfrey, Frank...Robbery; committed March, 1867; indicted April, same year.
Smith, Charley W...Rape; committed November, 1866; indicted April 1867.
Clark, C. C...Assault to kill; committed March, 1868; indicted April, same year.
Gunter, J. L...Assault to kill; committed March, 1868; indicted April, same year.
Alexander, Frank...Burglary.
Wilkinson, Shepard...Burglary. Theft (three cases); committed August, 1868; indicted October, 1867.
Phillips, Jos...Theft; committed May, 1868; indicted October, same year.
Christmas, J. W...Theft.
5

Davis, Marion.

Cox, S.

Brimley, Stephen H...Assault to kill; committed October, 1867; indicted October, same year.

Cox, Wm...Robbery (two cases); committed January, 1866; indicted October, 1867.

Johnson, Love...Robbery.

Guest, Elisha...Murder; committed May, 1866; indicted October, '68.

Roberts, Jas...Theft; committed January, 1868; indicted April, same year.

Roberts, Jno...Theft; committed January, 1868; indicted April, same year.

Staley, Thos...Assault to kill; committed August, 1868; indicted October, 1868.

Snow, Jas...Robbery; committed January, 1869; indicted April same year.

Parish, Leander...Robbery; committed February, 1865; indicted December, 1871.

Russell, H. R.. Murder.

Anderson, Robt. B...Murder; committed March, 1867; indicted April, same year.

Clack, Henry...Theft; committed February, 1868; indicted April. same year.

Johnson, Jno...Theft; committed September, 1868; indicted October, same year.

Allen, Gabriel...Murder; committed June, 1867; indicted October, same year.

Hicks, Corde...Murder; committed September, 1867; indicted October, same year.

Elmore, Wm...Committed May, 1867; indicted October, same year.

Cox, Geo...Robbery; committed January, 1866; indicted October, '67.

West, Kinch...Robbery; committed January, 1866; indicted October, 1867.

Sarvis, James...Robbery; committed January, 1866; indicted October, 1867.

Johnson, Wm...Murder; committed May, 1869; indicted October, same year.

Alexander, Robt...Murder.

Bradford, Autry...Assault to murder; committed September, 1869; indicted October, same year.

Winters, Nelson...Theft.

Stamper, Judd...Assault to kill; committed October, 1869; indicted October, same year.

Isbell, Jas...Assault to kill; indicted October, 1867. Burglary; committed May, 1869; indicted October, same year.

Ward, A...Murder; committed August, 1870; indicted November, same year.

Cole, Wm....Murder; committed August, 1870; indicted November, same year.

Seay, Thos...Theft; committed April, 1870; indicted November, same year.

Moseley, Isham.....Murder; committed December, 1870; indicted March, 1871.

Rogers, Wm....Theft, (two cases); committed October, 1870; indicted July, 1871.

Gramner, Payton...Theft; committed September, 1868; indicted October, same year.

Kirtland, Daniel...Theft; committed September, 1868; indicted October, same year.

Howard, F. B...Theft; committed November, 1870; indicted November, same year.

Carpenter, Thos. H...Assault to kill; committed December, 1870; indicted November, same year.

Barnett, Carey...Assault to kill.

Brown, Alfred...Assault to kill.

Alred, Alfred...Assault to kill.

McGinnis, Wm...Assault to kill.

Wisdom, Fred...Assault to kill; committed July, 1871; indicted July, same year.

Hudson, Call...Assault to kill.

Tinnin, Willis...Assault to kill; committed April, 1871, indicted April, same year.

Archer, Tobe...Assault to kill.

McCoy, Monroe...Assault to murder.

Holcomb, Merideth...Theft.

Birmingham, Pat...Assault to kill.

Nichols, Geo...Assault to kill; committed November, 1872; indicted December, same year.

Bland, A. T....Theft; committed February, 1873; indicted July, same year.

Blackburn, Thos...Theft.

Kavenaugh, A...Theft; committed December, 1871; indicted March, 1872.

Phillips, R. E....Theft; committed July, 1872.

Smith, Wm...Theft; committed November, 1872; indicted November, same year.

Dickerson, Sarah J...Murder.

Willis, Hampton...Murder; committed October, 1870; indicted November, same year.

Benson, Jno....Rape; committed March, 1869; indicted October, same year.

Roberts, Jno. L...Theft from house.

Green, I N...Murder.

Biggerstaff, H...Assault to kill.

Culberson, Geo...Theft; committed July, 1873; indicted July, same year.

Woodard, Chas...Theft; committed July, 1873; indicted July, same year.

Hill, G. H...Assault to kill; committed December, 1872; indicted August, 1873.

Fullerton, Thos...Threats to kill; committed April, 1873; indicted July, same year.

Suggs, Jno...Theft; committed March, 1873; indicted July, same year.

Armstead, K. W...Fraudulent disposal of mortgaged property.

Logan, David...Theft from a house; committed March, 1874; indicted April, same year.

Yates, Luke...Burglary; indicted March, 1870.

Scott...Burglary; indicted March, 1870.

Allen, Neal S. B...Theft; 2 cases.

McCarty, Clint...Assault to kill.

Orange, French...Burglary.

DeWitt, G. W...Embezzlement; committed May, 1873; indicted July, same year. False entry on record; committed May, 1873; indicted July, same year. False entry upon entry record; committed March, 1873; indicted July, same year.

Smith, Nathan (alias White)...Assault to kill; committed April, 1875; indicted June, same year.

Jones, Chas...Mayhem; committed May, 1875; indicted June, same year.

Maxwell, Jackson...Murder; committed January, 1875; indicted June, same year.

Simmons, Stephen...Assault to kill; committed September, 1873; indicted June, 1875.

Slim, Jim (alias James Moore)...Embezzlement.

Coker, John...Assault to kill; committed April, 1875; indicted June, same year.

Williams, John M...Assault to kill; committed July, 1875; indicted October, same year.

Rice, S. A...Assault to murder; committed August, 1875; indicted October, same year.

Thomas, Billie .Murder; committed July, 1875; indicted October, same year.

Griffin, Jas. R...Forgery (two cases); committed November, 1873; indicted October, 1875.

Cowan, J. W...Assault to kill; committed December, 1875; indicted February, 1876.

Battis, J...Murder; committed December, 1875; indicted February, 1876.

Dunn, Geo...Murder.

McDaniel, Jack...Assault to murder; committed February, 1876; indicted February, same year.

Sims, Campbell...Theft; committed January, 1876; indicted February, same year.

Hart, John...Murder; committed January, 1876; indicted February, same year.

Scott, Isham...Theft; committed September, 1873; indicted November, same year.

Baker, George (alias George Nichols, alias George Burke)...Murder; committed August, 1873; indicted December, same year.

Mason, Geo...Theft; committed January, 1874; indicted March, same year.

Smith, Chas...Robbery; committed January, 1874; indicted April, same year.

Pozzine, Chas...Arson; committed March, 1874; indicted April, same year.

McCarty, W. C...Assault to kill (2 cases); committed September, 1874; indicted November, same year.

Nelms, J. B...Assault to kill; committed September, 1874; indicted November, same year.

Davidson, Thos...Theft; committed September, 1874; indicted November, same year.

Scarborough, Wm....Theft; committed May, '73; indicted July, same year.

Redding, Sam...Theft (4 cases) ; committed October, '73 ; indicted November, same year.

Roberts, Jno. L...Theft; committed October, '70; indicted April, '74.

Knight, Maley...Perjury ; committed March, 74 ; indicted April, same year.

Taylor, Dick...Theft; committed September, '73; indicted July, '74.

Morrison, George...Assault to kill; committed July, '74 ; indicted July, same year.

Clayton, S. S...Assault to kill; committed September, '74; indicted November, same year.

Gibson, Isaac...Theft; committed November, '73; indicted November, '74.

Gates, Joseph...Murder; committed September, '74; indicted November, same year.

Simmons, Robert...Assault to kill; committed November, '74; indicted November, same year.

Smith, D. W....Theft; committed November, '74; indicted November, same year.

Urban, Davis...Assault to kill; committed December, '74; indicted December, same year.

Leir, Leteir...Murder.
Yates, Joseph...Murder.
Yarborough, E...Theft.
Schenck, John C...Seduction.
Dorzeter, Mary J...Assault to murder.
Burns, Polk...Resisting an officer ; 2 cases.
Shelling, Lindsey...Theft of gelding ; 2 cases.
McElya, W. A...Assault to murder.
Glasscock, John...Burglary and theft.
Maness, James...Theft of horse.
Price, John...Murder.
Pearce, Wesley...Murder.
Hearne, J. C...Murder.
Nowell, W. C...Forgery.
Gearon, L. G...Assault to murder.
Scarborough, Middleton...Forgery.
Pitt, W. P...Forgery.
Howard, E. B...Manslaughter.
Evans, S. E...Assault to murder.
Thompson, Bill...Robbery.
Isbell, Baley...Robbery.
Neal, Willis...Threats to take life.
Boswell, John, Jr...Assault to murder.
Armstrong, James...Assault to murder.
Eubanks, Nancy...Accessory to murder.
Fowler, Enoch...Assault to murder.
Mauldering, Berry...Murder.
Beavers, Jim...Accessory to murder.
Hodges, James...Accessory to murder.
Mayfield, W. E. C...Murder.
Wallace, Wm...Assault to murder.
O'Neal, James...Assault to murder.
Smith, D. D...Bigamy.

LAMPASAS COUNTY.

Short, G. W...Assault to murder; committed January, 1873; indicted January, same year. Height, 6 feet 1 inch; weighs 180 lbs, black hair and eyes and dark complexion.

Bowen, Bill...Murder; committed March, 1873; indicted May, same year; six feet high, weighs 170 lbs., dark hair and eyes, and dark complexion. Various other charges.

Keith, Charles...Murder; committed August, 1875; indicted November, same year; six feet high, weighs 160 lbs., sandy hair, grey eyes. Was convicted and escaped.

Brophy, M. A...Theft; committed August, 1875; indicted January, 1876; 5 feet 10 inches high, weighs 150 lbs., dark hair, artificial eye.

Douglass, W. S...Swindling; committed, 1875; indicted September, 1876; 5 feet 10 inches high, weighs 160 lbs., light hair, blue eyes, fair complexion. Other charges. Has been convicted to the Penitentiary for life in West Virginia.

Shroyier, Robert...Theft of cattle; committed March, 1876; indicted September, same year; 5 feet 8 inches high, weighs 150 lbs., dark hair and eyes and dark complexion.

Neal, J. V...Theft of cattle; committed March, 1876; indicted September, same year; 6 feet high, weighs 160 lbs., dark hair and eyes and dark complexion.

Labarte, E. A...Forgery; committed, '76; indicted March, '77; 6 feet high, weighs 150 lbs., dark hair, grey eyes and dark complexion; 12 cases.

Arnold, Allen...Murder; committed January, '76; indicted March, same year.

Arnold, William...Murder; committed January, '76; indicted March, same year.

Hess, Sam...Murder; committed January, '77; indicted September, same year.

Cooper, Toles...Theft of cattle; committed January, '77; indicted September, same year; 5 feet 8 inches high, weighs 150 lbs., dark hair and eyes, and dark complexion.

Carter, Tip...Theft of cattle; committed January, '76; indicted September, '77; 5 feet 8 inches high, weighs 150 lbs., dark hair and eyes. and dark complexion.

Brown, Ed....Aiding prisoners to escape; committed May, '76; indicted September, same year; 5 feet 6 inches high, weighs 140 lbs, dark hair and eyes, and dark complexion.

Redding, Wm. Z...Aiding prisoners to escape; committed May, '76; indicted September, '77.

Stedman, E. D....Aiding prisoners to escape; commited May, '76; indicted September, '77.

Dahoney, George...Murder; committed '76; indicted March, same year.

May, W. C....Theft of mules; committed '76; indicted March, '76; 5 feet 10 inches high, weighs 160 lbs., dark hair and eyes and dark complexion.

Massie, J. W...Theft from house; committed, '75; indicted May, same year; 5 feet 8 inches high, weighs 150 lbs., dark hair and eyes, and dark complexion.

Strange, William...Theft of cattle; committed, '72; indicted same year.

LAVACA COUNTY.

Insal, Richard...Murder; committed 1865; indicted same year; white.

McNeal, James; and Tanner, Samuel...Murder; committed 1867; indicted same year; white.

Hazel, James...Murder; committed 1867; indicted 1868; white.

Atkinson, Wm...Theft of neat cattle; committed 1868; indicted same year; white; supposed to be in Jackson county.

McKnight, Felix...Theft of gelding; committed 1869; indicted same year; white.

Williams, John...Grand larceny; committed 1870; indicted same year; white.

Hogan, Leonard...Murder; committed 1871; indicted same year; white.

White, Ben...Assault to kill; committed 1871; indicted same year; white, black hair, very dark skin; supposed to be in Johnson, Erath or Hood counties.

Smith, Wm...Theft of gelding; committed 1871; indicted same year: white.

Warren, John...Assault to rape; committed 1871; indicted same year; white.

Harvey, Richard...Murder; committed 1871; indicted same year; negro.

Gonier, Henry...Theft from house; committed 1872; indicted same year; white, about 30 years old.

Parr, Frank...Assault to kill; committed 1872; indicted same year.

Garrett, Wm...Theft from house; committed 1872; indicted same year.

Debord, Wm...Theft of gelding; committed 1873; indicted same year; white.

Smith, Wm. E...Assault to kill; committed 1873; indicted same year, white.

Isaacs, Albert...Theft of gelding; committed 1873; indicted same year; negro.

Roberts, James...Murder; committed 1873; indicted same year; near Eagle Pass.

Mangum, Wm...Murder; committed 1873; indicted same year; white.

Hanna, Zack...Murder; committed 1873; indicted same year; white.

Williams, Almstead; Young, John...Theft of horse; committed 1873; indicted same year; colored.

Aycock, Bill...Theft of gelding; committed 1873; indicted same year; colored.

Pace, Dave...Theft of gelding and murder; committed 1873; indicted same year; white.

Walton, Luther; Roberts, Dan.; and Olive, Perry...Theft of gelding; committed 1874; indicted same year; are supposed to be in either Kimble, Concho, or Menard counties.

Bolivar, John; and Perry, O...Theft of mule; committed 1874; indicted same year; gamblers, red complexion, in Kimble or Menard counties, 2 cases; white.

Robert, Elberts...Theft of hog; committed 1874; indicted same year.

Gause, L. A...Theft of two mares; committed 1874; indicted same year; white, supposed to be in Washington.

Porter, Isaiah...Theft of gelding; committed 1874; indicted same year; three cases, colored.

Scott, Wm...Theft of ox; committed 1874; indicted same year; white, supposed to be in Galveston; young man.

Brown, Mary...Theft of snuff-box; committed 1874; indicted same year; negro.

Haynes, George...Theft of cow; committed 1874; indicted same year; white.

Hitchcomb, Chas...Theft of horse; committed 1874; indicted same year; white.

Binkley, Joseph...Theft of a mare and mule; committed 1874; indicted same year; white.

Hodge, John...Theft of cow; committed 1874; indicted same year; white.

Pace, James...Assault to kill; committed 1874; indicted same year; white, heavy built, black hair and beard, about 35 years old.

Wright, Curtis...Theft from house; committed 1874; indicted same year; white.

Harris, Joe...Theft of estray; committed 1874; indicted same year; white, supposed to be in Gonzales or Bastrop counties.

Mayo, Sallie...Infanticide; committed 1874; indicted same year; negro.

Carter, John...Assault to kill and murder; indicted same year; two cases; white, in Bell county, young man, heavy built.

Samora, Joe; Samora, Green; and Brenningham...Theft of gelding; committed 1874; indicted same year; 6 cases; all of them are Mexicans, young men.

Philips, J...Selling mortgaged property; committed 1874; indicted same year; looks like " a Peter-Ben-Funk-Jew," glib with his tongue.

Mc Mullen, Frank...Theft of gelding; committed 1874; indicted same year; three cases; white man, about 23 years old, medium height.

Webb, Pressly...Assault to kill; committed 1875; indicted same year; two cases; white man.

Hogan, James...Theft of gelding; committed 1875; indicted same year; two cases; heavy set young man.

Cladonian, Wallace...Theft of gelding; committed 1875; indicted same year; white.

Hodge, Hum...Theft of colt; committed 1875; indicted same year; white.

Magee, James...Theft of beef steer; committed 1875; indicted same year; white.

Hatchet, Dock...Theft of beef steer.

Harvell, Wm...Theft from house; negro.

Hawkins, Charles...Assault to kill; committed 1875; indicted same year; two cases; white.

Sowery, John...Altering mark with intent to defraud; committed 1875; indicted same year; white.

Cole, Martin...Theft of hog; committed 1875; indicted same year; white.

Harper, J. P...Theft; committed 1875; indicted same year; white, and young man, black hair and eyes, very talkative and well educated.

Davis, W. H...Embezzlement; committed 1875; indicted same year; heavy set, black hair, about 30 years old, supposed to be in Louisiana.

Hanna, Jack...Murder; committed 1875; indicted same year; young man, white, slender built.

North, Ed...Murder; committed 1875; indicted same year; colored

Cox, A., Sr.; and Cox, A., Jr...Theft of cows; committed 1875; indicted same year.

Farmer, T. J...Murder; committed '75; indicted same year; white, fleshy.

Cole, Asa...Theft of meal; committed '75; indicted same year; white.

Gregory, Wm...Bigamy; committed '75; indicted '76; white, stout built, about 30 years old.

Skipton, George...Theft of gelding; committed '74; indicted same year; six cases; a dashing young man, dresses well, about 30 years old, fond of playing draw poker.

Valentine, Ed...Theft; committed '76; indicted same year; six cases; stout built, 30 years old, black hair and eyes.

Davis, George...Theft of hog; committed '76; indicted same year.

Franks, Thomas...Theft of cattle; committed '76; indicted same year; five cases; white, fond of whisky and likes to gab, very tall, sandy hair, 35 years old.

Criswell, Wm...Theft from house; committed '76; indicted same year.

Hawks, Frank...Murder; committed in 1877; indicted same year; heavy set, black hair and eyes, weighs about 190 pounds, 23 years old, scar on cheek.

Ryan, C...Theft of beef; committed in 1876; indicted in 1877; white, two indictments.

Holt, John...Theft of beef; committed in 1877; indicted same year, white.

Steward, John...Theft of gelding; committed in 1877; indicted same year, heavy set, white.

Hughes, Wm.; and Mass, Mack...Murder; committed in 1876; indicted same year.

Kuykendall, Cooper...Murder; committed in 1876; indicted same year; mulatto.

LEE COUNTY.

Middleton, William...Theft; committed June, 1874; indicted July, same year.

Morse, Dan. L...Theft; committed Jannary, 1875; indicted May, same year; about 32 years old, eyes somewhat grayish and considerably in-flamed, apparently from strong drink; about 5 feet 7 or 8 inches high, curly hair and usually shingled.

Ghent, Lid, alias Gentry...Assault with intent to murder; committed October 13, 1876; indicted March 8, 1877; about 22 years old, sandy complexion, weighs about 150 pounds, in Blanco county a short time since.

Axum, Joseph...Theft; committed April, 1876; indicted September, 1876; about 6 feet high, weighs 140 pounds, fair complexion, eyes hazel, hair auburn.

Lopez, Armstead...Theft; committed August, 1875; indicted December, same year; half Mexican, weighs 180 pounds, 6 feet high, and about 26 or 27 years old.

Doyle, Newton...Theft; committed June, 1874; indicted July, same year.

Stallings, Ben...Theft; committed December, 1874; indicted December, same year; in Blanco county.

Molette, Jim...Theft; committed September, 1875; indicted December, same year; negro, in Colorado county.

Purtle, Felix H...Assault with intent to murder; committed April,

1876; indicted September, 1876; about 36 years old, 5 feet 10 inches high, dark complexion, usually has whiskers all over his face, walks erect, pock-marked on the neck.

Sparks, Isaac...Assault with intent to murder; committed April, 1876; indicted March, 1876; about 20 years old, weighs about 175 pounds, hair light, complexion fair, about 5 feet 8 inches high, rather low and heavy built.

Wilkinson, John...Theft; committed January, 1877; indicted March, same year; about 5 feet 10 inches high, weighs about 150 pounds, complexion dark, about 22 years old, in Calhoun county.

Sanders, Richard M...Theft, highway robbery and rape; 6 feet high, weighs 150 pounds, medium build, erect in form, dark hair and eyes, prominent cheek bones; eyes deep set in head, eyebrows meet and quite heavy, dark moustache, light imperial, good appearance, well armed.

LEON COUNTY.

Walton, Wm.; and Walton, Thos....Murder; committed March 18, 1865; indicted May 17, 1865. William Walton is about 5 feet 7 inches high, light complexion, blue eyes, rather stooped, round shouldered, about 37 years of age, light hair; of slow speech, and not very bright. Thos. Walton is about 5 feet 10 inches high, sallow complexion, spare made; dark eyes and hair, furtive look; is about 40 or 45 years of age. When last heard from was in the neighborhood of Fort Scott, Kansas. Left Navarro county when they went there.

Philips, Nep. (*alias* Duncan); Philips, Dan...Murder; committed September 1, 1867; indicted December 26, 1867. Nep. Philips (negro), gingerbread color, round, fat face, about 5 feet 10 inches high; about 35 years old. Dan Philips, negro.

Alexander, Moffatt...Assault with intent to murder; committed September 1, 1867; indicted December 27, 1867. About 5 feet 8 inches high; ruddy complexion, light hair, grey eyes, sharp features, quick spoken; about 40 years of age. When last heard from was in Arkansas.

Johnson, Andy...Theft of a horse; committed March 8; indicted June 24, 1868. Negro.

Crawford, A...Murder; committed March 1, '68; indicted July 3, '68. Small, spare made man, about 40 years of age, thin visaged, dark hair, blue eyes.

Butler, John A...Assault with intent to murder; committed June 11, '70; indicted June 30, '70.

Ainsworth, Joab; Ainsworth, Tap.; Finch, Alfred...Theft of an ox; committed January 15, '70; indicted July 2, '70.

Keith, O...Murder; committed June, '69; indicted July 2, '70. Very heavy set man; 5 feet 8 inches high; sallow complexion, yellow hair, blue eyes, broad face; powerful man, strong. When last heard from was in Louisiana.

Graham, Duncan ; Brinkley, Thos.; and Shire, Jacob...Murder.

Linson, W. J...Assault with intent to murder; committed December 25, '70; indicted March 21, '71; small man; light hair, blue eyes; about 35 years old, ruddy complexion, weight about 130 pounds.

Mullins, Christopher...Murder; committed June 2, '70; indicted July 24, '70; about 5 feet 9 inches high, ruddy complexion, reddish hair and beard, thin visaged.

Harris, Jim; and Brown, Ed...Murder and assault to murder; committed November 15, 1871; indicted November 24, same year; negroes.

Densmore, Jerry...Burglary; committed February 7, 1873; indicted March 22, same year; negro; black, heavy set, weighs about 150 pounds, wide-mouth, about 5 feet 6 inches high, 22 years old.

Johnson, Merrett...Theft of hogs; committed February, 1873; indicted July 29, same year; negro; spare built, thin face, light color, thick lips, about 5 feet 6 inches high, about 25 years old; when last heard from was in Robertson county, on Brazos.

Stockings, J. B...Unlawful sale of mortgaged property; committed April 4, 1873; indicted November 25, same year; about 5 feet 10 inches high, spare made, weighs about 150 pounds, ruddy complexion, fair hair, blue eyes; when last heard from was in Hamilton county.

King, Barney; Lankford, Nathan...Theft of cattle; committed September 10, 1874; indicted September, 17, same year. King is a very small man, about 21 years old, crippled, cannot walk without crutch, dark, sallow complexion, dark hair and eyes. Lankford is about 5 feet 8 inches high, weighs about 150 pounds, dark complexion, long, dark hair. When last heard of were in Atascosa county.

Warren, Steve...Theft of hogs; committed September 5, 1874; indicted September 14, same year; negro; heavy built, moderately dark, round-faced, about 5 feet 10 inches high, about 30 years old. When last heard from was in Houston county.

Flournoy, George...Assault with intent to murder; committed August 10, 1873; indicted September, 1874; negro; yellow. When last heard from was in M'Lennan county.

Gelchrist, Thos...Theft of gelding; committed May 20, 1874; indicted September 15, same year; white. When last heard from was in Navarro county.

Culton, Houston, alias Houston Brooks...Theft of steer; committed June 18, 1874, indicted September 9, same year; a mulatto negro; heavy set, wide face, protruding lips, weighs about 160 pounds, about 30 years old. When last heard from was in Hearne, Robertson county.

Thomas, Philip H...Murder; committed January 11, 1875; indicted January 13, same year; about 5 feet 10 inches high, spare made, weighs about 150 pounds, blue eyes and light hair, rather thin visaged, about 45 years old. When heard from was in Arkansas.

Evans, John...Theft of hogs; committed December 20, 1874; indicted January 8, 1875; yellow negro; rather freckled, square-faced, kinky hair, weighs about 180 pounds, heavy set. When last heard from was in Washington county.

Goff, Jesse...Unlawful marriage; committed January 1, 1875; indicted April 20, same year; low, heavy set, weighs about 130 pounds, bad looking man generally, sallow complexion, dark hair and eyes. When last heard from was in Grimes county.

Boykin, W. P...Theft of cattle; committed August 5, 1875; indicted September, same year; tall man, about 6 feet high, light hair, blue eyes, small beard, large frame, weighs about 150 pounds. When heard from was in Navarro county.

Wiggins, John H...Theft from house; committed May 10, 1875; indicted September 14, same year; small, wiry-looking man, has chronic sore eyes, generally wears goggles, dark hair and eyes, ruddy complexion. When last heard of was in Arkansas.

Benson, George...Assault with intent to ravish; committed August 1,

1875; indicted September 11, same year; low set, chunky, griff negro, about 5 feet 6 inches high, aged about 25 years.

Ingall, Till...Theft of hogs; committed November 1, and November 20, 1876; indicted January 6, same year.

Burlison, Aleck, alias D. A. Burlison...Assault with intent to murder; committed December 25, 1875; indicted January, 1876; about 5 feet 8 inches high, ruddy complexion, blue eyes, weighs about 150 pounds, broad face, not much beard, generally wears small goatee.

Farrow, W. S...Assault with intent to murder; committed December 26, 1875; indicted January 6, 1876; medium size, about 5 feet 10 inches high, sallow complexion, dark hair, blue eyes, crippled in one hand, got cut in a gin. When last heard from was in Walker county.

Cannon, W. T...Assault with intent to murder; indicted June 16, 1876; light complexion, about 28 years old, dark hair and eyes, about 5 feet 8 inches high, quick spoken, and a devil of a fellow after women. When last heard from was in Austin.

Bergemann, John...Assault with intent to murder; committed July 26, 1876; indicted August 15, same year.

Shelton, Ben...Theft of hog; committed May 30, 1876; indicted August 15, same year; copper-colored negro, weighs about 150 pounds, 5 feet 10 inches high, pleasing appearance. When last heard from was in Walker county.

Harris, Erasmus...Arson; committed December 8, 1876; indicted December 14, same year; dark, very heavy set negro, square-faced, quick-spoken, rather impudent, very good teeth and shows them often. When last heard from was in Grimes county.

Harris, Morris...Wilful burning; committed December 4, 1876; indicted December 14, same year; tolerably black negro boy; about 15 years old, of shackly construction and not very strong-minded, is a son of Erasmus Harris and is with him. When heard of was in Grimes county, near Navasota.

Johnson, Alf...Assault with intent to murder; committed October 8, 1876; indicted December 14, same year; copper-colored negro, about 30 years old, heavy set, about 5 feet 7 inches high, extremely large lips, long hair. When last heard from was in Anderson county.

Collins, Bruce; and Collins, B. F...Assault with intent to ravish; committed July 26, 76; indicted December 14, '76. Bruce is a boy about 17 years old, light complexion, sandy hair, about 5 feet 7 inches high. B. F. Collins is a heavy set man, heavy red beard, light hair, ruddy complexion, about 24 years old, about 5 feet 8 inches. When heard from were in Johnson county.

McWilliam, Wm...Theft of gelding; committed September 9 and 10, '76; indicted December 16, '76. Tall, slim man, about 5 feet 11 inches high, thin features, dark hair, thin beard, grey eyes.

Cook, Mike...Assault with intent to murder; committed December 25, '76; indicted July 11, '77.

Saunders, Wm...Assault with intent to ravish; indicted July 12, '77.

Burke, George...Theft of cotton; committed November 29, '76; indicted July 13, '77.

Gooden, Warren...Forgery and attempt to pass forged instrument; committed April 25, '72; indicted July 17, '77. White. Believed to be indicted in Jefferson county for murder. Was at Lampasas Springs in April, '77. Probably under assumed name.

Cowherd, R. O...Forgery and attempt to pass forged instrument; committed January 7, '77; indicted July 18, '77. Spare made, about 5 feet 10 inches high; dark complexion, dark heavy eyebrows, about 45 years old; dark eyes, heavy beard, tolerably grey. When heard from was in Kentucky, near Clarksville.

LLANO COUNTY.

Redding, W. Z...Theft of cattle (two cases) and official misdemeanor in six cases; committed in '74; indicted August, same year; about 30 years of age, 6 feet high, slender built, light complexion, light hair, blue eyes, and light, thin beard.

Olney, Joseph...Theft of cattle (seven cases), and assault to murder; committed during the spring of '74; indicted August, same year; is about 30 years old, 5 feet 8 inches high, slender built, weighs about 130 pounds, red complexion, hair and beard almost white, light blue eyes.

Clark, John...Robbery; committed July, '74; indicted August, same year.

Williams, James; and Wagner, Peter...Theft of a beef steer; committed August 12, '74; indicted December, same year.

Worthing, Richard...Altering mark on hogs not his own; committed in '74; indicted December, same year; is about 20 years old, 5 feet 9 inches high, has black hair and eyes, has been seen in Hill county.

Cox, William Henry...Theft of hogs; committed in '74; indicted December, same year; he is about 18 years old, has light hair, blue eyes and light complexion, is about 5 feet 10 inches high.

Barrett, A. W., alias Barrett, Captain...Theft of cattle (two cases;) committed April 8, '75; indicted April, same year; is about 35 years old, 6 feet high, stoop-shouldered, weighs about 180 pounds, very dark hair and heavy dark beard, speaks slowly, is apt to be engaged in some speculation.

Lee, George...Assault to murder; committed in '74; indicted April, '75; is in Denton county often.

Taylor, Abe...Theft of cattle; committed in the summer of '75; indicted August, same year; he is about 32 years old, 5 feet 9 inches high, light build, auburn hair, gray eyes, has a nervous jerking about the cheeks when excited.

Brazeale, Juel...Killing a beef steer; committed August 15, '74; indicted August, '75; is about 20 years old, 5 feet 9 or 10 inches high, light hair and eyes, often runs cattle in Uvalde county.

Polk, R. T.; and Franklin, George...Theft of hogs; committed November 10, '74; indicted August, '75.

Miller, A. R...Murder; committed April '75; indicted August, same year; he is about 30 years old, 5 feet 10 inches high, weighs about 150 pounds, has auburn hair, light eyes, stammers badly while speaking.

Lamar, John...Theft of a gun from a house; committed January 15, '76; indicted February, same year.

Hilliard, James...Theft of a hog; committed April 1, '75; indicted February, '76; he is about 28 years old, 5 feet 9 inches high, dark hair and eyes, dark complexion.

Larrimore, Wm...Theft of a yearling; committed September 24, '75; indicted February, '76; he is about 30 years old, 5 feet 10 inches high, auburn hair, hazel eyes, weighs about 135 pounds, has his family with him wherever he is.

Sorrell, Tom...Theft of hog; committed December 15, '75; indicted February, '76.

Moss, Mat...Murder; committed October 4, '75; indicted February, '76; he is about 22 years old, 6 feet high, light hair and blue eyes, light complexion, weighs 180 or 190 pounds, coarse voice and rough manners, was in the Indian Territory a short time ago.

Daniels, Redman...Theft of a gelding; committed April 1, '76; indicted May, '76.

Peyton, Ed...Theft of cattle (two cases); committed April 1, '76; indicted May, '76; he is 22 or 23 years old, 5 feet 10 inches high, slender form, light hair and eyes.

Pritchard, Aaron...Theft of yearling; committed March, '76; indicted May, '76.

Baird, John...Murder; committed January 12, '76; indicted May, '76; he is about 30 years old, about 6 feet high, slender build, weighs about 150 pounds, has light, wavy hair, light beard, blue eyes, has a bravado expression on his countenance, is very restless, always seems to be watching for something.

Mosley, Geo.; and Sharp John...Theft of hogs; committed December 15, '75; indicted November, '76.

Mackey, Jiles...Murder; committed October, '76; indicted November, '76; he is 35 years old, looks to be part Indian, has black hair and eyes, and scattering black beard, repeats the words, "Well, well!" very often while talking; is in Wise county most of his time.

Watts, Ben...Assault to kill; committed February 20, '77; indicted March, '77, in San Saba county; venue changed to this county.

Cain, Wm...Theft of a calf; committed July 15, '76; indicted, '77; is a relative of the notorious Neal Cain, is said to be in Brown county.

Freeman, Wm. S...Theft of cattle; committed January, '77; indicted May, '77, in three cases; he is about 22 years old, 6 feet high, slender form, light hair, blue eyes, has very little beard.

Lott, David...Assault to murder; committed December 17, '76; indicted May, '77.

Mitchell, Ed...Theft of a beef steer; committed January 15, '76; indicted May, 77; he is about 18 or 19 years old, light hair, blue eyes, is badly hair-lipped, which causes an impediment in his speech; was in Fayette county, Texas, when last heard from, has relatives there.

McAdams, L. L...Assault to murder; committed September 30, '76; indicted May, '77; his postoffice is Pilot Point, Denton county, Texas.

Leapart, D. P...Theft of a yearling; committed June 27, '76; indicted May, '77; he is 25 or 30 years old, dark hair and eyes, very red face, about 5 feet 8 inches high.

Gardener, Mitchel...Theft of a heifer; committed October 15, '76; indicted May, '77.

LIVE OAK COUNTY.

Petty, Jno...Murder; committed August 1, '67; indicted November 4, '76.

Hadden, W. N...Murder; committed June 22, '67; indicted November 4, '69.

Bell, C. S...Murder; three cases; committed November 1, '69; indicted March 1, '72.

Rodriguez, Marcus...Theft of gelding; committed April 20, '72; indicted June 29, '72. Mexican.

Desidora, Juan...Theft of cow; committed February 1, '73; indicted June 25, '73. Mexican.

Ascosta, Antonio...Theft of a mare; committed September 1, '72; indicted June 25, '73. Mexican.

Clay, Dave...Murder; committed September 1, '72; indicted June 25, '73.

Houstamente, Gregoria...Theft of gelding; committed October 1, '73; indicted February 26, '74. Mexican.

Chaffer, Antonio...Theft of beef steer; committed September 1, '73; indicted October 29, '74. Mexican.

Daniel, Jno...Murder; committed April 5, '75; indicted June 30, '75.

Delian, Juan and Hanposa, Panch...Theft of geldings; two cases; committed September 19, '75; indicted October 28, '75. Mexicans.

Stevenson, John, *alias* Edenfield, John...Murder; committed October 4, '75; indicted October 28, '75.

Dyer, Robt...Assault to murder; two cases; committed October 24, '75; indicted October 29, '75.

Adams, H. L...Murder; committed October 2, '75; indicted October 30, '75.

Garcia, Dominico...Murder; committed July 8, '75; indicted October 30, 75. Mexican.

Walk, Thos.; and Dyer, Robt...Assault to castrate; committed October 18, '75; indicted October 30, '75.

Ferguson, E. L...Theft of gelding; committed August 1, '75; indicted February 29, '76.

Shannon, David...Theft of cattle; committed December 1, '74; indicted March 3, '76.

Longoria, Ruvinto...Theft of gelding; committed December 1, '75; indicted March 3, '76. Mexican.

Shannon, Lou...Theft of hogs; committed December 1, '75; indicted March 3, '76.

Cole, Frank...Theft of mare; committed May 29, '75; indicted June 15, '76.

Hobbs, W. J...Bigamy; committed January 17, '75; indicted June 15, '76; dark eyes, 5 feet 8 inches high, black hair, 25 or 28 years old.

Travino, Manuel...Theft of gelding; committed March 14, '76; indicted June 15, same year; Mexican.

Gonzales, Argustin...Murder; committed April 16, '76; indicted June 15, same year; Mexican.

Phillips, Gage...Theft of gelding; committed October 15, '75; indicted June 15, '76.

Sanchez, Marcus...Theft of gelding; committed November 15, '75; indicted 15, '76; Mexican.

Brown, Geo., alias, Jack Brown...Theft of gelding; committed May 1, '76; indicted June 15, same year.

Rogers, John (two cases)...Theft of gun and mule; committed May 17, '76, indicted June 15, same year.

Valreal, Ramajio...Theft of sheep; committed March 1, '76; indicted June 15, same year; Mexican.

Phillips, Ike...Altering brand; committed October 1, '76; indicted June 15, same year.

Shannon, Alonzo...Theft of ambulance; committed May 1, '77; indicted March 3, same year.

Sharp, Capt. Thos.; Lewis, W. H.; Fox, Chas...Murder; committed

August 1, '76; indicted March 3, '77. Sharp has black hair and whiskers, brown eyes, 5 feet 11 inches high, very fine-looking; in Lewisburg, Ark. Lewis is 6 feet high, blue eyes, light hair, slender built, crippled in right hand. Fox in penitentiary.

LIBERTY COUNTY.

Dunman, Caesar...Theft of watch; committed August 12, 1874; indicted December, same year; is a copper colored negro, a good sized man, about 5 feet 11 inches high, weighs 160 or 170 pounds, reads and writes, about 35 years old.

Dickinson, Rufus...Theft of beef; committed March 1, 1873; indicted December, 24, 1874; is a very black negro, quite slender, 6 feet high, sharp faced, weighs about 140 pounds, about 25 years old.

Pinson, Sam...Theft of mare; committed September 5, 1874; indicted December, same year.

Brigley, Thomas...Theft of mare; committed April 1, 1872; indicted December, 1874.

Taylor, J. W...Theft of beef; committed June 25, 1874; indicted December, 1874; spare build, about 5 feet 10 inches high, light complexion, weighs about 145 pounds, round shoulders, hair sandy.

Woods, Henry...Assault with intent to murder; committed September 10, 1874; indicted January, same year; about 40 years old, small, hatchet-faced, a keen eye, never looks you in the face while talking, likes to be with himself while walking, looks at the brim of his hat, weighs about 130 pounds, about 5 feet 6 inches high, red complexion, red sandy hair.

Walker, L. M...Theft of cattle; committed July 1, 1873; indicted January, 1875; old, dark-gray hair, quite small, about 5 feet 6 inches high, gray whiskers, weighs about 140 pounds, dark eyes, stoop-shouldered.

Parish, Wm.; and Allant, Edward...Theft of horse; committed May 1, 1875; indicted August, same year.

Lockhart, Irvin...Assault with intent to murder; also, theft; committed June 27, 1874; indicted December, same year; is a brown-black negro, about 6 feet high, weighs about 150 or 160 pounds, has a long scar across his right temple.

Burrell, Albert...Theft of bull; committed October 15, 1874; indicted December, same year; is a very black negro, weighs about 150 pounds, is about 45 years old, about 5 feet 10 inches high, compact.

Tubbs, Wm...Theft of a hog; committed March 10, '74; indicted December, same year; is a very black negro, about 5 feet 6 or 7 inches high, weighs about 170 pounds, heavy build, has an impediment in his speech, about 50 years old.

Perry, William...Theft of gelding; committed August 15, '76; indicted September, same year; about 5 feet 5 inches high, about 21 year-old, his carriage erect, light complexion, blue eyes, light, sandy hair, weighs about 130 pounds.

Moore, J. P.; Stripling, D...Theft of a gelding; committed August 30, '76; indicted September, '76. Moore is a small man, about 5 feet 6 inches high, red face, about 24 years old, inclined to stoop, fails to look at you while talking, blue eyes, dark brown hair, whiskers on his chin, weighs 130 pounds. Stripling is a young man, just 21 years old, stout build, 5 feet 10 inches high, weighs 140 pounds.

Hornsinger, John; Hines, Thomas...Theft of a hog; committed February 15, '76; indicted September, same year. Hornsinger is of Dutch origin, stout built man, weighs 160 pounds, very heavy built, about 5 feet 6 inches high, ruddy complexion, dark hair, heavy whiskers on chin but short. Hines is a young man, about 23 or 25 years old, tall and slim, quick spoken, has the look of a desperate man, wears a low-crowned hat with wide brim, goes armed and seems to be on the look-out, about 6 feet high, red face, light hair and blue eyes.

Lum, Pat.; Green, Ed...Murder; committed April 1, '75; indicted August, same year. Pat Lum is a young man, about 24 years old, tall, raw-boned, large frame, round shoulders, weighs about 175 or 180 pounds, dark brown hair, no beard when the murder was committed, has very large hands and feet, and is now out in the West with his relatives; reward has been offered for him. Ed. Green is very small and slim, about 24 or 26 years old, weighs about 125 pounds, light brown hair, wears a mustache and thin whiskers on chin, has small foot and hand; reward has been offered for him. Is now the West.

Scott, Dan...Rape; committed January 20, '77; indicted March, same year; very black negro, weighs about 140 pounds, about 5 feet 10 or 11 inches high, about 50 years old, face small, a great deal of white in his eyes.

Giles, Jody...Theft of hog; committed January 1, '75; indicted August, same year.

Lasame, Robert...Theft of beef; committed September 15, '75; indicted December same year.

Fruger, Frosan...Theft of hog; committed December 15, '75; indicted January, '76; of French descent, speaks the English language very brokenly, an athletic heavy set man, grey eyes, dark hair, about 25 years old, light whiskers, weighs about 160 pounds, about 5 feet 11 inches high; was convicted by a jury, obtained new trial, and fled the country.

Ellis, G. K...Murder; committed April 15, '76; indicted September, same year; about 25 years old, a medium sized man, weighs about 150 pounds, about 5 feet 10 inches high, dark hair, dark complexion, eyes sunk in his head. He is in Mississippi.

Lockhart, Shade and David...Theft of cattle; committed June 20, '76; indicted September, same year. Shade Lockhart is a very black negro, about 50 years old, a very large raw-boned, powerfully made man, a blacksmith, about 6 feet 3 inches high. David, a son of Shade Lockhart, is about 18 years old, chunky built, about 5 feet 10 inches high, round-faced, has a peculiar expression of the eye, weighs about 150 pounds.

Taylor, Charley...Theft of hogs; committed April 30, '76; indicted September, same year; bright mulatto, a medium sized man, weighs about 150 pounds, has long straight black hair, black eyes, about 5 feet 6 inches high, about 20 years old. Supposed to be in Harris county.

MONTAGUE COUNTY,

Greer, Morgan...Theft of a yearling heifer; committed August 25, '73; indicted November 1, same year.

Slaughter, Ben...Theft of a gelding; committed September 10, '73; indicted November 1, same year; is a very black negro, heavy built, about 5 feet 8 or 10 inches high, weighs 175 or 180 pounds, 30 years old, has some beard, has lived in Parker and Palo Pinto counties, left hand burned so that his little finger is drawn up, he once belonged to ——— Slaughter, of Palo Pinto county.

Whaley, Isaac...Assault to murder; committed March 31, '72; indicted June 27, '73.

McConnell, A...Theft of a steer; committed July 4, '73; indicted November 1, same year.

Williams, W. H...Theft of a steer; committed August 26, '73; indicted November 1, same year; about 45 years old, 5 feet 7 inches high, weighs about 140 pounds, dark hair and whiskers and dark complexion, is a great talker.

Wisdom, Joseph L...Theft of cattle; committed April 1, '75; indicted ——— 23, same year; is a small man, 5 feet 6 or 7 inches high, weighs about 140 pounds, is 23 years old, light complexion, blue eyes, light or sandy hair, freckled face, but little beard, which is red or sandy color, very boastful disposition and drinks whisky; he was married in Montague county, and probably has his wife with him, and he will likely be in company with Joseph Chambers, who is indicted for forgery, and was in Medina county when last heard from.

Story, John...Theft of a steer; committed January 1, '75; indicted March 20, same year.

Houston, John...Theft of a steer; committed January 1, '75; indicted March 20, same year.

Wilson, James...Theft of a steer: committed January 1, '75; indicted March 20, same year.

Turner, M. L...Theft of a gelding; committed April 1, '74; indicted March 19, '75; is 45 or 50 years old, about 5 feet 11 inches high, weighs 150 pounds, fair complexion, last heard of in Southern Texas, Mason and Llano counties, has a son by name of Palmer Turner, very talkative.

Steel, John...Theft of hog; committed March 4, '74; indicted November 21, same year.

Rodgers, Charles...Theft of a cow; committed January 1, '75; indicted March 20, same year; is 5 feet 10 inches high, weighs about 160 pounds, fair complexion, black hair, married, last heard from in Indian Territory.

Rodgers, John...Theft of a cow; committed January 1, '65; indicted March 20, same year; is about 30 years old, 5 feet 9 inches high, weighs about 130 pounds, slender made, small head and face, short nose, unmarried, and has an inferior countenance.

Perkins, Henry...Murder of L. Fleming; committed January 10, '73; indicted November 9, '74.

Chambers, Joseph...Forgery; committed May 1, '75; indicted July 26, same year; is about 30 years old, about 5 feet 11 inches high, weighs about 150 pounds, stoop-shouldered; light complexion, sandy beard and cross-eyed, is probably in company with J. L. Wisdom; charged with theft, last heard from in Medina county.

Waldrum, Wm...Assault to murder; committed November 1, '75, indicted November 20, same year.

Masoner, James...Theft of hogs; committed January 1, '75; indicted March 19, same year; is about 24 years old, about 6 feet high, weighs about 180 pounds, stout, well built, light complexion, blue eyes, red face, has but little beard, auburn hair and beard, generally very civil, and has a good appearance; is likely to be found on some ranche in Western Texas, and is probably with his brother, Geo. Masoner.

Johnson, Wm...Theft of hogs; committed January 1, '75; indicted March 19, same year; is about 21 years old, about 5 feet 8 inches high, has very little, if any, beard, light complexion, light hair and eyes, cross-eyed, has a green and awkward appearance, came from Red River county.

Minnis, L. C...Assault to murder; committed May 1, '74; indicted July 23, same year; is about 35 years old, about 5 feet 8 inches high, heavy built, black eyes, black hair and beard, generally wears heavy beard, generally goes neatly dressed, is apt to be keeping saloon, has family with him.

Fuller, W, M...Theft from a house ; committed December 12, '76 ; indicted March 17, same year.

Thompson, A. M...Murder of D. L. Fisher; committed March 14, '76 ; indicted June 10, same year.

Tinnon, John...Theft of cattle; committed March 17, '76; indicted June 6, same year; is about 21 years old, about 5 feet 8 inches high, weighs about 130 or 140 pounds, dark or swarthy complexion, black hair and eyes.

Dillworth, ——. ...Attempt to bribe; committed April 23, '76; indicted June 10, same year. Is about 6 feet high, spare built, light complexion, light hair and beard, blue eyes. Passed through this county in April, '76, with a herd of cattle from Southern Texas.

Freeman, Sam....Assault to murder; committed May 1, '75; indicted July 24, same year.

Smith, Sam...Assault to murder; committed May 1, '75; indicted July 24, same year.

Masoner, Geo...Theft of a gelding; committed July 4, '74; indicted March 17, '75. Is about 26 years old, about 6 feet high, weighs about 170 or 180 pounds, light complexion, light hair and beard, slow spoken. Has a family, and his wife has red hair.

Taylor, William...Theft of gelding; committed July 4, '74; indicted March 17, '75. Is about 22 years old, about 5 feet 8 or 10 inches high, weighs 140 or 150 pounds, black hair and eyes, swarthy complexion, drinks and gambles a good deal, is very profane and vulgar, smooth face.

Barry, N. S., alias Stokes Berry...Assault to murder ; committed July 18, '74 ; indicted July 25, same year. Is about 40 or 45 years old, 5 feet 8 or 10 inches high, heavy set, black hair and eyes, black beard, dark complexion, is probably a little grey. Has a large family ; came from Georgia, and has probably gone back.

Dyer, L. R...Assault to murder; committed September 1, '72; indicted June 23, '73. Is about 30 years old, black hair, eyes and beard, has but little beard, swarthy complexion, 5 feet 10 or 11 inches high, weighs 140 pounds. When last heard from was in Colorado.

Morehead, John...Theft of steers; committed September 1, '73; indicted November 1, same year. Is about 50 years old, 5 feet 11 inches high, weighs about 150 pounds, dark complexion, grey eyes, dark hair, and is a drunkard.

Lewallen, Mrs. Wiley...Assault to murder; committed March 1, '75 ; indicted July 26, same year. She is the wife of Wiley Lewallen, about 45 years old, light complexion and light hair. When last heard of was living on Red river, in Fannin county.

Inge, Sidney...Assault to murder; committed March 21, '76; indicted March 22, same year.

Club, Jo...Theft of yearling steer; committed July 1, '74 ; indicted November 20, same year; is about 23 years old, 5 feet 10 inches high, weighs about 150 pounds, fair complexion, black hair, has small head and large

neck, and straight form, single man.   Last heard from was in Southern
Texas.

Willis, John...Theft of yearling steer; committed July 1, '74; indicted
November 20, same year.

Henson, William...Assault to murder; committed December 2, '73;
indicted March 29, '74.   Is about 6 feet high, weighs about 160 pounds,
light complexion, light hair and eyes, sandy beard, about 26 or 28 years
old.   Has a family with him, and when last heard of was in Cherokee
county.

Slack, Jacob...Theft of a cow; committed May 10, '73; indicted November 1, same year.   Is about 25 years old, 5 feet 11 inches high, weighs
about 180 pounds, dark complexion, grey eyes, stout built.   Last heard
of was in Colorado Territory.

Ingam, B. L...Assault to kill; indicted June, '77.

Huitt, B. T...Assault to kill; indicted June, '77.

Harris, L. F...Uttering forged land titles; indicted June, '77. Lived
at Dallas. When indicted was Commissioner in Bankruptcy.

Waybourne, Robt...Assault to rape; indicted November, '76.

Thompson, J. C...Murder; (two cases;) indicted June, '76. Dark
complexion, hair and eyes; 165 or 175 pounds.

West, Wm...Assault to kill; (four cases); indicted November, '77, 28
years old; 160 pounds. Once belonged to Lieut. S. W. Campbell's
company of Rangers. Is with Millett & Mabry, Wilbarger county, Texas.

King, Jack...Assault to kill; (four cases;) indicted November, '77. Is
with Wm. West.

Copeland, Joe, and Ingsum, Henry...Theft; indicted November, '77.

Carrolton, Jack; Labaum, Bill; and Neaves, Walter J...Resisting officer; indicted June, '77.

Waller, M. B...Murder; (two cases ;) dark complexion, hair and eyes;
28 years of age, 5 feet 10 inches high; lame in one leg; walks on his toe.

Norton, John, and Mullin —...Murder; indicted June, '77.

West, ...—Theft; indicted June, '76.

White, Frank...Perjury; indicted June, '76. Red complexion and
hair, light whiskers, 180 pounds. When last heard from was in Harde-
man county.

Watson, Mat...Theft; indicted June, '76.

Skipworth, Jas...Theft; indicted June, '76.

Smith, J...Theft; indicted November '75. Light hair and complexion,
150 pounds, quick spoken, 26 years.

Reed, W. H....Bigamy; indicted June, '76. Sixty years of age. Now in
Cooke county.

Staunton, Mike...Assault to kill.

Ohair, R. T...Perjury; indicted October, '76; 6 feet 2 inches high;
dark hair; grey eyes, 180 pounds ; a mason by trade, and is sure to say
something about it. Usually wears long whiskers or Burnsides.

Bean, Wm...Murder; indicted October, '76.

Neal, Joe....Murder; indicted February, '72.

Norton, John...Murder; Dark skinned, black hair; 160 pounds.

McCallister, James...Assault to kill; indicted March, '76.

McKeever, John...Theft; indicted July, '74, dark complexion and
hair, black eyes, 45 years old, 6 feet high, weighs 170 pounds, drunkard,
and great talker, last heard of in Grayson county.

Medley, Frank...Theft; indicted July, '74.

Marshall, John...Theft; indicted November, '73.

Murray, Jack...Assault to kill; indicted October, '70; fair complexion, light hair, sandy beard, blue eyes, 5 feet 9 inches high, weighs 160 pounds, stooped-shoulders, heavy set, broke jail while his case was appealed to the Supreme Court, and penalty (2 years in the penitentiary) confirmed.

McKey, Giles...Theft of mules; indicted October, '72; dark complexion, hair and eyes, 6 feet high, weighs 180 pounds, 32 years old, features rough.

Jackson, J. W...Bigamy; indicted June, '76; dark complexion, dark hair, a little gray, eyes gray, 50 years old, weighs 160 pounds, 5 feet 9 inches high; carpenter.

Leuty, Bud...Assault to kill; indicted March, '76.

Jones, Selvas...Theft of mules; indicted October, '72; fair complexion, blue or gray eyes, 5 feet 10 inches high, 28 years old, good-looking, and gentlemanly in his manners.

Hudson, Simon...Theft of cow; indicted October, '73; fair complexion, light hair and eyes, 25 years old.

Harrison, Geo...Burglary; indicted February 12; dark complexion, hair and eyes, 6 feet 1 inch high, 30 years old, scar on forehead running into his hair, little or no beard; native of a New England State.

Harris, Wm...Murder; indicted February, '72; black negro, 6 feet high, 30 years old, weighs 180 pounds, formerly a U. S. soldier at Fort Sill.

Hancock, John...Assault to kill; indicted November, '73.

Gregg, Samuel...Assault to kill; indicted March, '76.

Douglas, Geo...Theft (2 cases); indicted November, '73; dark complexion, hair and eyes, 5 feet 10 inches high, 35 years old, talkative, and great boaster.

Down, Wm...Theft; indicted March, '75; fair complexion, light hair and eyes, weighs 180 pounds, 24 years old, heavy set and rough-looking; indicted for murder in Cooke county.

Cummings, Hattie...Assault with intent to kill; indicted March, '76; she has a good looking 7 year old boy with her.

Cobb, Benjamin...Theft; indicted June, '76; fair complexion, blue eyes, light hair, 25 years old, weighs 160 pounds, 6 feet high, upper teeth projects considerably, talks a great deal.

Craft, Dan...Accessory to assault to kill and theft; indicted March, '76; dark complexion and hair, hazel eyes, 24 years old, 5 feet 8 inches high, weighs 150 pounds.

Allen, L. M...Forgery and theft; indicted October, '76; dark complexion, hair and eyes, right hip dislocated, limps a great deal, 45 years old, 6 feet high, very talkative, school teacher, claims to have been a colonel in Confederate service.

Brown, John...Assault to kill and burglary; indicted July, '75; dark complexion, hair and eyes, straight hair, curls a little, weighs 165 pounds, 28 years old; somewhere in Brown or Collin counties; brother-in-law of J. W. Wilson, indicted in Clay county for murder.

MATAGORDA COUNTY.

Sheppard, Lee...Murder; indicted 1866; mulatto, resembling a Mexican; straight black hair and dark eyes, little beard (if any), rather slim build, and about 5 feet 8 inches high. Supposed to be near Houston.

Cross, James...Dueling; assault to kill and murder; murder; indicted '68; Scotchman; short thick build, light hair, blue eyes, about 50 years old, and about 5 feet 4 inches high. Supposed to be in Western Texas.

Franklin, James...Theft of mares; indicted '69; theft of gelding; indicted '69; negro.

Foster, John...Theft of gelding; indicted February, '71; theft of mule; indicted February, '71; negro; dark kinky hair, dark eyes, about 5 feet 10 inches high, and about 40 years old.

Johnson, Robert...Murder; indicted February, 71; light florid complexion, light hair and whiskers, blue eyes, about 5 feet 4 inches high, and about 40 years old. Last heard of in the U. S. army, near San Antonio.

Jones, Anson...Theft of a hog; indicted October, '71; supposed to be in the penitentiary at Huntsville.

Allen, J. R. (alias Dr. J. R. Jones); assault to kill and murder; indicted October, '72; light complexion, light hair, blue eyes, about 5 feet 4 inches high and of thick build; followed the profession of a doctor; supposed to be in Louisiana or Mississippi.

Jones, Hanson...Theft of hog; indicted February, '73.

Taylor, Thomas...Theft of a watch; indicted June, '73.

Boulden, Albert...Assault to murder; indicted October, '73.

Tipton, Bill...Theft of gelding; indicted October, '73.

Mathews, Martin...Theft of cattle; indicted October, '74; negro; about 40 years old, is quite intelligent, and talks pleasantly. Supposed to be in Colorado county.

Baptiste, Gordolphus...Theft of cattle; indicted October, '74; negro. Supposed to be in Colorado county.

Page, Henry...Theft of cattle; indicted October, '74; negro. Supposed to be in Colorado county.

Wiggins, Robert...Arson; indicted October, '74; indicted October, '74; negro. Supposed to be in Wharton county.

Monroe, Peyton...Theft of hog; indicted October, '74.

Burton, Frank...Theft, indicted February, '76; he is 27 or 28 years old, but looks younger; is about 5 feet 8 or 9 inches high, and slender, fair complexion, light brown hair, full blue eyes, has but little beard, and of rather genteel appearance, has worked at the carpenter trade, and was last heard from in Waller county.

Arnold, Levi...Theft of a cow; indicted May, '77; is 23 or 24 years old, 5 feet 8 inches high, and stoutly built, of fair complexion, and light brown hair, was a stock-raiser; whereabouts unknown.

Price, Wm. A...Forgery and swindling; indicted November, '77; is 28 or 36 years old, 5 feet 10 or 11 inches high, and very slender, is copper-colored, and in features is more white than negro, is a lawyer by profession, and until recently was County Attorney of Fort Bend county; supposed to have gone to Louisiana.

MORRIS COUNTY.

Jones, Emma...Murder; committed July 23, '75; indicted August 3, '75; a negro woman, black, about 26 years old, over medium size, and above medium height, quick spoken.

Bowers, Sam...Forgery; is about 18 years old, light hair, blue eyes, freckled and rather sallow complexion; committed about July, '75, and indicted in August same year; he is thought to be in some of the border counties west of this with his father, who has moved west from this county since the commission of the offense; white.

Pink, Wilson...Swindling; fair skin, light hair, blue eyes, ruddy complexion, well marked, sanguine temperament, about 27 or 28 years old, 5 feet 7 or 8 inches high, light; thought to be in Collin or Dallas counties.

Jones, Bill...Bigamy; about 5 feet 7 inches high, black, heavy build, and rather round face, about 40 years old.

Jones, Amanda...Bigamy; a bright mulatto, about 30 years old, rather fleshy, medium height, hair black and rather straight; was married to Bill Jones about May or June, '77, and indicted October, '77.

MENARD COUNTY.

Davis, George...Theft from house; indicted June, '74.

Baker, George...Assault to murder; indicted November, '74.

Clark, James...Theft of cow; indicted November, '74. Irishman; dark sandy hair, grey eyes, about 5 feet 9 inches high, about 30 years old, and weighs about 160 pounds.

Quinchan, Concalius...Theft of gelding; committed July, '74; indicted November, same year. Irishman; yellow grey eyes, auburn hair, Roman nose, about 5 feet 9 inches high, about 28 years old, and weighs about 140 pounds. Generally known by the name of Jim Sullivan.

Ward, W. A ..Embezzlement; committed September, '73; indicted November, '74. Is 5 feet 9 inches high, curly auburn hair, grey eyes, and weighs about 160 pounds.

Redding, Shelton...Theft from house; committed September, '74; indicted March, '75. Negro; about 5 feet 8¼ inches high, reddish hair, 35 or 40 years old, weighs about 145 pounds.

Barnes, S. H...Assault to murder; committed July, '75; indicted July, same year. Very dark complexion, coarse black hair, 30 or 35 years old, about 5 feet 10 inches high, dark eyes, ugly scar on face, weighs about 175 pounds.

Underwood, Nathan...Theft of cattle; committed May '75; indicted July, same year. Rather dark complexion, dark brown hair (sleepy looking), round shoulders, about 30 years old, weighs about 140 pounds, Formerly from Hood county. Recently reported to be on Devil's river. with a herd of cattle stolen from Mexico.

Baldwin, N. W...Theft of oxen; committed June, '75; indicted November, same year. About 5 feet 8 inches high, red hair, freckled face, blue eyes, weighs about 170 pounds. In Kimble county.

Martin John...Theft of gelding; committed April, '76; indicted June, same year.

Lancaster, Alexander...Theft of cattle; about 5 feet 8 or 9 inches high, weighs about 160 pounds, dark brown hair, dark eyes, and had one hair lip, had a hole just under the left nostril; about 28 years old.

Lancaster, Frank...Theft of cattle; about 17 years old, and about 5 feet 6 inches high, had red hair, sandy complexion, very freckled faced, eyes sky blue, very heavy set, weighs about 130 pounds.

Buckley, Charles...Theft of stallion; escaped from Menard county jail. has been a convict in the State Penitentiary, was sent there in the year 1875, in the month of November same year; was pardoned out abut

June, '77; is about 5 feet 7 inches high, dark brown hair, stoops in his shoulders, eyes blue or hazel, one eye is slightly crossed, has a hanging look, cannot look you in the face when speaking, about 20 years old, weighs about 130 pounds.

Owens, John...Theft of mare; about 5 feet 11 inches high, very light hair, light complexion, and light blue eyes, weighs about 160 pounds, and about 20 years old.

Lloyd, Frank...Murder; very broad shoulders, weights about 135 pounds, about 5 feet 7 inches high, very light hair, very light moustache and some whiskers, sometimes has his whiskers shaved off, square, heavy jaw, sky blue eyes.

MONTGOMERY COUNTY.

Clepper, John; Clepper, Lem C...Assault to murder; committed October 15, '66; indicted November 15, same year. John Clepper is 66 years old, 5 feet 10 inches high, weighs 160 pounds, grey hair, dark eyes and complexion. Lem C. Clepper is 32 years old, 5 feet 11 inches high, weighs 150 pounds, eyes, hair and beard black, dark complexion, is a photographer. Father and son supposed to be in Bosque county.

Baugh, Alex. R...Murder; committed February 3, '68; indicted May 20, same year; 45 years old, 5 feet 8 inches high, weighs 135 pounds, blue eyes, fair complexion, sandy hair and beard, stooped-shouldered. Escaped after conviction.

Abbott, Henry, alias Bill...Burglary; committed February 4, '68; indicted November 20, '68; 30 years old, 5 feet 8 inches high, weighs 160 pounds, copper-colored, low forehead.

O'Neil, James R...Assault to murder; committed March 5, '68; indicted November 20, same year; about 30 years old, 5 feet 8 or 9 inches high, weighs 130 pounds, blue eyes, light hair, fair complexion. In Robertson county, near Hearne.

Province, P. P...Murder; committed September 10, '69; indicted September 21, '70; about 30 years old, 5 feet 9 inches high, weighs 160 pounds; round face, dark hair, eyes and complexion. In Orange county.

Binferd, Mack; Theft of $100; committed December 27, '69; indicted February 11, '71; negro; about 45 years old, weighs 160 pounds, 5 feet 9 inches high.

Jones, Tom...Theft of hogs; committed December 31, '70; indicted February 11, '71; 35 years old, 5 feet 10 inches high, weighs 175 pounds, beard thin; negro.

Bateman, Otto, alias Wren...Assault to murder; committed March 26, '71; indicted June 12, same year; about 28 years old, light hair, blue eyes, fair complexion, 5 feet 8 inches high, weighs 155 pounds, quite stout.

Linton, Wallace; Johnson, Sam...Theft of two geldings; committed November 10, '70; indicted June 23, '71. Linton is 30 years of age, 5 feet 8 inches high, weight 140 pounds, spare made, light black or griff color, in Travis county. Johnson is 36 years of age, 6 feet high, weight 175 pounds; black.

May, J. Lew...Assault to murder; committed March 10, '71; indicted June 23, '71; 28 years old, 5 feet 11 inches high, spare built, weight 140 pounds.

Johnson, Frank...Assault to murder; committed November 10, '71;

indicted September 25, '71 ; about 35 years old, 5 feet 6 inches high, weight 140 pounds; black.

Higginbotham, J. W...Assault to murder; committed October 29, '71; indicted February 13, '72 ; 38 years of age, 5 feet 6 inches high, weight 165 pounds, sandy hair, blue eyes, fair complexion.

Harris, William...Theft of a mare ; committed February 9, '72; indicted February 17, '72 ; age 23 years, 5 feet 10 inches high, weight 140 pounds, dark hair, eyes and complexion.

Connell, Clem...Assault to murder; committed May 10, '72; indicted June 15, '72; very black, heavy set, 5 feet 6 inches high, weight 160 pounds, age about 24 years.

Sloan, William...Theft of a gelding; committed August 10, '72; indicted September 25, '72; 28 years old, 5 feet 8 inches high, light hair, eyes and complexion.

Harris, Alex...Murder ; committed November 1, '71; indicted February 7, '73 ; age 30 years, 5 feet 11 inches high, weight 165 pounds, dark hair, blue eyes, fair complexion ; a mechanic. Supposed to be at Holly Springs, Miss.

Jackson, Frank, *alias* McGuffin...Theft of a gelding; committed May 10, '73 ; indicted June 7, '73 ; about 30 years old, 5 feet 10 inches high, weight 165 pounds, black hair, white eyed.

Calloway, Roland...Murder; committed January 20, '74; indicted February 6, same year. About 24 years old, 5 feet 10 inches high, weighs about 155 pounds, dark hair, eyes and complexion.

Bruce, Nick, alias George Washington...Theft of cotton ; committed December 20, '73; indicted February 11, '74. Age, 40 years, 6 feet high, weighs 180 pounds, ginger-cake color.

Beauchamp, George...Assault to murder ; committed June 9, '74 ; indicted June 12, '74. Age, 27 years, 5 feet 10 inches high, weighs 145 pounds, light hair and and eyes.

Mackey, Willis...Theft of gelding; committed March 15, '75; indicted June 10, '75. About 30 years old, 5 feet 8 to 10 inches high, weighs 150 pounds, copper color.

Sands, J. B...Assault to murder; committed January 15, '75; indicted February 5, same year. Is 30 years old, 6 feet high, weighs 170 pounds, scar on forehead or face, blue eyes, light hair and complexion. Supposed to be in Harris county.

Sands, R. C...Assault to murder; committed January 15, '75; indicted February 5, same year. Is 34 years old, 6 feet high, blue eyes, auburn hair, fair complexion, light hair. Supposed to be in Harris county.

Dobie, Robert...Assault to murder; committed January 15, '75; indicted February 5, same year. Age, 28 years, weighs 140 pounds, 5 feet 6 inches high, blue eyes, fair complexion, light hair. Supposed to be in Harris county.

Simonton, Madison...Theft of hogs; committed May 15, '75 ; indicted June 10, same year. Low, stout, round-shouldered, griff color, cross-eyed, downcast look, 55 years old, 5 feet 6 inches high, weighs 145 to 150 pounds, stutters.

McRae, Dennis...Assault to murder ; committed March 15, '75; indicted January 16, '75; about 45 years of age, 6 feet 2 inches high, weighs 185 pounds, light black.

Kirby, John James...Assault to murder; committed August 4, '75 ; indicted September 16, '75; about 26 years old, 5 feet 10 inches high, weighs 135 pounds, hatchet-faced, gray eyes, dark hair and complexion.

7

Miller, Henry...Theft of cattle; committed April 15, '75; indicted June 14, same year. About 40 years of age, 5 feet 6 to 8 inches high, weighs from 160 to 180 pounds, heavy built and black. In Austin county.

Jones, Wm...Assault to murder; committed August 4, '75; indicted September 16, '75; 35 years old, 6 feet 1 inch high, weighs 185 pounds, blue eyes, dark hair, light complexion.

Cole, John...Assault to murder; committed September 10, '75; indicted September 16, '75; a mulatto, 40 years old, 6 feet high, weighs 200 pounds.

King, Joe., alias Williamson...Rape; committed June 15, '75; indicted September 21, '75; low, heavy set, bow-legged, 30 years old. 5 feet 5 inches high, weighs 130 pounds, lost several teeth, 2 broad front teeth.

Alford, J. P...Assault to murder; committed August 1, '75; indicted September 22, '75; about 28 years old, 5 feet 9 inches high, weighs 140 pounds, black hair and eyes, dark complexion; resides in Waller county.

Hayes, James H...Theft of cattle; committed January 1, '76; indicted February 22, '76; 50 years old, 5 feet 11 inches high, weighs 165 pounds, dark hair, turning gray, dark complexion, gray eyes, in Orange county.

Rogers, Lewis...Assault to murder; committed May 20, '76; indicted September 15, '76; about 30 years old, 6 feet high, weighs 190 pounds, wears moustache, is very black.

McKee, L. S...Theft of $100; committed February 5, '77; indicted February 10, '77; about 32 years old, 6 feet 2 inches high, weighs 185 pounds, dark complexion, black hair and eyes, high forehead, sloping backward, very large foot, wears a black moustache and goatee, lately arrested in Dallas for stealing a $5000 check in Chattanooga, Tennessee.

Moore, Thomas...Assault to murder; committed December. 27, '76; indicted February 13, '77.

Cheshire, Robert...Assault to murder and theft; committed March 27, '77; indicted September 6, same year; 52 years old, 6 feet high, weighs 160 pounds, stoop-shouldered, dark hair, blue eyes, fair complexion.

McRae, Alex...Theft of $1500; committed January 28, '75; indicted September 11, '77; about 24 years old, 5 feet 8 inches high, black eyes and hair, full face, weighs about 160 pounds, dark complexion. About Seguin.

Moses, Elbert...Assault to murder; committed February 10, '77; indicted September 8, same year. In Montgomery county.

Remington, Frank...Assault to murder; committed May 10, '76; indicted September 12, same year; about 30 years, 5 feet 10 inches high, 140 pounds, dark hair, eyes and complexion.

Gibson, Charles...Assault to murder; committed July 16, '77; indicted September 11, same year; about 35 years old, 5 feet 6 inches high, weighs 140 pounds, griff or copper-color, large red eyes.

Hicks, J. J.; Young, Wallace; Young, John...Theft of cow; committed March 17, '77; indicted September 11, same year.

Williams, Jackson; Harrall, Walter...Burglary; committed July 4, '77; indicted September 11, same year.

MARION COUNTY.

Peck, Wm...Rape; committed February 5, '70; indicted June 22, same year; negro.

Cross, Peter...Murder; committed October 10, '70; indicted October 15, same year; negro.

Jones, Simon...Perjury; committed October 22, '70; indicted October 28, same year; negro.

Johnson, Geo...Attempt to kill and murder; committed March 3, '71; indicted April 24, same year; negro.

Clarence, Harry...Burglary; committed February 20, '71; indicted April 24, same year; negro.

Pierce, Frank...Forgery; committed April 1, '71; indicted April 24, same year; negro.

Band, Pink...Theft of gelding; committed October 4, '68; indicted April 24, '71.

Looney, Isaac W...Theft of gelding; committed October 4, '68; indicted April 24, '71.

Spence, Tuge...Theft of gelding; committed October 4, '68; indicted April 24, '71. Supposed to be dead.

Crawford, J. B...Forgery; committed September 28, '70; indicted April 24, '71. Small size, painter.

Baxley, Jas...Burglary; committed December 2, '70; indicted April 26, '71.

Johnson, Henry C...Swindling; committed January 10, '71; indicted April 26, same year.

Ragay, Philip; Haraug, L. P...Swindling; committed January 10, '71; indicted September 1, same year; large size, of French birth or descent; both supposed be in Louisiana now.

Daley, John...Swindling; committed February 1, '71; indicted September 1, same year.

Benton, J. P....Theft of gelding; committed November 10, '71; indicted January 15, same year,

Cobb, W. P...Assault to murder; committed August 16, '72; indicted January 15, same year.

Smith, W. B...Arson; committed January 1, '72; indicted August 16, same year.

Allen, Jas...Theft; committed November 1, '72; indicted December 17, same year; tall, about 5 feet 11 inches high, yellow negro.

Thomas, Charles...Theft from house; committed October 5, '72; indicted December 7, same year.

Cobb, W. P...Assault to murder; committed October 5, '75; indicted December 17, '75.

Burley, George...Assault to murder; committed December 14, '72; indicted December 17, same year; negro.

Abernathy, West...Assault to kill; committed July 3, '76; indicted December 2, same year.

Filgore, ——...Murder; committed June 10, '76; indicted November 27, same year; white. Probably in Mississippi.

Smith, George...Theft of hogs; committed November 20, '76; indicted December 2, same year; negro.

Kimball, Sam...Theft of hogs committed March 1, '76; indicted December 2, same year; negro.

Griffin, Jesse...Murder; committed May 9, '73: indicted May 15, same year; negro.

Wood, Alonzo...Swindling; committed December 25, '73; indicted January 10, '74.

Hudson, Thos. J...Forgery; committed September 29, '74; indicted September 7, same year; is a lawyer by profession. Not in the State.

Glass, J...Murder; committed October 14, '74; indicted January 4, '75.

Dreeson, B. J...Swindling; committed February 26, 73; indicted January 10, '74. Jew, low stature.

Parker, Wade...Assault to murder; committed March 1, '74; indicted April 18, same year; negro.

Crawford, M...Assault to murder; committed February 5, '74; indicted June 2, same year; negro.

Nunn, Sam'l...Murder; committed June 24, '74; indicted August 27, same year.

Nevils, Albert...Theft of cattle; committed September 3, '74; indicted September 7, same year; negro.

Johnson, Ed...Assault to murder; committed May 1, '74; indicted September 9, same year; negro.

Johns, Perry...Burglary and theft; committed December 2, '74; indicted January 1, '75; negro.

Collins, John...Perjury; committed April 27, '76; indicted April 29, same year; 22 years old, dark complexion, deaf, 5 feet 9 inches high; Irish.

Johnson, John...Theft from house; committed December 9, '74; indicted January 7, '75.

Smith, Henry...Perjury; committed September 16, '74; indicted January 7, '75; negro.

Burnett, W. E...Theft; committed November 11, '74; indicted January 13, '75; about 5 feet 10 inches high, 45 years old.

Thomas, Wm...Burglary and theft; committed April 30, '75; indicted July 2, same year; negro.

Thomas, George...Theft from house; committed August 27, '75; indicted December 27, same year; negro.

Allison, John...Assault to murder; committed August 5, '75; indicted October 27, same year; negro.

Higgins, Sam...Theft from house; committed September 10, '75; indicted October 27, same year; negro.

Wright, Charles...Theft from house; committed August 19, '75; indicted October 27, same year; negro.

Andrews, Nervain...Theft from house; committed September 18, '75; indicted October 27, same year; negro.

Grandison, James...Theft from house; committed December 20, '74; indicted October 27, same year; negro.

Cloud, Chas. M...Forgery; committed June 30, '75; indicted November 4, same year; is about 13 years old.

Joplin, Giles...Assault to murder; committed January 30, 76; indicted March 3, same year; negro.

Owens, Walter...Theft from house; committed February 10, '76; indicted March 7, same year; negro.

McLENNAN COUNTY.

Jarrett, Henry...Theft of a mule; indicted June, 8, '70.

Watson, George...Murder; indicted July 13, '70.

Jennings, Mark...Theft of a mare; indicted December 3, '70.

Lindsey, E. E...Theft of oxen; indicted December 8, '70.

Sloan, Crocket...Assault with intent to murder; indicted December 9, '70.

Moore, B. T...Murder; indicted December 14, '70.

Evans, J. W...Assault with intent to murder; indicted April 7, '71.

Eaton, James E...Theft of a horse and buggy; indicted April 17, '71.

Pretty, Joseph...Assault with intent to kill and murder; indicted April 17, '71.

Wallace, S. W...Theft of a cow valued at $25; indicted August 18, '71.

Wallace, S. W...Theft of a cow valued at $25; indicted September 13, '71.

Boyd, Newton...Theft of a gelding; indicted December 15, '71.

Farris, Thomas...Theft of a mule; indicted December 16, '71.

Saunders, Dr. W. H...Unlawfully receiving stolen property; indicted December 20, '71.

Mare, A...Theft of a gelding; indicted December 20, '71; negro.

Tyer, Joseph...Assault with intent to murder; indicted April 20, '72.

Cathorn, G. W...Theft of a beef cow valued at $24; indicted May 1, '72.

Williams, Thos...Theft of a sorrel mare; indicted August 12, '75.

Daniels, F. M...Theft of a sorrel mare; indicted August 12, '72.

Williams, Thomas...Theft of a black mare; indicted August 12, '72.

Daniels, F. M...Theft of a black mare; indicted August 12, '72.

Harris, Chas...Theft of a saddle; indicted August 12, '72.

Williams, Thomas...Theft of a gelding or mare; indicted August 12, '72.

Keelam, William...Theft of a gelding or mare; indicted August 12, '72.

Binkley, Henry...Murder; indicted August 12, '72.

Fletcher, Jeff...Theft of a mare; indicted August 15, '72.

Allen, Lou...Altering mark and brand on a cow; indicted August 20, '72.

Haywood, Wm...Assault with intent to murder; indicted August 24, '72; negro.

Mullens, Jim...Theft of a gelding; indicted December 21, '72; negro.

Stephenson, Robert...Theft of a promissory note; indicted January 1, '73; in Georgia.

Green, John...Theft of a bay gelding; indicted January 2, '73; negro.

Green, John...Theft of a bay pony horse; indicted January 2, '73; negro.

Busues, Wm.; alias Burns, Bill...Theft of two bales of cotton; two cases; indicted January 3, '73.

Busues, Wm.; alias Burns, Bill...Theft of one bale of cotton; indicted January 3, '73.

Granberry, Sol...Theft of a mule; indicted January 3, 73; negro.

Hill, Jeff...Assault with intent to murder; indicted April 15, '73.

Rushing, W. J...Theft of a gray mule; indicted April 15, '73.

Morris, W. H...Permitting a prisoner to escape; indicted April 15, '73.

Morris, W. H...Permitting a prisoner to escape; indicted April 17, 73.

Shelton, Nat...Concealing stolen property; indicted April 17, '73; yellow man.

Juvenal,——...Theft of three cows and three yearlings valued at $39; indicted April 28, '73.

Morris, W. H...Embezzlement of public money; indicted April 29, '73.

Cooly, John W...Swindling; indicted August 16, '73.

Johnson, Ollie...Theft of a cow valued at $60; indicted July 17, '73.

Johnson, Ollie...Theft of a two-year-old heifer valued at $35; indicted August 17, '73.

Wilder, Vincent...Concealing stolen gelding; indicted July 19, '73.

High, Wm. A...Theft of a black gelding; indicted July 18, '73.

Harrington, Mat...Swindling; indicted December 12, '73.

Wortham, Henry...Assault with intent to murder; indicted December 19, '73.

Bowling, Harris...Assault with intent to kill; indicted December 19, '73.

Yancy, Tom...Theft of a bay mare; indicted December 19, '73.

Bowling, Harrison...Murder; indicted December 19, '73.

Black, Eugene...Assault with intent to murder; indicted December 24, '73; negro.

Griffian, John...Burglary; indicted December 24, '73.

Williams, John...Assault with intent to murder; indicted April 13, '74.

Hudson, W. T.; Hudson, N. S.; and Hudson, A. J...Theft of a cow, valued at $12, and one yearling, valued at $4; indicted April 13, '74.

Rable, Wm...Theft of cattle (four cases); indicted April 13, '74.

Warwick. Samuel...Theft of two twenty dollar gold pieces; indicted April 15, '74.

Cester, Wm...Theft of one white cow : indicted April 15, '74.

Johnson, William...Theft of a beef steer, valued at $15; indicted April 16, '74.

Turner, Jack...Assault with intent to murder; indicted April 18, '74.

Maclison, Chas., alias Temple...Unlawful marriage; indicted April 18, '74.

Fleming, James M...Theft of seven sewing machines; indicted April 18, '74.

Bledsone, ——...Assault with intent to murder; indicted April, '74.

Dean, Robert J...Forgery; indicted April 22, '74.

Smith, S. P...Theft of four yearlings; indicted April 22, '74.

Weaver, Bud...Assault with intent to murder; indicted April 22, '74.

Parsley, John...Theft of a sorrel mare; indicted April 30, '74.

Hammond, Thomas...Assault with intent to murder; indicted July 10, '74.

McCloud, Ben...Theft of a heifer, valued at $8; indicted July 10, '74.

Willis, Dock...Theft of a beef steer, valued at $15; indicted July 11, '74; negro.

Jackson, Samuel...Theft of one heifer yearling; indicted July 10, '74.

Grace, W...Theft of one bale cotton; indicted July 17, '74.

Shmidt, Jens...Theft of money from a storehouse; indicted July 17, '74.

Bowe, Joe...Theft of a bull yearling; indicted April 18, '74.

Stinson, Geo...Theft of a brown cow; indicted April 20, '74.

Green, Irvin...Theft of a mare; indicted July 21, '74; negro.

McCloud, H. C...Assault with intent to murder; indicted July, 23, '74.

Prather, Mose...Assault with intent to murder; indicted July 24, '74; negro.

McCloud, H. C...Perjury; indicted July 28, '74.

Jackson, Manuel...Theft of two hogs; indicted August 17, '74; negro.

Trout, John...Theft of a bay colt; indicted August 18, '74.

Smith, John...Assault with intent to kill and murder, indicted August 18, '74.

Wallace, Andrew...Theft of a horse; indicted August 20, '74.

Hess, J. B...Embezzlement; November 6, '74.

Williams, Jack....Theft of $28; indicted November 6, '74.

Williams, J. F.; Williams, Moses; and Young, ——...Theft of two mules, a mare and a gelding colt; indicted November 6, '74.

Horker, Wm...Murder; indicted November 21, '74.

West, Geo...Assault with intent to rape; indicted November 11, '74.

Steel, Simon...Assault with intent to kill and murder; indicted November 11, '74.

Bordeaux, A...Swindling; indicted March 5, '75.

Enochs, E...Theft from a house; indicted March 5, '75.

Williams, Jack...Theft of a cow; indicted March 5, '75.

Golden, Thomas...Assault to kill and murder; indicted March 12, '75.

Ferris, J. S...Theft of a mule; indicted March 16, '75.

Ruble, Gum...Theft of a cow; indicted March 16, '75.

Jackson, Chas...Theft of a sow hog, valued at $6; indicted March 16, '75.

Pitts, Thos...Theft of a hog; indicted March 16, '75; negro.

Lovelace, J. C...Theft of a gray gelding; indicted March 18, '75.

Cook, J. H...Theft of a work ox; indicted March 16, '75.

Stokes, Gaines....Theft of a roan gelding; indicted March 18, '75.

Hunter, Hal...Assault with intent to murder; indicted March 24, '75.

Jackson, Arkansaw...Theft of cedar posts, valued at $20; indicted March 25, '75.

Jackson, W. G...Theft of a gelding; indicted July 8, '75.

Parker, Robt...Theft of a mare; indicted July 10, '75.

Harris, J. B...Assault with intent to murder; indicted July 13, '75.

Cook, John...Theft of a mare and gelding; indicted July 13, '75.

Thompson, Verge...Theft of a cow and yearling: indicted July 16, '75.

Wilmer, Buck...Theft from a house; indicted July 16, '75.

Shepherd, J. D...Theft of a yearling; indicted July 17, '75.

Owens, Cos...Theft of one ox, valued at $25; indicted July 22, '75.

Little, Abe...Murder; indicted July 22, '75; negro.

Wilson, Chas...Theft of watch and money; indicted July 24, '75.

Cook, J. H., alias Cooper, J. H...Theft of ox; indicted August 12, '75.

Burnes, J. M...Assault with intent to murder; indicted August 14, '75.

Carrick, Chas...Murder; indicted November 3, '75.

Green, Robt. J...Swindling; indicted November 4, 75.

Williams, Shep...Serious threats against the life of Ben Banes; indicted November 5, '75.

Cook, J. M...Theft of two oxen.

Martin, A. P...Theft of a grey gelding; indicted November 8, '75.

Bingham, J. W...Swindling; indicted November 10, '75.

Thomas, Major...Assault with intent to murder; indicted November 10, '75; negro.

Brazeal, Allen...Theft of a cow; indicted November 12, '75.

Carter, B. F...Theft of an estray gelding; indicted November 18, '75.

Gaston, Oliver; and Gillard, Gabe...Theft of $15 in money; indicted November 20, '75.

Bell, George, alias Pitts, Martin...Theft of a mare; indicted November 20, '75; colored.

Longley, J. W., alias Patterson...Robbery; indicted November 20, '75.

Falkner, J. M.; Wright, James; Roach, Edward...Theft of a gelding; indicted November 24, '75.

Rushing, Robert; Roseberry, William...Theft of four bales of cotton; indicted November 24, '75.

Sims, A...Theft of a gelding; indicted November 25, '75.

High, Samuel...Theft of a gelding; indicted November 15, '75.

Crutcher, G. H...Embezzlement; indicted November 25, '75.

Muse, Geo...Theft of a gelding; indicted March 9, '75.

Horn, Reese...Assault with intent to murder; indicted March 9, '76; colored.

Wilburn, Albert...Theft of gelding, two cases; indicted March 11, '76.

Russel, J. P...Theft of a gelding; indicted March 14, '76.

Jackson, Bob, alias Whispering Bob...Swindling; indicted March 14, '76.

Wright, Reuben—Assault, intent to murder; indicted March 17, '76.

Willburn, J. W...Theft of a cow; indicted March 20, '76.

Gambreel, James...Theft of a gelding; indicted March 20, '76.

Gambreel, James...Theft of an ox; indicted March 20, '76.

Patterson, Sam...Theft of a watch and chain; indicted March 20, '76.

Robinson, Jeff...Theft of a beef steer; indicted March 24, '76.

Wright, Charles...Assault, intent to murder; indicted March 24, '76.

Vaums, P. B....Theft of $258; indicted March 28, '76.

Bill, Joshua...Theft of two bales of cotton; indicted March 28, '76.

Willburn, J. J...Altering marks and brands; indicted March 28, '76.

Foster, E...Theft from a house; indicted May 4, '76; negro.

Foster, E...Burglary; indicted May 4, '76; negro.

Johnson, Wm...Swindling; indicted May 4, '76; negro.

Randolfe, John P....Theft of $52 in money; indicted May 10, '76.

Williams, Henry....Theft of a mare mule; indicted May 9, '76.

Kurtz, Chris....Burglary; indicted May 10, '76.

Sweat, Green...Assault with intent to rape; indicted May 11, '76.

Pool, Elias S....Marrying a negro woman; indicted May 14, '76.

Dyer, W. R....Theft of a cow; indicted May 16, '76.

Crary, T. J....Theft of an ox; indicted May 16, '76.

Glasgo, alias Mixon...Theft of two cows; indicted May 16, '76.

Standifer, Burrell...Theft of a horse; indicted May 16, '76; negro.

Dyer, W. R...Theft of 1000 pounds cotton; indicted May 17, '76.

Boykin; and Hardin....Theft of a sorrel mare; indicted November, 27, '76.

Powers, Geo. W...Theft of a wagon valued at $125; indicted November 23, '76.

Lundy, John W...Theft of sorrel horse; indicted November 23, '76.

Lundy, John W...Theft of a cow; indicted November 23, '76.

Miller, James...Perjury; indicted November 29, '76.

Wilson, Jack....Forgery; indicted November 29, '76.

Thacher, Wm....Theft of a gelding; indicted March 9, '77.

Hall, Henry...Theft of a mare; indicted March 9, 77.

Barkley, Newton...Assault with intent to murder; indicted March 9, '77

Witherspoon, J. F...Forgery; indicted March 18, '77.

Allen, R. A...Theft of a cow; indicted March 28, '77.

Henderson, James...Swindling; indicted March 25, '77.

Meat, A...Assault with intent to murder; indicted March 25, '77.

Carry, alias Davis, alias John Wilson...Theft of two mules; indicted March 25, '77.

Witherspoon, J. F...Forgery; indicted March 26, '77.

Crain, A. G...Theft of 100 photographs; indicted March 26, '77.

Kellis, Wm...Murder; indicted November 7, '77.

Deason, Wm...Assault with intent to murder; indicted November 13, 77.

Foreland, J. W...Forgery; indicted November 15, '77.

Cardnel, Jack; Thompson, Reuben, alias Robinson; and Berry, Sol... Theft of heifer, neat cattle; indicted November 20, '77; all negroes.

Golden, Thos....Perjury; indicted November 20, '77.
English, Dixon...Theft of a gelding; indicted November 21, '77.
Boatwright, R. J...Forgery; indicted November 23, '77.
Sims, Austin...Murder; indicted November 23, '77.
Fillmore, Stephen....Theft of gelding; indicted November 23, '77; negro.
Pitit, J. W...Theft of two steers; indicted November 23, '77.

M'CULLOCH COUNTY.

Sanders, Lafayette; and Surcey, W. P...Theft of a cow; indicted September, 1876. Lafayette Sanders has fair complexion, hair light red, blue eyes, about 26 years old, height about 5 feet 10 or 11 inches, weighs about 150 or 160 pounds. W. P. Surcey has dark complexion, dark hair, height about 5 feet 7 inches, weighs about 180 pounds.
McMahan, ———...Theft of cattle (five indictments); indicted March, 1877; about 5 feet 10 inches in height, complexion sandy, weighs about 160 pounds.
Dougherty, Emanuel...Serious threats to take human life; indicted March, 1877; about 5 feet 8 or 9 inches high, light complexion, hair brown, inclined to be curly, heavy set, weighs about 150 or 160 pounds.
Hall, Caleb, alias Hall, Cail...Theft of cattle; indicted March, 1877; about 5 feet 11 inches in height, light complexion, hair brown, usually wears moustache and goatee, slim built, weighs about 160 pounds.
Smith, Monroe...Theft of a cow; indicted March, 1877; about 5 feet 6 inches high, weighs about 130 pounds, light complexion, blue eyes, about 23 years old.
Odom, Syens...Illegally altering marks and brands of a cow and theft of a cow (two indictments); indicted March, 1877.
Fuller, Bud...Theft of cattle; indicted March, 1877.
Ware or Weir, Bill...Unlawfully altering brands of a cow; indicted March, 1877.
Johnson, Willis; Johnson, Nat.; and Wicker, Bill...Six indictments, three for theft of cattle and three for illegally altering marks and brands of cattle; indicted March, 1877.
Parks, John...Three indictments, two for theft of cattle and one for illegally defacing brands of a cow; indicted March, 1877.

MADISON COUNTY.

McMillan, Neil, Jr...Murder; indicted December, 74; light complexion, heavy set, 5 feet 10 inches high, 45 or 46 years old.
Purvis, John...Murder; indicted August, '73; thin visage, black hair, blue eyes, 6 feet high, 25 or 26 years old.
Tyler, Jobe F...Murder; indicted August, '73; light complexion, small man, say 135 to 140 pounds in weight, about 35 years old.
Powlege, John N...Assault to kill; 5 feet 10 inches high, dark eyes and hair, rather slender, 25 years old.
Tell, Wm...Theft; indicted December, '73.
Mason, James P...Murder; indicted August, '74; black hair, low stature, 26 or 28 years old, dark skin.
McMillan, Theophlus...Murder; indicted December, '74; small man.

Mathis, Fred...Cattle stealing; three cases; light complexion, small stature, 24 or 25 years old.

Pigford, John...Cattle stealing; three cases; 6 feet high, slender, dark hair and eyes, 22 or 23 years old.

McIver, John R...Murder; committed December, '76; 27 or 28 years old, 5 feet 10 inches high, sandy complexion, heavy brows and very thick lips, and has rather a downward look when in conversation and contracts his brows when talking; has a soft and pleasant voice.

McIver, Dr. Joseph...Murder; indicted December, '76; is 5 feet 9 or 10 inches high, weighs 215 pounds, rather round form, fine address, excellent conversational powers, rather bald headed, teeth good, hazel eyes, round full face; is supposed to be in Kimble connty.

Lewis, Clint...Murder; committed June 6, '76.

Mosley, Ransom; Baker, Geo.; and Arnold, Hamp...Murder; committed June 6, '76.

Mattox, S. H...Murder; committed August 12, '74.

Scott, Elbert P...Murder; committed December 11, '74.

MAVERICK COUNTY.

Daniel, Encarnacion...Accessory to murder; indicted March, '73; Mexican, in Mexico.

Sandobal, Jesus; and Antonio...Murder; indicted March, '73; Mexicans, escaped to Mexico.

Gonzales, Pedro...Theft of a steer; indicted August, '74; Mexican, in Mexico.

Cabanas, Rafael...Swindling; indicted August, '74; fancy Mexican, speaks English, black moustache, and is 5 feet 6 inches high.

Lopez, Candelario...Burglary; indicted August '74.

Hill, S. A...Theft of geldings; indicted September, '75; dark hair, heavy set, small pale face, and has a goatee.

Seamon, James, alias Hanscum, James...Theft of money; indicted January, '76.

Centento, Victor...Theft of a gelding; indicted September, '75; Mexican, pock-marked, 5 feet 10 inches high, low forehead and has a guilty look, supposed to be in this county.

Villareal, Crescencio...Assault to murder; indicted May, 1875; two forfeitures of bond. In Piedras Negras or Rio Grande, Coahuila, Mexico.

Flores, Anastacio...Theft of cattle; indicted May, 1876; forfeited two bonds. Near Monclova or San Buena Ventura, Coahuila, Mexico.

Chavari, Solomon; Chavari, Cornelio; Trevino, Benito; and Seguin, Juan...Assault to murder; indicted November, 1876. Last heard from when in jail in Piedras Negras, for crimes committed in Mexico. The assault was made on E. Buschel, U.S. Revenue officer, when in discharge of his duty.

Belles, Blas de las...Theft of pistol; indicted November, 1876.

Belas, Antonio...Theft of a gelding; indicted November, 1876; broke jail in Maverick county. In Mexico or on Rio Grande below.

Hernandez, Simon...Theft of a colt; indicted May, 1876; broke jail in Maverick county. In Mexico.

Bitela, Lucas...Theft of a horse; indicted May, 1877; broke jail in Maverick county. In Mexico.

Frazier, Sam... Theft of a gelding; indicted May, 1877.

Escobar, Manuel, alias Escobero...Theft of gelding; indicted May, 1877; broke jail in Maverick county. In Mexico.

Garcia, Guadalupe...Driving cattle across the Rio Grande; indicted May, 1877. In Mexico, about Monclovo viejo, on Rio Grande, about 14 miles above Eagle Pass and Piedras Negras, generally known as "el Desmolado," tall, stout, not very dark, sickly complexion, upper front teeth out, and generally known in this county; did belong to Manuel Van's minute men.

Ozuna, Serapio; and Garcia, Andres...Robbery; convicted October term 1871, (10 years each); supposed to be about Monterey, Mexico.

NAVARRO COUNTY

Jones, Wm...Theft of money; committed '73; indicted same year; negro.

Brown, John...Theft of cotton; committed '73; indicted '73; black, 5 feet 8 inches high, heavy build.

Allen, W. A...Murder; committed '74; indicted same year.

Martin, N. B...Selling mortgaged property; committed '73; indicted '74; 6 feet high, ruddy complexion, light hair, blue eyes.

Benham, David...Theft of mule; committed '74; indicted same year.

Lawrence, Sam...Theft of saddle; committed '74; indicted same year.

McDaniel, John...Theft of yearling; committed '74; indicted same year.

Loupe, R. S...Theft of oxen; committed '74; indicted same year.

Jeffers, James...Theft of mule; committed '73; indicted '74.

Sheets, A. D...Theft of beef; committed '73; indicted '74.

Baptiste, John...Assault to murder; committed '74; indicted same year; negro; 6 feet, slim build.

Stroud, Beaton...Theft of heifer; committed '74; indicted same year.

Stroud, J. B...Theft of oxen; committed '74; indicted same year.

Crabtree, J. W...False swearing; committed '74; indicted same year.

Farrar, Robert; and Tom...Theft of beef; committed '74; indicted same year.

O'Keef, John...Theft of beef; committed '75; indicted same year.

Rushing, Alf...Theft of cattle (three cases); committed '74; indicted '75.

Polk, John....Theft of cattle (two cases), and theft of beef (two cases); committed '75; indicted same year.

Horn, Enoch...Theft of gelding; committed '75; indicted same year.

Curtis, Bill...Theft of gelding; committed '75; indicted same year; negro, 5 feet 8 inches high, 25 years old.

Cain, David...Obtaining money under false pretenses; committed '75; indicted same year.

Meader, Thos...Theft of beef; committed '74; indicted '75.

Hickey, Thos...Forgery; committed '74; indicted '75.

York, Frank...Theft of beef; committed '75; indicted same year.

Lee, John...Burglary; committed '75; indicted same year.

Elder, James...Murder; committed '75; indicted same year.

Haley, James H...Forgery; committed '75; indicted same year.

Bryant, J. A...Obtaining money under false pretense; indicted '75.

White, Ras...Theft of gelding; committed '74; indicted '75.

Barry, Adam...Uttering forged instrument; committed '75; indicted same year; negro.

Adams, Geo. W...Perjury; committed '75; indicted same year; said to be in Arkansas; 5 feet 8 inches high, slender, 22 years old, blue eyes and light hair.

Byers, Edmund....Theft from house; committed '75; indicted same year.

Poole, S. T...Assault to murder; committed '75; indicted same year.

Frazier, Sarah A...Incest; committed '75; indicted same year.

Kimbell, Ike...Theft of ox; committed '75; indicten same year.

Tickle, Geo...Theft of ox; committed '75; indicted same year.

Floyd, John T...Perjury; committed '75; indicted same year.

Sims, Dan ..Theft from house; committed '75; indicted same year.

McMatt, Jesse....Theft from house; committed '75; indicted same year.

Crawford, Bob....Threatening life of another, and theft of cattle; committed '75; indicted same year.

Ross, Dan...Theft of geiding; committed '75; indicted same year; negro.

Chapman, Lewis...Swindling; committed '75; indicted same year.

Parish, Abe....Theft of gelding and theft of beef (three cases); committed '76; indicted same year.

Smith, Thomas...Theft of cattle (three cases); committed '76; indicted same year.

Swink, James...Theft of cow; committed '76; indicted same year.

Lisp, Robert, Theft of cow; committed '76; indicted same year.

Burrus, Jack...Theft of cow (four cases); committed '76; indicted same year.

Moore, West...Assault to murder; committed '76; indicted same year.

Hamilton, Cain...Theft from house; committed '76; indicted same year.

Jackson, Henry...Theft of hog; committed '76; indicted same year.

Young, Caleb...Theft of beef; committed '76; indicted same year.

Lanning, Tony...Theft of mare; committed '76; indicted same year.

Swink, Henry...Theft of cattle; committed '76; indicted same year.

Walker, Amos...Assault to murder; theft of mare; theft of mule; committed '76; indicted same year.

Bowman, Lewis...Theft of beef; committed '75; indicted '76.

Griggs, Frank...Theft of cattle; committed '75; indicted '76; two cases; 5 feet 6 inches high, small, sandy hair, blue eyes.

Clark, Lewis...Assault with intent to murder; committed '75; indicted same year; 5 feet 10 inches high, slender, brown colored kinky hair; negro.

Fraley, Bud...Theft of cattle; committed '75; indicted '76; 5 cases; 5 feet 11 inches high, heavy built, dark hair and eyes.

Payne, Sam...Theft of hog; committed '76; indicted same year; 5 feet 8 inches high, slim build, black hair and eyes; negro.

O'Bannon, J. M...Theft of colts; committed '76; indicted '76; 6 feet high, weighs 150 pounds, light hair and eyes, sandy beard and moustache.

Anderson, J. P...Conspiracy and assault with intent to murder; committed '76; indicted same year; 6 feet 2 inches high; sallow complexion, stoop-shoulders, black hair and eyes, nearly always carries saddle-bags on his arm.

Williamson, Wm...Theft of cattle; committed '76; indicted same year; 6 feet high, slim build; white hair, blue eyes, ruddy complexion; 21 years old, supposed to be in Tennessee.

Tickle, Robt...Murder; committed '76; indicted '76; 5 feet 8 inches high, heavy build, full face, sallow complexion, light hair, blue eyes; $250 reward offered.

Tickle, James...Theft of ox; committed '75; indicted '76; 5 feet 8 inches high, slim build, dark hazel eyes, weighs 140 pounds, dark hair.

Tickle, George...Assault with intent to murder; committed '76; indicted same year.

Crouch, W. D...Theft of cow; committed '75; indicted same year.

Wattles, Z. T...Murder; committed '76; indicted same year; 5 feet 8 inches high, slender, light hair, blue eyes, about 28 years old, walks and talks hastily.

Swann, J. C...Assault with intent to murder; committed '77; indicted same year.

Lee, Sam...Murder; committed '77; indicted same year; about 19 years old; medium size.

Lee, John...Robbery; committed '77; indicted same year.

McWhorter, R. A...Theft of mare and gelding; committed '77; indicted same year.

Combs, W. P...Theft of yearling; committed '77; indicted same year.

Harris, Wm...Assault with intent to murder.

Samuel, R. P...Murder; committed '77; indicted same year; 5 feet 9 inches high, slender, sallow complexion, dark hair, one hand crippled.

NACOGDOCHES COUNTY.

Fuller, William...Murder; committed January, '69; indicted February, same year.

Kidd, John B...Murder; committed June, '69; indicted February, '70; medium size, 38 years old.

Crutchfield, John...Theft of horse; committed April, '70; indicted Ocber, same year.

Robinson, Isaac...Burglary; committed February, '69; indicted October, '70.

Day, Robt...Murder; committed May 1, '63; indicted July 8, '63.

Jarvis, J...Assault to murder; committed May, '71; indicted June, same year.

Shears, Vina...Assault to murder (two cases); committed October, '71; indicted October, same year.

Parmaley, Jack...Assault to murder (two cases); committed December, '71; indicted March, '72; negro, spare build and 30 years old.

Grayson, J. M...Assault to murder; committed December, '71; indicted November, '72; murder (2 cases); committed December, '71; indicted July, '72; small man, 40 years old.

McRoberts, James...Murder; committed December '71; indicted July, '72. Large man, 65 years old.

McClender, J. C...Assault to murder; commited February, '73; indicted February, same year.

White, W. L...Assault to murder; committed January, '73; indicted March, same year. Above medium size, and is 45 years old.

White, Steve...Theft of a hog; committed November, '73; indicted March, same year. Negro.

Blackburn, Frank...Murder; committed September '73; indicted October, same year. Fair complexion and blue eyes.

Greenwood, Marion...Burglary; committed October, '73; indicted October, same year. Heavy set, dark complexion, 45 years old.

Vawters, Dillard...Theft from house; committed August, '73; indicted November, same year.

Hazlet, Marion...Murder; committed December, '71; indicted November '72. Small man, 60 years old.

King, Jordan...Murder; committed December, '71; indicted November, '72. Tall negro,

Bullock, Henry...Theft from a house; committed January, '74; indicted May, same year.

King, Thomas...Theft from a house; committed December, '73; indicted May, '74.

Lewis, Thomas, alias Coney Lewis...Theft of a hog; committed November, '73; indicted May, '74.

William, John...Assault to murder; committed March, '74; indicted May, same year.

Chissum, Samuel...Theft of oxen and theft of beef steer; committed November, '75; indicted December, same year.

Carter, Marshall...Theft of a gun; committed April, 75; indicted May, same year.

Dickinson, Charles...Swindling; committed April '75; indicted May, same year; negro.

Jordan, Mat...Theft of cattle and assault to murder; committed November, '75; indicted December, same year; negro.

Hall, L. D...Swindling; committed October, '75; indicted December, same year; over medium size, 50 years old.

Fall, Lynn...Assault to murder; committed December, '75; indicted December, same year; medium size, dark complexion, 20 years old.

Hensen, T. J...Assault to murder (two cases); committed May, '75; indicted December, same year; medium size, 50 years old, florid complexion.

NEWTON COUNTY.

Roan, Henry...Assault to murder; committed December 1, '69; indicted August 21, '71.

Crawford, James...Theft of hogs; committed November 5, '71; indicted December 23, same year.

Beard, W. A...Assault to kill; committed September 4, '71; indicted December 23, same year; supposed to be in Louisiana.

Delany, Tobias...Robbery; committed January 10, '70; indicted December 23, '71, is supposed to be in the western portion of Texas.

Brooks, George...Theft from a house; committed November 1, '72; indicted December 20, same year.

Green, Charles...Assault to murder; committed April 1, '73; indicted December, 20, same year.

Foster, Dan...Assault to murder; committed February 1, '73; three indictments.

Green, Charles...Assault to murder; committed February 15, '73; indicted April 23, same year.

McFarland, Henry...Assault to murder; committed August 1, '73; indicted August 21, same year.

Haygood, John...Theft of hogs; committed December, 1, '73; indicted December 19, same year.

Sweatman, Green...Assault to murder; committed February 1, '74; indicted July 30, same year.

Sweatman, Ben...Assault to murder ; committed May 10, '74; indicted July 30, same year.

Landy, J. O...Swindling : committed December 1, '75; indicted November 27, same year; it is rumored Landy is in jail in Mississippi.

Brooks, Joseph...Theft of hogs; committed October 1, '75; indicted November 27, same year.

Jordan, James...Theft from a house; committed December 1, '75; indicted June 19, '76.

Bevel, Bayley...Assault to murder ; committed June 4, '76; indicted June 19, same year.

Smith, George...Assault to murder; committed November 25, 76; indicted December 22, same year.

ORANGE COUNTY.

Hanks, Horatio....Assault with intent to kill; committed February, '68; indicted Spring term, same year. Is about 5 feet 10 inches high, heavy made, weighs about 160 pounds, about 28 years old, black hair and dark complexion, wore a heavy dark moustache.

Gill, W. A...Murder; committed May 4, 69; indicted October 30, same year. Is about 5 feet 11 inches high, weighs about 175 pounds, 35 years old, heavy whiskers, dark complexion.

Wilson, D. W...Murder; committed May 4, '69; indicted October 30, same year.

Bill, Yellow...Murder; committed May 4, '69; indicted October 30, same year.

McGee, Richard...Threatening to kill; committed November 28, '71; indicted December, 8, same year. Is about 5 feet 9 inches high, auburn hair, gray eyes, about 28 years old, very slender, will weigh about 125 pounds.

Stewart, W. A...Forgery; committed January 10, '72; indicted August 12, same year. Is about 5 feet 8 inches high, weighs abut 160 pounds, about 40 years old, blue, red curly hair and red beard, heavy made and has a very red face.

Brown, Dan...Assault with intent to kill; committed November 19, '73; indicted December, 5, '73.

Ferguson, Angus...Assault to kill; committed January 5, '74; indicted August 9, same year. Lives in Louisiana.

MuCorquodale, Ephraim...Assault with intent to kill ; committed January 1, '74; indicted August 7, same year. Is 6 feet high, slender made, weighs about 140 pounds, 35 years old, hair very black, and piercing black eyes, complexion, dark, wore a light beard on his chin, has a slight stoppage in his speech.

Spain, Emanenl...Theft from a house; committed January 1, '76; indicted April 6, same year. Negro, very black, about 6 feet high, rather slender built, weighs 160 pounds, about 26 years old, very flat nose and large eyes.

Johnson, Jethro...Murder.

Addison, Doc...Assault to kill.

PANOLA COUNTY.

Winn, Thomas...Theft of a cow; committed May, '65; indicted June, same year.

Truelock, Samuel...Robbery; committed May, '65; indicted June, same year.

Kern, Polk...Robbery; committed May, '65; indicted June, same year.

Harris, John...Robbery; committed May, '65; indicted June, same year.

Corlin, G. W...Theft of cotton; committed October, '65; indicted December, same year.

Campbell, Columbus...Assault to murder; committed November, '65; indicted December, same year.

Booker, James...Theft; committed October, '65; indicted December, same year.

Turner, W. A...Theft of cotton; committed July, '65; indicted December, same year; about 38 years old, about 6 feet high, weighs 165 pounds, dark complexion; supposed to be in Robertson county.

Evans, N. S...Assault to murder; committed November, '65; heavy build, red face, weighs about 175 pounds; last heard of in Marion county.

Elder, John W...Robbery; committed October, '65; indicted December, same year; about 40 years old, small eyes, sharp features, about 5 feet high, weighs about 135 pounds, curly hair; last heard of in New York city.

Gibson, Charles...Theft; committed January, '66; indicted June, same year; negro.

George, ——...Theft; committed December, '65; indicted June, '66; negro.

McLendon, Joseph...Theft; committed March, '67; indicted March, same year.

Tatum, Thomas...Assault to murder; committed August, '65; indicted March, '67; last heard of in Rusk county.

Elijah, ——...Assault to murder; committed August, '65; indicted March, '67; negro.

Bickerstaff...Robbery; committed February, '67; indicted March, same year.

Alexander, Creed...Assault to murder; committed March, '67; indicted March, same year; about 28 years old, about 5 feet 7 inches high, weighs about 145 pounds, black hair, fair skin, may wear beard; lives in Middle Texas.

Garland, John...Assault to murder; committed March, '67; indicted March, same year; about 28 years old, about 6 feet high, weighs about 150 pounds, dark skin, black eyes (which are quite sharp), black hair, wears beard.

Coyle, Wm, alias True, Jno...Murder; assault to murder; committed January, '68; indicted March, same year; About 35 years old, weighs 180 pounds, light hair, fair skin, about 6 feet 2 inches high, quite a desperado; supposed to be in the Indian Territory; family living in Stringtown.

Cratick, Amos...Murder; committed January, '68; indicted March, same year; 35 years old; mother lives near Wynsborough, Wood county.

Henry, Willis...Murder; committed January, '68; indicted March, same year.

Coyle, Luther...Assault to murder; committed January, '68; indicted March, same year; negro.

Harrison, Thomas...Theft of a mule; committed July, '67; indicted March, '68; negro.

Langley, Stephen...Assault to murder; committed December, '66 indicted March, '68.

Allen, Wm...Theft; two cases; committed October, '67, and January, '68; indicted March, 68; about 22 years old.

Hains, Joshua and Ann...Murder; committed August, '67; indicted March, '68.

Hodge, Charles, alias Johnson, Charley...Murder; committed October, '67; indicted April, 68; about 28 years old, about 5 feet ten inches high, weighs about 160 pounds, sandy hair, blue eyes, talks considerably.

Jones, Samuel...Theft from a house; committed March, '68; indicted April, same year.

Wall, Charles...Murder; committed November, '67; indicted April, '68; negro.

Bateman, Wm...Robbery; committed, '67; indicted, '68; lives in Kaufman county.

Parish, Wm...Robbery; committed, '67; indicted April, '68.

Daniel...Theft of an ox; committed February, '68; indicted April, same year; negro.

McLoud, August...Assault to murder; committed October, '67; indicted April, '68; about 23 years old, about 5 feet 5 inches high, weight about 150 pounds, dark, sallow complexion, black hair, black eyes.

Donahoe, James...Theft of a cow; committed April, '68; indicted September, same year; about 35 or 40 years old, about 5 feet 3 inches high, weight about 130 pounds, sallow complexion, black hair and eyes.

Millstead, Peter...Assault to murder; committed October, '66.

Osburn, James...Adultery; committed, '65; indicted March, '69.

Guinn, Mary...Adultery; committed, '65; indicted March, '69.

Thompson, John...Theft; committed July, '69; indicted March, same year.

Oglesby, Julius...Theft of a horse; indicted March, '69.

Crawford, Andrew...Burglary; indicted March, '69.

Bevin, John...Burglary; indicted March, '69.

Chambliss, Rolla M...Theft of horse; indicted November, '69.

Barren, Alfred...Murder; indicted March, '69.

English, James...Assault to murder; indicted September, '68.

Wilson, T. H...Assault to murder; committed December, '69; indicted March '70.

Emberson, Julia...Murder; committed January, '70; indicted March, same year; female, about 35 years old, about 5 feet 4 inches high, light hair, fair skin, and of ill-fame.

Welch, James...Murder; committed December, '69; indicted April '70.

Wynne, William...Assault to murder; committed February, '70; indicted April, same year.

Staggers, Mrs. E...Swindling; committed January, '70; indicted April, same year.

English, G. W...Theft; committed March, '70; indicted April, same year.

Houston, Laurence...Assault to murder (two cases); indicted October, '70; indicted February, '71.

Bird, Willis...Theft of cotton; indicted October, '70.

8

Ware, Sigh...Adultery; committed October, '70; indicted February, '71

Womack, Lena...Adultery; committed October, '70; indicted February, '71.

Campbell, John W...Adultery; indicted February, '71.

Smith, Charles...Adultery; committed October, '70; indicted February, '71.

Reed, Mary...Adultery; committed October, '70; indicted February, '71.

Greenwood, Marion...Assault to murder; indicted October, '71.

Oliver, James...Robbery; indicted October, '71.

Darnall, John I...Murder; committed April, '71; indicted October, same year. About 29 years old, about 6 feet high, weighs 175 pounds, dark skin, black eyes, shows his upper front teeth when talking, has one tooth out on the upper set. Lives in or about Middle Texas, near Johnson, Tarrant, or Dallas county.

Kelley, James...Assault to murder; committed October, '71.

Washington, Irving...Perjury; committed September, '71; indicted October, same year.

Morris, Edmond...Theft; committed October, '71; indicted February, '72. Negro.

Bradley, John...Swindling; indicted February, '72. About six feet high, light complexion.

Smalley, Robert...Obtaining goods under false pretenses; indicted February, '72.

Taylor, Henderson...Theft; committed November, '71; indicted February, '72.

Gales, July...Theft; committed November, '71; indicted February '72.

Hilton, Nathan and Isaac...Swindling; committed October, '71; indicted February, '72.

May, Lee...Threats to do serious bodily injury; committed December, '71; indicted February, '72. Lives in Rusk, Shelby, or Nacogdoches county.

Self, Buck and Middleton...Threats to do serious bodily injury; committed December, '71; indicted February, '72. Live either in Rusk, Shelby, or Nacogdoches county.

Morris, James...Assault to murder; committed November, '70; indicted June, '72.

Driver, John...Assault to murder; indicted June, '72. About 40 years old, 6 feet high, dark skin, black eyes, weighs 145 pounds, right arm off close to shoulder, loves whisky.

Hodges, Shade...Murder; committed December '71; indicted June, '72. Negro.

Cooke, David...Burglary; committed August, '72; indicted October, same year. Negro, about 25 years old.

Robertson, Ky...Murder; indicted October, '72. Negro about 30 years old, 6 feet 2 inches high, weighs 180 pounds. Lives on Red River, in DeSoto parish, La.

Warmington, Sylvester...Theft; committed August, '72; indicted October, same year

Munday, Orison...Assault to murder; indicted October, '72.

Roberts, Stephen...Murder; indicted February, '73. Reward by Governer, $150. Lives at Olustee, Florida; short, heavy set, red complexion and hair.

Greenwood, Martin...Accessory to murder; committed November, '72; indicted February, 73.

Thompson, Jack...Assault to murder; indicted February, '72. About 25 years old, weighs about 165 pounds, about 5 feet 10 inches high, sandy hair, freckled face, usually wears his hair long, which is quite thick. Last heard of near Cedar Grove, Kaufman county.

Boren, Joseph...Theft; committed November, '72; indicted June, '73. Negro; about 23 years old, spare build, about 5 feet 4 inches high.

Story, Joseph...Sodomy; committed May, '73; indicted June, same year. About 35 year old, weighs about 160 pounds, about 5 or 6 feet high, fair skin, red whiskers and hair. Lives in Middle Texas.

Yarbourough, Richard...Assault to murder; indicted October, '73.

Carter, Peter, alias Peter Clark...Theft; indicted October, '73.

Allen, George...Theft; indicted October, '73.

Buckingham, Isham...Theft; indicted October, '73.

Haynes, Jack...Theft; indicted October, '73. Negro.

Nelson, George, alias George Williams...Theft; indicted October, '73. Negro.

Sullins, Bartholemew...Theft; indicted October, '73.

Scoggins, Richard...Assault to murder; indicted February, '74. One-legged Yankee pensioner. Last heard of in Shreveport, La.

Henry, ——...Burglary; indicted February, '74. Negro.

Coleman, Jack...Theft; indicted June, '74. Lives at Bethamy, La.

Gill, Vinck...Theft; indicted June, '74.   "   "   "

Boyd, Lary...Theft; indicted June, '74.   "   "   "

Stephens, Charles...Theft; indicted June, '74. "   "   "

Williams, Joe...Theft; indicted June, '74.   "   "   "

Birmingham, David...Theft; indicted June, '74. "   "   "

Jackson, Joe...Theft; indicted June, '74.   "   "   ".

Houston, Nettie...Theft; indicted June, '74.

Nichols, Ned...Assault to murder; indicted June, '74.

Spradley, John...Theft; indicted June, '74. About 23 years old, weighs about 140 pounds, dark skin, dark hair, about 5 feet 10½ inches high. Lives in Middle Texas.

Dunn, Frank...Assault to murder; indicted October, '74. About 60 years old, carpenter, about 6 feet high, weighs about 160 pounds, florid complexion, and is an ardent lover of strong drink.

Sheals, James...Theft; indicted October, '73. About 40 years old, about 5 feet high, weighs about 120 pounds, sandy hair and fair skin.

Kelly, Dick...Adultery; indicted February, '75.

Hardy, Mary...Adultery; indicted February, '75.

Grim, Charles...Assault to rape; indicted February, '75.

Lary, Lewis....Assault to murder; indicted June, '75.

Kay, Bedford...Theft; indicted June, '75.

White, Josh...Theft; indicted October, '75.

Moore, Wm...Assault to murder; indicted October, '75.

Keener, Wm...Assault to murder; indicted October, '75.

Standifer, Wm...Threats to kill; indicted February, '76.

Brown, James...Robbery; indicted February, '76.

Burnes, Pickens....Burglary, assualt to rape, and swindling; indicted February, '76.

Brown Jack...Murder; committed October, '76; indicted February, '77; bright mulatto, about 24 years old, weighs about 160 pounds, about the ordinary height, has a mole on his cheek, was tried at the August term of the District Court of Panola county, '77, and indicted of murder in the second degree, and punishment assessed at 99 years in the penitentiary, took an appeal and escaped pending same.

Herin, Samuel...Theft; indicted February, '77; is somewhere in Central Texas.

Johnson, Lum...Assault to murder; committed October, '76; indicted February, '77; is a slender, dark mulatto, about 20 years old, is perhaps in Harrison county, worked a while at the railroad shops at Marshall.

Wallace, George...Selling mortgaged property; indicted February, '77; is a very dark negro.

Crawford, Ellsbury ..Assault to murder; committed October, '76; indicted February, '77; is a slender man, slightly stooped, with sandy hair and whiskers, is a great singer, teaches singing schools, takes great interest in such things, has relatives living in Grimes and Fannin counties, has been lurking in both places, has a family with him, is now near Texarkana, in Arkansas.

Miller, Jerry...Threats to take life; indicted February, '77; is a tall man, with sandy whiskers and black hair.

Cottonredder, Kelse...Assault to rape; indicted August, '77; tried, convicted and punishment at seven years in the penitentiary, escaped pending appeal; is a slender negro man, about 24 years old, has a light moustache.

Johnson, Rector...Assault to murder; indicted August, '77; is a copper-colored negro man, about 25 years old, with a deformity in one leg, being shorter than the other.

Bourman, John...Assault to murder; indicted August, '77; negro.

Adams, John...Assault to murder; indicted August, '77; is about 19 years old, weighs about 130 pounds.

Davis, Bijot...Theft; indicted August, '77.

Appleton, James...Theft; indicted August, '77; negro.

Duke, James...Murder; indicted August, '77; about 24 years old, goes under various Christian names, but retains the surname, Duke.

Ingram, George...Burglary; indicted August, '77; negro.

Walteree, Till...Assault to murder; indicted August, '76; is a negro, lives in Louisiana, near the Harrison county line, and near Elysian Fields.

PECOS COUNTY.

Spencer, Wm...Murder; indicted October, '75; about 35 years old; formerly resided in Tom Green county.

Heredia, Cileto...Murder; committed December 9, '76; indicted October, '77; Mexican, about 35 years old.

Sand-Hill George (other name unknown)...Murder; indicted April 9, '76; reported to be driving a stage in Eastern Texas, about 35 or 40 years old.

PRESIDIO COUNTY.

Boyd, John; and Moulton, Edward...Murder; indicted April, 1877. Both white; Moulton is about 28 or 30 years old, 5 feet 8 inches high, thick set, weighs 170 or 180 pounds, and now in New Mexico. Boyd is now at Fort Clark.

POLK COUNTY.

Brooks, Evans...Murder; committed November, '70; indicted February, '73; negro.

Martin, Frank...Assault to murder; committed September, '70; indicted February, '73; negro, about 40 years old, about 5 feet 10 or 11 inches high, spare build. Last heard of near Hempstead.

Bruce, Guilford G...Murder; committed September, '69; indicted February, '73. Dark complexion, light hair and eyes, about six feet high, spare build, about 30 years old.

Bishop, W. R...Robbery; committed September, '72; indicted February, '73; 5 feet 8 inches high, 150 pounds, large scar on cheek, 28 years old, florid complexion, sandy hair.

McGinnis, Birt...Assault to murder; committed January, '73; indicted February, same year; dark complexion, black hair and eyes, about 21 or 22 years old, 5 feet 8 or 9 inches high; either in Kansas City, Mo., or Indiana. Weight 170 pounds.

Diggs, Wm...Assault to murder; committed August, '73; indicted October, same year; about 5 feet 8 or 9 inches high, weight about 140 pounds, about 27 or 30 years old. Last heard of in Mississippi.

Price, James H...Assault to murder; committed January, '74; indicted February, same year; about 24 or 25 years old, light complexion, light hair and eyes, about 6 feet high, spare build, weight about 140 lbs, ignorant and dissipated. Last heard of at Lake Charles, La.

Oats, John T...Perjury; committed June, '73; indicted February, '74; about 25 or 27 years old, dark complexion, 5 feet 10 inches high. Last heard of in Houston county.

Mann, Levi...Assault to murder; committed January, '74; indicted February, same year; about 17 or 18 years old. Last heard of in Washington county.

Mann, Archie...Assault to murder; committed January, '74; indicted February, same year; about 5 feet 7 inches high, about 45 years old, weight 145 to 150 pounds, light complexion, light hair, blue eyes, round face. Last heard of in Washington county.

Gassiott, Nick R...Theft of a hog; committed January, '74; indicted February, same year; 28 years old, 5 feet 10 inches high, hazel eyes, florid complexion, dark hair, weight 160 pounds.

Slade, Jerry...Theft of a beef; committed August, '74; indicted October, same year. Theft of a hog; committed June, '74; indicted October, same year; negro, about 5 feet 8 inches high, 50 years old, weight about 140 pounds. Last heard of in San Jacinto county.

Trowell, Jim...Assault to murder; committed June, '74; indicted October, same year; negro, nearly white, 5 feet 9 inches high, weight 150 pounds, 24 or 25 years old. Last heard of in Houston county, near Crockett.

Burch, Wash...Theft of a beef; committed January, '74; indicted October, same year; 5 feet 10 or 11 inches high, 25 years old, weight 140 or 150 pounds; negro. Last heard of in Houston county, near Lovelady.

Nelson, John H...Murder; committed November, '74; indicted February, '75; very dark complexion, black hair and eyes, about 26 years old, about 5 feet 11 inches high, weight 165 pounds, heavy set, large limbs, very strong, a kind of downcast expression, will not look a man straight in the face, has a peculiar laugh. Last heard of in Calcasieu parish, La.

Choate, Wm. M...Murder; willfully refusing to arrest a murderer while deputy sheriff; committed February, '75; indicted April, '76; 6 feet 2 inches high, weight 160 pounds, red complexion, 24 years old, light hair, blue eyes, Western cowman, very profane and dissipated. Last heard of in Karnes county, with Bill Taylor's gang.

Bill, Banjo...Murder; indicted, 1865; negro; heavy set.

Burnett, Jesse...Assault to rape. Lately escaped from penitentiary.

Haywood, Jordan...Assault to kill; indicted, 1876; negro; 5 feet 8 inches high, 140 pounds weight, a little hump-shouldered, 25 years old, broad mouth, prominent teeth.

Haywood Adam...Assault to kill; indicted April, 1877; negro; 5 feet 7 inches high, 45 years old, weighs 150 pounds.

McMahon, John...Murder; indicted October, '76; dark complexion, black hair and eyes, 5 feet 11 inches high, 25 years old, weighs 160 lbs.

Pickens, J., alias J. Pickens Burns...Forgery; indicted '76. Light complexion, hair and eyes, 5 feet 11 inches high, 30 years old, spare build.

Snell, Frank...Murder; two cases; indicted April, '77. Sallow complexion, black hair and eyes, 5 feet 11 inches high, 40 years old.

Walters, Napoleon...Theft; indicted October, '76.

Mitchell, Dennis...Negro; burglary; indicted April 19, '77; and theft of gelding; indicted October 18th, '77. About 28 years of age, 6 feet high, slender, small scar on left temple, also scar on left side, slow of speech, has a mean countenance, can't look in a man's face.

Jordan, Nash...Negro; theft of mare; indicted October 18, '77. Black, heavy build, scar on right side of face, about 5 feet 10 or 11 inches high, wears a little beard on side of face.

Cooper, Jenks...Negro; indicted October 18, '77; theft of hog.

Cain, Luke and Dick, and Frank Stuts...Theft of beeves; indicted October 18, '77. Luke Cain is about 5 feet 9 inches high, sandy hair, heavy red beard, very ignorant, some front teeth out, is about 35 years old. This description will apply to Dick, except that he is some taller, and has not as heavy beard and no front teeth out. Frank Stutts is 20 years old, and no beard.

Cherry, John...Negro; about 5 feet 10 inches high, heavy built, talkative, has an air of importance, a bright mulatto. Indicted October 18, '77. Theft of heifer.

PARKER COUNTY.

Staggs, Tobe; and Barringer, J. T...Theft; committed March 4, '73; indicted June 5, '73.

Cheeley, Jasper; Cheeley, Scott; Malber, John; and Washington, Jas... Murder; committed October 1, '73; indicted October, '73.

Pate, James...Theft; committed May 1, '74; indicted June 11, '74.

Prince, Ike...Theft; committed January 16, 74; indicted June 11, '74; negro.

Edmonds, Levi; and Edmonds, Frank...Murder; committed December 28, '72; indicted June 11, '74.

Anderson, James...Murder; committed January 10, '74; indicted Oct. 13, '74.

Hill, Monroe...Murder; committed June 10, '72; indicted June 18, '74.

Campbell, Ed...Theft; committed December 10, '73; indicted June 12, '74.

Taylor, Zach...Assault to murder; committed September 10, '74; indicted October 13, '74.

Moppin, G...Theft; committed September 10, '74; indicted October 13, '74.

Cornelius, Wm...Theft; committed December 10, '74; indicted February 2, '75.

Culwell, James...Theft; committed December 3, '74; indicted February 9, '75.

Meeks, John...Assault to murder; committed December 25, '74; indicted February 9, '75.

Nooner, A...Theft; committed November 10, '73; indicted February 10, '75; committed also for theft Nov. 1, '73; indicted Feb. 10, '73.

Cantrell, Robert...Theft; committed October 11, '74; indicted February 10, '75.

Brown, Thomas; Brown, Joseph; and Callis, Henry...Theft; committed May 6, '74; indicted February 10, '75.

Hooper, Wm...Theft; committed January 10, '75; indicted June 10, '75.

Wyley, Geo...Assault to murder; committed February 1, '75; indicted June 10, '75.

Brazil, Sim...Assault to murder; committed October 10, '74; indicted June 11, '75.

Taylor, C. A...Assault to murder; committed May 10, '75; indicted June 14, '75.

Harbert, Wm...Theft; committed February 10, '75; indicted June 14, '75.

Beck, A.; and Porter, Winfield...Theft; committed November 1, '71; indicted October 7, '75.

Whitsell, Eldridge....Serious threat to take life; committed September 5, '75; indicted October 7, '75.

Prince, Wesley...Theft; committed December 30, '75; indicted April 20, '76.

Brooks, Geo.; and Cantrell, Robert....Theft; committed October 20, '74; indicted April 20, '76.

Whetstone, J...Assault to murder; committed August 25, '76; indicted September 15, '76.

Harris, Joe...Swindling; committed December 20, '75; indicted September 15, '76.

Harris, Joe....Theft; committed December 15, '75; indicted December 15, '76.

Burnes, O. B...Assault to murder; committed July 22, '76; indicted September 15, '76.

Hill, Geo...Assault to murder; committed January 1, '75; indicted September 19, '76.

Phillips, James....Theft; committed November 10, '76; indicted April 8, '77.

Carloch, Thomas; and Fandren, John...Theft; committed March 1, '75; indicted October 12, '75.

Harris, Eli....Burglary; committed April 2, '77; indicted April 24, '70; negro.

Harris, Eli....Theft; committed April 2, '77; indicted April 24, '77; negro.

Harris, Eli....Theft; committed April 2, '77; indicted April 24, '77; negro.

Lofton, Bud; and Smith, Riley...Assault to murder; committed September 24, '76; indicted April 20, '77.

Marsh, M. D...Fraudulently disposing of mortgaged property ; committed December 1, '76; indicted April 24, '77.

Burleson, James...Theft; committed November 24, '76; indicted April 24, '77.

Robertson, Wm....Assault to murder; committed September 15, '77 ; indicted September 18, '77.

Smith, Riley....Theft; committed July 30, '77 ; indicted September 18, 77.

Robertson, Wm....Assault to murder; committed September 15, '77 ; indicted September 18, '77.

Rothschild, Absalom...Assault to murder ; committed July, '77 ; indicted September 18, '77.

Gentry, Chas....Murder ; committed March 19, '74; indicted September 18, '77.

Odum, M. V....Theft; committed December 10, '73; indicted June 12, '74.

Green, Thos....Assault to murder; committed September 2, '77 ; indicted September 19, '77.

ROCKWALL COUNTY.

McReynolds, Geo...Murder of W. A. Beddinfield, May 28, '76; dark hair, 6 feet high, 24 years old, short nose (end turns up with deep crease in center), gray eyes, right fore-finger off above second joint, smooth face, rather dark complexion, bold and daring appearance, weighs about 170 pounds ; $500 reward offered by J. D. Beddingfield.

Howeth, Emily...Infanticide ; indicted October, '76.

Wells, Mary...Infanticide ; indicted October, '76.

Cannon, Embury...Assault to murder; indicted '75 ; bond forfeited, 6 feet high, 52 years old, dark hair somewhat gray, dark eyes, full beard tolerably gray, moustache trimmed, limps, leg has been broken and is bent outward, large rough hands, rather thin visage, talks rather fine and slow, nose slightly Roman, fond of drinking, lively and overbearing when under influence of liquor, has been wounded with a knife in the right side in region of liver; has been also indicted as accessory to murder of A. C. Starks, October 1, 1876.

Cannon, W. C...Assault to murder; indicted '75 ; 5 feet 10 inches high, dark eyes, hair and complexion, 22 years old, large eyes, beard thin and black, generally clean shaved, weighs about 150 pounds, square built, very reserved and has but little to say.

RED RIVER COUNTY.

Guest, Elisha...Murder; committed in '69; indicted same year; 28 years old, fair complexion, blue eyes, about 6 feet high, weight about 170 pounds.

Jones, Hugh...Murder; committed '67; indicted '68; 30 years old, about 5 feet 10 or 11 inches high, weight 140 pounds, florid complexion, light hair, blue eyes, which have a peculiar expression, near-sighted.

Harrist, James A...Murder; committed '69; indicted '70; 40 or 45 years old, light complexion, red hair and beard, thin visage, lame in one leg, weight about 140 pounds.

Bagwell, Wm...Murder; committed '71; indicted same year; light complexion, blue eyes, about 27 years old, 6 feet 1 or 2 inches high, weight 180 of 200 pounds, supposed to be in Western Texas.

Woods, Alex...Murder; committed '73; indicted August, same year; negro, 22 years, heavy set, 5 feet 5 or 6 inches high, weight 160 pounds, supposed to be in the Choctaw Nation.

Jacks, J. H...Murder; committed '75; indicted April, same year; 26 or 27 years old, weight 150 or 160 pounds, 5 feet 10 inches high, black hair, light complexion, blue eyes; in Arkansas.

Chappell, Joseph...Murder; committed '76; indicted May, same year; 20 years old, light complexion, light hair, blue eyes, about 5 feet 10 inches high, weight about 130 pounds, a scar on his face.

Milor, Volney V...Murder; committed '76; indicted May, same year; 5 feet 9 inches high, about 22 or 23 years old, square build, weight 130 pounds, blue eyes, light hair, whiskers light and thin when not shaved.

Covington, James A...Murder; committed '76; indicted May, same year; 28 years old, 5 feet 10 inches high, weight 165 pounds, light complexion.

Fenton, John...Theft from a house; committed '73; indicted February, '74; about 6 feet high, weight 160 or 170 pounds, dark skin, black hair, black eyes, large nose, peaked face, rather good looking.

Caton, Cato...Theft of hog; committed '74; indicted June, same year.

Bates, Frank...Murder; committed '73; indicted February, same year.

Mitchell, Jake...Theft from a house; committed '74; indicted October, same year; negro; about 20 years old, spare build, full face, 5 feet 10 inches high, weight 140 pounds. In Arkansas.

Reed, Harrison...Theft from a house; committed '74; indicted October, same year; negro, small size; about 30 years old, 5 feet 10 or 11 inches high, weight 140 or 150 pounds.

Retherford, Taul...Theft of hog; committed '74; indicted October, same year; negro; 40 or 45 years old, weight 155 or 160 pounds, about 5 feet 9 or 10 inches high, some beard.

Holtzclaw, Gus...Assault to murder; committed '73; indicted October, same year; 6 feet high, weight 190 or 200 pounds, light complexion, blue eyes, dark hair, 28 years old. In Arkansas.

Wilburn, Rachel...Burglary; committed '73; indicted October, '74; negress; 35 or 40 years old, weight 130 or 140 pounds. In Titus county.

Black, Wm...Theft of cattle; committed '74; indicted August, '75.

Chastine, Mat...Theft of cattle; committed '74; indicted August, '75.

Wilson, John...Theft; committed '75; indicted August, same year.

Mahalla, Robert...Murder; committed '75; indicted August, same year; Choctaw Indian; about 6 feet high, light complexion for an Indian, black hair and eyes, weight 160 pounds.

Rice, Robert...Murder; committed '75; indicted December, same year; 5 feet 6 inches high, light hair, blue eyes, fair complexion, spare build, weight 125 or 130 pounds.

Hensley, Lewis W...Assault to murder; indicted May 25, '77; about 28 years old, about 5 feet 6 inches high, weighs about 150 pounds, light hair, long sharp nose, blue eyes, small whiskers on chin, is now in Cook county.

Watts, Julius...Murder; indicted May 25, '77; 21 or 22 years old, 5 feet 9 inches high, slender in form, weighs about 135 pounds, dark hair, brown eyes, no beard, in Choctaw Nation.

Carroll, William...Assault to murder; indicted May 25, '77.

Pitman, George...Embezzlement; indicted May 29, '77.

Caldwell, Otho; and Jones, Ike...Assault to murder; indicted May 20, '77.

Keith, Jack...Theft of horse; indicted June 2, '77.

Buchanan, T. J...Assault to murder; indicted May 25, '77; about 45 years old, 5 feet 8 or 9 inches high, dark complexion, gray hair and whiskers, heavy set, weighs about 150 pounds, supposed to be in Louisiana.

Bryson, Sam...Theft of a horse; indicted May 25, '77.

Chastine, Mack...Theft of a horse; indicted May 25, '77.

Moony & Crawford...Theft of a box of boots; indicted May 25, '77.

Smith, John...Assault to murder; indicted May 25, '77.

McCrary, John.. Theft of a horse; indicted June 2, '77; about 26 years old, about 5 feet 9 inches high, slender in form, red hair, freckled faced, small blue or gray eyes.

Scales, J. H...Rape; indicted November, '76.

Allen, Augt. A...Swindling; indicted February '73; 5 feet 7 inches high, 34 years, old, blue eyes, slender, weighs 140 pounds, quick spoken.

Allen, Chas...Swindling; indicted February, '73.

Loughery, B...Swindling; indicted February, '73.

Fletcher, Howard...Murder; indicted December, '75.

Fletcher, Robert...Murder; indicted December, '75.

Gordon, Wm...Murder; indicted November, '76; 30 years old, 5 feet 8 inches high, black curly hair, short, black and thick whiskers dark, brown eyes, weighs 140 pounds.

RUSK COUNTY.

Murray, Joseph...Assault to murder; committed November 14, '75; indicted December 18, same year; white.

Payne, Ed...Assault to murder; committed September 1, '75; indicted December 18, same year; white.

Dea, Nic...Assault to murder; committed September 18, '75; indicted December 18, same year; white.

Payne, Ed...Murder; committed October 2, '75; indicted December 2, same year.

Williams, David...Assault to murder; committed December 18, '73; indicted December 22, same year.

Gadison, Robert...Theft of a hog; committed December 1, '75; indicted December 22, same year.

Ivry, Winwright...Assault to murder; committed April 3, '76; indicted April 7, same year. Is about 21 years old, fair complexion, light hair, supposed to be in Louisiana.

Redwine, Isham...Forgery; committed September 17, '75; indicted April 13, '76. Thick, heavy-set negro.

McClane, Peyton...Robbery, committed December 1, '75; indicted April 13, '76. Black, thick-lipped negro, heavy-set.

Carroll, George...Assault to murder; committed March 18, '76; indicted April 13, same year.

Williamson, Alexander...Assault to murder; committed March 18, '76; indicted April 13, same year.

Hale, Mansel...Burglary; committed December 24, '75; indicted April 13, 76. Is about 5 feet 10 inches high, 20 years old.

Todd, George...Burglary; committed December 24, '75; indicted April 13, '76.

McGraw, Wm...Burglary; committed December 24, '75; indicted April 13, '76.

Robertson, Thomas...Burglary; committed December 24, '75; indicted April 13, '76. Is about 20 years old.

Van Dyke, Jefferson...Theft of money; committed July 14, '74; indicted July 16, same year; negro.

Shelton, Adaline...Perjury; committed July 14, '74; indicted July 17 same year.

Grey, John...Murder; committed January 5, '74; indicted July 17, same year; negro.

McCord, Oliver...Incest; committed May 1, '74; indicted July 17, same year; negro.

McCord, Sarah...Incest; committed May 1, '74; indicted July 17, same year; negress.

Runnells, Richard...Theft of a beef steer; committed August 15, '74; indicted November 7, same year; negro.

Brown, Eugene...Assault to murder; committed October 24, '74; indicted November 7, same year.

Talbert, John, alias Talleferro, John...Murder; committed September 16, '74; indicted January 12, same year; negro.

Presnel, Jim...Sodomy; committed September 8, '74; indicted November 17; same year; white.

Johnson, John...Assault to murder; committed December 25, '74; indicted April 15, same year; white.

Pope, James...Obtaining money under false pretences; committed February 8, '75; indicted April 15, same year. Is 23 years old, 5 feet 10 inches high, weighs about 135 pounds, rather dark hair, light complexion, blue eyes, short turn-up nose, talks loquaciously and quick, his people live in Coryell county.

Hogan, Frank...Assault to murder; committed July 1, '75; indicted August 11, same year.

Ash, Thos...Theft of a beef steer; committed September 30, '74; indicted August 13, same year.

Rhodes, George...Murder; committed June 3, '75; indicted August 16, same year. About Denison.

Buckhannan, Albert...Murder; committed April 15, '75; indicted August 16, same year.

Bradley, Dock...Theft of a mare; committed April 20, '75; indicted August 16, same year.

Hopkins, W. O...Theft of a mare; committed December 30, '73; indicted August 16, same year.

Hardie, Dock...Assault to murder; committed October 1, '76; indicted December 11, same year.

Hardie, Wiley...Assault to murder; committed October 1, '75; indicted December 11, same year.

Stokes, Wm...Assault to murder; committed October 30, '72; indicted December 12, same year.

McGlaughlin, John...Assault to murder; committed October 30, '72; indicted December 12, same year.

Jones, John...Theft; committed March 8, '73; indicted May 23, same year.

Farmer, H. H...Threat to take life; committed May 20, '73; indicted May 28, same year.

Flynn, Thos.; and Flynn, Jas...Murder; committed October 5, '72; indicted November 27, same year.

Moss, Henry...Swindling; committed December 25 '72; indicted September 10, same year.

Anderson, Wm...Assault to murder; committed September 13, '73; indicted September 18, same year.

Tipps, Blake...Theft of a hog; committed December 28, '73; iudicted January 9, '74.

Brewer, Caleb; and Blackburn, Col...Assault to murder; committed December 20, '73; indicted January 15, '74.

Jackson, Andrew...Theft of a mare; committed September 11, '73; indicted January 15, '73; negro.

Gallaway, A. L...Swindling; committed November 1, '73; indicted January 19, '74.

Mayfield, Frank...Assault to murder; committed December 24, '73; indicted January 19, '74.

Jamerson, Frank...Theft; committed March 1, '73; indicted January 19, '74.

Lindsay, Joel...Assault to murder; committed April 30, '74; indicted July 10, same year.

Grimes, M. H...Threat to take life; committed December 7, '73; indicted July 15, '74.

Gallaway, Alford...Theft of a hog; committed November 1, '73; indicted July 15, '74.

Stone, Enoch...Assault to murder; committed October 1, '68; indicted October 28, same year.

Johnson, Geo...Assault to murder; committed June 1, '68; indicted October 28, same year.

Isaacs, Thos...Assault to murder; committed March 1, '68; indicted October 28, same year.

Harris, Wm...Theft; committed July 1, '68; indicted April 16, '69.

Little, Wm...Assault to murder; committed December 5, '68; indicted April 17, '69.

Roberts, Jesse...Assault to murder; committed January 1, '69; indicted April 17, same year.

Girtman, Norman...Assault to murder; committed July 1, '68; indicted April 17, '69.

Sanders, Zachary...Murder; committed August 1, '65; indicted April 20, '69.

Johnson, Bill...Theft of a gelding; committed November 1, '68; indicted April 23, '69.

Milton, Geo. W...Theft of a gelding; committed October 1, '68; indicted April 23, '69.

Fuller, Houston...Assault to murder; committed February 1, '69; indicted April 23, same year.

Calhoun, Patrick W. H...Theft of a mare; committed February 1, '69; indicted April 23, same year.

Butler, Thos. M...Assault to murder; committed June 11, '69; indicted October 16, same year.

Moore, Jas. A...Assault to murder; committed August 15, '69; indicted October 16, same year.

Stanford, Adolphus...Assault to murder; committed September 10, '69; indicted October 20, same year.

Higgs, Jere., Jr...Murder; committed February 20, '70; indicted December 9, same year.

Taylor, Henry...Assault to murder; committed April 1, '70; indicted December 9, same year. Negro.

Mimms, Chas...Assault to murder; committed March 1, '70; indicted December 9, same year.

Thurmond, Jos...Assault to murder; committed June 5, '70; indicted December 9, same year. Negro.

Smith, Thos...Assault to murder; committed January 10, '70; indicted December 10, same year.

Adams, Wm...Assault to murder; indicted December 10, '70.

Thomas, Wm...Assault to murder; committed August 10, '70; indicted December 10, same year.

Murphy, John...Assault to murder; committed October 20, '70; indicted December 13, same year.

Fisher, Richard....Assault to murder; committed October 25, '70; indicted December 13, same year.

Greenwood, J. T...Assault to murder; committed October 27, '71; indicted December 20, same year. Blue eyes, weight 150 pounds.

Carr, Allen...Murder; committed August 1, '71; indicted December 20, same year. Sallow complexion, round face, grey eyes.

Roberts, Jesse...Assault to murder; committed November 30, '71; indicted January 4, '72. Small, 26 years old, fair complexion.

Baldre, James....Assault to murder: committed November 1, '71; indicted January 4, '72.

Stewball, Jas...Assault to murder; committed November 1, '71; indicted January 4, '72.

Pilcher, John D...Assault to murder; committed November 1, '71; indicted January 4, '72.

Ham, Wm...Assault to murder; committed November 1, '71; indicted January 4, '72.

Roquemore, Aaron...Perjury; committed January 4, '72; indicted June 2, '73. Yellow negro, 40 years old.

Johnson, Frank...Theft; committed August 1, '71; indicted January 6, '72. Negro.

Nelson, John W., Sr...Murder; committed December 25, '71; indicted January 6, '72. Dark complexion, 60 years old.

Dempsey, Thos., alias J. E. Dempsey...Assault to kill and murder; committed February 10, '72; indicted April 10, same year. Heavy set.

Adams, Jos....Assault to kill and murder; committed January 29, '72; indicted April 10, same year.

Ewing, April....Assault to kill and murder; committed March 15, '72; iudicted April 10, same year. Negro.

Smith, Geo...Assault to kill and murder; committed April 11, '72; indicted April 13, same year.

Greenwood, Pinckney H....Assault to kill and murder; committed April 11, '72; indicted April 13, same year.

Thompson, J. S....Theft; committed November 1, '72; indicted August 14, same year.

Turner, Wm...Theft; committed November 1, '72; indicted August 14, same year.

Hampton, Wm...Assault to murder; committed May 25, '72; indicted August 14, same year.

Roland, Willis...Assault to murder; committed August 3, '72; indicted August 19, same year.

McDonald, Frank...Assault to murder; committed August 3, '72; indicted August 19, same year.

Merchant, Jas...Assault to murder; committed July 15, '72 ; indicted August 19, same year.

May, Chas...Murder; committed June 9, '72; indicted August 27, same year.

Goodwin, O. W...Hog stealing; committed October 17, '72; indicted December 7, same year.

Clifford, Wm...Hog stealing; committed October 17, '72; indicted December 7, same year.

Butler, Thos...Assault to murder; committed June 11, '70; indicted April 24, '71.

Brown, Geo...Murder; committed June 24, '71; indicted August 18, same year.

Walton, Austin...Assault to murder; committed August 8, '71; indicted August 18, same year.

Deason, John...Assault to murder; committed July 20, '71; indicted August 18, same year.

Greenwood, P. H...Assault to murder; committed June 23, '71; indicted August 18, same year.

Hamilton, Rufus...Assault to murder; committed May 27, '71; indicted August 18, same year.

Hamilton, Jefferson...Assault to murder; committed May 27, '71; indicted August 18, same year.

Neal, Sarah....Murder; committed June 1, '71; indicted August 17, same year. Negro.

Gentry, Abby...Murder; committed April 10, '71; indicted August 17; same year.

Salmon, Henry....Incest; committed January 1, '71; indicted August 17, same year.

Salmon, Mary...Incest; committed January 1, '71; indicted August 17, same year.

Little, Wm...Assault to murder; committed December 5, '68; indicted August 18, '71.

Bagley, Warner...Assault to murder; committed January 15, '71; indicted August 22, same year.

McDonald, Thos....Assault to murder; committed December 1, '70; indicted August 23, '71.

Walker, Wm...Burglary; committed July 20, '71 ; indicted August 25, same year. Negro.

Mayfield, Dudley...Sodomy; committed June 15, '71; indicted August 30, same year.

Rogers, Dock...Assault to murder; committed January 1, '70; indicted August 30, '71.

Hurn, Stephen...Assault to murder; committed December 25, '70; indicted August 30, '71.

Mays, Martin...Assault with intent to ravish; committed August 1, '71; indicted August 30, same year.

Harlan, Dwight...Assault with intent to murder; committed February 1, '65; indicted February 18, same year.

Whaley, Chas. E...Robbery; committed January 30, '66; indicted February 17, same year.

Whaley, Thos...Robbery; committed January 30, '66; indicted February 17, same year.

Tutt, Ed....Assault to murder; committed December 20, '66; indicted April 20, '67. Has only one leg, rather tall, black hair.

Carter, Ben...Theft of two mares; committed February 1, '66; indicted April 20, '67.

Tatum, H. W...Murder; committed November 10, '65; indicted April 27, '67.

Chisum, Talbert F...Murder; committed January 25, '66; indicted April 24, '67. Is a small man, black eyes, black hair, heavy moustache, quick nervous temperament, weighs about 125 pounds, between 35 and 40 years old, loves to play the fiddle, favorite tune, " Black Jack Grove," with vocal accompaniment, 5 feet 8 or 10 inches high, last heard from in some of the extreme northwestern counties, has an uncle by his name, who is a large stock-owner in some of said counties, rumored recently that he was seen in McLennan county.

Dickson, Aaron....Theft; committed December 1, '66; indicted April 24, '67.

Taylor, Robert...Assault with intent to murder; committed September 1, '66; indicted April 24, '67.

Russell, T. J...Murder; committed April 10, '63; indicted April 27, '67.

Moore, Chas...Murder; committed December 24, '66; indicted April 27, '67.

Lynch, Joe...Assault with intent to murder; committed December 10, '65; indicted April 27, '67.

Berry, James, Jr...Assault with intent to murder; committed September 10, '66; indicted April 27, '67.

West, John...Assault with intent to murder; committed December 10, '65; indicted April 27, '67.

Laud, Wm...Murder; committed April 1, '67; indicted April 27, same year.

Mackey, Wm...Murder; committed April 1, '67; indicted same month.

Hardie, Ann...Negress; perjury; committed January 8, '67; indicted April 27, same year. |

Wyche, Drew...Assault with intent to murder; committed June, 1, '67; indicted April 24, '68.

Smith, Peter (freedman)...Theft of a mare; committed April 2, '68; indicted the same month.

Hudson, Martin...Theft committed April 2, 68; indicted April 24, same year.

Crawley, Zadocks...Theft of two mules; committed January 1, '68; indicted April 25, same year.

Fortune, J. W...Assault with intent to murder; committed January 20, '68; indicted April 25, same year.

Child, Lewis...Theft of a beef steer; committed April 1, '68; indicted April 25, same year.

Coleman, C. E...Theft of a gelding; committed November 1, '67; indicted October 17, '68.

Shaden, A. A...Murder; committed September 16, '68; indicted October 17, same year.

Shadden, Wm...Murder; committed September 16, '68; indicted October 17, same year.

Shadden, Joseph...Murder; committed September 16, '68; indicted October 17, same year.

Shadden, Hans...Murder; committed September 16, '68; indicted October 17, same year.

Colly, Henry...Murder; committed September 16, '68; indicted October 17, same year.

Nevils, Paul...Murder; committed September 16, '68; indicted October 17, same year.

Shankles, James...Murder; committed September 16, '68; indicted October 17,.same year.

Coats, Wm...Assault to murder; committed August 1, 70; indicted December 15, same year.

Reed, Jos...Assault to murder; committed December 10, '69; indicted December 25, same year.

O'Conner, John...Assault to murder; committed November 20, '70; indicted December 15, same year.

Robinson, Frank...Assault to murder; committed November 20, '70; indicted December 15, same year.

Welch, Chas....Theft; committed February 1, '70; indicted December 15, same year.

Canterberry, Henry...Theft; committed February 1, '70; indicted December 15, same year.

Daniels, Benj...Murder; commftted December 18, '69; indicted December 15, '70; negro.

Hutchings, Joseph...Murder; committed December 10, '69; indicted December 15, '70.

Turner, Levi...Murder; committed February 5, '70; indicted December 15, same year.

Adams, John...Assault to murder; committed June 12, '70; indicted December 15, same year.

Earle, Noah....Extortion; committed August 1, '70; indicted December 15, same year.

Brown, Eli...Assault to murder; committed September 20, '70; indicted December 15, same year.

Earle, Isaiah...Assault to murder; committed August 10, '70; indicted December 15, same year.

Jackson, Reuben...Theft of a gelding, committed July 10, '69; indicted December 16, '70; negro.

Hester, Jos...Assault to murder; committed July 12, '70; indicted December 16, same year.

Jeffreys, Terrell...Assault to murder; committed April 15, '70; indicted December 16, same year; negro.

Robinson, Frank G...Assault to murder; committed June 10, '70; indicted December 16, same year.

Tyler, Willis...Assault to murder; committed February 27, '70; indicted December 16, same year.

Prewitt, W, J....Theft of a hog; committed March 1, '70; indicted April 19, '71.

Bromley, James...Attempt to rape; committed July, '66; indicted April 24, '67; white; heavy set, light complexion and hair, 30 years old, weighs 165 pounds.

Cordray, David...Accomplice of Jas. Bromley; dark complexion, hair and eyes, heavy set, weighs 150 pounds.

Prewitt, W. J...Perjury; committed April, '71; indicted April, same year; 40 years old, weighs 140 pounds, red complexion and hair.

Taylor, George...Assault to kill; committed May, '76; indicted September, same year; weighs 200 pounds, fine looking man, fair complexion, 5 feet 10 inches high, corpulent.

Mapps, David...Assault to kill; committed August, '76; indicted September, same year; black negro; heavy set.

Johnson, Ranse...Assault to kill; committed August, '76; indicted September, same year; negro; round face, weighs 150 pounds.

Rutherford, Frank...Assault to kill; committed June, '76; indicted September, same year; negro; supposed to be in Harrison county.

Grover, Matt...Murder; committed September, '76; indicted September, same year; weighs 120 pounds, red face, 5 feet 7 inches high, 21 years old.

Lowrie, Robt...Assault to kill; committed January, 77; indicted January, same year.

Hines, Dock...Theft of hog; committed October, '76; indicted January, '77; negro; 5 feet 8 inches high, weighs 150 pounds.

Smith, J. T...Perjury; committed September, '76, indicted January, '77; 25 years old, weighs 150 pounds, fair complexion.

Brown, R. E...Threat to take life; committed December, '76; indicted January, '77; 5 feet 10 inches high, weighs 150 pounds, dark skin, hair and eyes, 40 years old.

Brown, Bartlett...Robbery; committed November, '76; indicted January, '77.

King, Burton...Assault to kill; committed July, '77; indicted July, same year; negro.

Smith, Calvin...Theft; committed June, '77; indicted July, same year.

Gray, Wm., and Ellen...Incest; committed January, '77; indicted July, same year.

Simmons, Wash...Theft of hog; comitted January, '77; indicted January, same year.

ROBERTSON COUNTY.

Davis, A. R...Murder.
Barker, N. W...Murder.
Harris, Jack...Assault to murder.
Hanna, Fred...Theft from a house.
Nelson, Richard...Theft of horse.
Ferguson, Aaron...Theft of horse.
Davis, London...Theft from a house.
Hord, James R....Theft of horse.
McDonald, John K...Assault to murder.
Roberts, Bill...Theft.
Arnett, John...Theft.
Brashear, Seaborn...Murder.
Fuller, Wm....Murder.
Hendley, James...Murder.
Davis, Theodore...Murder.
Thompson, Alex...Theft (two cases).
McDonald, Bailey...Assault to murder.
Cochran, E...Murder.
Moody, G. W...Assault to murder.
Elliott, Thomas...Manslaughter.
Counsel, Ike...Burglary.
Jordan, John....Aggravated assault and battery.
Cook, James B....Assault to murder.
9

Ludlow, Sidney...Rape.
Robertson, Henry...Murder.
Gallagher, John...Theft from a house.
Wilson, James...Assault to murder.
Smith, Taylor...Assault to murder.
Campbell James...Theft of horse.
Matthews, L. L...Theft of horse.
Wilson, W. H...Assault to murder.
Freedman, Wm...Swindling.
Day, M. J...Assault to murder.
Dirr, Robert...Theft of a horse; 2 cases.
Allen, Smith...Theft of a horse; 2 cases.
Ables, J. M...Theft of goods.
Pugh, Charles...Murder.
Smith, Wm...Murder.
Walker, Joel...Murder.
Richardson, S. C...Assault to murder.
Williams, Lum...Theft of a horse.
Putnam...Assault to murder.
Bramlett, Augustus...Assault to murder.
Knapp, Wm...Theft of a cow.
Middleton, James...Unlawfully using an estray.
McCulloch, Horace...Assault to murder.
Harris, James (two cases); Bridges, Jas.; Stallcup, E. B.; Milton Brothers...Theft of cattle.
Calhoun, Dennis...Disturbing worship.
Happe, E. H...Assault to murder.
Waddell, Wm...Assault to rob.
Lindsay...Theft of gelding.
Rains...Theft of mule.
Willis...Assault to murder.
Porter, Ben...Theft of gelding.
Grissom, Rome...Removing hide from an ox not his own.
Taylor, David M...Theft of a hog.
Dial, Steve...Murder.
Bouy, Geo...Assault to murder.
Smith, Alf.; Hardy, Horace...Theft of a gelding.
Jenkins, Jas...Theft.
White, Robert...Murder.
Walker, Albert...Theft of gelding.
Perry, Richard...Theft of cotton.
Wilson, Moses...Murder.
Gamble, John...Theft from a house.
Wilkerson, Allen...Theft of steer.
Merriman, Jas...Assault to murder.
Morrell, Zack; Bennett, Henry...Affray.
Childers, T. M...Forgery.
Black, John...Theft from a house; theft of a mule; 2 cases.
Bonner, Bob...Assault to murder.
Johnson, Sam....Assault to murder.
Block, Bill...Theft of an estray mare.
Wilson, Alex...Theft of chattels.
Newton, Aaron...Theft of cattle.
Maddox, Joe...Rape.

Metts, Marion...Theft of a gelding and saddle.
Dailey, K...Theft of hog.
Cavenaugh, Jas...Assault and battery.
Wilson, John...Unlawful trespass of stock; unlawfully pulling down fence; permitting stock to go into field.
Wilburn, Borney, alias Boney Welbourne...Murder.
Thomas, Geo...Theft of hog.
Townsend, Louis...Theft of hogs.
Townsend, Logan...Theft of cattle.
Harrell, Alexander...Theft of money.
Hardin, Geo...Theft of money.
Cobb, Rola...Murder.
Chisem, Lewis...Carrying a pistol.
Pierce, Ben...Theft of plow and chian.
Bucklau, W. B...Embezzlement.
Avant, Wm...Murder.
Turner, Frank...Theft of bridle and saddle.
Hill, C. L...Forgery.
Howell, T. J...Theft of cow.
Davin, John, alias John Darton...Theft of mare.
Robinson, Ike...Assault to murder.
Johnson, Elijah...Theft from a house.
Hearne, Tim. R...Theft of cotton.
Morris, Charles...Theft of hog.
Salter, Reuben...Murder.
Steele, L. V...Theft of cotton.
Reed, Albert...Theft of gelding.
Beall, John...Theft of cotton; theft of a bag of cotton.
Shoats, Chris...Arson.
Estis, Eugene...Murder.
Cox, J. P., Russum, John...Theft of an estray steer.
Lewis, Philip...Theft from a house.
Holt, Samuel...Murder.
Overstreet, Frank...Murder.
Young, John...Theft of work steers.
Preston, George...Assault to murder.
Reynolds, Samuel...Theft of hog.
Davis, Henry...Assault to murder.
Gardner, Stephen...Passing counterfeit money, coin.
Deer, Ed...Theft of hog.
Herring, Frank...Assault to rape.
Johnson, Leonard...Murder of his wife; indicted May, '77;
Davis, John...Murder; indicted June, '77.
Erwin, W. H...Murder; indicted January 3, '77.
Johnson, Fed...Murder; indicted May, '76.
Ford, Al...Theft of cow; indicted May, 77.

SAN JACINTO COUNTY.

Norman, Bill...Theft from house; indicted November, '71. Negro; about 28 years old, 5 feet 6 inches high, weighs about 140 pounds, big mouth, thick lips, flat nose.
Hines, Charles....Theft from house; indicted March, '75. Negro; 30

years old, 5 feet 5 inches high, dark copper-color, prominent eyes, round shoulders, weighs 140 pounds, rather fancy.

Hoot, Manuel...Theft from house (2 cases); indicted March, '75. Negro boy; about 14 years old.

McCall E. H...Forgery (2 cases); indicted July, '72. 5 feet 6 inches high, 30 years old, black eyes and hair. In Louisiana.

Williamson, Abe...Theft of hog; indicted November, '76. Negro; 55 years old, 6 feet high, weighs 150 pounds, wool gray.

Horn, H. M...Theft of mules and wagon; indicted November, '73. One leg shorter than the other, about 28 or 30 years old, low, weighs 120 or 130 pounds. Land trader and speculator.

Stewart, Jacob...Theft of beef; indicted March, '74. Negro ; 60 years old, gray wool, slight build.

Anderson, Wm...Theft from house; indicted July, '75. Light hair, blue eyes, weighs 125 pounds, 20 years old, 5 feet 8 inches high.

Mitchel, Rube...Theft of hog; indicted July, '75. Negro; big mouth, flat nose, 21 years old, weighs 135 pounds, 5 feet 8 inches high.

Luvis, E. M...Theft of a bale of cotton; indicted March, '76. 5 feet 7 inches high, slight build, blue eyes, dark hair, one eye cocked, preacher by profession, lawyer, poker-player, a horse-racer, cock-fighter, etc.

Davinson, Ned...Rape. Negro ; 22 years old, 6 feet high, weighs 160 pounds,

Lowe, Bob...Indicted October 10, '77 (two charges); aiding in escape of prisoners from jail, and an assault with intent to murder the Sheriff of San Jacinto county; black negro, 20 years of age, 5 feet 6 inches high, droop shoulders and pleasant face, smiles when he speaks.

McGowan, Bob Ambrose...Charged with same offense as Bob Lowe in same bill of indictment; very black, 21 years old, broad mouth and thick lips, weighs about 175 pounds, has a peculiar whine or drawl when speaking.

Pope, Alfred...Theft; indicted October 12, '77.

Pope, John...Theft; indicted October 12, '77.

Sprutt, Austin...Theft of cotton, and theft of beef; indicted October 12, '77; 6 feet two inches high, very stout, light hair, gray eyes, usually has beard all over his face, sandy red complexion, has a peculiar voice, a prominent mole on his left cheek, claims to have the asthma, 28 or 30, years old.

Sprutt, J. D...Theft of cotton and theft of hides ; indicted October 12, '77, and April, '77; brother to Austin Sprutt, 5 feet 10 or 11 inches high, droop shoulders, stout made, light hair, heavy eyebrows, wears beard all over his face, beard a shade darker than his hair, about 35 years old, slightly peculiar voice.

Hamilton, John...Burglary; indicted April, '77; about 26 or 30 years old, 5 feet 9 inches high, copper color, has but little to say, rarely speaks without being spoken to.

SHELBY COUNTY.

Oliver, J...Assault to murder ; committed '65.

Holt, H. L...Murder; is about 30 years old, supposed to be in Bosque county.

Oliver, Malichia...Theft; committed in '66; supposed to be in Hill or Milam counties, a very old man.

Loud, James...Bigamy; committed in '68.

Adams, Calhoun...Theft; committed in '68; is a freedman, supposed to be in Louisiana.

Hall, Samps...Theft; committed in '68; freedman, is in Louisiana.

Connon, H. P...Theft; committed in '69; is in Louisiana.

Woolam, James...Theft; committed in '69.

Thurman, Flem...Assault to murder; committed in '69.

Fuller, Wm...Assault to murder; committed in '69.

Tines, James...Assault with intent to kill; committed in '69.

Tucker, Tillman; indicted '70; freedman in Louisiana.

Hudgins, Wm...Assault to kill; indicted in '70; supposed to be dead.

McAdams, Jack...Murder; indicted in '70; is a freedman; in Louisiana.

Payne, W. H...Murder; indicted in '70; supposed to be dead: Payne is also indicted for assault with intent to murder.

Parmer, David...Theft; indicted '70; is tall, broad shouldered, raw boned, about 40 years old.

Smith, W. B...Assault to kill; indicted in '70.

Thurman, Flem...Perjury; indicted '70; is over medium size, about 30 years old.

Rankin, Flax...Assault to murder; indicted '70.

Dill, Wm...Theft; indicted '70; is low, square shouldered, heavy set, dark complexion, 25 or 30 years, supposed to be in Arkansas; there is another indictment against the same party.

Swindoll, Alex...Theft; indicted '70; is a long, slim, black freedman, supposed to be in Louisiana; there is another indictment for theft against him.

Tatum, Alex...Theft; indicted '71; freedman, is in Louisiana.

Goodwyn, Solomon...Assault to kill; indicted '71; is low of stature, about 21 years old, supposed to be in Louisiana.

Mayers, Eph...Murder; indicted '71.

Greer, Jacob...Buggery; indicted '71; freedman, in Louisiana; Greer was also indicted for murder in '71.

Parker, John...Assault to kill; indicted '71; is a boy; he was also indicted for rape in '71.

Cravey, Newton...Assault to kill; is about 6 feet high, red complexion, about 24 years old.

Eakin, John...Scraggling a mule; indicted '71; is low and heavy set, about 30 years old.

Wheeler, Cicero...Murder; indicted '71; is about 6 feet high, dark complexion, dark eyes, about 23 years old; is in Indian Territory.

Johnson, Thos...Theft; indicted '72; dead.

Crutchfield, John...Theft; indicted '72; supposed to be in Nacogdoches county.

Cole, Wm...Theft; indicted '72; is about 25 years old.

Cozim, H. C...Swindling; supposed to be hung.

Thomason, D. B...Theft of a hog; indicted '72.

Alford, John D...Theft; indicted '72.

Goodwyn, Joel...Is a jail bird; broke out and went to Louisiana.

Biggs, Lewis...Theft; indicted '73; is a freedman, very black, big lips.

Graham, Sam...Assault to murder; broke jail, supposed to be in Louisiana, copper complexion, about 35 years old, above the medium size; was indicted in '73.

Greer, Ned...Theft; indicted '73; supposed to be in Jefferson, Texas, or in Louisiana, freedman.

Words, Ed...Burglary; indicted '74.

Pormir, Bud...Assault to murder; indicted '74; is about medium size.

McClelland, Isaac...Theft; indicted '75; freedman.

Brooks, Smith...Theft; indicted '74; freedman.

Harper, Mid...Theft; indicted '74; freedman.

Hordu, Wm...Theft; indicted '74.

Blunt, Ben...Theft; indicted '74; freedman.

Holman, Jack...Attempt to rape; indicted '74; is a large mulatto, about 21 years old, residence unknown.

Truett, Jacob...Bigamy; indicted '74; freedman.

Sanford, John...Threats to kill; indicted '75; is about 35 years old, residence unknown.

Halbert, Joe...Rape; indicted '74.

Johnson, Lit...Murder; indicted '75; is about 30 years old; medium size, supposed to be in Mississippi.

Samples, John...Murder; indicted in '77. He is of rather swarthy complexion, about 5½ feet high, 20 or 25 years old.

Bussy, Dick...Theft; indicted in '77. Negro; supposed to be in Van Zandt, Smith, Harrison, or Gregg county.

Bates, Ned...Theft and burglary; indicted in '76. Negro; of low stature and tolerably small, very black. Supposed to be in Nacogdoches or San Augustine county.

Cock, Charles R.; Spradly, J. Monroe...Murder; indicted in '75. They are each what is usually termed gentlemen of elegant leisure, both raised in Panola county, they are each about 30 years old, of medium size, tolerably good looking, hawk noses, 5 or 5½ feet high.

SAN SABA COUNTY.

Baird, John...Theft of cattle (2 cases); indicted August, '75.

Barrett, A. W.; Nichols, Wm...Theft cattle (4 cases); indicted December, '74.

Connor, Frank; Connor, Wm., Jr...Murder; indicted August, '75.

Henson, Thomas...Theft of cattle; indicted April, '75.

Knight, R. S...Theft of cattle; indicted December, '74.

Jones, Calvin...Theft of cattle; indicted October, '75.

McMullins, John, alias Dillard, John...Theft of cattle; indicted April, '75

Middleton, J. W...Selling cattle without power of attorney; indicted August, '75.

Neighbors, Wm...Assault with intent to murder; indicted April, '75.

Patterson, Bill; Richets, —— ...Theft of cattle; indicted April, '75.

Redding, W. Z...Theft of cattle; indicted May, '74.

Shaw, John...Theft of cattle; indicted August, '74.

Spencer, George...Theft of cattle; indicted April, '72.

Smith, James W...Assault with intent to murder; indicted August, '75.

Neal, Chas...Theft of cattle; indicted October, '75.

Williams, Samuel...Theft of cattle; indicted April, '74.

Stanfield, W. B...Theft of cattle; indicted September, '76.

Nichols, Knox...Theft of cattle (6 cases); indicted September, '76.

Jones, John...Theft of cattle (6 cases); indicted September, '76.

Vandyke, Wilson...Theft of a gelding; indicted September, '76. Is an escaped convict to the penitentiary from Coryell county, Texas.

Barnett, H. S...Theft of cattle ; indicted September, '76.
Lee, John...Embezzlement ; indicted September, '76.

SMITH COUNTY.

Birge, Bird...Assault to murder; committed '67; indicted January, same year. Blue eyes, 45 or 50 years old, has been shot in the breast.

Middleton, A. A. J ..Murder; committed '67; indicted June, same year.

Weatherby, Richard...Murder; committed '67; indicted December, same year.

Warren, Thos. F....Murder; committed '68; indicted May, same year.

Allen, Hardin...Theft; committed '68; indicted December, same year.

Walker, Jackson...Theft; committed '68; indicted December, same year.

Hill, Martin...Murder; committed '68; indicted December, same year.

Hudgins, Zachariah...Assault to murder; committed '68; indicted December, same year.

Gilliam, Jas...Murder; committed '69; indicted May, same year,

Gilbert, Marsh...Theft; committed '70; indicted December, same year. Negro.

Lucas, Gilbert...Theft; committed '70; indicted December, same year. Negro.

Dennis, Ephraim...Rape; committed '70; indicted December, same year. Negro.

Medlin, Wm...Murder; committed '71; indicted March, same year.

Davis, John...Theft; committed '71; indicted April, same year. Negro.

Weeks, Tip...Murder; committed '71; indicted August, same year. Dark skin, gray eyes, about six feet high, slim build, inclined to be round-shouldered.

Simpson, N. K...Murder; committed '71; indicted August, same year.

Black, Joseph...Murder; committed '71; indicted August, same year.

Jarmon, Joseph...Murder; committed '71; indicted August, same year.

Thompson, Molly...Theft; committed '71; indicted August, same year. Negress.

Landers, Wm...Assault to murder; committed '71; indicted August, same year. White.

Harper, Wm...Assault to murder; committed '71; indicted August, same year. White.

Parker, John...Murder; committed '71; indicted August, same year. White.

Kelly, John...Murder; committed '71; indicted August, same year. Dark skin, black eyes, about 30 years old, slim build, downcast look.

Scales, J. H...Obtaining money falsely; committed '71; indicted August, same year; white.

Bruton, J. C...Murder; committed '71; indicted December, same year.

King, A. W...Theft; committed '71; indicted December, same year; white.

Reaves, John...Assault to murder; committed '71; indicted December, same year; white.

Walker, J. P...Theft; committed '71; indicted March, '72.

Check, Thos...Assault to murder; committed '72; indicted December, same year; negro.

Johnson, Randal...Murder; committed '72; indicted April, same year; negro, short and stout.

Evans, Douglass...Murder; committed '72; indicted April, same year; negro.

Sharpe, George...Murder; committed '72; indicted April, same year. Resisting officer; committed '74; indicted May, same year; negro.

Johnson, Paul...Murder; committed '72; indicted April, same year; negro.

More, Ed.....Murder; committed '72; indicted April, same year; negro.

Evans, Crawford...Murder; committed '72; indicted April, same year; negro.

Scott, Archie...Murder; committed '72; indicted July, same year; negro.

Edwards, Sue...Murder; committed '72; indicted July, same year; negress.

Jones, Thomas...Theft; committed '72; indicted July, same year.

Gardner, Sol...Theft; committed '72; indicted July, same year.

Hill, Randill...Theft; committed '72; indicted November, same year; negro, not very dark. Supposed to be in McLennan county, at a plantation on the Brazos.

Baxter, James...Theft; committed '72; indicted November, same year.

Moss, Richard...Assault to murder; committed '72; indicted December, same year.

Wayland, Timothy...Robbery; committed '72; indicted December, same year.

Martin, E...Theft; committed '72; indicted March, '73.

Daniels, Bob...Theft; committed '73; indicted March, same year; negro.

Standford, Peter...Murder; committed '73; indicted March, same year.

Moran, Pat...Theft; committed '73; indicted March, same year; Irishman.

Clark, R. S., and C. J...Assault to murder; committed '73; indicted March, same year; white.

Kay, John...Arson; committed '73; indicted March, same year; negro.

Thomas, Alfred...Theft; committed '73; indicted March same year.

Allan, Obediah...Theft; committed '73; indicted April, same year.

Johnson, Polk...Theft; committed '73; indicted April, same year.

Johnson, Charles...Theft; committed '73; indicted July, same year; Norwegian.

King, Robert....Assault to murder; committed '73; indicted July, same year.

Carter, James...Assault to murder; committed '73; indicted July, same year.

Hughes, Wm...Murder; committed '73; indicted July, same year.

Benton, James....Theft; committed '73; indicted July, same year.

Robertson, J. T. M....Theft; committed '73; indicted July, same year.

Oliver, Charles.....Theft; committe l '73; indicted August, same year.

Simpkins, Ben...Theft; committed '73; indicted August, same year; negro.

Richardson, John...Murder; committed '73; indicted August, same year.

Johnson, Gabriel...Theft; committed '73; indicted November, same year; negro.

Owens, Oscar....Theft; committed '73; indicted December, same year; negro.

Weaver, Henry...Murder; committed '73; indicted August, same year.

Jones, Pink...Assault to murder; committed '73; indicted August, same year.

Simms, Thos...Assault to murder; committed '73; indicted August, same year.

Taylor, W. L.... Theft; committed '73; indicted November, same year.

Helton, Geo., and Harry....Theft; committed '73; indicted November same year.

Loftin, Aaron...Assault to murder; committed '73; indicted November, same year; negro. In Harrison county.

Mills, James...Murder; committed '73; indicted December, same year; white.

Hambrick, John...Murder; committed '73; indicted December, same year; white.

Miles, J. M...Murder; committed '73; indicted December, same year; white.

Lewis, Jas. L...Theft; committed '74; indicted May, same year; white.

Wallace, Aaron...Theft; committed '74; indicted May, same year; white.

Melvin, Hardy...Bigamy; committed '74; indicted May, same year.

Clark, J. T...Assault to murder; committed '74; indicted September, same year.

Fenton, Long John...Theft; committed '74; indicted September, same year.

Green, Frank...Theft; committed '74; indicted September, same year.

Jiles, Jas...Assault to murder; committed '74; indicted September, same year.

Johns, Richard...Theft; committed '74; indicted September, same year.

Milburn, Moore...Assault to murder; committed '74; indicted September, same year.

Liddell, Dan...Assault to murder; committed '74; indicted September, same year. In Alabama.

Tate, Jas...Theft; committed '74; indicted September, same year.

Whitman, E. G...Theft; committed '74; indicted September, same year.

Faught, A. H...Theft; committed '74; indicted September, same year.

White, James...Theft; committed '74; indicted September, same year.

Taylor, Frank...Theft; committed '74; indicted September, same year.

Dobbins, H. M...Swindling; committed '74; indicted September, same year.

Millege, Anderson...Sodomy; committed '74; indicted September, same year.

Grisham, A. B...Murder; committed '74; indicted September, same year. Small, 30 years old.

Williams, Joe...Assault to murder; committed '75; indicted January, same year.

Butler, Henry...Bigamy; committed '75; indicted January, same year. Negro.

Dodson, Cornelius...Theft; committed '75; indicted January, same year.

Lavas, John...Assault to murder; committed '75; indicted January, same year.

Lugan, Tom...Assault to murder; committed '75; indicted January, same year.

Cesil, W. A...Assault to murder; committed '75; indicted January, same year.

Swinney, Ransom...Assault to murder; committed '75; indicted July, same year.

Rurton, Robert...Theft; committed '75; indicted July, same year.

Lindsey, Joel...Murder; committed '75; indicted July, same year.

Boyd, Ike...Murder; committed '75; indicted July, same year. Negro.

Yarbrough, George...Assault to murder; committed '75; indicted August, same year. Negro.

Robertson, Dick...Assault to murder; committed '75; indicted August, same year.

Ellsworth, George...Assault to murder; committed '75; indicted August, same year.

Napoleon, Ed...Theft; committed '75; indicted August, same year. Negro.

Owens, Henry...Theft; committed '75; indicted August, same year. Negro.

Strickland, John...Theft; committed '75; indicted August, same year.

Robinson, Sam...Theft; committed '75; indicted November, same year. Negro. Supposed to be in Dallas, at a Mr. Ross'.

Odom, Jas...Assault to murder; committed '76; indicted March, same year.

Weeks, Ferney, alias Coley Weeks...Murder; committed '71; indicted August, same year; white.

Sharp, Geo...Resisting an officer; committed '74; indicted May, '74; negro.

Williams, Green...Murder; committed '74; indicted July, '75; negro.

Brown, Robt...Assault to murder; committed '75; indicted July, same year.

Coleman, Luke...Assault to murder; committed '75; indicted August, same year.

Porter, Creed, alias Taylor...Assault to murder; committed '76; indicted March, same year; negro.

Wooten, Edy...Bigamy; committed '76; indicted September, same year; negro.

Holbrook, D. M...Assault to kill; committed '76; indicted October, same year; white.

Morman, Ben...Assault to kill; committed '76; indicted October, same year; white.

Rainbow, J. W...Theft; committed '76; indicted October, same year; white.

Taylor, Robt...Murder; committed '76; indicted September, same year; white, 50 or 60 years old.

Cranshaw, Jim...Assault to kill; committed '76; indicted September, same year.

Shaw, M. V...Assault to kill; committed '76; indicted March, '77.

Horton, J. M...Robbery; committed '76; indicted March, '77; white.

Brisby, Claiborn...Assault to rape; committed '77; indicted March, same year; white.

Payne, Doc...Rape; committed '77; indicted March, same year; white.

Simpson, W. B...Assault to kill; committed '77; indicted March, same year; white.

Dingler, B. F...Selling mortgaged property; committed '77; indicted March, same year; white.

Hill, A. W...Selling mortgaged property; committed '77; indicted March, same year; white.

Hudgins, Wm. A...Selling mortgaged property; committed '77; indicted March, same year; white.

Hudnall, J. B...Selling mortgaged property; committed '77; indicted March, same year; white, 23 years old, light hair and eyes.

Kelly, Henry...Assault to kill; committed '77; indicted April, same year.

TARRANT COUNTY.

Carrigan, A...Assault to murder; committed '74; indicted April, '76; 6 feet high; sandy hair and moustache, ruddy complexion, bony face, prominent nose; last heard of in Lampasas county.

Hawkins, Wm...Robbery; committed in '75; indicted in August '75.

Fudge, Wm...Assault to murder; committed in '76; indicted in '76; 6 feet high, spare built, ruddy complexion, gray hair and whiskers, about 50 years of age; supposed to be in California.

Thomas, Joe R...Theft of cattle; committed in '76; indicted in '76; escaped from jail in March, '77; about 30 years of age, 5 feet 6 inches high, spare made, sandy hair and whiskers.

Halbert, C. M...Theft of a yearling; committed in '76; indicted in '76.

Scott, A. G...Theft of mare; committed in '76; indicted in '76.

Allen, John...Theft of gelding; committed October, '73; indicted August, '76; last heard of on the Gaudalupe river.

Trimble, Marion...Theft of gelding; commited in '73; indicted in '76; last heard of on the Gaudalupe river.

Reynolds, Stake...Theft of gelding; committed in '73; indicted in '76; last heard of on the Gaudalupe river.

Sansom, Fletcher...Theft of mare; committed in '76; indicted in '76.

Parker, Monroe...Theft of gelding; committed December, '73; indicted August, '76.

Kelly, James...Assault with intent to murder; committed March '73; indicted August, '76.

Whatley, M...Murder; committed February, '73; indicted August, '76; supposed to be Arkansas.

Stockton, Sam...Robbery; committed in '76; indicted in '76.

Brummett, C. T...Theft of yearling; committed in '76; indicted in '76.

Billings, Chas...Theft of gelding; committed in '76; indicted in '76; lives in Southern Texas.

Hawkins, Heuse...Robbery; committed in '75; indicted in '76.

Goldsmith, John...Robbery; committed in '75; indicted in '76.

Cresswell, James...Murder; committed '69; indicted March, '77.

Snow, Wm...Murder; committed '76; indicted same year.

Cook, Geo...Assault with intent to murder; committed '76; indicted 1877.

Byrd, J. P...Theft of horse; committed '74; indicted March, '77.

Rose, Jas...Assault with intent to murder; committed September, '76; indicted March, '77.

Sour, Ben...Theft of $200; committed October, '76; indicted March, 1877.

Hudson, John T...Filing for record fraudulent land title; committed '76; indicted '77.

Spain, Joe....Theft of horse; committed '75; indicted '77.

Mosely, B. F...Theft of gelding; committed '77; indicted same year.

Brinnen, James...Theft of mare; committed '77; indicted same year.

Miller, O. M...Murder; committed '77; indicted same year.

Morehead, Doc...Swindling; committed '77; indicted same year.

Benjamin, D. W....Robbery; committed April, '77; indicted August, same year.

Smith, A. T...Theft of gelding; committed May, '77; indicted August, same year.

Briggs, H. G...Theft and forgery; committed January, '77; indicted March, same year. Was page of the Senate in the 12th Legislature, and was subsequently employed in Secretary of State's office in Austin.

Nathan, Leopold...Swindling; committed '76; indicted March, '77.

Lockhart, A. P...Swindling; committed '77; indicted same year.

TRINITY COUNTY.

Wingate, Edward T...Assault to murder; committed September, '72; indicted February, '73. Thirty years old, 5 feet 10 inches high, weight 160 pounds, red complexion, red hair, stands erect.

Shuler, Wm...Murder; committed August, '72; indicted February, '73.

Thompson, Alford...Murder; committed June, '72; indicted February, '73; 28 years old, 5 feet 9 inches high, weight 140 pounds, fair complexion, light hair, stands very erect.

Baldwin, Goldwin...Murder; committed June, '72; indicted February, '73; 30 years old, 5 feet high, weight 150 pounds, fair complexion, blue eyes, quick spoken.

Bates, Hockley...Assault to murder; committed January, '72; indicted February, '73. Negro.

Walker, Amos...Murder; committed March, '74; indicted October, same year; 45 years old, 6 feet high, weight 175 pounds, dark complexion, black hair, does not have much to say.

Lacy, Charles...Murder; committed September, '74; indicted October, same year; 35 years old, six feet high, weight 175 pounds. Negro.

Stanley, Aaron...Assault to murder; committed May, '73; indicted October, '74.

Wingate, Frank...Murder; committed June, '66; indicted October,

'74; 35 years old, 6 feet high, weight 160 pounds, fair complexion, red hair, freckled face, white eyebrows.

Avery, R. E...Murder; committed in '70; indicted February, '75; 45 years old, 5 feet 8 inches high, weight 150 pounds, fair complexion, dark hair, whiskers turning gray.

Cain, David...Murder (two cases); committed September, '68; indicted February, '75; 30 years old, 6 feet high, weight 160 pounds, fair complexion, sandy hair.

- Tullas, Willowby...Theft of hogs; committed January, '76; indicted February, same year; 50 years old, 6 feet high, weight 175 pounds, dark complexion, dark hair, which curls.

Lowe, Wm...Assault to murder; committed November, '75; indicted February, '76.

Brownlee, Alfonso...Theft of hogs; committed November '75; indicted February, 76; 30 years old, 5 feet 4 inches high, weight 125 pounds, fair complexion, sandy hair, two upper front teeth gone; doctor.

Odum, Wm...Theft of a cow; committed May, '75; indicted June 10, same year.

Hambric, Alfred...Murder; committed October 19, '76; indicted March, '77; 30 years old, 5 feet 8 inches high, weighs 165 pounds, blacksmith.

Ruff, Sam...Murder; committed July 24, '76; indicted September, same year; 30 years old, 5 feet 6 inches high, weighs 150 pounds, very fair complexion, white hair.

Raspberry, Wm...Theft of hogs; committed January 20, '75; indicted February, '76.

Meredith, Bud...Murder; committed September 8, '76; indicted September, '77; 17 years old, has relatives in McLennan county.

UPSHUR COUNTY.

Booth, J. W...Assault to murder; committed April 1, 1868; indicted May 21, same year.

Smith, Henry...Murder; committed October 1, 1865; indicted November 21, 1868.

Smith, Jeff...Murder; committed October 1, 1868; indicted November 21, same year.

Gilchrist, Geo...Murder; committed October 1, 1868; indicted November 21, same year.

Walker, Kirk...Theft of $300; committed June 1, 1869; indicted November 19, same year.

Anderson, Wm...Theft; committed March 20, 1868; indicted October 14, 1870.

Pitts, Obidah...Assault to murder; committed May 25, 1870; indicted February 9, 1871.

Bolton, Wash...Theft; committed May 22, 1871; indicted June 7, same year.

Fowler, Jos...Assault to murder; committed May 10, 1871; indicted June 12, same year.

Wilkes, Peter...Theft; committed August 28, 1870; indicted June 13, 1871.

Harris, Constantine...Theft; committed November 19, 1870; indicted June 13, 1871.

Massey, H. C...Murder; committed March 20, 1871; indicted July 12, same year.

English, Jas...Assault to murder; committed September 23, '71; indicted October 12, same year.

English, Wm...Assault to murder; committed September 23, '71; indicted October 12, same year.

Robertson, Jas...Assault to murder; committed July 2, '71; indicted October 13, same year.

Anderson, J., Jr....Rape; committed October 7, '71; indicted October 16, same year.

Burns, A. P...Assault to murder; committed September 20, '71; indicted October 16, same year.

Hughes, Benj...Bigamy; committed January 4, '72; indicted February 11, '72.

Reel, Wm...Assault to murder; committed December 28, '71; indicted February 10, '72.

Strickland, Don...Bigamy; committed February 20, '70; indicted February 10, '72.

Reaves, Robt...Assault to murder; committed December 1, '71; indicted February 12, '72.

Fulkerson, Chas...Assault to murder; committed April 12, '72; indicted June 7, '72.

Moran, Hugh...Theft; committed May 11, '72; indicted June 8, '72.

Reel, Elisha...Murder; committed July 28, '72; indicted October 9, '72.

Counsil, Orvin...Rape; committed July 14, '72; indicted October 10, '72.

Woods, Chas...Rape; committed July 13, '72; indicted October 10, same year.

Brown, Kit...Rape; committed July 13, '72; indicted October 10, same year.

White, Geo., alias Johnson....Murder; committed September 10, '72; indicted October 15, same year.

Bryant, Nelson...Theft; committed March 28, '71; indicted June 5, '73.

Easley, D. T...Threats to take life; committed March 8, '73; indicted June 5, same year.

Caughlin, Edward...Theft; committed January 6, '73; indicted June 9, same year.

Caton, John...Assault to murder; committed December 10, '72; indicted June 9, same year.

Scott, David...Assault to murder; committed January 15, '73; indicted June 11, same year.

Bush, John...Theft; committed July 7, '73; indicted October 9, same year.

Stoddard, Thos...Theft; committed July 7, '73; indicted October 9, same year.

Young, Frank...Theft; committed October 30, '73; indicted June 11, '74.

Sexton, Samuel...Theft; committed July 7, '73; indicted October 9, same year.

Smith, Jas...Bribery; committed March 15, '73; indicted October 9, same year.

Kelly, Pat...Murder; committed February 24, '73; indicted June 11, same year.

Reese, H.•B...Theft; committed July 7, '73; indicted October 9, same year.

Benton, John...Theft; committed October 15, '72; indicted June 11, '73.

Lagrone, D. H...Theft; committed November 9, '72; indicted June 11, '73.

Scott, Alfred...Theft; committed February 6, '73; indicted June 11, '73.

Hall, Buck...Murder; committed May 24, '73; indicted June 11, '73.

Pinson, W. S...Assault to murder; committed February 9, '74; indicted February 10, '74.

Jennings, Jos...Theft; committed August 10, '73; indicted October 9, same year.

King, Robert...Kidnapping; committed November 24, '73; indicted February 10, '74.

Vaughn, Gadrid...Assault to murder; committed January 15, '71; indicted October 15, same year.

Johnson, Wm...Theft; committed December 21, '73; indicted October 7, '74.

Jewell, Henry...Theft; committed January 15, '74; indicted June 11, '75.

Thompson, Edmond...Assault to murder; committed September 20, '75; indicted October 7, same year.

Hill, Henrietta....Poisoning; committed April 26, '75; indicted June 11, same year.

Richards, T. J...Bigamy; committed September 29, '75; indicted February 10, '76.

Williams, Elisha...Murder; committed September 3, '74; indicted October 7, same year.

Ducket, Andy...Murder; committed September 3, '74; indicted Oct. 7, same year.

Springs, Lucien...Swindling; committed June 20, '76; indicted July 1, same year.

Smith, Geo...Threats to take life; committed May 20, '76; indicted June 28, same year.

Wallace, M. L...Assault to murder; committed June, '69; indicted October, '70.

Wallick, J. E...Murder; committed March, '71; indicted June, same year.

Brown, Henry...Theft; committed October, '71; indicted October, '72. Negro.

Carter, F. M...Using estray; committed December, '73; indicted February, '74.

Bird, Wm...Assault to kill; committed January, '75; indicted February, same year.

Davis, Moses...Assault to kill; committed May, '76; indicted July, same year.

Fowler, Alpha...Murder; committed November, '76; indicted January, '77.

Wilburn, Dan...Rape; committed July '76; indicted January, '77.

Fenlord, Jno...Rape; committed September, '76; indicted January, '77.

Davenport. Jas...Rape; committed September, '76; indicted January, '77

McGuflin, Jno...Rape; committed September, '76; indicted January, '77.

UVALDE COUNTY.

Wall, Geo. W...Murder of R. W. Black; committed October, '67; indicted January, '68.

Hernandez, Dateo...Theft; committed June, '67; indicted November, same year.

Thacker, Ezekiel...Accessory to murder of R. W. Black; committed October, '67; indicted December, same year.

Hancock, Jasper J...Murder of G. T. Nimmo ; committed September, '68; indicted November, same year.

Mosly, James...Murder of Richard Grimes; committed January, '70; indicted October, same year.

Horde, E...Murder of John Craft; committed January, '68; indicted January, '70.

Roque, Angel...Theft of mule; committed January, '71; indicted June, same year.

Gibbons, John...Theft of gelding; committed August, '72; indicted May, '73.

Miller, John D...Robbery; committed April, '72; indicted May, '73.

Garza, Elijo...Theft of a watch; committed July, '73; indicted January, '74.

Ubanks, Gabe...Theft of gelding; committed July, '74; indicted September, same year. Negro, about 35 years old, 5 feet 9 or 10 inches high, weight 190 or 200 pounds, very slow, speaks like there was mush in his mouth, pop-eyed. Supposed to be in Mexico.

McKinney, Collin...Theft of gelding; committed September, '75; indicted September, same year; 25 years old, weight 130 or 135 pounds, black hair, dark complexion, dark brown eyes, almost black, tolerably quick spoken.

Lopez, Pedro...Murder and assault to murder ; committed August, '75; indicted September, same year.

Samano, Felipe...Assault to murder; committed September, '75; indicted September, same year.

Spencer, Andrew J...Murder of James O. Bryant; committed July, '75; indicted September, same year; 5 feet 8 inches high, weight 170 or 175 pounds, 33 or 34 years old, dark complexion, black hair, dark brown whiskers and eyes, round face, slow spoken, open countenance, intelligent appearance, genteel and unassuming manners.

Stapps, A. J...Assault to murder; indicted January, '76; light hair, worn long, light blue eyes, a small freckled face, about 35 or 36 years old, 5 feet 8 inches high, weight 135 or 140 pounds.

(Of the foregoing named fugitives the greater portion are supposed to have crossed the Rio Grande.)

Rimeras, Trinidad...Theft; committed March '75; indicted May '75; Mexican, 19 years, quite intelligent looking.

Barnes, Pink...Theft; committed September, '75; indicted January, '76; convicted and sentenced to the penitentiary for five years, appealed and escaped, dark complexion, brown curly hair, 30 years old, weighs 160 pounds, looks like he is one-quarter or one-eighth negro.

Beverly, Lou...Theft; committed September, '75; indicted January, '76.

Joines, H. S.. Assault to kill; committed January, '77; indicted April, same year; 28 years old, brown hair, light eyes and complexion, weighs 150 pounds, 5 feet, 7 inches high.

Contreras, Bruno...Theft of oxen; committed August 4, '76; indicted October 4, same year, Mexican.

Keonio, Miguel...Theft of gelding and three mules; committed April 3, '77; indicted October 23, same year; convicted and sentenced to penitentiary for 10 years, appealed and escaped, Mexican, weighs 180 pounds, heavy set, 40 years old, bad countenance, heavy beard, lived about Laredo.

Sheely, James...Theft of gelding; committed in '77; indicted October, same year; 20 years old, weighs 160 pounds, 5 feet 9 inches high.

Juan, ——...Theft of a gelding; committed July, '77; indicted July, same year.

Powell, Bant...Theft of cattle (two cases); committed in June and September, '77; indicted October, same year; 21 years old, 5 feet 10 inches high, large round face, fair complexion, weighs 180 pounds, pleasant countenance.

Sanchez, Marion...Theft; committed September, '65; indicted October. '66.

House, Thelbert...Murder; committed January, '68; indicted November, '71.

Bascus, Martina...Theft; committed July, '70; indicted February, '71.

Pedro, ——...Theft of cattle; committed March, '74; indicted May, '74.

Williams, Harry...Theft; committed July, '73; indicted May, '74.

Estabon, ——...Theft; committed May, '74; indicted September, same year.

VICTORIA COUNTY.

Jasper, Thos...Passing false instrument of writing; committed January 8, '76; indicted March 14, same year. Negro, very black, thick, heavy set, about 6 feet high, weighs about 175 or 180 pounds, 21 or 22 years old.

Anderson, John...Theft of horse; committed January 1, '76; indicted March 17, same year.

Davidson, Jesse...Theft of cattle; committed October 26, '75; indicted November 11, same year. Is a young man about 21 years old, dark complexion, black eyes, about 5 feet 8 inches high, weighs 130 pounds, convicted and escaped.

Lee, George...Theft of gelding; committed September 18, '75; indicted November 12, same year; 5 feet 10 inches high, sandy whiskers, ex-U. S. soldier.

DeBorde, Wm...Theft of gelding; committed June 5, '75; indicted November 13, same year.

Hall, Ferdinand...Theft of cattle; committed May 30, '75; indicted July 7, same year. Is about 5 feet 10 inches high, red hair, very much freckled, about 22 years old, wide space between the two front teeth in upper jaw.

Drake, Tom...Assault with intent to murder; committed May 29, '75; indicted July 7, same year. Five feet 6 inches high, brown eyes, dark complexion, very talkative when drinking, queer shaped mouth.

Coleman, Wm...Murder; committed April 22, '75; indicted July 10, same year. Between 5 and 9 inches and 6 feet high, hazel eyes, stiff brown beard mixed with gray, rather bony, coarse voice, gambles.

McDaniel, Bill...Murder; committed June 1, '75; indicted July 10, same year. Is about 5 feet 8 or 10 inches high, slim build, dish faced,

10

black eyes and brown hair, dark complexion, weighs about 130 or 135 pounds, is about 21 or 22 years old.

Milam, Geo, alias Gibson...Murder; committed June 1, '75; indicted July 10, same year. Is 21 or 22 years old, inclined to be fleshy, light complexion, white hair, black eyes, about 5 feet 6 inches high, weighs 150 pounds.

Marshall, Sam...Theft of cow; committed February 29, '75; indicted March 10, same year. Negro, very black, about 6 feet high, weighs about 160 or 165 pounds, about 26 years old, supposed to be about Jefferson.

Lava, Candelario...Murder; committed December 29, '74; indicted March 11, same year. Mexican.

Fuller, Jas...Theft of horse; committed November 30, '74; indicted March, '75. Is about 25 years old, light complexion, about 5 feet 10 inches high, has small wicked-looking black eyes, black hair, when last seen had heavy black beard on face, he will weigh about 145 or 150 pounds.

Garza, Frank...Swindling; committed May 1, '75; indicted July 5, same year. Mexican, is about 5 feet 7 or 8 inches high, yellow complexion, will weigh about 140 or 150 pounds, broad shouldered, and walks stoop shouldered, smooth face, about 30 or 35 years old, has small, black eyes, talks peculiar and fast, has served under Cortina, gambles, convicted and escaped.

Carter, Si. G...Embezzling a gelding valued at $50; committed January 24, '75; indicted July 6, same year.

Williams, C. M...Swindling; committed June 2, '75; indicted July 7, same year.

Kawalksy, J. B...Obtaining money under false pretenses; committed December 3, '73; indicted January, '74. Is a Jew, slender build, a little stooped, very black hair and eyes, weighs about 130 pounds, about 5 feet 9 inches high, dandy.

Scott, Nero, alias Marshall, freedman...Theft of steer; committed January 14, '74; indicted January, same year. Is a negro about 5 feet 10 inches high, weighs about 150 or 160 pounds, sometimes goes by the name of Nero Marshall, supposed to be about Jefferson.

Brown, Chas., a freedman...Theft of beef steer; committed June 4, '74; indicted July 3, same year.

Sterne, George, alias Elliott...Theft of mare; committed June 4, '74; indicted July 6, same year. Is a negro, very black, about 5 feet 8 or 10 inches high, full faced, weighs about 150 or 160 pounds, when walking carries his head up.

Thomas, Justus...Theft of cattle; committed June 20, '74; indicted July 9, same year. Is a young man about 21 or 22 years old, dark complexion, has coarse jet black hair curling at the ends, is about 5 feet 6 or 7 inches high, weighs about 140 or 145 pounds, has a large black mole on the back of his neck, black whiskers, if any, and might be taken for a negro.

White, Henry, freedman...Assault with intent to commit rape; committed August 15, '74; indicted November 19, same year. Is a large black negro, about 6 feet high, very heavy set, weighs about 180 pounds.

Clark, W. S...Theft of $20 from a house; committed February, 10, 1873; indicted September 16, same year. Is between 30 and 40 years of age, tolerably good looking, dark complexion, black eyes, long dark hair, dark whiskers, has a long face, is about 5 feet 7 or 8 inches high, weighs about 140 or 150 pounds, drinks.

Ivory, Dave...Theft of hog of the value of $25; committed September 5, 1873; indicted September 16, same year; negro.

Fry, Alex, alias Reid...Theft of a mare; committed November 30, 1873; indicted January, same year.

Graham, Thomas...Obtaining money under false pretenses; committed January 7, 1872; indicted January 19, 1874; is about 5 feet 8 inches high, lived about St. Louis, Mo.

Reid, Phil, alias Phil Thomas...Passing a forged order; committed September 2, 1871; indicted September 20, same year; negro.

Hicks, Oliver...Theft of mule; committed March 1, 1869; indicted March 21, 1870.

Hussatz, Frank H...Theft of horse and buggy; committed July 10, 1870; indicted September 16, same year. German; about 5 feet 9 inches high, very talkative, light blue eyes.

Miller, J. P...Theft of horses; committed October 10, 1866; indicted March, 1867.

Fowler, G. W...Theft of horses; committed October 10, 1866; indicted March, 1867.

DeMorse, H. L...Theft of horses; committed October 10, 1866; indicted March, 1867.

Miller, Frank...Murder; committed December 17, 1866; indicted March, 1867.

Patterson, Jas...Murder; committed December 17, 1866; indicted March, 1867.

McCarthy, Andrew...Murder; committed June 5, 1866; indicted October, 1866. Is about 5 feet 10 or 11 inches high, red complexion, brown whiskers, is about 40 years old. Supposed to be in Matamoros practicing medicine.

Craig, James...Embezzlement; committed August, 1868; indicted August, same year.

Pierce, Frank...Assault with intent to murder; committed November 1, 1869; indicted March 19, 1870.

Gallon, Martin...Theft of ox valued at $20; committed December 15, 1869; indicted March 20, 1870.

Seymour, Godfred...Murder; committed June 1, '63; indicted August, 1869.

Phillips, Dick....Assault to kill; committed October 15, '69; indicted March, '70. Negro.

Lee, Frank...Theft of beef; committed March 1, '70; indicted September, same year. Negro.

Burson, E.; and Estus, Thos...Theft of cattle; committed January, '76; indicted March, same year.

James, Felix...Assault to kill; committed August, '76; indicted November, same year. Low, thick and heavy set.

Richards, John...Theft of gelding; committed September, '76; indicted November, same year. Freckled, 19 or 20 years old.

Jernigan, James...Theft of gelding; committed April, '76; indicted November, same year. Medium size, brown hair, formerly lived on Golden Rod Creek, Jackson county.

Castro, Caruto...Theft of oxen; committed August, '76; indicted November, same year.

Townsend, Lee...Assault to kill; committed November, '76; indicted November, same year.

Lewis, Alex...Theft of mare; committed August, '76; indicted May 1877. Black, thick-set, 160 pounds weight

Lewis, Neil....Theft of gelding; committed December, '76; indicted May, '77.

Hanson, J. H....Theft of gelding; committed February, '77; indicted May, same year. Small, 135 pounds weight, printer, poet and sewing machine agent.

WOOD COUNTY.

Andrews, Isaac...Theft (2 cases); committed April and May, '71; indicted November, same year.

Burnett, John...Theft; committed December, '66; indicted May, same year. Thirty years old, weighs 140 pounds, 5 feet 8 inches high, dark complexion, gray eyes, dark hair. Last heard of in Lafayette county, Arkansas.

Burke, Jack...Illegal use of estray, committed November, '70; indicted March, '71.

Brannon, Richard...Assault to murder; committed April, '71; indicted June, same year.

Boyle, Thomas...Theft; committed March, '73; indicted June, same year. Thirty years old, weighs 160 pounds, 5 feet 8 inches high, fair complexion, blue eyes, light hair; Irishman. Last heard of in Bowie county.

Carter, Wm...Bigamy; committed, '71; indicted March, same year. 25 years old, weighs 160 pounds, 6 feet high, swarthy complexion, dark eyes, dark hair.

Corgan, James...Assault to murder; committed March, '72; indicted November same year.

Carter, James...Theft; committed January, '74; indicted October, same year. Twenty-three years old, weighs 150 pounds, 5 feet 10 inches high, black eyes, black hair.

Campbell, W. A...Murder; committed May '74; indicted October, same year; 35 years old, weighs 130 pounds, 5 feet 8 inches high, fair complexion, gray eyes, dark hair; physician.

Carter, France...Removing estray; committed May, '74; indicted June, same year.

Connor, Phil...Murder; committed December, '72; indicted June, '73: 30 years old, weighs 140 pounds, 5 feet 10 inches high, fair complexion, blue eyes, auburn hair; Irishman.

Christopher, J. P...Theft; committed December, '74; indicted July, '75; 23 years old, weighs 150 pounds, 5 feet 8 inches high, fair complexion, blue eyes, red hair; last heard of in Sevier county, Arkansas.

Conley, John...Theft; committed September, '75; indicted November, same year.

Eaton, John...Murder; committed May, '70; indicted October, same year; 40 years old, weight 140 pounds, 5 feet 9 inches high, dark complexion, black eyes, black hair, bad countenance, slightly hump-shouldered.

Grayson, Thos...Theft; committed April, '74; indicted June, same year.

Howell, W. T...Murder; committed May, '73; indicted June, same year; 35 years old, weighs 150 pounds, 5 feet 10 inches high, dark complexion, black eyes, dark hair, knock-kneed, laughs without expression.

Hendrix, Wm. H...Assault to murder; committed August, '71; indicted October, same year.

Harris, George, Theft; committed October, '72; indicted November same year; 30 years old, weighs 160 pounds, 5 feet 8 inches high, black hair, black eyes; negro.

Hodges, Joel...Assault to murder; committed May, '65; indicted November, same year; 30 years old, weighs 160 pounds, 5 feet 9 inches high, fair complexion, blue eyes, auburn hair; last heard of near Texarkana, Arkansas.

Hughey, Willis H...Murder; two cases; committed January, '67; indicted November, same year.

Harry, Dick...Forgery; committed April, '74; indicted July, same year.

Hunnicut, Jas...Theft; committed June, '75; indicted June, same year.

Hazard, Robert...Theft; committed October, '72; indicted June, '73.

Kennel, Henry...Burglary and theft; two cases; committed April, '72; indicted April and June, same year.

Keyes, George...Assault to kill; committed August, '69; indicted November, same year; 40 years old, weighs 150 pounds, 5 feet 10 inches high, black eyes, black hair; negro.

Moore, Joe...Theft; committed September, '75; indicted November, same year; 27 years old, weighs 175 pounds, 5 feet 10 inches high, red complexion, gray eyes, dark hair, fine looking, fond of dress.

McAnally, Dick...Theft; committed August, '71; indicted October, same year.

McMillan, Taylor...Theft; committed December, '72; indicted June, '73; 30 years old, weighs 180 pounds, 6 feet high, black eyes and hair; last heard of at Fulton, Arkansas; negro.

Morris, Wm.; alias Farris, Wm...Murder; committed September, '71; indicted October, same year; 30 years old, weighs 160 pounds, 5 feet 10 inches high, yellow complexion, black eyes and hair; negro.

Mintz, J. C...Forgery; committed February, '74; indicted March, same year; 28 years old, weighs 160 pounds, 5 feet 10 inches high, sallow complexion, gray eyes, dark hair, hair-lipped.

Nunn, Wm...Assault to murder; committed November, 73; indicted March, 74; 30 years old, weighs 140 pounds, 5 feet 8 inches high, sallow complexion, dark hair.

Nance, Prior B...Murder; committed October, '69; indicted November, same year; 33 years old, weighs 140 pounds, 6 feet high, fair complexion, gray eyes, dark hair.

Prince, Hense...Assault to murder; committed June, '75; indicted July, same year; 30 years old, weighs 175 pounds, 6 feet high, black eyes and hair; negro; last heard of at Marshal.

Renfroe, John...Theft; committed March, '75; indicted July, same year; 28 years old, weighs 130 pounds, 5 feet 5 inches high, dark complexion, gray eyes, dark hair.

Rhine, Boone...Theft; committed October, '68; indicted November, same year.

Smith, Alfred...Theft; committed May, '73; indicted July, same year.

Smith, R. H...Assault to murder; committed October, '74; indicted November, same year; 45 years old, weighs 140 pounds, 5 feet 5 inches high, sallow complexion, gray eyes, gray hair, very fond of whisky; supposed to be in Mississippi.

Smith, Peter...Robbery; false imprisonment; committed January, '69; indicted January and June, '71; supposed to be dead.

Sharper, Wiley...Theft; committed June, '73; indicted June, same year; negro, 26 years old, weighs 150 pounds, 5 feet 8 inches high, black eyes and hair.

Speck, Marshall...Assault to murder; committed September '71; indicted October, same year; 28 years old, weighs 145 pounds, 5 feet 6 inches high, fair complexion, blue eyes, light hair, head large and bushy.

Smith, Jeff...Assault to murder; committed May, '74; indicted June, same year.

Sanders, W. B...Theft; committed December, '73; indicted November, '74; 30 years old, weighs 180 pounds, 6 feet high, fair complexion, blue eyes, light hair.

Tisdale, J. W...Assault to murder; committed April, '73; indicted July, same year.

Tracy, Charles...Assault to murder; committed April, '74; indicted June, same year.

Thompson, James...Assault to murder; committed November, '71; indicted February, '72; negro, 30 years old, weight 160 pounds, 5 feet 8 inches high.

Turner, Frank...Theft; committed '69; indicted November, same year; 34 years old, weight 150 pounds, 5 feet 5 inches high, fair. complexion, gray eyes, dark hair, last heard of at Napoleon, Arkansas.

Towles, Andy...Theft; committed November, '72; indicted June, '73; negro, 19 years old, weight 130 pounds, 5 feet 5 inches high, copper color.

Wilson, R. D...Theft; committed June, '75; indicted July, same year; 26 years old, weighs 150 pounds, 5 feet 6 inches high, red complexion, blue eyes, red hair, on the Texas frontier.

Williams, Martha...Theft; committed December, '74; indicted July, '75; 50 years old, weight 125 pounds, 5 feet 2 inches high, sallow complexion, gray eyes, gray hair, last heard of in Sevier, county, Ark.

Wilson, Mack...Theft; committed June, '75; indicted July, same year; 28 years old, weight 150 pounds, 5 feet 6 inches high, sallow complexion, gray eyes, dark hair, on Texas frontier.

Warmack, Hope...Assault to murder; committed October, '74; indicted November, same year.

Watson, Lee...Adultery; committed November, '73; indicted November, '74; negro.

Yarbrough, Cela...Adultery; committed November, '73; indicted November, '74; negress.

Gunter, J. H...Murder; indicted November 12, '65; 40 years old, weighs 160 pounds, 5 feet 11 inches high, light complexion and hair, blue eyes, supposed to be in the Indian Nation.

Fowler, John C...Murder; indicted '66; weight 150 pounds, 5 feet 8 inches high, light complexion, blue eyes, sandy hair, supposed to be in Mississippi.

Carson, B. F...Selling mortgaged property; committed September 23, '76; indicted December 14, same year; 25 years old, weight 160 pounds, 6 feet high, fair complexion, blue eyes, light hair.

Bellah, John...Selling mortgaged property; committed June 23, '76; indicted December 14, same year; 30 years old, weight 140 pounds, 5 feet 10 inches high, fair complexion, blue eyes, light hair, a little hump-shouldered.

Sweeden, Lee....Theft; committed September 7, '74; indicted November 4, same year; 32 years old, weight 140 pounds, 5 feet 8 inches high dark complexion, black eyes, dark hair.

WHARTON COUNTY.

Claudius, Jas...Murder; committed January 29, '68; indicted August, 25, same year.

George, Alsop...Murder; committed July 26, '72; indicted August 10, same year. Black, is 5 feet 10 inches high, wears a small moustache, is a barber by trade, talks plain, uses good language, gaudy in dress, 24 years of age, weighs 135 or 140 pounds.

Smith, Byron...Assault with intent to murder; committed July 30, '70; indicted December 9, '71. Is about 6 feet high, well formed, weighs 140 pounds, dark hair and moustache, aquiline nose. Is supposed to be in Fort Bend county, Texas. Rough cow boy.

Oliver, John...Assault with intent to murder; committed December 25, '72; indicted April 11, '73.

Callaway, Lemuel...Arson; committed March 30, '73; indicted April 14, same year. Very old and feeble, spare made, iron gray hair and whiskers, bald-headed, stoop shoulders, walks with a cane, a preacher by profession. Last heard of was in Terrebonne Parish, Louisiana.

McDowell, Tink...Defacing a brand; committed January 1, '73; indicted August 14, same year. Is a small, black negro, 5 feet 7 inches high, clean face, weighs 135 pounds. Last heard of was in Brazoria county.

Jackson, Chas...Theft of a gelding and two colts; committed July, 10, '73; indicted August 14, same year.

Brown, Alfred...Theft of a horse; indicted December 8, '73.

Gibson, John...Theft of a horse; committed July 19, '74; indicted April 9, '75. Negro, dark, copper-colored, spare made, weighs about 149 pounds, 5 feet 11 inches high, 24 years old, has a French accent. Last heard of in Louisiana.

Chinn, Jim...Theft of mare; committed November 20, '73; indicted April 9, '74.

Jones, Madison ..Theft of a hog; committed October 1, '73; indicted August 8, '74. Negro, bright mulatto, 5 feet 10 inches high, weighs about 140 pounds, Caucasian features.

Praylor, Jack...Assault with intent to murder; committed June 1, '75; indicted August 6, same year. Black negro, 5 feet 11 inches or 6 feet high, large white eyes, thick lips, heavy moustache, a carpenter by trade. Last seen in San Antonio.

Brown, Columbus...Murder; committed January 15, '75; indicted August 7, same year. Light complexion, about 17 years old, freckled face, sandy hair, very near red, a cow boy by trade. Last seen in Fayette county.

Smith, Bob...Assault with intent to kill; committed September 14, '73; indicted April 14, same year. About same as Byron Smith.

Stewart, J. H. T...Assault with intent to murder; committed May 4, '76; indicted August 26, same year; very bright mulatto, about 30 years old, weight 130 or 140 pounds, straight hair and features, talks a great deal and very fast, can read and write very well.

Townsend, Beth...Theft of a cow; committed January 15, '77; indicted June 11, same year.

Williams, Dave...Theft of yearling; committed June 15, '76; indicted August 25, same year; copper colored mulatto, about 5 feet 8 inches high, weight 140 pounds, straight features, fond of horse racing and gambling.

Jackson, Clarrissa...Murder; indicted June 6, '77.

Lyon, Thos...Theft of a cow; committed January 15, '77; indicted June 11, same year.

Northington, John T...Murder; committed October 10, '71; indicted December 9, same year; curly white hair, light complexion, blue eyes, 5 feet 8 inches high, weight 125 pounds, white fuz on lip and chin.

Phœnix, Jim...Burglary; committed October 21, '76; indicted December 15, same year; negro, very near black, straight features, wears mustache and goatee, talks slow and has little to say; jack-leg carpenter, fiddler by profession. Last heard of as a deck hand between Galveston and Houston.

Bowers, E., alias E. Parker...Swindling; committed December 19, '76; indicted April, '77; short, 135 pounds, fair complexion, blue eyes, very short white curly hair, neat in dress, no whiskers, little to say, mild mannered. Last heard of in San Francisco.

Ballard, Ples...Theft of a cow; committed July 16, '76; indicted August 31, same year. Mulatto, 5 feet 7 inches high, weighs 135 pounds, squints his eyes while talking, has a scar on his forehead, last seen on Kyle and Terry's sugar place, in Fort Bend county.

Brown, Tom...Theft of a hog; committed Nov. 13, '76; indicted December 12, same year.

Brown, Jack...Theft of hog; committed November 13, '76; indicted December 12, same year.

Jones, Warner...Disposing of mortgaged property; committed December 10, '72; indicted August 15, '73.

Brown, Alfred...Theft of a horse; committed September 13, '73; indicted December 8, same year.

Horan, L...Swindling; committed October 19, '75; indicted April 10, '76.

Mitchell, Charles...Theft of hog; committed July 21, '76; indicted August 25, same year.

McCambey, J. M...Murder; committed January 21, '76; indicted December 5, same year. White man, is 45 years old, weighs 160 pounds, about 5 feet 11 inches or 6 feet high, iron grey hair and whiskers, wears full beard, has an old running wound in the hip, causing him to limp slightly, well informed and has a pleasant address. Last heard of was in command of a regiment in Mexico.

Martin, Floyd...Theft of a beef; committed December 4, '76; indicted December 6, same year. Negro, dark copper colored, 5 feet 10 inches high, weighs 160 pounds, light whiskers on chin, drawling accent, round face, short chin.

WALLER COUNTY.

Bell, Matt...Assault to murder. Blue eyes, about 35 years old, shot through one foot, walks lame, black hair, talks about horse races and six-shooters, a good drinker.

Stifflemeyer, Wesley...Assault to murder. Light hair, about 25 years old, blue eyes, about 5 feet 6 or 8 inches high.

Richardson, Jack...Assault to murder. Negro.

Groce, Watt...Burglary. Negro; about 35 or 40 years old, about 5 feet 8 inches high, lame in one arm.

Clara, Jack...Perjury. Negro.

Haley, John...Theft of gelding. Light hair, light complexion, about 6 feet 1 inch high, about 28 years old.

Smith, Sam...Assault to murder. Negro.

Bories, Robert...Swindling. Negro.

Taylor, Robert...Theft from a house (2 cases). Negro; copper-colored, about 5 feet 10 inches high, about 25 years old.

Bird, Louis...Murder. Negro; copper-colored, about 5 feet 8 inches high, weighs about 160 pounds.

Landry, Wesley...Theft. Negro.

Buchanan, Nan...Theft from house; committed March 17, '73; indicted July 31, '74; heavy built negro, 45 years old, 6 feet high, is a great bugler, and has a dish face.

Hagan, Ed...Theft; committed December 12, '73; indicted May, '74.

Saunders, Fayette....Theft of saddle; committed June '74; indicted July, '74.

Blake, Lewis...Theft of cattle; committed March, '75; indicted May, '75.

Mayhan, Dick...Theft of cattle; committed May, '75; indicted May, '75.

Hampton, Wade...Theft of mare; committed November, '75; indicted December, '75.

Hall, Dan...Arson; committed November, '75; indicted December, '75.

Glass, Jess...Murder; committed January, '76; indicted July, '76; white boy, 16 years old, polite address.

Bishop, Alfred....Theft of cattle; committed June '76; indicted July, '76.

WILLIAMSON COUNTY.

Aldridge, John...Theft of cattle; committed October, '72; indicted March, '73; about 33 years old, auburn hair, freckled face 5 feet 9 or 10 inches high.

Baker, Wesley; and Baker, William...Forgery; committed December, '72; indicted March, '73.

Weinert, E. H...Theft of a gelding; committed August, '73; indicted March, '74.

Hill, James...Theft of a mare (three cases); committed August, '73; indicted March, '74.

Barton, Lum....Assault to murder; committed March, '74; indicted July, same year.

Davis, Sercy....Swindling; committed March, '74; indicted July, same year.

Brown, J. C...Murder; committed September, '74; indicted November, same year.

Bond, Dennis; Cox, John...Theft of cattle; committed June, '74; indicted November, same year.

Snow, Thomas...Assault to murder; committed February, '75; indicted March, same year.

Smith, R. D...Theft of cattle (three cases); committed '74; indicted same year; about 33 years old, nearly 6 feet high, blue eyes, light thin skin, weight 175 pounds, high cheek bones, slow to speak, supposed to be in Kansas, or near Fort Worth, Texas.

Smith, James A...Theft of cattle (three cases); committed '74; indicted same year; father of R. D. Smith and Pulaski Smith, 48 or 50 years old, weight 170 pounds, red complexion, beard turning gray.

Smith, Pulaski...Theft of cattle; committed '74; indicted same year; about 18 years old.

Roberts, John...Theft (felony); committed December, '74; indicted March, '75.

Rolen, R. H...Theft of a gelding; committed April, '75; indicted July, same year; about 35 years old, 5 feet 9 inches high, weight 160 pounds, scar over one eye, from hair going to temple, struck with a shot-gun.

Harris, Austin....Theft of cattle; committed May, '75; indicted July, same year; negro.

Woolem, C. M...Theft of a gelding; committed June, '75; indicted July, same year; about 50 years old, dark complexion, beard gray, 5 feet 11 inches high, weight 160 pounds, supposed to be in Erath county, Texas.

Roberts, Weldon....Theft of cattle; committed April, '75; indicted July, same year; about 21 years old, light complexion.

Beaty, G. W....Theft; committed March '75; indicted July, same year.

Wilcox, E. S....Theft of cattle; committed June, '75; indicted July, same year.

Beard, John...Murder, and theft of cattle and horses (five cases); committed October, '75; indicted January, '76; 5 feet 8 inches high, 23 years old, light complexion and blue eyes, two or three moles on face, thin beard, was in Western Texas, about Dogtown.

Pearce, John....Theft of a gelding; committed April, '75; indicted September, same year.

George, Dave, alias Dallum, Dave...Theft of a gelding; committed April, 75; indicted September, same year.

Middleton, George....Theft of a gelding; committed April, '75; indicted September, same year.

Lea, Luke...Assault to murder; committed August, '75; indicted September, same year. About 35 years old, tall and slender, red complexion, last heard of in Fayette county.

McCarroll, Sylvester....Arson; committed December, '75; indicted January, '76; 28 years old, short and stout built.

Jagelke, Henry...Burglary; committed November, '75; indicted January, '76; German, 45 years old, one wooden leg, last heard of in Hill county, Texas.

Rose, Mitchell...Theft; committed September, '75; indicted January, '76; negro, in penitentiary from Falls county, perhaps.

Solomon, W. E...Theft; committed October, '75; indicted January, '76.

Potts, John...Theft; committed October, '75; indicted January, '76.

Freeman, Sol...Theft of cattle; committed July, '75; indicted January, '76; negro, ginger colored, shrewd, 6 feet high, escaped from penitentiary, was heard of about Waco, November, '76.

Anderson, John....Theft of a gelding; committed August, '76; indicted September, same year; 18 years old, boyish face, his father is in Stephens county, beardless.

Berry, Silas...Theft of a gelding; committed May, '76; indicted September, same year; 5 feet 8 inches high, blue eyes, sallow complexion, right arm off near elbow; about 32 years old, can be convicted, supposed to be in Coleman county, Texas.

Bybee, William...Theft of a gelding; committed May, '76; indicted September, same year; 6 feet 2 inches high, 24 years old, blue eyes, stooped shoulders, can't look a man in the face when talking.

Brady, J. T...Theft of cattle; committed April, '76; indicted September, same year; black hair, 5 feet 11 inches high, weighs 150 pounds, 24 years old.

Connell, Geo...Burglary ; committed September, '76 ; indicted September, same year.

Dunn, Lee...Assault to murder ; committed August, '76 ; indicted September, same year ; tall, fair skinned, about 25 years old, was arrested in Dennison, November, '76, but released before our telegraph warrant could get there.

Hardin, J. T...Theft of gelding ; committed April, '76 ; indicted September, same year ; 23 years old, light complexion, stout built, round shouldered, came from Coryell county.

Hardin, Meredith...Theft of a gelding ; committed April, '76 ; indicted September, same year ; 19 years old, dark skin, dark eyes, sharp nose, 5 feet 7 inches high, from Coryell county.

Oliver, Robt...Murder ; committed January, '76 ; indicted January, same year.

Durant, A. J...Theft of cattle ; committed August, '76 ; indicted September, same year.

Diffitt, Marion...Assault to murder ; committed May, '76 ; indicted September, same year.

Roberts, James...Assault to murder ; committed April, '76 ; indicted September, same year ; 20 years old.

Baker, W. H.; Baker, D. P...Theft of a gelding ; committed April, '75 ; indicted September, '76.

Snyder, John, alias Childress, John...Theft of a gelding, four cases ; committed October, '76 ; indicted March, '77 ; 28 years old, height 5 feet 10 inches, heavy built, thick through shoulders, blue eyes, heavy eyebrows, No. 9 boot, weight 180 or 190 pounds, looks like a fool, talks like a simpleton, but sharp as a briar for all that, legs crooked, bends back in knees when standing.

Bertram, John...Assault to murder and burglary ; committed February, '77 ; indicted March, same year. Negro.

Sanders, Moses...Assault to murder ; committed February, '77 ; indicted March, same year. Negro.

Crohn, Morris...Theft of a mule ; committed February, '77 ; indicted March, same year ; pedler; supposed to be in Milam county.

O'Connor, John...Assault to murder ; committed February, '77 ; indicted March, same year.

Moore, Jack...Assault to murder ; committed February, '77 ; indicted March, same year.

Gary, F. S., alias Charles Lee...Theft of mule ; committed July, '76 ; indicted March, '77 ; rather dark complexion, dark hair and eyes, rather portly, weight 180 pounds, speaks frequently of —. Millett, stockman, and thinks he may go with his herd. His father lives 62 miles from Kansas City, Mo.

Rowlet, Samuel ; and Dunbar, Wm....Murder ; indicted '71.

Eastwood, Frank....Theft of mare ; indicted '76.

Jones, J. G...Theft of cattle ; indicted '73.

Kidd, Webb...Theft of cattle ; indicted '72.

Williams, A. J...Theft of cattle ; indicted '74.

Williams, Jack....Pleasant, open countenance, blue eyes, light complexion, weighs 125 pounds.

Ratliff, James...Theft of a mare ; committed '77 ; indicted '77.

Ratliff, Jack...Theft of gelding ; committed '77 ; indicted '77.

Kennedy, John...Assault to murder, committed '77 ; indicted '77.

Crim, Wm...Theft of cattle ; committed '77 ; indicted '77.

Armstrong, Nealy...Theft of cattle; committed '77; indicted '77.

Burns, Tom...Theft of cattle; committed '77; indicted '77.

Carlston, John...Murder; indicted '66.

Reed, James...Murder; indicted '67.

Barber, Charles...Murder; indicted '68.

Craig, Alex.; and Waller, Andrew...Murder; indicted '68.

Spoorland, Samuel...Theft of a mare; indicted, '70.

Spoorland, Samuel...Arson; indicted, '70.

Lemmons, Poley...Theft of a mare; indicted, '71.

George, Charles...Murder; indicted, '71.

Keyes, James...Arson; indicted, '71.

Cox, Bluf...Murder; committed '71; indicted, '71. Now on the Belknap, 15 miles from Red River Station; calls himself Davis (sometimes), deputy sheriff (?) of Montague knows him. He is 6 feet high, weighs 175 pounds, dark complexion, black hair, 28 or 30 years old, rough and profane, low forehead.

Wills, Wm., alias Hamilton, alias Pritchard, alias, &c., &c...Theft of cattle; committed '73; indicted, '73. Five feet 6 inches high, blue eyes, heavy moustache which he keeps colored, round, red face, has been wounded in thigh, wears No. 5 boots or shoes, goes well dressed.

Mankins, Pete (2 cases)... Theft of gelding; committed, '73; indicted, '74. Five feet 10 inches high, light complexion, blue eyes, light hair.

Peyton, William...Murder; committed, '65; indicted, '65.

WISE COUNTY.

Collins, D...Theft of hog; indicted December, '75. Thirty years old, six feet high, dark complexion.

Askey, Milton...Murder of W. W. Miller; indicted May, '76. 19 years old, light complexion, front teeth wide apart, weighs 160 pounds, wears number 9 boots, slow of speech.

Tibbet, Vigil...Theft; indicted December, '75.

Burns, Sam...Theft; indicted December, '75.

Kuykendall, R. T...Theft of steer; indicted December, '75. 18 years old, 5 feet 7 inches high, dark skin and dark eyes.

Banis, R. T...Theft of steer; indicted December, '75. Spare build, 5 feet 8 inches high, red complexion, about 35 years old.

Jolly, Rich...Theft of steer; indicted December, '75.

Crockett, Ruth...Murder; indicted August, '75. About 40 years old, rather good looking, rather dark hair, hazel eyes, about medium size, prostitute. Supposed to be at Buel's, near San Antonio.

Stewart, John...Burglary; indicted August, '75.

Morris, John...Assault to murder; indicted August, '75. 55 years old, rough looking, heavy build, 5 feet 11 inches high, dark complexion, quite gray.

Wiley, David....Theft of horse; indicted August, '75. About 21 years old, 5 feet 10 inches high, rather light complexion.

Tobias, George...Theft; indicted April, '75.

Halsell, Sam...Theft; indicted April, '75. Negro, copper-colored, about 23 years old, about 5 feet 11 inches high, square build, Roman nose.

Jones, R. F...Theft of steer; indicted December, '74.

Porter, Harvy...Assault to murder; indicted December, '74.

Ballard, Edward...Theft; indicted December, '74.

Miller, Bud...Theft of steer; indicted August, '74. About 6 feet high, dark complexion, about 27 years old.

Stephens, Henry, John, and Ed...Theft of steer; indicted August, '74.

Jack, W. T...Theft of gelding; indicted April, '74. About 26 years old, 5 feet 8 inches high, spare made, heavy, sandy moustache, photographer by profession.

Roach, Lucius...Assault to murder; indicted April, '74.

Simpson, Isaac...Theft; indicted April, 74.

Williams, T. J...Murder of Rimner; indicted April, 74. About 5 feet 10 inches high, weighs 130 pounds, fair complexion, 30 years old, blue eyes, sandy hair, Roman nose; gambler.

Lytle, Richard...Burglary; indicted April, '75. About 20 years old, light complexion, full features, inclined to spreeing.

Shy, C. W...Theft; indicted April, '75.

Harper, Thos...Theft of steer; indicted August, '74.

Verner, James...Theft of steer; indicted August, '74. About 25 years old, 5 feet 10 inches high, dark complexion and eyes.

Hines, Edward...Assault to murder; indicted November, 73.

Moffit, Austin, and Joseph...Theft; indicted November, '73.

Taylor, B. F...Indicted May 14, '77, for theft of steer on December 9, same year. Is about medium size, middle age, dark complexion.

Richards, William, alias "Wild Bill"...Indicted for murder May 9, '77. Is low, heavy set, dark hair and eyes, about 30 years old, and has heavy beard, usually wears a "gotee," and has an English brogue in his talk. Helped to murder Dock Malone on 12th of April, '77.

Arp, Bill...Murder; indicted May 9, '77. Is about 30 years old, rather tall, light complexion, light eyes, has a family. His mother is a widow; has a younger brother that has a pecular natural defect in his right ear. Are likely all near together, and in Southern or Southwestern Texas.

Brock, J. T....Indicted May 14, '77, for theft of hog, committed in April, same year. Is a rather small, dark-complexioned man, about 32 years old; has a wife and two children. Last heard from was in Johnson county.

Daniels, Dock...Assault to murder in '77; indictment filed May 14. '77. Is about 23 years old.

Garet, C. A...Theft of horse in '77; indictment filed May 9, same year, Is a young man, and in Arkansas.

Ashbell, Joe M...For assault to murder in '77; indictment filed May 14, same year. Is about 28 years old, medium size, light complexion, light eyes, has but little to say, generally about saloons, and is a carpenter by trade.

Curry, John...Theft of horse in '76; indictment filed October 8, same year. Is about 30 years old, good size and light complexion, and has "St. Vita's Dance."

WASHINGTON COUNTY.

Atkinson, Randle...Bigamy; indicted February 3, '73; colored.

Bean, D...Murder; indicted June, '73; supposed to be in Bell county; white.

Brozell, James...Forgery; indicted January, '77; white.

Collins, J. B...Theft of a gelding; indicted July, '77; white.

Davis, Phil...Theft of a hog; indicted January, '77; colored.

Hogan, Wash...Theft of a gelding; indicted January, '77; colored.
Hill, Ben...Assault with intent to murder; indicted July, '77; colored.
Jones, Elijah...Murder; indicted January, '77; white.
Mognus, Bill...Murder; indicted February, '76; colored.
Sanders, Richard, Jr...Theft of a gelding; indicted June, '74.
Smith, Conrad...Assault with intent to kill; indicted July, '76; white.
Vanu, Thomas...Theft of a gelding; indicted June, '74; colored.

WALKER COUNTY.

Helliary, alias Tucker Blackburn...Murder; committed August 29, '71; indicted November 8, same year. Is 5 feet 8 inches high, spare built, dish-faced, dark hair and beard, dark eyes, weighs about 130 or 140 pounds, 25 or 26 years old, very quiet, bad countenance.

Stewart, W. H...Embezzlement of public money; committed October 1, '70; indicted April 15, '71. Is about 37 or 38 years old, light complexion, light hair which is inclined to curl, heavy set, about 5 feet 10 inches high, weighs about 170 pounds, Irish accent in speaking, formerly sheriff of Walker county.

Montgomery Sam...Theft from a house of $160 gold; committed October 1, '71; indicted November 17, same year. Is a negro, about 6 feet high, about 40 or 45 years old, weighs about 165 pounds, had no beard.

McGar, Moses...Theft of a mare; committed July 30, '71; indicted November 17, same year.

Norris, Jack...Assault with intent to murder; committed March 10, '72; indicted March 22, same year.

Powell, A. J...Assault with intent to murder; committed March 10, '72; indicted March, 22, same year.

Hendley, Isaac...Forgery; committed January 9, '72; indicted April 4, '72. Irish; light complexion, light-redish hair which is very coarse, a broad, square face, broad front teeth, about 6 feet high, weighs 175 or 180 pounds, large eyes, quick spoken, blacksmith by trade, about 27 years old, large mouth. Supposed to be at Keachi, DeSoto parish, La.

Tullis, James...Theft from a house; committed February 17, '72; indicted April 4, same year. Is a negro, slick-looking, no beard, about 30 years old, weighs about 190 pounds; ex-convict. When last heard of was in Houston county, Texas.

Hightower, Henry...Theft from house; committed June 10, '72; indicted July 17, same year.

Birdlow, Wm...Theft from a house; committed December 24, '72; indicted July 16, '73.

Colburn, Fill...Assault with intent to murder; committed July 27, '73; indicted August 2, same year.

Cowan, Jas. A...Theft of property over $20 in value; committed July 15, '73; indicted August 2, same year.

Lawrence, Primus...Rape; committed August 6, '73; indicted November 20, same year; is of a copper color; about 20 or 22 years old, spare made, about 5 feet 5 inches high, weighs 120 or 125 pounds.

Haynes, Geo., Alias Duckworth...Murder; committed October 16, '73; indicted November 24, same year; is a black negro, about 50 years old, weighs 175 or 180 pounds, heavy beard, one eye out, spare build and quick spoken, about 5 feet 8 or 10 inches high.

Townley, Wm...Swindling; committed February 15, '73; indicted November 26, same year.

Smith, Martin...Theft of a hog; committed October 1, '73; indicted November 26, same year. Is a black negro, heavy set weighs 160 or 170 pounds, is about 5 feet 8 inches high, 40 or 45 years old.

Sewell, John...Theft of hog; committed October 1, '73; indicted November 26, same year. Is a black, slick negro, about 5 feet 10 inches high, 35 or 40 years old, weighs about 140 pounds.

King, Theodore...Theft from a house; committed September, '73; indicted November 28, '73. Is about 20 or 22 years old, light complexion, red sandy hair, will weigh 135 or 140 pounds.

McCants, George...Theft from a house; committed November, 15, '73; indicted, same month.

Garrett, Willis...Theft of hogs, value of $25, three indictments; committed November 27, '73; indicted November 28, same year. Is a black negro, about 5 feet 8 or 10 inches high, weighs about 160 pounds, prominent cheek bones, about 40 or 45 years old.

Tipton, J. W...Theft of beef steer; committed September 1, '73; indicted December, same year. Has blue eyes, light complexion, sandy hair, about 40 years old, weighs 175 or 180 pounds, sandy beard.

Moon, Austin...Assault with intent to commit rape; committed November, '73; indicted March 19, '74. Has light complexion, light hair, blue eyes, spare made, weighs about 135 pounds, 25 years old, crippled in one foot by railroad train, was said to be at Hot Springs, Arkansas, in July last, driving a hack.

Wiley, Anderson...Theft from a house; committed March 8, '74; indicted March 25, same year.

Cottrell, Amanda...Theft from a house; committed February 1, '74; indicted March 26, same year.

Pettit, Millard...Theft from a house; committed December 5, '73; indicted April 2, '74.

Altum, H. L...Murder; committed June 12, '74; indicted July 15, same year. Is about 25 or 30 years old; heavy set, weighs about 140 pounds, about 5 feet 5 or 6 inches high, dark complexion, dark hair, gray eyes, very little beard.

Dupree, K...Theft of beef steers; committed May 8, '74; indicted July 17, same year. Said to be dead.

Ridley, Solomon...Theft of mule; committed May 30, '74; indicted July 21, same year.

Murtos, Stephen...Theft of gelding; committed July 15, '74; indicted July 30, same year. Is in penitentiary, sent from another county on another charge.

Roe, Frank...Theft from a house; committed October 25, '75; indicted November 18, same year. Dark complexion, dark hair and eyes, about 5 feet 8 or 10 inches high, about 40 or 45 year old, weighs about 160 or 170 pounds, No. 1 mechanic, ex-convict.

Stubblefield, Nelson...Theft of hog; committed November 5, '74; indicted November 25, same year. Negro, about 45 or 50 years old, both legs deformed, when walking knees strike and feet about 36 inches apart, weighs about 160 pounds. Said to be in Hill county.

Palmer, Abe...Feloniously and seriously threatening to take life; committed March 10, '75; indicted April 1, same year. Negro, about 25 or 30 years old, eyes large and show a good deal of white, weighs about 150 pounds, quarrelsome disposition. Supposed to be in Grimes or Montgomery county.

Davis, Arthur...Murder; committed May 2, '75; indicted July 28, same year. Dark skin, hair and eyes, heavy beard, about 5 feet 6 or 7 inches high, weighs 140 pounds, about 40 or 45 years old.

Taylor, Geo...Theft from a house; committed October 1, '75; indicted November 18, same year. Dark copper colored negro, about 5 feet 8 or 9 inches high, weighs 175 or 180 pounds, ex-convict sent from Leon county to penitentiary.

Parks, James...Theft from house; committed November 8, '75; indicted November 24, same year.

Dees, John...Theft from house; committed November 1, '75; indicted November 24, same year.

Alston, Drea...Theft of hog; committed June 30, '75; indicted November 24, same year. Copper-colored negro, about 5 feet 8 inches high, weighs 145 pounds, 35 or 40 years old.

Thompson, Fountain...Theft of hog; committed June 30, '75; indicted November, same year.

Gillaspie, Joc...Assault with intent to murder; committed September 6, '75; indicted November 26, same year. Negro, nearly black, about 6 feet high, weighs about 160 pounds, spare built, very talkative when drinking, usually wears his hair and beard wrapped, lower front teeth protrude.

Warren, Jas...Assault with intent to murder; committed February, 13, '76; indicted March 3, same year.

Thomas, Fountain ..Theft of hog; committed June 10, '75; indicted April 1, '76.

Shields, Reed...Murder; committed February 15, '76. Black, low and chunky, 5 feet 7 or 8 inches high, weighs 160 pounds, 25 or 30 years old, peculiar voice, speaks down in chest, very deep voice, sounds like he was talking in a barrel.

Vowell, A. J....Assault to kill; committed March 10, '72; indicted March 22, same year,

Wood, Austin...Assault to rape; committed November 1, '73; indicted March 19, '74; light complexion and hair, blue eyes, spare made, weighs 135 pounds, 25 years old, crippled in one foot.

Dees, John...Theft from house; committed November 1, '75; indicted November 24, same year; dark hair and eyes, weighs 160 pounds, 5 feet 8 or 10 inches high, 35 or 40 years old.

Tucker, Albert, Jr...Assault to kill; committed May 3, '76; indicted October 25, same year; 5 feet 10 inches, weighs 135 pounds, sandy hair, red, freckled face, blue eyes, thin, sandy whiskers.

Ashworth, Moses....Murder; committed June 16, '76; indicted October 25, same year; white.

Hall, Sam...Assault to kill; committed March 15, '77; indicted April 12, same year; negro.

Taylor, Wm...Murder; committed January 28, '77; indicted April 23, same year; negro.

Johnson, Sam...Theft of hog; committed December 1, '76; indicted April 20, same year; negro.

Kent, Granville...Theft of gelding; committed July 21, '77; indicted October 18, same year; negro pracher.

Booker, John...Theft of hog; indicted December 5, '73; negro; 25 years old, weighs 140 pounds, 5 feet 6 inches high.

YOUNG COUNTY.

Lumley, John...Theft; indicted '75.

Southerland, J...Theft; indicted '75.

Cooper, J...Theft; indicted '75. Cooper is on the buffalo range, west.

Boyd, A. L...Assault with intent to murder; indicted October, '77; about 45 years old, beard on face, bald headed, small blue eyes, about 5 feet 10 inches in height, great talker.

Vandever, Robt...Assault with intent to murder; indicted October, '77; about 5½ or 6 feet high, light complexion, blue eyes, long, sandy hair, don't talk much.

WEBB COUNTY.

Schule, Irvan C. A...Theft from a house; committed April 1, '68; indicted January, '70.

Whetstone, C. A...Cattle stealing; committed June, '70; indicted December, same year.

Zito, John...Burglary; committed March, '71; indicted July, same year.

Tarnes, Angell...Burglary; committed May, '70; indicted July, '71.

Luvo, Cipriano...Assault with intent to commit murder; committed March, '72; indicted March, same year.

Gonzales, Jose Ma...Theft; committed June '72; indicted November same year.

Reina, Jacobo...Theft; committed August, '72; indicted July, '73.

Martinez, Pancho...Assault with intent to commit rape; committed November, '73; indicted March, '74.

Sanchez, Doroteo...Murder; committed July, '73; indicted March, '74.

Valdez, Filomeno...Swindling; committed February, '75; indicted March, same year.

DeOllos, Adrian...Assault with intent to commit murder; committed October, '75; indicted October, same year.

Benavides, Manuel...Theft of geldings; committed January, '76; indicted March, same year.

Arzola, Benigno...Murder; committed November, '75; indicted April, '76. In New Laredo, Mexico.

Aguirre, Librado...Assault to kill; commited November, '75; indicted April, '76.

Fisher, J. King...Theft of geldings; committed February, '76; indicted April, same year.

Guerrero, Manuel...Theft of geldings; committed March, '76; indicted April, '77.

Aldopa, Vedo...Theft of mare; committed July, '77; indicted October, same year.

BEE COUNTY.

Brown, James...Theft of money; 26 years old, dark hair, eyes and complexion, thin beard, 5 feet 8 or 9 inches high, slender, awkward appearance.

Arthur, Robt...Theft of money; 25 years old, dark complexion, medium height, slender build, $25 reward by Sheriff Walton.

11

Holly, T. J...Theft of mare; 25 years old, slight build, fair complexion, grey eyes, one of them a shade lighter than the other, and can't see out of it, Roman nose, hair dark and inclined to curl, 5 feet 10 inches in height, weight 145 pounds, tolerable fair education; under sentence to 5 years in penitentiary; $50 reward by Sheriff Walton.

Holly, W. H. H...Theft of mare; 30 years old, near 6 feet high, 150 pounds, light complexion, dark eyes and hair, brother of T. J. Holly, and both from Louisiana; $25 reward by Sheriff Walton.

Dykes, D. P. or L. P...Theft of hogs.

Phelps, J. A...Murder; 37 years old, 5 feet 10 inches high, fair complexion, light hair, large teeth, blue eyes, talks rather long, and is fond of whisky.

Buckingham, M. J...Theft of horse.

Munroe, J...Murder; mulatto, 30 years old, 5 feet 8 inches high, yellow complexion, good looking, quick spoken, 160 pounds. Last heard of in Galveston in 1876.

Dominguez, Cicere...Theft of mare.

Kay, Eli...Theft of gelding; 25 years old, 5 feet 8 inches high, dark complexion, black hair worn straight, black eyes, 165 pounds. Last heard of in Robinson county.

Bailey, Henry...Theft from house.

Yeater, Henry...Murder; 27 years old, 5 feet 10 inches high, slim built, fair complexion, getting to be heavy set.

Garrelt, A. J...Assault to kill.

Perez, Raman...Theft of gelding.

Burns, Robt...Theft of money.

Henry, Jas...Theft of colt; 20 years old, 5 feet 6 inches high, dark complexion, slim built.

Geland, Narcisso...Assault to kill.

Salero, Juan...Murder.

Tunny, Alvin...Theft of mare.

Balderos, Rafael...Theft of colt; 45 years old, 5 feet 4 inches high, black hair and eyes, weight 115 pounds; scar on mouth, some front teeth missing, speaks broken English. Mexican.

BOWIE COUNTY.

Hewitt, John W...Murder; committed October, '70; indicted October, same year; dark complexion, dark hair, about 6 feet high, rather slim built, and about 40 or 50 years old.

McCowan, John...Murder; committed February, '71; indicted June, same year. Supposed rather light or auburn hair, and some 28 or 30 years old.

Tisdale, Charles...Murder; committed February, '71; indicted June, same year. Supposed to have dark or black hair, under medium size, and about 33 years old.

Wilson, Joseph...Assault to murder; committed December, '70; indicted June, '71. White man, some 30 years old, 5 feet 9 inches high, black hair, weighs 160 pounds, pock-marked, restless and excited appearance.

Lee, H. T...Assault to murder; committed December, '70; indicted October, '71. About 5 feet 8 or 9 inches high, black hair, black eyes, weighs about 145 or 150 pounds, and is about 30 years old.

Woods, David...Assault to murder (two offenses); committed July, '71; indicted October, same year. About 5 feet 10 inches high, spare built, black hair and eyes, heavy eyebrows, and about 30 years old.

Morris, Woods...Assault to murder (two offenses); committed July, '71; indicted October, same year. About 5 feet 7 or 8 inches high, rather light hair and eyes, top of head very sharp, slender built, and about 25 years old.

Love, Louis...Hog stealing; committed January, '71; indicted June, same year. Mulatto negro, about 5 feet 9 or 10 inches high, some 45 years old, and weighs about 150 or 160 pounds.

Nanney, J. C...Assault to murder; committed July, '71; indicted October, same year. White.

Moore, S. M...Assault to murder; committed July, '72; indicted October, same year. About 35 years old, near 6 feet high, and weighs about 150 or 160 pounds. Last heard of in Lamar county, Texas.

Kitchens, Joe...Burglary; committed February, '73; indicted June, same year. White.

Weaver, Louis...Hog stealing; committed June, '75; indicted July, same year. Negro, black, some 35 years old, about 6 feet high, and rather slender built.

Garety, Pat...Assault to murder; committed March, '73; indicted June, same year. Irishman, some 45 years old, about 6 feet high, black hair and eyes, and weighs about 180 pounds. Escaped from Bowie county jail.

Alsobrook, Ned...Assault to murder; committed February, '73; indicted June, same year. Negro; last heard of in Jefferson, Texas.

Woods, Tim...Assault to kill; committed, '71; indicted, same year; 5 feet 5 inches, light hair, blue eyes, weighs 130 pounds.

Whitefield, Wash...Rape; committed December '72; indicted June, '73. Negro.

Hill, John...Hog stealing; committed April, '73; indicted June, '74. Negro, black, near 6 feet high, 28 or 30 years old, and weighs some 170 or 180 pounds. Broke Bowie county jail.

Malone, T. J...Theft from house; committed March, '74; indicted June, same year. About 5 feet 7 or 8 inches high, thin visage, dark complexion, black hair and eyes, about 25 years old, and weighs about 130 pounds.

Britton, J. H...Murder; committed May, '74; indicted June, same year. About 6 feet high, sallow complexion, auburn hair, blue eyes, weighs about 160 pounds, and is some 30 years old. Escaped Bowie county jail.

Grady, Henry...Theft of gold watch; committed April, '74; indicted July, same year. Mulatto negro, 5 feet 6 inches high, under medium size, and about 25 years old.

Smith, Steve...Assault to murder; committed February, '74; indicted July, same year. Negro, black, about 6 feet high, some 45 or 50 years old, one foot off, and walks with a crutch. Shoemaker.

Pruitt, Robert...Assault to murder; committed '74; indicted July, same year. Low heavy built, dark complexion, dark hair and eyes, and about 30 years old.

Knight, Henry...Horse stealing; committed July, '74; indicted July, same year, White, some 25 years old.

Garland, Bud...Horse stealing; committed July, '74; indicted July, same year. Negro.

Dalby, W...Assault to murder...committed July, '74; indicted July, same year. Negress, dark.

Thelps, Joseph...Hog stealing; committed November, '74; indicted February, '75.

Runnels, Ellis...Hog stealing; committed April, '75; indicted July, same year. Negro, black, about 6 feet high, rather slender, and some 35 years old; whiskers straighter than is common with negroes.

Brooks, David...Theft from house; committed November, '74; indicted February, '75. Negro, copper colored, medium size, and 18 or 20 years old. Last heard of near Paris, Texas.

Matthews, Ellison...Hog stealing; committed September, '74; indicted October, same year. Negro.

Weaver, Frank...Theft of cattle; committed September, '75; indicted November, same year. White.

Johnson, R. M. (Sheriff)...Embezzlement, swindling, etc. (three causes); committed June, '75; indicted July, same year. About 5 feet 9 inches high, some 35 or 40 years old, black curly hair, a little bald headed, whiskers a little gray, and weighs about 140 pounds. Appointed deputy sheriff of McCulloch county February, '76; arrested August, '77; gave bail, which he forfeited.

Greenhill, Allen...Assault to murder (two causes); committed June, '75; indicted July, same year. Negro.

Clements, George...Hog stealing; committed April, '75; indicted October, same year.

Johnson, Elijah...Theft of a hog; committed December, '75; indicted March, '76; negro, black, about 25 years old.

Parker, Calvin...Murder; committed '76; indicted same year; about 35 years old, weighs about 140 pounds, sandy hair and whiskers, slender built, and of a quiet, retiring appearance.

Faukner, F. M...Receiving and concealing stolen goods; committed '77; indicted same year; broke from Bowie county jail, about 30 years old, about 5 feet 11 inches high, black hair, square features, gray or black eyes, frequents saloons and billiard halls.

Wallace, Wm...Assault to murder; black hair and eyes, about 35 years old, loves whisky, is quarrelsome when drunk, about 5 feet 10 inches high, weight 140 pounds.

Walker, George...Committed '76; indicted same year; about 25 or 30 years old, weighs 145 pounds, dark hair and eyes, about 5 feet 10 inches high, has a small moustache.

Atkinson, Charles...Murder; committed '77; indicted same year; 6 feet 1 or 2 inches high, whiskers, hair and complexion red, weighs perhaps 150 pounds.

Christopher, George...Murder; committed '77; negro, copper colored.

BRAZOS COUNTY.

Hardin, John...Murder; indicted '68.

Wilson, C. C...Forgery; indicted '68.

Griffin, Wm...Theft of a mule; indicted '68.

Stanford, Jeff...Theft of a mule; indicted '68.

Perkins, L. J...Theft of a mule; indicted '68.

Gallaway, Capt...Burglary; indicted '68.

Cornnich, N. A...Embezzlement; indicted '69; said to be in Hood county.

Shields, Frank...Assault with intent to murder; indicted '69.
Shields, John...Assault with intent to murder; indicted '69.
Walker, Amos...Murder; indicted '70.
Walker, Andrew...Murder; indicted '70. (Same party indicted in Black and Walker case.)
Walker, Thos...Murder; indicted '70.
Rose, ——...Murder; indicted '70.
Courice, ——...Murder; indicted '70.
Hilburn, Robert...Murder; indicted '70.
Jones, Tom...Robbery; indicted '70.
Johnson, Jas. and Hy...Burglary; indicted '70.
Hamilton, Wm...Embezzlement; indicted '70.
Morrison, Amos...Theft of a gelding; indicted '70.
Tompkins, Wash...Burglary; indicted '70; chunky, heavy-set, black negro.
Moore, Geo...Theft of a gelding; indicted '70.
Sasser, Jas...Assault with intent to murder; indicted '70.
Miller, Vic...Assault with intent to murder; indicted '70.
Price, Geo...Assault with intent to murder; indicted '70.
Ham, Rich...Assault with intent to murder; indicted '70.
Harn, S. D...Swindling; indicted '70; small, fair complexion, light hair, conviction probable.
Harvey, F. H...Embezzlement; indicted '70; Englishman.
Price, Geo...Robbery; indicted '70.
Hines, Milton...Assault with intent to murder; indicted '70.
Heaven, Ferd...Theft of a gelding; indicted '70.
Jones, Henry...Theft of money; indicted '70.
Rodgers, Josiah...Accessory to murder; indicted '70.
Bulloch, Fanny, Murder; indicted '70; a negro woman; said to be in Mexico.
Harris, Sam...Assault with intent to murder; indicted '70; negro.
Ball, Jas...Assault with intent to murder; indicted '70.
Allard, Peter...Theft of a cow; indicted '70.
Thomas, Rodney...Theft from a house; indicted '70.
Kirk, Miles...Theft; indicted '70.
Bickham, Lewis; Theft; indicted '70; negro.
Jones, Paul...Theft; indicted '70.
Lynn, Chas...Theft; indicted '70.
Stribling, Geo...Theft; indicted '71; negro.
Glaze, Billy...Passing counterfeit money; indicted 71; white man fair complexion, ordinary size, dark hair and eyes; said to be in Northern Texas; has a family.
Robinson, Lewis...Theft; indicted '71.
Bowen, J. R...Theft of a gelding; indicted '71; below medium size, dark hair, eyes and complexion; thought to be in Louisiana.
Robertson, Thos...Robbery; indicted '71.
Huntsman, Henry...Burglary; indicted '71.
Miller, John...Theft from a house; indicted '71.
Davis, Wm...Theft of a gelding; indicted '72; negro.
Hogwood, Isaac...Theft from a house; indicted '72; negro.
Williams, Frank...Theft; indicted '72; negro.
Williams, John...Theft; indicted '72; negro.
Blackwell, Mitch...Theft; indicted '72; negro.
Lyon, W. T...Theft; indicted '72; white man, former revenue officer of this district; said to be in N. Y.

Ford, Wm...Theft from a house; indicted '72.

Uphalt, Lewis...Theft of cattle; indicted '72.

May, Mallory...Theft of an ox; indicted '72.

Foster, Chas. B...Bigamy; indicted '72. A negro preacher, dark complexion. In Louisiana or Eastern Texas.

Goldsberg, Frank...Theft; indicted '73. A German peddler.

Hearne, Thos...Swindling; indicted '73. A black negro, about 25 years old; said to be in Alabama.

Boykin, Jno...Theft of a horse; indicted '73.   A white man; said to be in West Texas.

Davis, Jno...Theft from person; indicted '73.

Prasia, Martin...Assault with intent to murder; indicted '73. A German.

Nelson, I. A...Murder; indicted '74; tall, dark complexion, dark hair and eyes; was a sewing machine agent here.

Shaw, W. M...Theft of a gelding; indicted '74.

Armbritten, Boney...Theft of a hog; indicted '74.

Scott, Jno...Burglary; indicted '74.

Robinson, Frank...Perjury; indicted '74; negro.

Brown, Jno...Theft; indicted '74; negro.

Miller, J. I...Assault with intent to murder; indicted '74.

Harrold, Thos.; and Harrold, Mary...Theft of a sack of coffee; indicted '75; negroes.

Beson, Jno...Theft of a colt; indicted '75.

Cavitt, Jack...Assault with intent to murder; indicted '75; negro.

Webber, Lewis...Theft of a watch; indicted '75; German peddler.

New, Wm. J...Assault with intent to murder; indicted '75.

Arthur, Henry...Theft; indicted '75; negro.

Anderson, Dave...Murder; indicted '75; negro man; said to be in Milam county.

Warren, Jas...Assault with intent to murder; indicted '75; tall, spare made; white man.

Dudley, J. B...Theft of mare; indicted '75; white, about 24 years old.

Batte, Jas.; Finch, M...Theft of a cow; indicted '76; white, about grown; both said to be in West Texas; both engaged in a robbery case in this county.

English, Dickson...Assault with intent to murder; indicted '76; white man, fair complexion, light hair, and said to be in West Texas.

Janks, Wiley...Assault to murder.

Johnson, Logan...Theft of a cow; indicted '76; white, about 21 years of age.

Ross, Wm...Theft of a gelding; indicted '76.

Bunger, W. G...Embezzlement; indicted '76; white, 38 years old, rather light complexion, heavy set, well proportioned man, has a family who live in Hill county.

Easters, Ike...Assault with intent to murder; indicted '76; negro.

Randle, W. H...Seriously threatening to take life; indicted '76; white, about 30 years old, good looking, black, rather curly, hair, and eyes very dark; face was powder-burned when he left.

Hall, Len...Theft of cattle; indicted '76; negro.

Vaughn, Fed...Assault with intent to murder; indicted '76; negro.

Erwin, Wm...Assault with intent to murder; indicted '76; white, 30 years of age, 6 feet tall, well built, dark hair and eyes, black moustache and beard, a doctor by profession. He is also indicted for murder in Robertson county.

McMillan, Wm...Assault with intent to rob; indicted '76; fair complexion, light beard, blue eyes, 25 years old; said to be in West Texas.

Finch, Mann; Batte, Jas...Robbery; indicted '76; both said to be in West Texas.

McNiel, Wm.; Burrows, Geo...Theft of gelding; indicted '76; Burrows is the same who murdered the Sheriff of Montgomery county.

Lattimore, Henry...Assault to murder; indicted '76; negro.

Stanley, Young...Assault to murder; indicted '76.

Taylor, Dave...Burglary; indicted '76.

Hoag, Antony...Assault with intent to murder; indicted '76; negro.

Taylor, Major...Theft; indicted '76; negro.

Hamilton, Robt...Murder; indicted '76; a dark negro, about grown; medium size, and somewhere on the International railroad, between Hearne and Palestine.

Williams, Chas...Theft of a gelding; indicted '76; negro.

Williams, Henry...Theft from house; indicted '76; negro.

Washington, Henry...Theft of a cow; indicted '76; negro.

Bedgood, J. M...Assault with intent to murder; indicted '76.

Williams, Lum...Assault with intent to rob; indicted '76.

Hicks, Lush...Assault with intent to murder; indicted '76; negro.

Smiley, Munroe...Theft of money; indicted '76; a small, black, chunky negro, about 40 years old.

Courtney, Sam.; Hicks, Frank...Swindling; indicted '76; both negroes, and were working on the H. & T. C. R. R.

Windling, —...Theft of a hog; indicted '76.

Davis, Aaron...Assault with intent to murder.

Thomas, Isaiah...Murder; a negro of copper color, about 5 feet 9 inches high; said to be near Gonzales.

Goodright, Dr. Wm. H...Theft of a horse.

Pilet, Warren...Theft of a gun; a negro, about 18 years old.

Reeves, Joseph...Rape; a chunky negro; said to be in Waller county.

Evans, Berry...Assault with intent to murder; negro.

Oats, Willis...Murder; negro.

Jones, Wesley...Embezzlement; negro.

Goodwin, John...Theft of neat cattle; the same for whom the Governor has offered a reward for murder in Hamilton county.

EASTLAND COUNTY.

Turnan, Jack...Assault with intent to murder; committed August 15, '76; indicted August 20, same year; is about 6 feet high, well built.

Mansker, P. C...Theft from a house; committed May 14, '76; indicted August, 10, same year; red complexion, about 30 years old.

Tanzey, Marion...Theft of a gelding; committed March 4, '76; indicted August 8, same year; below medium height, very light complexion, light hair, about 22 or 23 years old.

Straum, Thos...Assault with intent to murder; committed July 20, '76; indicted August 10, same year.

Townsend, ———...Murder; committed July 4, '75; indicted November 9, same year.

Hines, M. M...Murder; indicted November 9, '75.

Hines, L. M...Murder; indicted November 9, '75.

John, Henry...Theft from a house; indicted November 9, '75.

Grounds, Dock...Assault with intent to kill; indicted November 5, '75.

Moore, Jessie...Theft of cattle; committed March 6, '75; indicted March, same year.

Gillam, Wm...Theft of gelding; committed May 1, '74; indicted June 5, same year.

Ford, ———...Theft of gelding; committed September 4, '74; indicted November 5, same year.

Moody, George...Assault with intent to murder; committed July 1, '74; indicted November 5, same year.

Thompson, Henry...Assault with intent to murder; committed June 3, '75; indicted June 3, same year.

Atwood, ———...Theft of yearling; indicted June 2, '77.

Ester, David...Theft of mare, and assault with intent to murder (two cases); indicted June 21, '77; about 30 years old, light thin hair, light whiskers, rather large gray eyes, about 5 feet 9 inches high, talks hurriedly, is very familiar, a braggadocio, a villain of the first-class.

Olney, W. W...Swindling; indicted June 21, '77.

Hale, H. N...Embezzlement (two cases); indicted June 21, '77.

GRAYSON COUNTY.

Breedlove, George...Assault to murder; committed July, '73; indicted July, same year.

Evans, Berry...Threat to take life; committed October, '74; indicted November, same year.

DeGraffenreid, S...Assault to murder; committed July, '75; indicted July, same year.

Holmes, R. T...Assault to murder; committed March, '75; indicted March, same year.

Hatley, Wm...Assault to murder; committed November, '75; indicted March, '76.

Jarvis, M...Assault to murder; committed March, '76; indicted March, same year.

Shields, Wm...Assault to murder; committed April, '74; indicted July, same year.

Sims, John...Assault to murder; committed June, '76; indicted July same year.

Short, Ed...Murder; committed November '75; indicted November, same year.

Roberts, E. H...Assault to murder; committed February, '75; indicted March, same year.

Oglesby, J. P...Swindling; committed January, '75; indicted March, same year.

McNight, A...Assault to murder; committed November, '74; indicted March, same year.

Watson, M...Theft of steer; committed May, '75; indicted November, same year.

Watkins, A...Assault to murder; committed December, '75; indicted March, '76.

Vanalstyne, J. T...Theft of gelding; committed January, '73; indicted July, '76.

Cavenaugh, John...Murder; committed May, '73; indicted June, same year.

Ward, H. L...Theft of gelding; committed July, '73; indicted September, same year.

Chase, Joseph...Murder; committed February, '69; indicted February, same year.

Crocker, Jack...Murder; committed March, '74; indicted March, same year.

Stevens, Thomas,...Murder; committed February 24, '77; indicted March 27, same year.

Thompson, James...Murder; committed November 28, '76; indicted March 28, '77.

Patton, George...Assault to murder; committed December 5, '76; indicted March 15, '77.

McNeal, Jno. T...Assault to murder; committed December 10, '76; indicted April 14, '77.

Roan, Frank...Assault to murder; committed December 25, '76; indicted March 15, '77.

Sloan, Doss...Assault to murder; committed December 15, '76; indicted March 30, '77.

Glover, A. C...Swindling; committed October 8, '76; indicted April 21, '77.\

Godfrey, Samuel...Robbery; committed December 22, '76; indicted March 27, 77.

Godfrey, George...Robbery; committed December 22, '76; indicted March 27, '77.

Parsons, Z. L...Embezzlement; committed March 25, '77; indicted April 11, same year.

Yates, Joseph...Theft of mare; committed January 15, '75; indicted April 14, '77.

Thompson, Richard...Theft of cow; committed January 10, '77; indicted March 21, same year.

Mann, John...Theft; committed January 15, '77; indicted May 24, same year.

Thompson, Doc...Theft; committed January 15, '77; indicted May 24, same year.

Carter, S. M., alias Bryant, J. W...Theft of mule; committed April 21, '77; indicted May 23, same year.

Brown, M. C...Murder; committed July 5, '73; indicted September 13, same year.

Armstrong, J. N...Murder; committed July 5, '73; indicted September 13, same year.

Hawkins, Marion...Rape; committed August 4, '77; indicted September 20, same year.

Booer, John...Assault to murder; committed September 7, '77; indicted September 20, same year.

Tate, Thomas...Theft of gelding; committed April 26, '77; indicted October 16, same year.

Hardy, William...Bigamy; committed November 21, '76; indicted '77.

Savage, William A...Assault to murder; committed December 11, '75; indicted October 17, '77.

Anderson, George...Theft of gelding; committed June 15, '77; indicted September 24, same year.

Wollens, J. S...Passing forged order; committed November 27, '77; indicted October 9, same year.

Newcome, Robert...Assault to murder; committed August 12, '77; indicted September 24, same year.

Richards, Trass...Theft of cattle; committed April 1, '77; indicted October 13, same year.

Richards, Wesley...Assault to murder; committed October 7, '77; indicted October 13, same year.

Brooks, Henry...Theft of mare; committed March 1, '77; indicted October 9, same year.

Hays, George...Theft of mare; committed March 1, '77; indicted October 9, same year.

Carlton, Leonard...Murder; committed February 10, '74; indicted October 10, '77.

Carlton, Mat...Murder; committed February 10, '74; indicted October 10, '77.

Weeks, Fursen...Murder; committed February 10, '74; indicted October 10, '77.

McGlothlin, John...Theft of mare; committed July 5, '77; indicted September, 22, same year.

Saunders, Dick...Theft of mare; committed October 1, '76; indicted October 16, '77.

Terrill, Dave...Theft of mare and mules; committed June 28, '77; indicted October 13, same year.

Campbell, Brandon...Theft of hogs; committed June 15, '77; indicted October 16, same year.

Vaughn, John...Theft of hogs; committed June 15, '77; indicted October 16, same year.

KIMBLE COUNTY.

Caught Cathey, Lewis...Murder; committed April 16, '77.

Killed Dublin, Richard...Murder; committed April 16, '74; indicted same year; also indicted for theft of cattle in three cases.

Elliott, John...Theft.

Mason, Jas. P...Murder of Rance Moore.

Killed Reynolds, Stark...Theft of a gelding.

MASON COUNTY.

Killed Baird, John...Murder; indicted May, '77; about 5 feet 8 inches high, 28 years old, fair complexion, spare built. *Reward $500*

Faulkner, R. C.; Williams, Nat.; and Wilder, Charles...Theft of beef; indicted November, '76.

Faulconer, Thomas...Murder, also assault with intent to murder; indicted July 8, '72; 20 years old, dark complexion, small in size.

Ake, John...Theft of cattle; indicted May 17, '77.

RAINES COUNTY.

Hampton, S. A...Assault to kill; committed September 1, '70; indicted March 22, '71.

Case, Wm...Burglary and robbery; committed May, '72; indicted July, same year; tall, slender, blue eyes, light hair, 30 years old, weight 140 pounds, quick spoken.

Burns, Sam...Theft of cattle; committed July '71; indicted November, same year; tall, slender, blue eyes, light hair, 40 years old, weight 150 pounds, in Denton county.

Tollett, Sam...Murder; committed September, '72; indicted November, same year; negro, 5 feet 10 inches high, weighs 160 pounds, quick spoken, bad countenance.

Slatter, Fred...Theft of a horse; committed June, '72; indicted November, same year; light hair and complexion, blue eyes, 5 feet 7 inches high, weighs 140 pounds, supposed to be in the Nation.

Byford, Wesley...Assault to kill; committed September, '72; indicted July, '73.

Holmesley, M. F...Murder; committed December, '72; indicted July, '73; 5 feet 7 inches high, weighs 150 pounds, blue eyes, auburn hair, in Western Texas.

Bray, A. J...Murder; committed May, 75; indicted July, same year; 24 years old, dark hair, eyes and complexion, weighs 150 pounds, supposed to be in Waco.

McFadden, J. N...Murder; committed June, '75; indicted July, same year.

Ivy, Lee; Ivy, Marion; and Shoemake, Joe...Theft of a steer; committed October, '74; indicted November, same year; all of them about 22 years old; the two Ivys have dark hair and eyes; the other has blue eyes.

Tutt, Ben...Assault to kill; committed February, '75; indicted March, same year; 5 feet 8 inches high, dark hair and eyes, weight 135 pounds, 25 years old.

Calhoun, Levi...Theft of cattle; committed January, '75; indicted March, same year; tall and slender, rather stooped shoulders, 35 years old, blue eyes, auburn hair.

Moss, Pinkney...Theft of hogs; committed December, '73; indicted March, '75.

Adams, P. A...Incest; committed June, '75; indicted July, same year; 5 feet 10 inches high, blue eyes, very light hair and complexion, stooped shoulders and pox-marked.

Parker, Joe...Assault to kill; committed April, '76; indicted June, same year; 5 feet 10 inches high, blue eyes, heavy set, light hair, 175 pounds, quick spoken.

Taylor, Floyd...Rape and perjury; committed January, '77; indicted March, same year; 5 feet 11 inches high, blue eyes, auburn hair, light complexion, rather downcast look, 145 pounds.

McCullar, E...Theft of hogs; committed January, '77; indicted April, same year; 45 years old, 6 feet high, rather stooped, blue eyes, auburn hair, down look, spare made, 140 pounds.

Campbell, Henry...Rape; convicted and appealed to Supreme Court, and escaped pending appeal; negro, 5 feet 4 inches high, chunky, 150 pounds, bad looking, don't talk plainly.

Anderson, Ralph...Theft of saddle; committed September, '77; indicted September, same year; tall, slender rawboned negro, 30 years old, quick spoken.

McDaniel, John...Theft of cattle; committed May, '75; indicted July, same year; 25 years old, 5 feet 10 inches high, black hair and eyes; near Fort Griffin.

REFUGIO COUNTY.

Griffin, Henry, alias Bully...Murder; committed May, '68; indicted February, '69. Black, heavy set, 5 feet 10 inches high, weighs 180 pounds, 31 years old.

Randolph, L. B...Indicted February, '70. White, 5 feet 11 inches high, light complexion, weighs 170 pounds.

McGrew, Burrell...Murder; indicted May, '72. Dark mulatto, 5 feet 9 inches high, 46 years old, weighs 160 pounds, heavy, stout build, scar on jaw, stoppage in his speech, middle finger of one hand gone, impudent, and quick in movements and speech.

Andres, Charles...Theft of horse and murder. Supposed to be an American.

Cortez, Ellervardo...Theft of gelding; indicted October, '73.

Castillo, Severo...Instigating murder. Is 23 years old, 5 feet 11 inches high, straight, squarely built, head slightly thrown back, rather fidgety appearance when walking, and light complexion for a Mexican, dark hair and eyes, large mouth, talks loud, short square chin, likes to dress well.

Saldanio, Elijo...Murder. Is 21 years old, low, heavy set, 5 feet high, very dark, Roman nose very crooked, cross, wild appearance, looks furtively at another, weighs 150 pounds, broad full face, little to say unless spoken to, speaks slow, dresses rough, and rough appearance.

Amien, Pedro...Murder; indicted May, '75. Very bow-legged, 5 feet high, ruptured.

Flores, Andres...Theft of saddle; indicted May, '74.

Ridgeway, Willis...Theft of cattle (14 indictments); indicted May, '73. Is 26 years old, 6 feet high, weighs 190 pounds, round build, elegant form, upper lip tolerably short and a little curled, may be detected on his countenance, brown hair. His mother married J. N. Huddlestone, " Old Newt," of bad reputation.

Ridgeway, Matt...Theft of cattle (14 indictments); indicted May, '73. Is 27 years old, square built, large limbs, weighs 185 pounds, 5 feet 10 inches high, red complexion and hair, eyebrows and eyelids white, blue eyes, round face, lips tolerably short and thick, and appear rolled up, dull intellect, reserved.

Edwards, H. C...Theft of cattle (14 indictments); indicted May, '73.

SAN AUGUSTINE COUNTY.

Morris, ——...Murder; indicted October 5, '64. Negro; is in Harris county.

Miller, Robert F...Murder; indicted October 5, '74. Generally said to be in the State of Missouri; so informed by private letter.

Alexander, Squire...Murder; indicted October 10, '66. Said to be in Louisiana.

Levi, Washington...Murder; indicted October 10, '66. Said to be in Louisiana.

Jourdan ——...Murder; indicted October 10, '66. Negro; said to be in Louisiana.

Broocks, Reuben...Murder; indicted October 10, '69. Said to be in Louisiana.

Cullen, Henry...Assault to murder; indicted August 28, '68. Negro; left the State.

Garrett, Richard...Forgery; indicted September 1, '68. Negro.

Nethery, William...Murder; indicted March 4, 70. Fled to Palo Pinto county.

Flournoy, Mitch...Rape; indicted March 4, '70.

Farrow, Aaron; Baker, Geo (negroo,)...Arson; indicted March 9, '70. fled to Louisiana, Nachitoches parish.

Stanley, Marshall...Assault to murder; indicted February 9, '71. Negro; lives, or supposed to be near Hempstead. Notorious horse thief.

Garrett, Harry...Assault to murder; indicted June 13, '71. Negro; in Louisiana.

Rushing, James...Theft of a horse and bigamy; indicted February 16, '72; Fled to Northern Texas.

Perkins, Edmond...Theft of a hog; indicted October 17, '73. Negro; in Shelby county.

Gamble, Dick...Theft of a hog; indicted February 10, '74. Negro; fled to Louisiana.

Jones, Zack...Perjury; indicted February 11, '74. Negro; in Louisiana.

Davis, Hiram...Theft of a hog; indicted February, '74; fled to Louisiana.

Mintloe, Jourdan...Murder of a woman; indicted February 11, '74; negro; in Louisiana,

Goodwin, J. B...Theft of a horse; indicted October 16, '74; said to be in Limestone county.

Wallis, Frank P...Robbery; indicted October 16, '74; lives in Fayette county.

Gamble, Richard...Murder; indicted December 2, '74; negro; fled to Louisiana.

Stanley, Adam...Threat to take life; indicted December 2, 74; negro; believed to be in Van Zandt county.

Saunders, G. W...Selling mortgaged property; indicted December 2, '74; said to live in Milam county.

Busby, Daniel...Selling mortgaged property; indicted December 2, '74; said to be in Limestone or Freestone county.

Smith, P. H.; Palvadore, Nick (convict)...Theft of hogs; indicted March 26, '75.

Allen, James...Theft; indicted August 6, '75; supposed to be in Louisiana.

SAN PATRICIO COUNTY.

McDonald, John...Murder; indictment found October 15, '59.

Pratt, Joseph...Assault with intent to kill; indictment found April, 30, 1868.

Curtis, W. H...Assault with intent to murder; indictment found October 30, '73.

Bass, George (colored)...Theft of a gelding; indictment found May, 29, '74; sentenced to the Penitentiary from Goliad county and escaped from Huntsville.

WILSON COUNTY.

Garza, Miguel...Theft of a gelding; committed February 1, '65; indicted May 31, '67; Mexican.

Peralles, Silverio...Assault with intent to murder ; committed September 4, '70 ; indicted March 27, '72.

Hines, John...Theft of gelding ; committed November 1, '71 ; indicted March 29, '72.

Thomas, Henderson...Theft of a mare ; committed December 1, '71 ; indicted July 25, '72 ; about 20 years old, about 5 feet 6 inches high, dark complexion, dark wavy hair, high cheek bones, and is quick spoken.

Martin, Pedro...Theft of a cow ; committed October 30, '72 ; indicted November 29, same year.

Elkins, Lucien...Murder ; committed July 1, '72 ; indicted July 29, '73.

Montgomery, Cato...Burglary ; committed May 15, '73 ; indicted July 31, same year ; black negro, about 6 feet high, about 23 years old, quick spoken, and generally very impudent, weighs 180 pounds.

Williams, Jacob...Assault with intent to murder ; committed November 10, '73 ; indicted November 25, same year ; negro.

Holstein, Henry...Assault with intent to murder ; committed August 22, '73 ; indicted November 27, same year ; light complexion, sandy hair, about 5 feet 8 inches high, about 23 or 24 years old, weighs about 130 or 140 pounds,

Johnson, Henry...Theft of cow ; committed January 1, '74 ; indicted March 27, same year ; negro.

Williams, Jake...Theft of a gelding ; committed March 22, '74 ; indicted March 27, same year ; negro.

Orono, Albino...Theft of a cow ; committed April 5, '74 ; indicted July 30, same year ; Mexican.

Orono, Marin...Theft of cow ; committed April 5, '74 ; indicted July 30, same year ; Mexican.

Gutierres, Francisco...Theft of mule ; committed April 1, '74 ; indicted November 25, same year ; Mexican.

Robbins, G. D...Theft of beef steer ; committed April 1, '74 ; indicted November 28, same year ; light complexion, about 25 or 30 years old, about 5 feet 6 inches high, weighs about 140 pounds, said to be in Bandera county, or in or near Creed Taylor's Ranch, on prong of Llano river.

Edwards, Jas...Theft of gelding ; committed September 2, '74 ; indicted November 28, same year.

Jimenes, Jose Ma...Theft of a gelding ; committed January 15, '75 ; indicted March 29, same year ; Mexican.

Garcia, Jose Ma...Murder ; committed June 17, '75 ; indicted July 30, same year ; Mexican.

Gonzales, Luciano, and Cembranes, Francisco...Theft of a gelding ; committed July 4, '75 ; indicted July 30, same year ; Mexican.

Sutton, Frank...Murder ; committed November 18, '75 ; indicted November 25, same year ; sallow complexion, about 6 feet 2 or 3 inches high, very slender, light hair, small blue eyes, slow spoken. When last heard from was in Gonzales county.

Owens, W...Assault with intent to murder ; committed February 20, '76 ; indicted June 6, same year.

Moore, S...Assault with intent to murder ; committed February 20, '76 ; indicted June 6, same year.

Taylor, Jas...Theft of gelding ; committed August, '76 ; indicted December, same year.

Kimble, Bud...Murder ; indicted June, '77.

Gonzales, Andres...Theft of cattle; indicted June, '77; tall, light complexion, slow of motion.

Escobedo, Nicolas...Theft of cattle; indicted June, '77.

SHACKELFORD COUNTY.

Statecap, Wesley...Theft of mule; committed August, '74; indicted June, '75; 22 years old, 5 feet 7 inches high, round face, hair and complexion light, eyes same, obtusive countenance, very little beard.

Harris, Jack...Assault with intent to kill; committed October, '75; indicted November 19, '75.

Harden, Francis...Assault with intent to murder; committed April, '76; indicted May, same year; 45 years old, 5 feet 5 inches high, hair and complexion dark, clean shaved, saddler by trade.

Durham, Harvey...Murder; committed November, '76; indicted May, same year; 30 years old, weighs 125 pounds, complexion and eyes light, physique slim, features sharp, sanguine temperament. Last heard of in Arkansas.

Oglesby, Jas...Murder; committed December, '75; indicted May, '76; 6 feet high, weighs 160 or 170 pounds, black hair, either dark or blue eyes, carries heard on one side from wound in the neck, one-fourth or one-eight Indian, nose large and very red, wears moustache. Last heard of in Fort Smith, Arkansas. Well acquainted in the Indian Territory.

McKinney, R. B. E...Theft of cattle; committed May, '76; indicted October, same year.

Martin, Wm. A. (commonly known as Hurricane Bill)...Assaut with intent to murder; committed June, '76; indicted October, same year; 6 feet high, well proportioned, light hair, blue eyes, fine looking, weighs probably 100, face rather sharp, fine address, usually well dressed.

Aulthouse, Jas...Theft of gelding; committed February, '75; indicted June, '75; 21 years.

White, Jas...Murder; indicted October, 76; 55 years old, 6 feet high weighs 170 pounds, top of head bald, iron grey hair and whiskers, dark eyes; buffalo hunter. Last heard of in Northwest range of Texas.

Foster, Jas...Theft of gelding; committed December, 76; indicted April, '77.

Reed, Chas...Murder; committed January, '77; indicted April, same year; 25 years of age, weight 145 pounds, 5 feet 8 inches high, black hair and eyes, harbored by Millet Bros., cattle men,

Nance, Jas...Murder; committed April, '77; indicted April, same year.

Walker, Nolan, alias Walker, Jas, alias Walker, Notton...Theft of gelding; committed March, 77; indicted April 77; medium height, lost one or two front teeth, shot in the arm with buckshot; last heard of in Grayson county.

Taylor, Geo...Robbery; committed April, '77; indicted October, same year.

Owens, ——...Theft of cattle; committed February, '77; indicted April, same year.

Clay, George; and H. Kahn...Forgery; committed August, '77; indicted October, same year. Clay is 6 feet high, well built, inclined to be corpulent, dark hair and eyes, wears a moustache, scar on his face, has a wife living in Parker or adjoining county; last heard of in Fort Worth.

Kahn is a Jew, 5 feet, 8 inches high, slim build, no whiskers, light complexion, dark eyes; last heard of in Fort Worth; has relatives living in Dallas, (Kahn Bros.,) doing business there.

Jones, L. J...Theft; committed December, '76; indicted October, '77.

Hardee, W...Murder; committed April, '77; indicted October, same year; aggravated case; last heard from on the Wichita river with a cow herd.

Wallack, Julius...Forgery; committed June, '77; indicted October, same year; 5 feet 5 inches high, weighs 145 pounds, wears moustache and goatee, black hair and eyes; Jew; supposed to be in Germany.

Hightower, W....Theft of cattle; committed June, '77; indicted October, same year; 28 or 30 years old, dark hair and eyes, features sharp, sluggish expression; previous residence in Hood county; has a family; last heard of in Tarrant county.

TRAVIS COUNTY.

Alexander, Aurora...Murder; committed November, '66; indicted same year.

Goen, ——...Murder; committed August '68; indicted same year.

Carpenter, Mrs. Ara, and J. H....Murder; committed September, '68; indicted same year.

Bryant, C. W...Assault to rape; committed January, '69; indicted March, same year.

Gatlin, ——...Theft of beef steer; committed October, '68; indicted March, '69.

Hamilton, Jim...Murder; committed October, '68; indicted March, '69.

Neal, J. M...Theft of neat cattle; committed April, '69; indicted, same year.

Moore, Charley...Theft of a mare; committed September, '70; indicted October, same year.

Lane David...Theft of steer; committed May, '70; indicted October, same year.

Losson, Wm...Theft of steer; committed June, '70; indicted October, same year.

Allen, Geo. W...Swindling; committed September, '70; indicted October, same year.

Barnes, Thos...Resisting an officer with arms; committed September, '70; indicted October, same year.

Miller, ——...Swindling; committed November, '70; indicted February, '71.

Kenner, Peter...Theft of harness; committed November, '70; indicted February, '71.

Wimberly, Ezekiel...Assault to murder; committed October, '70; indicted February, '71.

Caviness, Pole...Theft of an ox; committed August, '70; indicted June, '71.

Davis, Andrew...Theft of cow; committed March, '71; indicted June, same year.

Gage, George...Theft of cow; committed March, '71; indicted June, same year.

Leggett, Wells W...Bribery; committed November, '71; indicted February, '72.

Kellow, Jas...Murder; indicted February, '72.

Clark, Wm...Murder; committed May, '72; indicted June, same year.

Schubart, Wm., alias Byfield, Wm...Murder; committed April, '72; indicted June, same year.

Barefoot, Isaac D., alias Byfield, James...Assault to murder; committed May, '72; indicted June, same year.

Glasscock, Wm...Assault to murder; committed February, '72; indicted June, same year.

Piper, Bill...Theft of cattle; committed May, '72; indicted June, same year.

Blair, Thos...Theft of gelding; committed May, '72; indicted June, same year.

Kirk, Jas...Theft of gelding; committed May, '72; indicted June, same year.

Ishner, Zacharias....Assault to kil,; committed June, '72; indicted June, same year.

Mahony, Jack, alias Geo. Mahoney...Assault to kill; commited Aug., '72; indicted October, same year.

Rains, Tom...Theft of stallion; committed August, '72; indicted October, same year.

Black, Chas...Theft of gold watch and chain; committed August, '72; indicted October, same year. Negro.

Butler, Ben...Theft from a house; committed February, '73; indicted February, same year.

Bennis, Harry, alias Wild Harry...Theft from a house; committed February, '73; indicted February, same year.

Davidson, Gen. Jas...Embezzlement (three cases); theft of carbines (two cases); committed October, September and August, '72; indicted February, '73.

Martin, Robert...Passing forged document; committed August, '72; indicted June, '73.

Kessee, Thos...Passing forged document; committed October, '72; indicted June, '73.

Stone, Al...Theft of a mare; committed April, '73; indicted June, same year.

Galloway...Theft of a mare; committed April, '73; indicted June, same year.

Robinson, Eugene...Swindling; committed December, '72; indicted October, '73.

Auterass, Jose...Theft of gelding; committed January, '74; indicted February, same year. Mexican.

Fuller, Jas...Theft of gelding; committed June, '74; indicted February, same year.

Davis, Thos...Theft of mare; committed December, '73; indicted February, '74. Negro.

Ezelle, D. M...Theft of steer; committed August, '73; indicted February, '74.

Evy, John...Theft of steer; committed August, '73; indicted February, '74.

Cox...Theft of steer; committed August, '73; indicted February, '74.

Garner, Alfred...Perjury; committed September, '73; indicted February, '74.

Coleman, Andrew...Theft from house; committed November, '72; indicted February, '74.

12

Hill...Theft of gelding; committed May, '74; indicted June, same year.

Johnson, Isaiah, alias Jim Johnson...Theft from house; committed June, '74; indicted June, same year.

Stewart, B. K...Perjury; committed May, '74; indicted June, same year.

Larsen, N. P...Swindling; committed November, '73; indicted June, '74.

Green, W. H....Forgery (two cases); committed November, '73, and January, '74; indicted June, '74.

Duff, Ed. F...Embezzlement; committed August, '74; indicted October, same year.

Johnson, Thos...Theft from house; committed September, '74; indicted October, same year.

Wynn, P. W...False swearing; committed July, '73; indicted October, '74. Uttering forged document (two cases); committed September, '74; indicted October, same year.

Cree, Thos...Uttering forged promissory note; committed October, '74 indicted October, same year.

Middleton, Sam...Assault to kill; committed July, '74; indicted October, same year.

Swipes, Jacob...Theft from house; committed September, '74; indicted October, same year.

Burns, Jas. A...Theft of gelding; committed October, '74; indicted October, same year.

Ruble, Montgomery...Theft of gelding; committed January, '74; indicted October, same year.

Morgan, Isaac...Theft of gelding; committed September, '74; indicted October, same year.

Ames, John...Assault to kill; committed January, '75; indicted February, same year.

Woods, J. M., and S. W...Theft from house; committed January, '75; indicted February, same year.

House, Jas...Murder; committed February, '75; indicted February, same year.

Daniels, Dan...Murder; committed February, '75; indicted February, same year.

Benton, Wm...Theft of work oxen; committed October, '72; indicted February, '75.

Finlay, —...Theft from house; committed December, '74; indicted February, '75.

Smith, Jim...Robbery; committed December, '74; indicted February, '75.

Thomas, John...Receiving a bribe; committed July, '74; indicted February, '75.

Huddlerton...Theft of a cow; committed December, '74; indicted February, '75.

Lazy, Jim...Theft of a cow; committed December, '74; indicted February, '75.

Cain, Jim...Assault to murder; committed June, '75; indicted February, same year. Negro.

Matthewson, Frank...Theft of gelding; committed January, '75; indicted February, same year.

Van Welde, Julius, alias New York John...Theft of gelding; committed June, '75; indicted February, same year.

Roberts, Buck...Theft of gelding; committed May, '75; indicted February, same year.

Walker, George...Theft of gelding; committed June, '75; indicted February, same year.

Matthews, E. C., alias " Crist " Matthews...Theft of bull calf; committed April, 75; indicted February, same year.

Powers, John P...Assault to kill; committed April, '75; indicted February, same year.

Monroe, John...Assault to kill; committed April, '75; indicted February, same year.

Chepman, Jim, alias Jim Pease....Theft from house; committed February, '75; indicted February, same year; negro.

Hamilton, Bob....Theft f gelding; committed April, '75; indicted February, same year.

Mitchell, John, and Mary....Theft of gelding; committed May, '75 indicted February, same year.

Durst, Mat. T...Theft of a mare and colts; committed April, '74; indicted February, '75.

Brown, Wm....Adultery; committed October, '74; indicted February, 1875.

Clark, Mrs. Wm...Adultery; committed October, '74; indicted February, '75.

Griffin, John...Assault to rape; committed April, '75; indicted June, same year.

Wardlow, T. D...Embezzlement; assault to kill (2 cases); robbery; committed April and July, '75; indicted June, same year.

Davis, Warren...Theft of gelding; committed October, '74; indicted June, '75.

Brown, Joe...Theft of hog; committed June, '75; indicted June, same year.

Crawford, Tom...Theft of heifer; committed May, '75; indicted June, same year.

Williams, Lewis...Assault to kill; committed July, '75; indicted June, same year.

Framen, John, and Joseph...Murder; committed September, '75; indicted October, same year.

Brittain, L. G...Theft of steer; committed August, '75; indicted October, same year.

Britton, G. L...Theft of mules; committed August, 75; indicted October, same year.

Leach...Assault to murder; committed November, '75; indicted February, '76.

Harris, Martin...Assault to murder; committed January, '76; indicted February, same year. Assault to kill; committed June, '75; indicted February, '75.

Cook, Henry...Theft from a house; committed November, '76; indicted February, '77.

Rueger, Theodore....Murder; committed January, '76; indicted February, same year.

Golden, John ..Assault to kill; committed October, '75; indicted February, '76.

Townsley, Webb...Assault to kill; committed October, '75; indicted February, '76.

Bates...Theft of a wagon; committed January, '76; indicted February, same year.

Peter, Tic...Theft of gelding; committed January, '76; indicted February, same year.

Smith, Bill...Burglary; committed February, '76; indicted February, same year.

Stroud, Jas...Theft of steer; committed January, '76; indicted February, same year.

Gage, George F...Embezzlement; committed February, '76; indicted February, same year.

Beers, Minnie...Theft of money; committed November, '75; indicted February, '76.

Garland...Assault to kill; committed December, '75; indicted February, '76.

Esmund, J. H...Murder.

Edwards, C. W...Murder.

Graham, Jessie...Murder.

Carpenter, Wm...Murder.

Chamberlain, A...Murder.

Martin, John...Murder.

Whittington, Wm...Theft.

O'Brien, D. J...Theft.

Wells, Bill...Theft.

Scott, John...Assault to kill.

Kelson, Bart...Theft.

Murphy, Reuben...Theft.

Sullivan, J. J...Assault to kill.

Barrett, W. H...Bigamy.

Bateman, V...Theft.

Horst, Geo...Theft.

Mattison, M. J...Perjury.

Williams, Sam...Theft.

Kissam, Webb...Burglary.

Seimers, F...Theft.

McGinness, Bill...Theft.

Fields, John...Theft.

McLeary, Henry...Assault to kill

McDonald, John...Kidnapping.

Carpenter, Geo.; and Robinson, Wm...Murder.

Elliott, L. C...Assault to kill.

Williams, John D.; and Johnson, Dick...Murder.

Dooling, Bud...Assault to kill.

Freeman, Billy...Murder.

Scroggins, Alf...Assault to kill.

Forales, Grancincio...Theft.

Hamilton, R. R...Swindling.

Ruby, Geo...Murder.

Golden, John...Theft.

Dow, James...Assault to kill.

Sneed, Bill...Theft.

Franklin, Geo...Theft.

Owens, Wm...Assault to kill.

Montgomery, Jas....Counterfeiting money.

Tague, ——...Counterfeiting money.

Brady, Wm....Assault to rape.

Hearne, C. C...Forgery.

White, Frank....Assault to kill.
Houston, Isaac...Theft.
Cottingham, P....Theft.
Milam, Geo....Assault to kill.
Hearne, James....Assault to kill.
Stockman, John....Assault to kill.
Henderson, Chas....Theft.
Barnett, Geo....Murder.
Terrell, G. A...Swindling.
Henderson, Walter...Theft.

REWARDS OFFERED BY THE GOVERNOR.

Baltzell, Wm...Murder; Februaay 7, '74 ; Gonzales county, $500.
Cotton, Mitchell...Murder; February 24, '74; Limestone county, $750.
Morris, Wm. H...Allowing escape of prisoner; March 5, '74; McLennan county, $250.
Dickerson, N. T...Marder; March 14, '74; Kaufman county, $500.
Stokes, Jos.; Stokes, Wm.; Cooper, Thos...March 17, '74; Assault to murder; Bandera county, $150 each.
Fleming, Alfred; Vance, Thomas...Theft of horses, etc.; March 18, '74; Washington county, $100 each.
Gentry, Chas...Murder; March 26, '74; Parker county, $500.
Stage Robbers...Robbing mail and passengers; April 8, '74; Travis county, $1000 each.
Gustine, Jack, alias Woods...Murder; April 13, '74; San Jacinto county, $250.
Long, Wm...Murder; April 17, '74 ; Madison county, $250.
Purvis, John...Murder; Madison county, $250.
Wilkerson, Allen...Murder; April 20, '74; Grimes county, $250.
Cline, Joseph...Murder; May 9, '74; Orange county, $250.
Unknown murderer of Dr. White; May 14, '74; Grayson county, $500.
Parker, Joseph...Murder; May 23, '74; Hunt county, $100.
Unknown murderers of J. B. Scobee; Milam county, $250 each.
Unknown parties burning Madison county Courthouse; June 16, '74; Madison county, $500.
Tucker, Sim...Murder; June 17, '74; Caldwell county, $150.
Gulbreth, M. C...Murder; June 17, '74; Bosque county, $250.
Irwin, John...Murder; June 18, '74; Washington county, $200.
Unknown murderers of Jas. P. Farmer...June 23, '74; Brazos county, $250.
Jones, Hugh...Murder; June 27 '74 ; Red River county, $150.
Gustine, Jack, alias Jack Woods...Murder; April 13, '74; San Jacinto county, $250.

Hamilton, Mack...Murder; July 14, '74; Johnson county, $250.

Lackey, John or Jake; Lackey, Joel...Theft of mule; July 15, '74; Fannin county, $150 each.

Murderers of Joe Beck and Mrs. Wolf...July 29, '74; Bexar county, $500.

Shadden, A. A.; Shadden, Wm.; Shadden, Joseph; Shadden, Hans; Shankle, James...Murder; August 3, '74; Rusk county, $300 each.

King, Dick...Murder; August 14, '74; Fayette county, $200.

Williams, T. J...Murder; Wise county, $250.

Unknown parties burning Mrs. A. Jones' stables...August 29, '74; Fayette county, $1000.

Washington, Alfred...Murder; September 8, '74; Grimes county, $250.

McMillor, Neil...Murder; September 9, '74; Madison county, $500.

Shelton, Ed...Murder; September 21, '74; Guadalupe county, $350.

Armitage, Henry...Murder; September 24, '74; Madison county, $500.

Yates, Joseph...Murder; September 25, '74; Lamar county, $250.

Linson, Tom...Murder; October 10, '74; Bell county, $500.

Stone, John...Murder; October 15, '74; Dallas county, $250.

Jones, Z. F...Murder; October 21, '74; Collin county, $500.

Culver, A., alias Jones...Murder; November 14, '74; Bastrop county, $250.

Unknown murderer of Pierre Chossard...November 16, '74; Medina county, $250.

Scott, Elbert P...Murder; November 24, '74; Madison county, $250.

Rather, Jas...Murder; November 24, '74; Bell county, $300.

Hughes, J. W. W...Murder; November 25, '74; penitentiary, $500.

Alexander, John...Murder; December 2, '74; Lamar county, $125.

Walters, A. W...Murder; December 28, '74; Hardin county, $300.

Nelson, John H...Murder; January 16, '75; Polk county, $250.

Vance, Joseph...Murder; January 23, '75; Grimes county, $250.

Hazlett, Columbus...Murder; January 28, '75; Nacogdoches county, $500.

Solomon, Cox...Murder; March 9, '75; Bosque county, $200.

Mackey, Nat...Murder; March 10, '75; Comanche county, $250.

Jeffries, Wm...Murder; March 10, '75; Comanche county, $250.

Murderers of Simon J. Majanor...March 13, '75; Houston county, $500.

Wright, Thomas; Wright, Wiley...Murder; March 19, '75; Ellis county, $400 each.

Murderer of Luke Moore...March 23, '75; McLennan county, $500.

Lindsey, Joel C...Murder; March 29, '75; Smith county, $350.

Murderer of Eugene Carter; April 5, '75; McLennan county, $1000.

Murderer of Magdelene Zatopeck...April 8, '75; Fayette county, $500.

Murderer of unknown man...April 26, '75; Ellis county, $250.

Miller, A. R...Murder; April 27, '75; Travis county, $250.

Foster, Wm.; Kendall, Jos. K...Murder; Bosque county, $200 each.

Collon, Adolphus...Murder; April 29, '75; Limestone county, $250.

Murderer of Mrs. Ratliff Morrow...May 5, '75; Montague county, $1000.

Pardue, Henry...Murder; June 5, '75; Bell county, $200.

Johnson, Randall...Murder; June 10, '75; Smith county, $500.

South, Bester...Murder; June 25, '75; Brazos county, $150.

Ballinger, Vincent...Murder; June 29, '75; Grimes county, $150.

Adkins, Lemuel, O...Murder; June 29, '75; Grimes county, $200.

Williams, Green...Murder; July 3, '75; Smith county, $150.

Kunde, Taylor; Kunde, Albert; and Kunde, Julius...Murder; July 5, '75; Guadalupe county, $250 each.

Colbath, Ambrose...Murder; July 9, '75; Gillespie county, $200.

Thompson, ——...Murder; July 14, '75; Travis county, $100.

Murderer of Freeman Batchelor...Montague county, $500.

Lamaster, Billy; and Musselwhite, Elzo...Murder; July 23, '75; Fannin county, $150 each.

Townsend, W. R...Murder; August 18, '75; Eastland county, $150.

Davis, Josiah H.; Whitley, Nathan...August 18, '75; Austin county, $150 each.

Rays, Damen...Murder; August 30, '75; DeWitt county, $200.

Caruthers, H. M...Murder; September 14, '75; Bastrop county, $200.

Durr, D. L...Murder; September 17, '75; Collin county, $200.

Lewis, James...Murder; September 20, '75; Kinney county, $200.

Murderer of Wm. Parsons...October 7, '75; Hamilton county, $300.

Nunez, Calixto; Mondragon, E...Embezzlement; October 25, '75; Bexar county, $200 each.

Manchaca, Cesario...Murder; October 25, '75; Bexar county, $200.

Short, Ed...Murder; November 11, '75; Grayson county, $200.

Culbreth, T. L...Murder; December 14, '75; Milam county, $200.

Hunter, Yance...Murder; December 27, '75; Burnet county, $100.

Beard, John...Murder; December 29, '75; Williamson county, $250.

Buchanan Dudley...Murder; January 13; '76; Dallas county, $200; and $500 by A. W. Perry.

Teal, Eli...Murder; January 14, '76; Van Zandt county, $250.

Murderers of Anthony Smith...January 24, '76; Milam county, $500.

Murderers of G. W. Schoby...February 19, 75; Bastrop county, $250.

Rains, W. A...Murder; February 21, 76; Kaufman county, $200.

Montgomery, Wm...Theft of cattle; February, 29, '76; Harrison county, $100.

Parker, W. C...Murder; March 3, '76; Houston county, $350.

Brittain, Wm. P...Assault to murder; Cherokee county, $200.

Barrow, Geo...Murder; April 12, '76; Montgomery county, $300.

Miles, Thos...Murder; April 14, '76 : Freestone county, $200.

Crowson, Wm...Murder; April 19, '76; Fannin county, $150.

Stage robbers between San Antonio and Kingsbury...May 12, '76; Guadaloupe county, $500.

Murderers of Henry Ferro...May 15, '76; Bexar county, $500.

Downs, Wm. F...Murder; May 25, '76; Cooke county, $250.

Askey Milton...Murder; May 26, '76; Wise county, $300.

Woods, Aleck...Murder; June 3, '76; Red River county, $100.

Milor, Volney V...Murder; June 2, '76; Red River county, $100.

Stage robbers between Dallas and Fort Worth...June 5, '76; Dallas county, $1000.

Graves, Milt.; Mitchell, Wm...Murder; June 6, '76; Hood county, $500 each.

Murderers of Jas. Gillyard; June 12, '76; Van Zandt county, $500.

Stephens, John...Allowing escape of prisoners; Clay county, $200.

Brown, John...Murder; June 10, '76; Clay county, $200.

Wilson, Jno. W.; Smith, Wm...Murder; Clay county, $300 each.

Packwood, Jesse...Murder; June 16, '76; Henderson county, $500.

McReynolds, Geo...Murder; June 26, '76; Rockwall county, $500.

Williams, T. J...Murder; July 7, '76; Wise county, $300.

Murderers of Christiana Beehring; July 8, '76; Fayette county, $500.

<Allen, Dike...Murder; July 10, '76; Caldwell county, $750.

Lum, Pat.; Green, Ed...Murder; July 10, '76; Liberty county, $250 each.

Irwin, A. D....Murder; July 10, '76; Panola county, $200.

Gregg, Herman...Murder; July 19, '76; Grimes county, $500.

Rosford, Thos...Murder; July 20, '76; Fannin county, $200.

Erwin, Wm...Murder; July 25, '76; Brazos county, $350.

Burners of Hays county C. H...Hays county, $750.

Murderers of Anderson Helms...Washington county, $300.

<Burton, Henry...Murder; August 25, '76; Travis county, $250.

Murderer of Otho Wells...September 4, '76; Coryell county, $250.

Williams, Sam...Murder; September 5, '76; Kimble county, $250.

Tickle, Robt...Murder; Navarro county, $250.

Lockhart J. W...Murder; September 18, '76; Marion county, $200.

Petty, John Thomas...Murder; Marion county, $200.

McLeod, Norman...Murder;	"	"	200.
Dreson, B. J...Swindling;	"	"	100.
Nunn, Sam'l... Murder;	"	"	200.
Renfro, G. B...Embezzlement;	"	"	50.
Jones, Berry...Burglary and theft;	"	"	50.
Smith, Henry...Perjury;	"	"	50.
Barnett. W. E...Theft;	"	"	50.
Thomas, Geo...Theft;	"	"	50.
Allison, John...Theft;	"	"	100.
Higgins, Sam...Theft;	"	"	50.
McCloud, Chas...Forgery;	"	"	100.
Tefire, Adam, alias Telfore...Murder; "		"	200.
Owens, Walter...Theft;	"	"	50.

Collins, John...Perjury; September 18, '76; Marion county, $100.

Burners Blanco county C. H.; October 20, '76; Blanco county, $1000.

Little, Aaron...Murder; October 28, '76; Kerr county, $500.

Christopher, Geo...Murder; Bowie county, $300.

Pearson, Jas. D...Murder; October 31, '76; Montgomery county, $300.

Wilson, Geo...Murder; November 6; Denton county, $750.

Arnold, Allen; Arnold, Wm., Jr...Murder; Lampasas county, $350 each.

Yarborough, H. B...Murder; November 20, '76; Brown county, $150.

Bates, Geo., alias Wm. Meek...Murder; November 29, 76; Medina county, $300.

Gordon, Wm...Murder; December 13, '76; Red River county, $200.

Boyles, Jas. W...Murder; December 26, '76; Milam county, $500.

Jackson, John...Rape; December 27, '76; Harrison county, $300.

Henderson, H. A...Murder; Coryell county, $250.

Sparks, Isaac...Attempt to murder; January 8, '77; Lee county, $200.

Moore, A., alias Munroe...Murder; February 8, '77; Marion county, $500.

Thurber, Henry E...Murder; February 13, '77; Bell county, $250.

Murderers of Alex. R. Stephen; February 16, 77; Wilson county, $300.

Bell, Wm...Murderer; February 23, '77; Dallas county, $200.

Barrington, James; Barrington, Esther; Koozier, Ed...Murder; March 13, '77; Clay county, $66 66 each.

Murderers of Dr. J. S. Webb; March 19, '77; Freestone county, $500.

Farrow, Aaron, alias Buford ; Baker, Geo....Arson ; March 20, '77 ; San Augustine county, $75 each.

Netherly, Wm. M...Murder ; San Augustine county, $175.

Mintlo, Jordan...Murder : San Augustine county, $250.

Squire, Alexander ; Washington, Levi ; and Brooks, Reuben...Murder ; March 20, '77 ; San Augustine county ; $50 each.

Ellis, J. R.; and Roach, James...Murder ; March 26, '77 ; Liberty county, $250 each.

Ronley, Columbus...Murder ; March 29, '77 ; Hays county, $350.

West, Solon...Murder ; April 3, '77 ; Harris county, $500.

Boyd, Ike...Murder ; Smith county, $350.

Cavin, W. T...Murder ; April 9, '77; Burnet county, $250.

Stage Robbers between Fort Worth and Cleburne ; April 11, '77 ; $250 each.

Hearne, J. C...Murder ; April 12, '77 ; Lamar county, $250.

Robbers of J. W. Hill...April 14, '77 ; Smith county, $250.

Robbers of T. J. Owens...Smith county, $250.

Robbers —— Wheat...Smith county, $250.

Robbers of the house of W. J. Deaton...Smith county, $250.

Carlin, Wm. A...Murder ; April 19, '77 ; Bosque county, $250.

Jail breakers and murdering prisoners...May 11, '77 ; Bosque county, $500 each.

Murderers of M. R. Green...May 18, '77 ; Comanche county, $400.

Murderers of Clinton Watkins...May 19, '77 ; Falls county, $500.

Thompson, J. C. ; Waller, M. B...Murder ; May 23, '77 ; Montague county, $300 each.

Robinson, Tom ; Owens, Henry, alias Hoodle ; and Peterson, Bell... Murder ; May 25, '77 ; Bastrop county, $200 each.

Yates, Joe...Murder ; May 26, '77 ; Lamar county, $300. *Negro*

Kimble, Bud...Murder ; Wilson county, $400.

Davis, Joshua H...Murder ; Washington county, $400.

Wilson, Geo...Murder ; June 2, '77 ; Denton county, $500.

Hawks, Frank...Murder ; June 4, '77 ; Lavaca county, $400.

Parker, Calvin.. Murder ; June 19, '77 ; Bowie county, $300.

Brittain, J. H...Murder ; Bowie county, $300.

Walker, Geo...Murder ; Bowie county, $300.

Miller, O. M...Murder ; June 20, '77 ; Tarrant county, $400. *Negro*

Pickett, Chas...Murder ; June 29, '77 ; Travis county, $400.

West, Robt...Murder ; July 2, '77 ; Bell county, $500.

Murderer of Geo. W. Tetric...July 9, '77 ; Hamilton county, $500.

Murderers of Wm. Parsons...Hamilton county, $500.

Anderson, Sam...Murder ; July 13, '77 ; Wilson county, $300.

Province, P. P...Murder ; July 18, '77 ; Montgomery county, $500.

Gentry, Chas...Murder ; July 19, '77 ; Parker county, $500.

Rowley, J. F.; Rowley, Napoleon...Murder ; July 23, '77 ; Hays county, $350 each.

Bell, C. S...Murder ; July 28, '77 ; Live Oak county, $500.

Cannon, E...Murder ; July 31, '77 ; Rockwall county, $400.

Gibson, Let...Murder ; August 7, '77 ; Fannin county, $300.

Nash, Richard...Murder ; August 18, '77 ; Cass county, $500.

Mayfield, W. E. C...Murder ; August 13, '77 ; Lamar county, $500.

Tuttle, W. S...Murder ; August 15, '77 ; Brown county, $300.

Kellis, Wm...Murder ; August 20, '77 ; McLennan county, $500.

McIver, Joseph...Murder ; August 27, '77 ; Madison county, $300.

12

178 LIST OF FUGITIVES FROM JUSTICE.

McIver, Jno. R...Murder; Madison county, $300.
Parker, W. C...Murder; August 29, '77; Houston county, $500.
Dovalina, Edwardo...Murder; September 1, '77; Webb county, $500.
Coyle, Wm.; and Roberts, Stephen...Murder; September 11, '77; Panola county, $500 each.
Carrick, Chas...Murder; September 12, '77; McLennan county, $400.
Johnson, Jim...Murder; September 17, 1877; Marion county, $500.
Hewitt, John W.; McCowan, John; and Tisdale, Chas...Murder; September 18, '77; Bowie county, $400 each.
Walters, David...Murder; September 20, '77; Fayette county, $150.
Darden, Moses; and Brown, Wesley...Burning storehouse; September 21, '77; Harrison county, $50 each.
Rodriguez, Martin...Murder; September 25, '77; Nueces county, $300.
Lewis, Clint...Murder; October 6, '77; Madison county, $200.
Shaver, J. W...Rape; Clay county, $500.
Watts, Julius...Murder; October 8, '77; Red River county, $150.
Norton, John; and Muller, —...Murder; October 11, '77; Montague county, $200 each.
Miller, Geo. W...Forgery; Travis county, $350.
Biggs, Henry H...Murder; October 16, '77; Shelby county, $300.
Collins, Harac...Murder; October 17, '77; Shelby county, $200.
Magnus, Bill...Murder; November 1, '77; Washington county, $200.
Halford, Nathaniel...Murder; November 8, '77; Gonzales county, $350.
Gardner, John J....Murder; November 12, '77; Hamilton county, $400.
Gardenhire, A. J...Murder; Tarrant county, $350.
Long, John; and McGibben...Murder; November 13, '77; Jack county, $250 each.
McMullan, Michael...Murder; November 13; Jack county, $250.
Talmage, C. H...Forgery; Travis county, $250.
Adams, Tom, alias Weekins...Murder; November 21, '77; Travis county, $300.
Bean, Russell...Murder; November 22, '77; Gonzales county, $300.
Graham....Murder; November 26, '77; Hopkins county, $500.
Irvin, A. D...Panolo county, $400.
Williams, Thos. J...Murder; December 4, '77; Bell county, $250.
Owensby, Gus...Murder; December 6, '77; San Saba county, $500.
Cordova, Feliciano...Murder; Bexar county, $400.
Thompson, James...Murder; December 10, '77; Grayson county, $300.
Beard, John...Murder; December 12, '77; Marion county, $500.
Rushing, Alfred; and Scruggs, Harde...Murder; Freestone county, $300.
Henderson, Gus...Murder; December 13, '77; Montgomery county, $350.
Turner, Sug...Murder; December 3, '77; Lampasas county, $350.
Ruby, George...Murder; December 11, '77; Travis county, $400.
Nelson, John H...Murder; December 21, '77; Polk county, $400.
Gillum, —...Allowing prisoner to escape; December 24, '77; Lampasas county, $300.
Swafford, John B.; and Marksbury, Allen...Escaped from jail; December 26, '77; Bosque county, $250 each.
Perkins, Henry...Murder; December 28, '77; Montague county, $500.
Gillum, —...Allowing prisoners to escape; Lampasas county; (on conviction, $300.)
Swofford, Jno. B.; Allen, Marksbury...Bosque county; escaped from jail; $250 each.

Perkins, Henry...Murder; Montague county; on delivery, $250; on conviction, $250.

Jossey, Wm...Murder; Cass county; on delivery, $300; on conviction, $200.

Kay, John...Arson; Smith county; $200.

Kemper, Wm...Murder; Montague county; $300.

Goodman, Ben...Murder; Wilson county; $500.

Tate, Ed...Murder; Houston county; $300.

Rasco, Jesse...Murder; Navarro county; on delivery, $300; on conviction, $200.

Adams, James...Murder; Fayette county; $150.

Goodwin, Benj...Murder; Wilson county; on delivery, $250; on conviction, $250.

Harris, Henry...Murder; Harrison county; $400.

INDEX.

A

	PAGE		PAGE
Atascosa County	3	Anderson, Jim	45
Ainsley, Wm	4	Alexander, Wm	46
Alcorta, Severe	4	Agnew, Lewis H	47
Aransas County	5	Atkins, Ira B	47
Allen, Noah	7	Amberg, James	49
Abbott, James C	8	Anderson, Wm	51
Adkins, Ed	9	Abernathy, John	51
Anderson, Felix	14	Anderson, Richmond	53
Alsop, A. M	15	Anderson, Bob, alias Walker	53
Autry, Robt	16	Anderson, Andrew	54
Ashlin, John	16	Alexander, ——	54
Achone, Pamphilio	4	Alexander, Peter, alias Reed	58
Ainsworth, Levin	18	Atkisson, Thos	60
Armstrong, G. W	21	Adams, John 63,	61
Adams, Frank	22	Anderson, Doc	64
Adams, David	23	Autizer, Wm	54
Abney, Jerry	23	Allen, ——	55
Andings, Wm	23	Armstrong, James	69
Allen Geo	24	Arnold, Allen 176,	70
Andrews, Felix	25	Arnold, Wm 176,	70
Allison, Neal	27	Atkinson, Wm	71
Anderson, C. B	28	Aycock, Bill	71
Austin, James	30	Alexander, Frank	65
Airy, Thos	32	Anderson, Robert B	66
Adrienne, Chas	33	Allen, Gabriel	66
Andrada, Julian	33	Alexander, Robt	66
Almares, Jesus	33	Alred, Alfred	67
Austin County	33	Archer, Tobe	67
Armstrong, Stephen	33	Armstead, K. W	67
Anderson County	34	Allen, Neal, A. B	68
Atkinson, Robt	34	Anderson, M. J., alias Widener	65
Arnold, Isaac	34	Asum, Joseph	73
Andrews, J. J	35	Alexander, Moffatt	74
Atwood, Wm	38	Ainsworth, Joab	74
Anderson, Mike	40	Ascosta, Antonio	79
Arnold, Mose	42	Adams, H. L	79
Ayers, Thos	42	Allen, L. M	85
Alsop, Joe, alias Drew	43	Allen, J. R., alias Jones	86
		Arnold, Levi	86

	PAGE		PAGE
Abbott, Henry, alias Bell	88	Arzola, Benigne	153
Ainsworth, Tap	74	Aguirre, Lilwado	153
Allent, Edward	80	Aldopa, Vede	153
Alford, J. P	90	Arthur, Robt	153
Allen, James	91	Alsolrook, Ned	155
Abernathy, West	91	Atkinson, Chas	156
Allison, John 176,	92	Allard, Peter	157
Andrews, Nervain	92	Armbritten, Boney	158
Allen, Lou	93	Arthur, Henry	158
Allen, R. A	96	Anderson, Dave	158
Allen, W. A	99	Atwood, ——	160
Adams, Geo. W	100	Armstrong, J. N	161
Anderson, J. P	100	Anderson Geo	161
Addison, Doc	103	Ake, John	162
Alexander, Creed	104	Adams, P. A	163
Arnold, Hamp	98	Anderson, Ralph	163
Allen, W	105	Andres, Chas	164
Allen, Geo	107	Amein, Pedro	164
Adams, John	108	Alexander, Squire 177,	164
Appleton, James	108	Allen, James	165
Anderson, James	110	Aulthouse, James	167
Allen, August, A	114	Alexander, Aurora	168
Allen, Chas	114	Allen, Geo. W	168
Ash, Thos	115	Auterass, Jose	169
Anderson, W	116	Ames, John	170
Adams, Wm	117	Armitage, Henry	174
Adams, Joseph	117	Alexander, John	174
Adams, John	120	Adkins, Lemuel, O	174
Arnett, John	121	Allen, Dike	176
Allen, Smith	122	Anderson Sam	177
Ables, J. M	122	Adams, Tom, alias Weekins	178
Avant, Wm	123	Adams, James	179
Anderson, Wm	124		
Adams, Calhoun	125		
Allen, Hardin	127	**B**	
Allan, Obediah	128	Brown, John	5
Allen, John	131	**Blanco County**	5
Avery, R. E	133	Ballard, Andrew, J	5
Anderson, Wm	133	Bundick, Chas	6
Anderson, J., Jr	134	**Bosque County**	6
Alford, Jno. D	125	Brady, S. W	6
Anderson John	137	**Burleson County**	7
Andrews, Isaac	140	Burton, ——	7
Aldridge, John	145	Brown, Harris	7
Anderson, John	146	Brown. J. Wesley	9
Armstrong, Nealy	148	Bolin, Alick	9
Askey, Milton 175,	148	Blo dgood, Martin	9
Arp, Bill	149	Beeman, A. L	9
Ashbell, Joe. M	149	Banks, Chas	9
Atkinson, Ranole	149	Byars, Cass	9
Altum, H. L	151	Buel, D. A	9
Alston, Drea	152	Berry, John	9
Ashworth, Moses	152	Butterworth, Walter	9

	PAGE		PAGE
Boil, Chas	10	Bledsoe, Sol	31
Butler, Gabe	10	Braziel, Bob	31
Barrington, Manly	10	Baker, John	31
Burns, Cook	10	Blair, Doe	31
Burleson, Ike	12	Bassett, Jack	32
Bishop, Thos	12	Bassett, Reuben	32
Bateman, Bell	12	Burns, Pink	32
Blalock, Thadeus	12	Brunsen, John	33
Branch, Ike	13	Byers, Alex	33
Barney, Wm., alia Barney		Butler, Oliver	34
Williams	14	Brooks, N. S	34
Hung Baily, D	16, 15	**Bandera County**	35
Baily, James	15	Brown, Geo. C	35
Boyd, G. W	15	**Burnet County**	35
Bell, Wm	15	Barnes, Thomas	35
Bryant, John	15	Barton, Al	36
Brown, Noah	16	Brown, James	37
Barney, Wm	14, 16	Baily, Mort	38
Borders, J. G	16	Baird, Jno *Killed*	38
Bass, Jordan	16	Brown, W. P	39
Balch, A. W	16	**Brazoria County**	40
Beck, Webb	16	Brown, Natt	40
Brossell, J. W	16	Bar, Santee Ed	40
Butler, Wm. H	17	Brown, Ben	40
Barnes, J. S	18	Bonner, Augustus	40
Brandon, John	18	**Bastrop County**	40
Beaty, John	19	Barker, Joseph	40
Bushby, Jas	19	Borra, ——	41
Brown, Thos	19	Bird, W. H	41
Burnett, James	20	Boese, Henry	41
Berry, Chas. P	22	Burlin, Calhoun	44
Beggers, Robt	22	Branton, Ben	44
Brown, Elisha	22	Botlon, Rufus	45
Bond, Geo	22	Boyd, Richard	46
Brown, Gabe	23	Broughton, Ch	46
Burleson, M. P	23	Brittain, Wm. P	175, 47
Bryan, Jerry	23	Brownlee, Henry	47
Bryan, Reuben	23	Barrington, James	176, 48
Brooking, W. H	24	Blanton, Jno. D	48
Brock, John	25	Brown, John	175, 48
Bell, L. S	25	Ball, Thomas	42
Barton, Geo	26	Burdell, Dr	49
Bateman, Henry	26	Blythe, Lemuel	49
Brown, Jas	27	Bacon, Sam	49
Burton, Sam	27	Brinlee, David	50
Barker, Jas	27	Bishop, ——	50
Blythe, Calvin	29, 27	Boren, Jack	50
Bell, A. D	28	Bartin, W. R	50
Bennett, W. H	28	Boren, Robt	50
Bell, Jas	28	Blalock, James	50
Bevens, Allen	28	Bean, Henry	50
Burdett, Lewis	29	Bounds, Joseph	51
Bryant, John	30	Baltzell, Wm	173, 51

	PAGE		PAGE
Brady, Hut............................	52	Benson, Jno............................	67
Bean, Russell................178,	52	Biggerstaff, H.......................	67
Brown, Sam	52	Battis, J.............................	68
Bobo, Young.........................	52	Baker, Geo., alias Geo. Nichols,	
Brimsbury, James.................	53	alias Burke......................	68
Bunton, Fred., alias Jack Davis	54	Burke Geo., alias Baker, alias	
Bowden, Chs.........................	54	Nichols..........................	68
Banta, Jacob............	56	Boswell, Jno., Jr.................	69
Benson, Jehu......................	56	Binkley, Joseph..................	72
Burnham, Wm......................	56	Brenningham, ——...............	72
Birkley, M..........................	56	Butler, Jno. A....................	74
Bockley, C. R......................	56	Boykin, W. P......................	75
Barton, Jerry......................	56	Benson, Geo.......................	75
Ballenger, V................174,	56	Burlison, Alick, alias D. A.....	76
Brown, Sawney....................	57	Bergeman, John..................	76
Boller, Caleb......................	57	Burke, Geo.........................	76
Bartlett, J. D......................	57	Barratt, A. W., alias Captain...	77
Bowden, W. W......................	58	Brazeale, Jual....................	77
Brown, Samuel.....................	58	Baird, John Killed...............	78
Banks, James......................	59	Bell, C. S..................177,	78
Brooks, W. W	59	Brown, Geo., alias Jack..........	79
Brady, John.........................	59	Brigley, Thos......................	80
Brady, Lundy......................	60	Burrell, Albert.................... ..	80
Beard, Moses.......................	60	Barry, N. S., alias Stokes.......	83
Brady, Nas.........................	60	Bean, Wm.........................	84
Burns, T. J.........................	61	Brown, John.......................	85
Baldwin, Wm........	61	Boulden, Albert...................	86
Brady, ——..........................	61	Baptiste, Gordolphus............	86
Bailey, Mat.........................	62	Burton, Frank.....................	86
Boba, John.........................	62	Bowers, Sam.......................	86
Bonesteele, ——....................	64	Baker, Geo.........................	87
Bird, James.........................	49	Barnes, S. H.......................	87
Bevry, Silas........................	56	Baldwin, N. W.....................	87
Berry, Wm..........................	56	Buckley, Chas......................	87
Bait, ——.............................	56	Baugh, Alex R.....................	88
Burns, Polk........................	69	Binferd, Mack.....................	88
Beavers, Jim.......................	69	Bateman, Otto, alias Wren......	88
Bowen, Bill.........................	70	Brinkley, Thos.....................	74
Brophy, M. A......................	70	Brown, Ed..........................	75
Brown, Ed..........................	70	Brooks, Houston, alias Cultor.	75
Bolivar, John......................	71	Bruce, Nick.......................	89
Brown, Mary.......................	72	Beauchamp, Geo..................	89
Bluett, Isaac.......................	65	Band, Pink........................	91
Bell, John..........................	65	Baxley, James.....................	91
Baker, R. L........................	65	Benton J. P........................	91
Burton, Hardy............... ..	65	Burley, Geo........................	91
Brimley, Stephen H.............	66	Burnett, W. E.............176,	92
Bradford, Autry...................	66	Boyd, Newton...	93
Barnett, Cary......................	67	Binkly, Henry.....................	93
Brown, Alfred......................	67	Busues, Wm., alias Bill Burns	93
Birmingham, Pat..................	67	Burns, Bill, alias Wm. Busues	93
Bland, A. T.........................	67	Bowling, Harris...................	94
Blackburn, Thos..................	67	Bowling, Harrison................	94

	PAGE		PAGE
Black, Eugene	94	Bill, Banjo	110
Bledsone, —	94	Banjo, Bill	110
Bowe, Joe	94	Burnett, Jesse	110
Bordeaux, A	95	Brown, Thos	111
Burnes, J. M	95	Brazil, Sim	111
Bingham, J. W	95	Beck, A	111
Brazeal, Allen	95	Brooks, Geo	111
Bell, Geo., alias Martin Pitts	95	Burnes, O. B	111
Bill, Joshua	96	Burleson, James	112
Boykin, —	96	Bagwell, Wm	113
Barkley, Newton	96	Bates, Frank	113
Boatwright, R. J	97	Black, Wm	113
Belles, Blas de Las	98	Buchanan, T. J	114
Belas, Antonio	98	Bryson, Sam	114
Bitela, Lucas	98	Brown, Eugene	115
Benham, David	99	Buckhannan, A bert,	115
Baptiste, John	99	Bradley, Dock	115
Bryant, J. A	99	Brewer, Caleb	116
Barry, Adam	99	Blackburn, Col	116
Byers, Edmund	100	Butler, Thos. M	116
Burrus, Jack	100	Baldre, James	117
Bowman, Lewis	100	Butler, Thos	118
Blackburn, Frank	101	Brown, Geo	118
Bullock, Henry	102	Bagley, Warren	118
Beard, W. A	102	Berry, Jams, Jr	119
Brooks, Geo	102	Brown, Eli	120
Brooks, Joseph	103	Bromley, James	120
Bevel, Bailey	103	Burns, J. Pickens	110
Bill, Yellow	103	Barringter, J. T	110
Brown, Dan	103	Brown, R. E	121
Booker, James	104	Brown, Bartlett	121
Bickerstaff, —	104	Barker, N. W	121
Berry, Sol	96	Brashear, Seaborn	121
Baker, Geo	98	Rramlett, Augustus	122
Brown, John	99	Bony, Geo	122
Bateman, W	105	Black, John	122
Bevin, John	105	Bonner, Bob	122
Barren, Alfred	105	Block, Bill	122
Bird, Willis,	105	Bucklan, W. B	123
Bradley, John	106	Beall, John	123
Boren, Joseph.,	107	Biggs, Lewis	125
Buckingham, Isham	107	Brooks, Smith	126
Boyd, Lary	107	Blunt, Ben	126
Birmingham, David	107	Bussy, Dick	126
Brown, James	107	Bates, Ned	126
Burnes, Pickens	107	Baird, John	126
Brown, Jack	107	Barrett, A. W	126
Bowman, John	108	Barnett, H. S	127
Boyd, John	108	Birge, Bird	127
Brooks, Evans	109	Black, Joseph	127
Bruce, Guilford G	109	Bruton, J. C	127
Bishop, W. R	109	Baxter, James	128
Burch, Wash	109	Benton, James	128

	PAGE		PAGE
Butler, Henry	130	Beard, John. *Killed*	175, 146
Boyd, Ike	177, 130	Berry, Silas	146
Brown, Robt.	130	Bybee, Wm.	146
Brisby, Claiborne	131	Brady, J. T.	146
Brummett, C. T.	132	Baker, W. H.	147
Billings, Chas.	132	Baker, D. P.	147
Byrd, J. P.	132	Bertram, John	147
Brinnen, James	132	Burns, Tom	148
Benjaman, D. W.	132	Barber, Chas.	148
Briggs, H. C.	132	Burns, Sam	148
Baldwin, Golden	132	Banis, R. T.	148
Bates, Hockley	132	Ballard, Edward	148
Brownlee, Alfonso	133	Brock, J. T.	149
Booth, J. W.	133	Bean, D.	149
Bolton, Wash	133	Brozell, James	149
Burns, A. P.	134	Birdlow, Wm.	150
Brown, Kit	134	Booker, John	152
Bryant, Nelson	134	**Bee County**	153
Bush, John	134	**Bowie County**	155
Benton, John	135	**Brazos County**	156
Brown, Henry	135	Boyd, A. L.	153
Bird, Wm.	135	Benavides, Manuel	153
Barnes, Pink	136	Brown, James	153
Beverly, Lou	136	Buckingham, M. J.	154
Bridges, James	122	Bailey, Henry	154
Bennett, Henry	122	Burns, Robt.	154
Bascus, Martina	137	Balderos, Rafael	154
Brown, Chas.	138	Britton, J. H.	155
Burson, E.	139	Brooks, David	156
Burnett, John	140	Ball, James.	157
Burke, Jack	140	Bickham, Lewis	157
Brannon, Richard	140	Bowen, J. R.	157
Boyle, Thos.	140	Blackwell, Mitch	157
Bellah, John	142	Boykin, John	158
Brown, Alfred	143	Brown, John	158
Brown, Columbus	143	Beson, John	158
Bowers, E., alias Parker	144	Batte, James	159, 158
Ballard, Ples	144	Bunger, W. G.	158
Brown, Tom	144	Bedgood, J. M.	159
Brown, Jack	144	Breedlove, Geo.	160
Brown, Alfred	144	Brown, M. C.	161
Bell, Matt	144	Booer, John	161
Bories, Robt.	145	Brooks, Henry	162
Bird, Louis	145	Baird, John	162
Buchanan, Nat	145	Burns, Sam	163
Blake, Lewis	145	Byford, Wesley	163
Bishop, Alfred	145	Bray, A. J.	163
Baker, Wesley	145	Broocks, Reuben	177, 164
Baker, Wm.	145	Busby, Daniel	165
Barton, Lum	145	Bass, Geo.	165
Brown, J. C.	145	Bryant, C. W.	168
Bond, Dennis	145	Barnes, Thos.	168
Beaty, G. W.	146	Bullock, Fanny	157

13

PAGE

Burrows, Geo......................159
Bryant, J. W., alias Carter, S.
    M.................. 161
Baker, Geo.......................177, 165
Barefoot, Isaac D., alias By-
    field, James..................... 169
Byfield, Jas., alias Barefoot, I.
    D........................... 169
Blair, Thos........................... 169
Black, Chas............ 169
Butler, Ben...... 169
Bennis, Harry, alias Wild
    Harry................... 169
Burns, Jas. A........ 170
Benton, Wm......................... 170
Brown, Wm......................... 171
Brown, Joe......................... 171
Brittain, L. G...... 171
Britton, G. L....................... 171
Bates, ——........................ 171
Beers, Minnie...................... 172
Barrett, W. H........ 172
Bateman, V......................... 172
Brady, Wm......................... 172
Barnett, Geo......... 173
Byfield, Wm., alias Schubert.. 169
Beck, Joe, murderer of. 174
Batchelor, Freeman, murderer
    of........... 175
Buchanan, Dudley.............. 175
Barrow, Geo........................ 175
Beehring,Christiana, murderer
    of......... 175
Burners of Hays Co. Court-
    house............... 176
Burton, Henry.................... 176
Burners of Blanco Co. Court-
    house.......... 176
Bates, Geo., alias Wm. Meek... 176
Boyles, James...................... 176
Bell, Wm........................... 176
Barrington, Esther.............. 176
Brittain, J. H..................... 177
Biggs, Henry M........... 178
Beard, John........................ 178
Burners Madison Co. Court-
    house............ 173
Burners Mrs. A. Jones' stables 174
Blanco Co. Courthouse, burn-
    ers of.............. 176
Brown, Wesley...... 178

C

PAGE

Cruz, Narcio....................... 3
Cantoon, Ramon.................. 4
Cornet, Joe........................ 4
Casinova, Santano............... 4
Coy, Cecilio Hernandez. 4
Connelly, Michael............... 5
Cox, Solomon.......... ....174, 6
Cook, E. T........................ 7
Collins, Monroe................... 7
Colorado County.............. 8
Conner, Tom...... 9
Crane, L. P......................... 9
Caldwell County.... 10
Currier, Richard.................. 12
Chambers County. 13
Church, Rollin..................... 13
Comal County................ 13
Comanche County............ 14
Coryell County................ 15
Crow, Pinckney................... 15
Cox, James...................... 16
Carodine, John.................... 16
Clifford, Wesley.................. 18
Cox, Joe......... 18
Cross, A. J......... 19
Cork, B. B......................... 20
Coates, James......... 21
Childers, James.................. 22
Childers, Chas.................... 22
Cunningham, Teige.............. 23
Canisse, Jas....................... 23
Chambliss, Geo 23
Cunningham, F. M.............. 25
Chapman, John G.............. 25
Coudray, Wm.......... 26
Coudray, L. C..................... 26
Cotner, H. C......... 29
Cornelius, Wm......... 31
Covington, W. B.................. 32
Corley, John....................... 22
Collins, Eli........................ 28
Coffee, Shadrick.................. 31
Cregg, Ben......................... 31
Clay, Robt......................... 33
Caden, Edwara. 36
Caden, Wm. T......... ......177, 36
Carver, Geo., Sr................... 35
Carver, Geo., Jr................... 35
Clark, Wm 38
Campbell, Geo..................... 39
Conroy, ——, alias Ross......... 39

	PAGE		PAGE
Campbell, W. E	39	Cooper, James	60
Caffae, Thos	39	Cantwell, Robt	61
Cruz, ——	39	Collins, John	62
Coward, Richard M	40	Callison, J. C	62
Curtis, Joseph	40	Collins, Joe	62
Crayton, Bob	41	Cotton, Mitchell 173,	63
Coulson, Bart	41	Cox, Green	63
Calhoun, W. E	42	Clendenan, Benj	63
Clanton, James	43	Cornelius, A. C	64
Clark, Lewis, alias Whiten	43	Callens, Adolphus...........174,	64
Caruthers, Henry M 175,	43	Caldwell, Samuel	64
Coulson, Nelson	44	Cooper, E. C	65
Commus, James	44	Conelias, Thos	65
Coleman County	45	Carico, W. B	65
Carter, G. V	45	Clark, C. C	65
Clark, P. J	45	Christinas, J. W	65
Calhoun County	45	Cox, S	66
Clark, ——	45	Cox, Wm	66
Camp County	45	Clack, Henry	66
Campbell, G. W	46	Cox, Geo	66
Cherokee County	46	Cole, Wm	66
Crunk, Wm	47	Carpenter, Thos. H	67
Clayton, Ed	47	Culberson, Geo	67
Clay County	48	Coker, John	68
Clark, Charley, alias Hart	36	Cowan, J. W	68
Cox, Roland	49	Clayton, S. S	69
Collin County	49	Cooper, Toles	70
Collins, John	49	Carter, Tip	70
Connelly, Ben	50	Carter, John	72
Cole, F. P	50	Cladonian, Wallace	72
Cobston, Thos	50	Cole, Martin	72
Cobston, Hence	50	Cox, A., Sr	72
Cartwright, J. J	51	Cox, A., Jr	72
Cary, ——	64	Cole, Asa	73
Cravy, Ike	64	Criswell Wm	73
Campbell, Floyd	51	Crawford, A	74
Coyle, M. S	51	Culton, Houston, alias Brooks	75
Coulter, Chas	52	Cannon, W. T	76
Chambers, John (3 times)	52	Collins, Bruce	76
Cottingham, Thos	52	Collins, B. F	76
Cooley, Richard (twice)	52	Cook, Mike	76
Crenshaw, Nick	54	Cowherd, R. O	76
Cochran, Buck	55	Clark, John	77
Clemons, Frank	55	Cox, Wm. Henry	77
Callison, Thos	55	Cain, Wm	78
Carroll, Lewis, alias Jas. Henry	55	Clay, Dave	79
Clements, Manning	56	Chaffer, Antonio	79
Cadwel, John	56	Cole, Frank	79
Colbath, Ambrose...........175,	56	Chambers, Joseph	82
Chatham, W. L	56	Club, Jo	83
Coline, W. H	58	Copeland, Joe	84
Cowan, Jack	60	Carrolton, Jack	84
Coy, Wm	60	Cummings, Hattie	85

	PAGE		PAGE
Cobb, Benj.	85	Coyle, Luther	105
Craft, Dan	85	Crawford, Andrew	105
Cross, James	86	Chambliss, Rolla M	105
Clark, James	87	Campbell, John W	106
Clepper, John	88	Cooke, David	106
Clepper, Lem. C.	88	Coleman, Jack	107
Connell, Clem	89	Carter, Peter, alias Clark	107
Callaway, Roland	89	Clark, Peter, alias Carter	107
Cole, Jno.	90	Crawford, Ellsburry	108
Cheshire, Robt.	90	Cottenredder, Kelse	108
Cross, Peter	91	Choate, Wm. M	110
Clarence, Harry	91	Cooper, Jenks	110
Crawford, J. B.	91	Cain, Luke	110
Cobb, W. P. (twice)	91	Cain, Dick	110
Crawford, M.	92	Cherry, John	110
Collins, John 176,	92	Cheely, Jasper	110
Cloud, Chas. M	92	Cheeley, Scott	110
Cathorn, G. W	93	Campbell, Ed	110
Cooley, Jno. W	93	Cornelius, Wm	111
Cester, Wm	94	Culwell, James	111
Cook, J. H.	95	Caubrell, Robt.	111
Cook, John	95	Carlock, Thos.	111
Cook, J. H., alias Cooper	95	Cannon, Embury 177,	112
Carrick, Chs 178,	95	Cannon, W. C.	112
Cook, J. M	95	Chappell, Joseph	113
Carter, B. F.	95	Covington, Jas. A	113
Crutcher, G. H	95	Caton, Cato	113
Crary, T. J	96	Chastine, Mat.	113
Carry, alias Davis, alias John		Carroll, Wm	114
Wilson	96	Caldwell, Otho	114
Craine, A. G	96	Chastine, Mack	114
Cardrell, Jack	96	Carroll, Geo	114
Cabanas, Rafael	98	Calhoun, Pat W H	116
Centento, Victor	98	Carr, Allen	117
Chavarii, Solomon	98	Clifford, Wm	118
Chavari, Cornelio	98	Carter, Ben	119
Crabtree, J. W Killed	99	Chisum, Talbert, F	119
Curtis, Bill	99	Crawley, Zadock	119
Cain, David	99	Child, Lewis	119
Crawford, Bob	100	Coleman, C. E	119
Chapman, Lewis	100	Colly, Henry	120
Clark, Lewis	100	Coats, Wm	120
Crouch, W. D	101	Canterberry, Henry	120
Combs, W. P	101	Cordray, David	120
Crutchfield, John	101	Cantrell, Robt.	111
Chissum, Samuel	102	Crawford ——	114
Carter, Marshall	102	Counsel, Ike	121
Crawford, James	102	Cook, James B	121
Carlin, G. W	104	Campbell, James	122
Campbell, Columbus	104	Childers, T. M	122
Coyle, Wm., alias Jno.True, 178,	104	Cavanaugh, James	123
Cratick, Amos	104	Cobb, Rola	123
Coney, Lewis, alias Thos Lewis	102	Chisem, Lewis	123

PAGE
Cox, J. P................ 123
Connon, H. P............ 125
Cravey, Newton......... 125
Crutchfield, John....... 125
Cole, Wm............... 125
Cozim, H. C............. 125
Cock, Chas. R.......... 126
Conner, Frank.......... 126
Conner, Wm............ 126
Cheek, Thos........... 128
Clark, R. S............. 128
Clark, C. J............. 128
Carter, James.......... 128
Clark, J. T............ 129
Cesil, W. A............ 130
Coleman, Luke......... 130
Cranshaw, Jim......... 131
Carrigan, A............ 131
Cresswell, James....... 132
Cook, Geo............. 132
Cain, David........... 133
Counsil, Orvin........ 134
Caughlin, Edward...... 134
Caton, John........... 134
Carter, F. M........... 135
Cochran, E............ 121
Calhoun, Dennis....... 122
Contreras, Bruno...... 137
Coleman, W........... 137
Carter, Si G........... 138
Clark, W. S........... 138
Craig, James.......... 139
Castro, Caruto........ 139
Carter, Wm........... 140
Corgan, James........ 140
Carter, James......... 140
Campbell, W. A....... 140
Carter, France........ 140
Connor, Phil.......... 140
Christopher, J P...... 140
Conley, John.......... 140
Carson, B. F.......... 142
Claudius, James....... 143
Callaway, Lemuel..... 143
Chinn, Jim............ 143
Clara, Jack........... 144
Connell, Geo.......... 147
Crohn, Morris........ 147
Crine, Wm........... 147
Carlston, John........ 148
Craig, Alex.......... 148
Cox, Bluff........... 148
Collins, D............ 148

PAGE
Crockett, Ruth........ 148
Curry, John........... 149
Collins, J .B........... 149
Colburn, Fell......... 150
Cowan, Jas. A........ 150
Cottrell, Amanda..... 151
Cox, John............ 145
Childress, Jno., alias Snyder... 147
Cooper, J............ 153
Clements, Geo........ 156
Christopher, Geo.......176, 156
Cornich, N. A........ 156
Cowrice, ——......... 157
Cavitt, Jack.......... 158
Courtney, Sam....... 159
Cavenaugh, John..... 161
Chase, Joseph........ 161
Crocker, Jack........ 161
Carter, S. M., alias J.W. Bryant 161
Carlton, Leonard..... 162
Carlton, Mack....... 162
Campbell, Brandon... 162
Cathey, Lewis....... 162
Case, Wm........... 162
Calhoun, Levi....... 163
Campbell, Henry..... 163
Cortez, Ellervardo... 164
Castillo, Severo..... 164
Cullen, Henry....... 165
Curtis, W. H........ 165
Clay, Geo........... 167
Carpenter, Mrs. Ara.. 168
Carpenter, J. H..... 168
Caviness, Pole...... 168
Cembranes, Francisco.. 166
Clark, W........... 169
Cox, ——.......... 169
Coleman, Andrew.... 169
Cree, Thos......... 170
Cain, Jim.......... 170
Chepman, Jas., alias Pease.. 171
Clark, Mrs. Wm.... 171
Crawford, Tom..... 171
Cook, Henry....... 171
Carpenter, W...... 172
Chamberlain, A.... 172
Carpenter, Geo.... 172
Cottingham, P..... 173
Cline, Joseph...... 173
Culver, A., alias Jones.. 174
Chossard, Pierre, murderers of 174
Carter, Eugene, murderers of. 174
Culbreth, T. L..... 175

	PAGE		PAGE
Crowson, Wm	175	Davis, Eli	49
Collins, Harac	178	Duncan, James	49
Cordova, Feliciana	178	Duncan, S. L	49
Cooper, Thos	173	Doggett, John	50
Carlin, W. A	177	Dearing, B. F	51
		Deer, Drew	51
		Darden, John	52
D		Dikes, Lewis	52
		Dorris, Miles	52
Domingo, Murro	4	Davidson, John, twice	55
Doran, Thos	11	Davis, Samuel	55
Davis, Tom	13	DeRusk, Samuel	56
Darby, Harman	13	Doss, Samuel	56
Dublin, Richard A	15	Deveraux, Julius	56
DeWitt County	16	Dawson, Moses	57
Demonett, Michael	16	Dillinger, L. D	57
Dickson, Wm	14	Davis, D. C	58
Day Alf	71	Durham, Harry	59
Davis, Burrell	17	Drummond, Chs	61
Dickson, Ed	18	DeBoard, Wm	62
Duncan, W. B	20	Davis, Jack, alias Fred. Bunton	55
Dennis, Ludd	23	Day, Alfred	55
Davis, Sam	23	Dill, Lum	60
Douglass, Hill	24	Daughtery, E. C	65
Deaton, J. M. *Killed*	25	Davis, Marion	66
Deaton, Geo	25	Dickerson, Sarah J	67
Driskill, Tilman, *Killed*	25	DeWitt G. W	68
Davis, Ben	27	Dunn, Geo	68
Dunlap, Robt	28	Davidson, Thos	68
Duncan, Milton	28	Dorzeter, Mary J	69
Duke, Kit	30	Douglass, W. S *in the Pen*	70
Doran, Thos	33	Dahoney, Geo	70
Deggs, Richard	33	Debord, Wm	71
Deggs, Prince	33	Davis, W. H	72
Dibble, Dan	34	Davis, Geo	73
Delano, Oll	34	Doyle, Newton	73
Davis, Dood	34	Denemore, Jerry	75
Davis, Dock	34	Daniels, Redman	78
Donnell, Jno	34	Daniel, John	79
Dickum, Jno	34	Delian, Juan	79
Daniels, Wm	37	Dyer, Robt. (twice)	79
Dale, Miny	38	Dunman, Caesar	80
Davis, E. L	40	Dickinson, Rufus	80
Davis, Blucher	41	Dillworth, ——	83
Dock, ——	43	Dyer, L. R	83
Drout, ——	45	Douglas, Geo	85
Davis, Geo	46	Down, Wm	85
Dickson, Alfred	46	Duncan, Nep., alias Phillips	74
Duncan, James	46	Desidora, Juan	79
Daniels, John	47	Davis, Geo	87
Dial, Wm	47	Dobie, Robt	89
Dodd, James	48	Daley, John	91
Davis, Aleck	34	Dreeson, B. J	176, 92

PAGE
Daniels, F. M. (twice)............ 93
Dean, Robt. J 94
Dyer, W. R........ 96
Deason, Wm...................... 96
Dougherty, Emanuel............. 97
Daniel, Escarnacion............. 98
Day, Robt.................... 101
Dickinson, Chs.................. 102
Delaney, Tobias 102
Davis, alias Carry, alias John
  Wilson 96
Daniel, ——.................... 105
Donahoe, James.................. 105
Darnell, Jno. J.................. 106
Driver, John................... 106
Dunn, Frank...................... 107
Davis, Bijot....... 108
Duke, James.................... 108
Diggs, Wm...................... 109
Dea, Nick...................... 114
Dempsey, Thos, alias J. E...... 117
Deason, John................. 118
Dickson, Aaron.................. 119
Daniels, Benj................... 120
Davis, London.................. 121
Davis, Theodore............... 121
Day, M. J..................... 122
Dirr, Robt.................... 122
Dial, Steve.................... 122
Daily, K...................... 123
Davin, John, alias Darton...... 123
Davis, Henry................... 123
Deer, Ed...................... 123
Davis, John................... 123
Davinson, Ned............. 124
Dill, Wm....................... 125
Dennis, Ephriam............ 127
Davis, John.................... 127
Daniels, Bob......... 128
Dobbins, H. M...... 130
Dodson, Cornelius.............. 131
Dingler, B. F.................. 131
Ducket, Andy.................. 135
Davis, Moses.................. 135
Davenport, James.............. 135
Davis, A. R.................... 121
Dillard, John, alias McMullen. 126
Davidson, Jesse................ 137
DeBorde, Wm...... 137
Drake, Tom.................... 137
DeMorse, H. L...... 139
Davis, Serey 145
Dunn, Lea..................... 147

PAGE
Durant, A. J...................... 147
Diffett, Marion......... 147
Daniels, Dock......... 149
Davis, Phil......... 149
Dupree, K...................... 151
Davis, Arthur 151
Dees, John (two times)......... 152
Dallum, Dave, alias George.... 146
Dunbar, Wm.................... 147
Duckworth, Geo., alias Haynes 150
DeOllos, Adrien......... 153
Dykes, D. P., or L. P... 154
Dominguez, Cicero............. 154
Dalby, W...................... 156
Davis, Wm.................... 157
Davis, John.................... 158
Dudley, J. B........ 158
Davis, Aaron...... *Killed* 159
DeGraffenreid, S........ 160
Davis, Hiram.................. 165
Durham, Harvey................ 167
Davis, Andrew................. 168
Davidson, Gen'l James.......... 169
Davis, Thos.................... 169
Duff, Ed. F.................... 170
Daniels, Dan................... 170
Durst, Mat T.................. 170
Davis, Warren................. 171
Dooling, Bud.................. 172
Dow, James................... 172
Dickerson, N. T................ 173
Davis, Josiah H................ 175
Durr, D. L.................... 175
Downs, Wm. F.................. 175
Deaton, W. J., robbers house of 177
Davis, Joshua H................ 177
Dovalina, Edwardo............. 178
Darlen, Moses................. 178

E

Elgo, J. R., alias Ogle............ 45
Escontreas, Peter................. 9
Eafron, Geo.................... 9
Elmore, Henry................. 11
Edwards, Allen................. 11
Ellis, James................... 13
Ellis County.................. 18
Estes, ——.................... 18
Erath County.................. 20
Edwards, Joe................... 21
Elliott, J. M.................. 21

	PAGE
Easley, Hardy H	22
Eastham, Claude	26
Evans, Bud	27
Estus, James	27
Ethel, Chas., alias Thos. Smith	32
Estus, Joe	29
Elliott, John	35
Eldridge, Bud	38
Edwards, Geo	40
Ellis, Jack	41
Eisenbach, John	42
Elston, Chs	45
Elder, Turner	49
Elliott, Alfred	50
Evans, David	55
Ethridge, Wm	62
Exline, Thos., alias Houston	54
Elmore, Wm	66
Evans, S. E	69
Eubanks, Nancy	69
Evans, John	75
Ellis, G. K	81
Edenfield, Jno., alias Stevenson	79
Evans, J. W	93
Eaton, James E	93
Enochs, E	95
Escobar, Manuel, alias Escobaro	98
Elder, James	99
Evans, N. S	104
Elder, John W	104
Elijah, ——	104
English, Dixon	97
English, James	105
Emberson, Julia	105
English, G. W	105
Edmonds, Levi	110
Edmonds, Frank	110
Ewing, April	117
Earle, Noah	120
Earle, Isaiah	120
Elliott, Thos	121
Estes, Eugene	123
Erwin, W. H	123
Eakin, John	125
Evans, Douglas	128
Evans, Crawford	128
Edwards, Sue	128
Ellsworth, Geo	130
English, James	134
English, Wm	134
Easley, D. T	134
Estabon, ——	137
Eaton, Jno	140

	PAGE
Eastwood, Frank	147
Elliott, Geo., alias Sterne	138
Eustis, Thos	139
Eastland County	159
English, Dick on	158
Easters, Ike	158
Erwin, Wm	176, 158
Evans, Berry	160, 159
Ester, David	160
Elliott, John	162
Edwards, H. C	164
Elkins, Lucien,	166
Edwards, James	166
Escobedo, Nicholas	167
Ezelle, D. M	169
Evy, John	169
Esmund, J. H	172
Edwards, C. W	172
Elliott, C	172
Ellis, J. R	177

F

	PAGE
Fulton, Clay	4
Fernandez, Casinova	4
Fulkenson, Wm	6
Foster, Wm	174, 7
Franklin, Burrel	7
Foster, Adam	10
Foley, Patrick, H	11
Freeland, Isaac	15
Fisher, King *killed*	16
Fawcet, Wm	9
Foreman, Thos	13
Foster, R	20
Furguson, Nick	21
Francis, Jas	21
Fade Willis	21
Franklin County	22
Frazier, Jas	22
Freestone County	22
Furlow, Miles	23
Fulcrod, Chas	24
Ferguson, Lark	24
Furguson, Ault	25
Fields, J	26
Filley, Frank	27
Fisher, W. F	30
Futhey, G. W	30
Franks, John	30
Fuller, A. J	31
Fawcett, Wm	31
Ferguson, Dock	17

	PAGE		PAGE
Fains, Thos. R	22	Falkner, J. M	95
Francis, Morris	34	Foster, E	96
Freeman, Foster	34	Foreland, J. W	96
Farris, Charlie	37	Fillmore, Stephen	97
Farris, Henry	37	Fuller, Bud	97
Freeman, Geo	37	Flores, Anastasio	98
Fezelle, Balus J	39	Frazier, Sam	98
Fowler, Dock	42	Farrar, Robt	99
Fuller, James	42	Farrar, Tom	99
Fast, Frank, alias Ferris	45	Frazier, Sarah A	100
Ferris, Frank, alias Fast	45	Floyd, Jno. T	100
Florence, Robt	48	Fraley, Bud	100
Freeman, Bill	48	Fuller, Wm	101
Flournoy, W. B	49	Foster, Dan	102
Fuell, Corn	50	Ferguson, Angus	102
Frost, Wm	50	Fall, Lynn	102
Ford, John	50	Fenton, John	113
Feagle, Wm	51	Fletcher, Howard	114
Franklin, T. J	53	Fletcher, Robt	114
Franklin, W. Rhett	54	Farmer, H. H	116
Fones, Joseph	54	Flynn, Thos	116
Franks, Bud	55	Flynn, James	116
Felder, Stephen	58	Fuller, Houston	116
Fairfax, Israel	59	Fisher, Richar	117
Finley, Nancy	60	Fortune, J. W	119
Foster, Ed	60	Faudren, John	111
Fields, Wm	60	Ferguson, Aaron	121
Ford, Henry	60	Fuller, Wm	121
Fraulkner, Billy	61	Freedman, Wm	122
Fondren, John	61	Ford, Al	123
Fielder, John	64	Fuller, Wm	125
Freeland, ——	56	Fenton, Long John	129
Fuller, Miles	65	Faught, A. H	129
Fullerton, Thos	67	Fudge, Wm	131
Fowler, Enoch	69	Fowler, Jos	133
Farmer, T. J	73	Fulkerson, Chas	134
Franks, Thos	73	Fowler, Alpha	135
Flournoy, Geo	75	Fenlord, Jno	135
Farrow, W. S	76	Fuller, James	138
Freeman, Wm. S	77	Fry, Alex., alias Reid	139
Ferguson, E. L	79	Fowler, G. W	139
Fruger, Frosan	81	Fowler, John C	142
Fuller, W. M	83	Freeman, Sol	146
Freeman, Sam	83	Farris, Wm, alias Morris	141
Foster, John	86	Fisher, J. King	153
Finch, Alfred	74	Faukner, F M	156
Franklin, Geo	77	Ford, Wm	158
Fox, Chas	79	Foster, Chas. B	158
Filgore, ——	91	Finch, Mann	158, 159
Farris, Thos	93	Ford, ——	160
Fletcher, Jeff	93	Faulkner, R. C	162
Fleming, James M	94	Faulconer, Thos	162
Ferris, J. S	95	Flores, Andres	164

	PAGE
Flournoy, Mitch	165
Farrow, Aaron, alias Buford	177, 165
Foster, James	167
Fuller, James	169
Finlay, ——	170
Framen, Jno	171
Framan, Jos	171
Fields, Jno.	172
Freeman, Billy	172
Forales, Grancincio	172
Franklin, Geo	172
Fleming, Alfred	173
Farmer, J. P., murderers of	173
Ferro, Henry, murderers of	175

G

	PAGE
Garcer Albert	3
Garza, Carpio	3
Garza, ——	3
Gatlin, James	4
Goins, Reuben	4
Gomez, Abaristo	4
Garcia, Luciano	4
Garza, Refugio	4
Gleason, John	5
Gibson, Wm	6
Goff, Wm	6
Galbreath, M. H., alias Bud	6
Gorman, John	7
Green, ——	10, 7
Graves, Henry	9
Gray, Malcom	9
Gatewood, P. M	11
Gilham, Wm	16
Gilmore, Jno., alias Williams	9
Gober, James	18
Goode, Milton	19
Gass, Sam	20
Gass, Mary	20
Gibbs, Jno. A	21
Granbury, Oscar	23
Graham, J. F	23
Goliad County	24
Gilcrease, Chas	24
Gill, Samuel	24
Green, Wm	27
Glenn, David	27
Glenn, Wm	28
Glenn, James	28
Greer, Nat	28
Gregory, Wm	29
Gatewood, P. M., alias Jno	30

	PAGE
Gatewood, Jno., alias P. M	30
Graves, Mit	175, 31
Garner, Wesley	32
Garza, Martina	24
Griner, Dallas	33
Green, A. A	33
Goode, Wm	33
Gage, Jno., alias Steve Sneling	33
Gilbreath, Wm	33
Groce, Ellison	34
Giles, Eastland	34
Grimes, Sya	34
Green, Bird	34
Griffin, Moses	34
Grindstaff, John	35
Gibson, Felix	39
Glover, Augustus	40
Gordon, Jeff	41
Glasscock, Wm	41
Gould, Ed. Uriah	41
Griffin, Lee	42
Gorman, Dr. S	43
Gardner, Wm	43
Glasscock, John	43
Gage, Geo	44
Gentry, Chs	44
Gradington, Richard	44
Gould, Jake	44
Gerdner, Mike	45
Garrett, Enoch	46
Goodwin, Wm. T	47
Gentry, Wm	44
Green, John	50
Green, James	51
Garcia, Antonio	54
Giddings, Verastus	55
Gillespie County	56
Gilson, Samuel	56
Gilson, Robert	56
Glenn, James	56
Grimes County	56
Garrett, Thos	57
Greer, Stephen	57
Garrett, J. D	57
Gregg, Harmon	176, 59
Gibson, R. B	60
Green, A. J	60
Gibson, J. A	61
Gibbons, J. W	61
Greenwood, John	62
Gintz, John	62
Good, Isham	63
Goodman, Wm., alias J. M	63

Name	Page	Name	Page
Goodman, J. M., alias Wm.....	63	George, —..	104
George, W. R.......................	64	Garland, John.....	104
Gonzales County.................	51	Grandison, James....	92
Goodin, Jno. D.....................	54	Guinn, Mary.......................	105
Gunter, J. L........................	65	Greenwood, Marion...............	106
Guest, Elisha.......................	66	Gales, July.......................	106
Gramner, Payton..................	67	Greenwood, Martin.............	106
Green, I. N.........................	67	Gill, Vinck......................	107
Griffin, Jas. R.....................	68	Grim, Chas.......................	107
Gibson, Isaac......:.............	69	Gassiott, Nick, R.............	109
Gates, Joseph.......................	69	Gentry, Chas............177,173,	112
Glasscock, John....................	69	Green, Thos......................	112
Gearon, L. G.......................	69	Guest, Elisha....................	112
Gonier, Henry.....................	71	Gordon, Wm 176,	114
Garrett, Wm.......................	71	Gadison, Robt....................	114
Gause, L. A........................	71	Grey, John.......................	115
Gregory, Wm.......................	73	Galaway, A. L....................	116
Ghent, Lid, alias Gentry........	73	Grimes, M. H.....................	116
Gentry, Lid, alias Ghent........	73	Gallaway, Alford.................	116
Graham, Duncan.	74	Girtman, Norman......	116
Gelchrist, Thos....................	75	Greenwood, J. T..................	117
Goff, Jesse......	75	Greenwood, Pinkney H...118,	117
Gooden, Warren	76	Goodwin, O. W....................	118
Gardener, Mitchell...............	78	Gentry, Abby...:.......	118
Garcia, Dominico.........	79	Grover, Matt........	121
Gonzales, Augustin...............	79	Gray, Wm.........................	121
Giles, Jody......	81	Gray, Ellen.........	121
Greer, Morgan.....................	81	Gallagher, John.........	122
Green, Ed.......................176,	81	Grissom, Rome.........	122
Gregg, Samuel......................	85	Gamble, John......	122
Gibson, Chas........	90	Gardner, Stephen.................	123
Griffin, Jesse........	91	Goodwyn, Solomon...........	125
Glass, J............................	92	Greer, Jacob.....................	125
Green, John......................	93	Goodwyn, Joel....	125
Granberry, Sol.....................	93	Graham, Sam.....................	125
Griffian, John........	94	Greer, Ned.......................	125
Grace, W.........	94	Gilliam, James........	127
Green, Irvin.......................	94	Gilbert, Marsh...................	127
Golden, Thos...... 97,	95	Gardner, Sol.....................	128
Green, Robt. J.....................	95	Green, Frank.....................	129
Gaston, Oliver.....................	95	Grisham, A. B....................	130
Gillard, Gabe......................	95	Goldsmith, John..................	132
Gambreel, James......	96	Gilchrist, Geo...................	133
Glasco, alias Mixon......	96	Gibbons, John....................	136
Gonzales, Pedro....................	98	Garza, Elijo........	136
Garcia, Guadelupe.................	99	Garza, Frank.....................	138
Garcia, Andres....................	99	Graham, Thomas...................	139
Griggs, Frank.....................	100	Gallon, Martin...................	139
Grayson, J. M.....................	101	Grayson, Thos...	140
Greenwood, Marion................	102	Gunter, J. H.....................	142
Green, Chas.......................	102	George, Alsop....................	143
Gill, W. A	103	Gibson, John.....................	143
Gibson, Chas........	104	Groce, Watt	144

	PAGE		PAGE
Glass, Jess	145	Gillyard, Jas., murderers of	175
George, Dave, alias Dallum	146	Green, M. R., murderers of	177
Gary, F. S., alias Chas. Lee	147	Gibson, Lit	177
George, Chas	148	Gardner, John J	178
Garet, C. A	149	Gardenhire, A. J	178
Garrett, Willis	151	Graham, ——	178
Gillaspie, Joe	152	Gillum, ——	178
Gibson, Geo., alias Milam	138	Goodman, Ben	179
Grayson County	160	Goodwin, Benj	179
Gonzales, Jose Ma	153		
Guerrero, Manuel	153		
Garrelt, A. J	154	**H**	
Geland, Narcisse	154		
Garety, Pat	155	Hernandez, Saferino	3
Grady, Henry	155	Haskell, Allen	3
Garland, Bud	155	Hampton, John	3
Greenhill, Allen	156	Humphries, Wm	5
Griffin, Wm	156	Headspeth, Wm	5
Gallaway, Capt	156	Hoover, Wm	6
Glaze, Billy	157	Howard, M. D	6
Goldsberg, Frank	158	Harvie, Nicholas, alias Dock	6
Goodright, Dr. Wm. H	159	Heusen, Albert	7
Goodwin, John	159	Heusen, Henry	7
Grounds, Dock	160	Hobbs, Joseph	7
Gillam, Wm	160	Holden, Henry	9
Glover, A C	161	Hill, Alick	9
Goodfrey, Samuel	161	Harbert, John	9
Goodfrey, Geo	161	Howard, B. A	9
Griffin, Henry, alias Bully	164	Hunt, Rowan	10
Garrett, Richard	165	Hall, Jno. W	10
Garrett, Harry	165	Haynes, Alvin	11
Gamble, Dick,	165	Hynes, Jube	11
Goodwin, J. B	165	Hisaw, Green	11
Gamble, Rich'd	165	Harris, Jim	12
Garza, Miguel	165	Hodge, Ben	12
Gutierres, Francisco	166	Henson, Adam	12
Garcia, Jose Ma	166	Howard, Ben	12
Gonzales, Luciana	166	Holmes, Sci	13
Gonzales, Andres	167	Hart, Zan	13
Goen, ——	168	Harper, Granison	13
Gatlin, ——	168	Haywood, Chas	13
Gage, Geo	168	Harris, Lewis	13
Glasscock, Wm	169	Hogue, Geo	14
Galloway, ——	169	Huff, Branch	15
Garner, Alfred	169	Hall, Andrew	15
Green, W. H	170	Hall, Frank	15
Griffin, John	171	Harris, Artemus	15
Golden, John 172,	171	Hamby, E. M	16
Gage, Geo. F	172	Hill, Philip	16
Garland, ——	172	Hardwick, C. T	16
Graham, Jessie	172	Henderson, H. A 176,	16
Gustine Jack, alias Woods	173	Houston, Jack	3
Gulbreth, M. C	173	Harris, Anderson	14

	PAGE		PAGE
Harris, Will	17	Henson, Jack	33
Horrett, Vol	17	Hodge, Hamilton	33
Hollan, Jerry	17	Hemmel, Robt	34
Humphreys, Wm	17	Hoffman, H	34
Henderson, Chas	18	Healy, J. H	34
Henderson, J. A.	18	Horn, Pink	34
Harrell, Wm	19	Hudgens, Harrison	36
Herring, Owen	19	Hart, Charly, alias Clark	36
Hurst, W. H	19	Huddleston, ——	38
Hodge, W. J	20	Higgins, Chris. C	40
Hines, Ben	20	Hall, David J	40
Hurrier, Joseph	20	Hanley, Fred	41
Hughes, Jos. H	21	Hall, John	41
Hill, Richard	21	Hazel, James	41
Head, Lorenzo	22	Holt, Thos	42
Hall, Thos	22	Hoffman, Bonny	42
Harris, John	22	Hoffman, Geo	42
Holden, Amos	23	Harris, Wesley	45
Harper, Henry	23	Hoffman, C. W	46
Halbert, J. M	24	Holloway. W. M	48
Hill, J. T	24	Hill, Dudley, alias Bull Williams	43
Hughes, Wm. F	24		
Hamilton County	25	Hardie, Mit	49
Hughett, James	25	Hamilton, M. M	50
Highsaw, James	25	Hunt, Wm	50
Hughes, J. W. W	25	Henry, Chas	50
Hays County	25	Hawkins, Theme	50
Henderson, James	25	Hill, Chas	50
Halford, Jerry	26	Houston, John	51
Holland, Ellen	26	Hicks, David	51
Hill, T. L	26	Halford, Nathaniel. 178, 53, 52
Hill County	26	Harrison, Austin	53
Harrington, Dell	26	Houston, Geo	53
Hancock, John	27	Holmes, J. F	53
Hardin, John W	27	Holmes, Thos	53
Herring, R. F	28	Heart, Joseph	54
Herring, J. W	28	Haynes, Peter	54
Hays, Wm	28	Houston, Thos., alias Exline	54
Haynes, Geo	29	Hilliard, Elias	55
Hollace, Thos	30	Hedrick, Geo. W	55
Hinton, J C	30	Hadley, Barney	57
Haskey, Boss	30	Harn, S. M	57
Hurkey, Boss	30	Hightower, Simon	58
Harrison, J. D	30	Hardy, Wm	58
Hall, D. N	30	Howard, Sam	58
Haley, James	31	Hays, R. H	59
Hood County	31	Hill, Wm	59
Henry, Wm	32	Hopkins, Thos	60
Hamilton, Robt	32	Hendrix, John	60
Harrison, Henry	32	Halsell, Jennie	61
Hill, Douglas	24	Hickman, Chas	62
Hall. Cabel	33	Hues, Robt	62
Hunt, Henry	33	Hamilton, Robt	63

15

	PAGE
Hoag, Martin	63
Hall, Wm. N.	63
Hood, Willie	64
Hill, Dick, alias Sullivan	49
Halford, Nathaniel	53
Harris, Geo.	54
Herndon, Jas. T.	54
Hanes, Wm.	56
Hutchinson, Geo.	56
Hunt County	59
Heifler, Augustus	65
Hicks, Harvey	65
Harman, Thos. N. B.	65
Hicks, Corde..	66
Howard, F. B.	67
Hudson, Call	67
Holcomb, Meredith	67
Hill, G. H.	67
Hart, John	68
Hearne, J. C. 177,	69
Howard, E. B.	69
Hodges, James	69
Hess, Sam	70
Hazel, James	71
Hogan, Leonard	71
Harvey, Richard	71
Hanna, Zack	71
Haynes, Geo.	72
Hitchcomb, Chas	72
Hodge, John	72
Harris, Joe	72
Hogan, James	72
Hodge, Hum.	72
Hatchett, Dock	72
Harvel, Wm.	72
Hawkins, Chas.	72
Harper, J. P.	72
Hanna, Jack	72
Hawks, Frank 177,	73
Holt, John	73
Hughes, Wm.	73
Harris, Jim	75
Harris, Erasmus	76
Harris, Morris	76
Hilliard, James	77
Houstamente, Gregoria	79
Hobbs, W. J.	79
Hornsinger, John	81
Hines, Thos.	81
Houston, John	82
Heuson, Wm.	84
Huitt, B. T.	84
Harris, L. F.	84

	PAGE
Hudson, Simon	85
Harrisson, Geo.	85
Harris, Wm.	85
Hancock, John	85
Hadden, W. N.	78
Hariposa, Pauch	79
Higginbotham, J. W.	89
Harris, Wm.	89
Harris, Alexander.	89
Hayes, James H.	90
Hicks, J. J.	90
Hudson, Thos. J.	91
Higgins, Sam 176,	92
Harris, Chas.	93
Haywood, Wm.	93
Hill, Jeff.	93
High, Wm. A.	94
Harrington, Mat.	94
Hudson, W. T.	94
Hudson, N. S.	94
Hudson, A. J.	94
Hammond, Thos	94
Hess, J. B.	94
Horker, Wm.	95
Hunter, Hal.	95
Harris, J. B.	95
High, Samuel.	95
Horn, Reese.	96
Hall, Henry.	96
Henderson, James.	96
Hall, Caleb, alias Cail.	97
Hill, S. A.	98
Hernandez, Simon	98
Horn, Enoch	99
Hickey, Thos.	99
Haley, J. H.	99
Hamilton, Cain.	100
Harris, Wm.	101
Hazlet, Marion	102
Hall, S. D.	102
Heuson, T. J.	102
Haygood, John	102
Hanks, Horatio	103
Harris, John.	104
Henry, Willis.	104
Harrell, Walter.	90
Harang, L. P.	91
Hardin, ——.	96
Hanscune, Jas. alias Seamon..	98
Harrison, Thos.	105
Hains, Joshua.	105
Hains, Ann.	105
Hodge, Chs., alias Johnson....	105

	PAGE
Houston, Lawrence	105
Hilton, Nathan	106
Hilton, Isaac	106
Hodges, Shade	106
Haynes, Jack	107
Henry, ——	107
Houston, Nettie	107
Hardy, Mary	107
Herin, Samuel	108
Heredia, Cileto	108
Haywood, Jordan	110
Haywood, Adam	110
Hill, Monroe	110
Hooper, Wm	111
Harbert, Wm	111
Harris, Joe	111
Hill, Geo	111
Harris, Eli	111
Howeth, Emily	112
Harrist, Jas. A	112
Holtzclaw, Gus	113
Hale, Mansel	115
Hogan, Frank	115
Hopkins, W. O.	115
Hardie, Dock	115
Hardie, Wiley	115
Harris, Wm	116
Higgs, Jere, Jr	117
Ham, Wm	117
Hampton, Wm	117
Hamilton, Rufus	118
Hamilton, Jefferson	118
Hurn, Stephen	118
Harlin, Dwight	118
Hardie, Ann	119
Hudson, Martin	119
Hutchings, Joseph	120
Hester, Jos	120
Hensley, Lewis W	113
Hines, Dock	121
Harris, Jack	121
Hanna, Fred	121
Hord, James R	121
Hendley, James	121
Harris, James	122
Happe, E. H	122
Harrell, Alex	123
Hardin, Geo	123
Hill, C. L	123
Howell, T. J	123
Hearne, Tim R	123
Holt, Samuel	123
Herring, Frank	123
Hines, Chas	123
Hoot, Manuel	124
Horn, H. M	124
Hamilton, John	124
Holt, H. L	124
Hall, Samps	125
Hudgins, Wm	125
Harper, Mid	126
Hordu, Wm	126
Holman, Jack	126
Halbert, Joe	126
Heuson, Thos	126
Hill, Martin	127
Hudgins, Zachariah	127
Harper, Wm	127
Hill, Randell	128
Hughes, Wm	128
Helton, Geo	129
Helton, Harry	129
Hambrick, John	129
Holbrook, D. M	130
Horton, J. M	131
Hill, A. W	131
Hudgins, Wm. A	131
Hudnall, J. B	131
Hawkins, Wm	131
Halbert, C. M	131
Hawkins, Hense	132
Hudson, John T	132
Hambric, Alfred	133
Harris, Constantine	133
Hughes, Benj	134
Hall, Buck	135
Hill, Henrietta	135
Hernandez, Datio	136
Hancock, Jasper J	136
Horde, E	136
House, Thelbert	137
Hall, Ferdinand	137
Hicks, Oliver	139
Hussatz, Frank H	139
Hanson, J. H	140
Howell, W. H	140
Hendrix, W. H	140
Harris, Geo	141
Hodges, Joel	141
Hughey, Willis H	141
Harry, Dick	141
Hunnicut, James	141
Hazard, Robt	141
Horan, L	144
Haley, John	144
Hagan, Ed	145

	PAGE		PAGE
Hampton, Wade	145	Harden, Francis	167
Hall, Dan	145	Hardee, W	168
Hill, James	145	Hightower, W	168
Harris, Austin	146	Hamilton, Jim	168
Hardin, J. T	147	Hardin, John	156
Hardin, Meredith	147	Hogwood, Isaac	157
Halsell, Sam	148	Hicks, Frank	159
Harper, Thos	149	Hurricane, Bill, alias W. A.	
Hines, Edward	149	Martin	167
Helliary, alias Tucker Black-		Hill, ——,	170
burn	150	House, James	170
Hendley, Isaac	150	Huddleston, ——,	170
Hightower, Henry	150	Hamilton, Bob	171
Haynes, Geo., alias Duckworth,	150	Harris, Martin	171
Hall, Sam	152	Horst, Geo	172
Hamilton, Wm., alias Wills,		Hamilton, R. R	172
alias Pritchard	148	Hearne, C. C	172
Hogan, Wash	150	Hearne, James	173
Hill, Ben	150	Henderson, Walter	173
Holly, T. J	154	Houston, Isaac	173
Holly, W. H. H	154	Henderson, Chas	173
Henry, James	154	Hamilton, Mack	174
Hewitt, John W	178, 154	Hughes, J. W. W	174
Hill, John	155	Hazlett. Columbus	174
Hilburn, Rob't	157	Hunter, Yance	175
Hamilton, W	157	Helms, Anderson, murderer of	176
Ham, Rich	157	Hill, J. W., robbers of	177
Harn, S. D.	157	Harris, Henry	178
Harvey, F. H	157	Hays Co. Courthouse, burners	
Hines, Milton	157	of	176
Heaven, Ferd	157	Henderson, Gus	178
Harris, Sam	157		
Huntsman, Henry	157		
Hearne, Thos	158	**I**	
Harrold, Thos	158		
Harrold, Mary,	158	Ingram, Thos	11
Hall, Lew	158	Isbell, John	22
Hoag, Antony	159	Inman, Eli	24
Hamilton, Rob't	159	Inins, Joel	25
Hicks, Lush	159	Ivey, G. W	28
Hines, M. M	159	Irvin, Bill	41
Hines, L. M	160	Irvine, Joe	45
Hale, H. N	160	Isham, Joe	46
Holmes, R. T	160	Irvine, Anthony (twice)	50
Hatley, Wm	160	Irvin, Gus	53
Hawkins, Marion	161	Ivey, Ben	55
Hardy, Wm	161	Isbell, James	66
Hays, Geo	162	Isbell, Baley	69
Hampton, S. A	162	Insal, Rich'd	71
Holmesley, M. F	163	Isaacs, Albert	71
Hines, John	166	Ingall, Till	76
Holstein, Henry	166	Inge, Sidney	83
Harris, Jack	167	Ingam, B. T	84
		Ingsum, Henry	84

	PAGE
Ingram, Geo	108
Isaacs, Thos	116
Ivry, Winwight	114
Ivory, Dave	139
Ivy, Lee	163
Ivy, Marion	163
Ishner, Zacharias	169
Irwin, John	173
Irwin, A. D	178

J

	PAGE
James, J. T	4
Joiner, J. W	7
Jones, Carter	7
Jackson, John	8
Jennings, Thomas	11
Johnson, James	11
Johnson, J. C	14
Jenkins, Wm	15
Jeffries, Wm	15
Jeffries, Sam	15
Jenkins N. A	15
Jones, Jeff	6
Jackson, John	17
Jackson, W. R	20
Jones, James	22
Johnson, R. C	23
Jackson, Daniel	23
Jackson, Seaf	23
Jackson, Geo	23
Jones, John	23
Jordan, John	25
Johnson, F. E	25
James, J. W	27
Johnson, J. R	27
Johnson County	29
Jones, J. E	30
Jordan, T. W	30
Johnson, John W	30
Jefferson County	32
Jones, J. S	32
Johnson, Henry	33
Jackson, Wm	33
Jones, Sehen	34, 33
Johnson, J. M	34
Jackson, Antona	35
Jones, Sam	39
Johnson, Ben. F	40
Jones, Lisbon	40
Johnson, Jeff	41
Jones, Adolph	42
Jackson, John	42

	PAGE
Johnson, John	44
Jackson, A. J	44
Junkins, Jo	44
Jackson, Wm	45
Judd, F. R	50
Johnson, G. B	50
Jennings, W. S	50
Jones, Z. T	51
Jones, Jack	51
Jolly, Logan (two times)	51
Johnson, Wm	52
Johnson, Ben., alias Sam	54
Johnson, Chas. D	55
Jones, Hamp	57
Jones, Charles	57
Jackson, John	58
Jackson, Ike	58
Johnson, Willis	59
Johnson, Morris	59
Jones, Pat	59
Jackson County	60
Jack County	60
Jones, Elmira	61
Jeffries, Preston	63
Jacobs, Bass	63
Jones, Benj	64
James, Henry, alias Lewis Carroll	55
Jackson, Ceaf	65
Jenkins, A. M	65
Johnson, Love	66
Johnson, John	66
Johnson, Wm	66
Jones, Chs	67
Johnson, Andy	74
Johnson, Merritt	75
Johnson, Alf	76
Johnson, Wm	82
Jackson, J. W	85
Jones, Selves	85
Johnson, Robt	86
Jones, Anson	86
Jones, Hanson	86
Jones, Emma	86
Jones, Bill	87
Jones, Amanda	87
Jones, Tom	88
Johnson, Sam	88
Johnson, Frank	88
Jones, Dr. J. R., alias Allen	86
Johnson, Sam	88
Jackson, Frk., alias McGuffin	89
Jones, Wm	90

202

INDEX.

	PAGE		PAGE
Jones, Simon	91	Johnson, Elijah	123
Johnson, Geo	91	Johnson, Leonard	123
Johnson, Henry C.	91	Johnson, Fed	123
Johnson, Ed	92	Johnson, Thos	125
Johns, Perry	92	Jones, Calvin	126
Johnson, John	92	Jones, John	126
Joplin, Giles	92	Jarmon, Joseph	127
Jarrett, Henry	92	Johnson, Randal	174, 128
Jennings, Mark	92	Johnson, Paul	128
Juvenal, ——	93	Jones, Thomas	128
Johnson, Ollie	93	Johnson, Polk	128
Johnson, Wm	94	Johnson, Chas	128
Jackson, Samuel	94	Johnson, Gabriel	129
Jackson, Manuel	94	Jones, Pink	129
Jackson, Chs	95	Jiles, James	129
Jackson, Arkansaw	95	Johns, Richard	129
Jackson, W. G	95	Jennings, Joseph	135
Jackson, Bob., alias Whispering Bob	96	Johnson, Wm	135
Johnson, Wm	96	Jewell, Henry	135
Johnson, Willis	97	Joines, H. S	136
Johnson, Nat	97	Johnson, Lit	126
Jones, Wm	99	Johnson, Geo., alias White	134
Jeffers, James	99	Juan, ——	137
Jackson, Henry	100	Jasper, Thos	137
Jarvis, J	101	James, Felix	139
Jordan, Matt	102	Jernigan, James	139
Jordan, James	103	Jackson, Chas	143
Johnson, Jethro	103	Jones, Madison	143
Jones, Samuel	105	Jackson, Clarissa	144
Jackson, Joe	107	Jagelke, Henry	146
Johnson, Lum	108	Jones, J. G	147
Johnson, Rector	108	Jones, R. F	148
Jordan, Nash	110	Jack, W. T	149
Jones, Hugh	173, 112	Jones, Elijah	150
Jacks, J. H	113	Johnson, Sam	152
Johnson, John	115	Jones, Warner	144
Jones, John	115	Jolly, Rich	148
Jackson, Andrew	116	Johnson, R. M	156
Jamerson, Frank	116	Johnson, Elijah	156
Johnson, Geo	116	Jones, Tom	157
Johnson, Bill	116	Johnson, James	157
Johnson, Frank	117	Johnson, Henry	157
Jackson, Reuben	120	Jones, Henry	157
Jeffreys, Terrell	120	Jones, Paul	157
Johnson, Charley, alias Chas. Hodge	105	Janks, Wiley	158
		Johnson, Logan	158
Jones, Ike	114	Jones, Wesley	159
Johnson, Ranse	114	John, Henry	160
Johnson, John	121	Jarvis, M	160
Jordan, John	121	Jourdan, ——	164
Jenkins, James	122	Jones, Zack	165
Johnson, Sam	122	Johnson, Henry	166
		Jimenes, Jose Ma	166

	PAGE
Jones, L. J	168
Johnson, Isaiah, alias Jim	170
Johnson, Thos	170
Johnson, Dick	172
Jones, Z. F	174
Jeffries, Wm	174
Jones, Berry	176
Jackson, John	176
Jailbreakers and murdering prisoners	177
Jossey, Wm	179
Jones, Mrs. A., stables, burners of	174
Jones, A., alias Culver	174
Johnson, Jim	178

K

	PAGE
Kay, Geo	7
King, Alfred	7
Knight, Clinton G	7
Kalb, Allen	9
Kirk, John	9
Kyle, Bur	9
Kirksey, Peter	12
King, S. R	14
Kyrkendall, Jos	7
Kinsey, Noah	10
Knowles, A. J	14
Kelley, Abe	16
Kerliks, John	17
Knowles, R. E	19
Kalb, John	23
Kirkland, Aaron	25
Kinney County	32
Key, Pinkney	34
Knighton, K. M	46
Killough, Chas	46
Kendrick, Samuel	48
Kennedy, John	50
Kiggin, John	50
Key, James	52
Kinney, Jno. D	55
Kirchner, Johan	56
King, ——	61
Karnes County	62
Kendall County	63
Kuttner, J	64
Kindred, Sam, alias McCall	54
Kent, ——	56
Kirtland, Daniel	67
Kavenaugh, A	67
Knight, Maley	69

	PAGE
Keith, Chas	70
Kuykendall, Cooper	73
Keith, O	74
King, Barney	75
King, Jack	84
Kirby, Jno. James	89
King, Joe, alias Williamson	90
Kimball, Sam	91
Keelam, Wm	93
Kurtz, Chris	96
Kellis, Wm	177, 96
Kimbell, Ike	100
Kidd, Jno. B	101
King, Jordan	102
King, Thomas	102
Kern, Polk	104
Kelley, James	106
Kelley, Dick	107
Kay, Bedford	107
Keener, Wm	107
Keith, Jack	114
King, Burton	121
Knapp, W	122
Knight, R. S	126
Kelly, John	127
King, A. W	127
Kay, John	179, 128
King, Rob't	128
Kelly, Henry	131
Kelly, James	131
Kelly, Pat	134
King, Rob't	135
Keonio, Miguel	137
Kawalsky, J. B	138
Kennel, Henry	141
Keyes, Geo	141
Kidd, Webb	147
Kennedy, John	147
Kuykendall, R. T	148
Kent, Granville	152
Keys, James	148
King, Theodore	151
Kimble County	162
Kay, Ely	154
Kitchens, Joe	155
Knight, Henry	155
Kirk, Miles	157
Kimble, Bud	177, 166
Kahn, H	167
Kenner, Peter	168
Kellow, James	169
Kirk, James	169
Kessee, Thos	169

	PAGE
Kelson, Bart	172
Kissam, Webb	172
Kunde, Taylor	175
Kunde, Albert	175
Kunde, Julius	175
Kemper, Wm	179
King, Dick	174
Kendall, Joseph K	174
Koosier, Ed	176

L

Lane, Samuel	3
Lemon, Savino	4
Lopez, Dionicio	4
Lindsly, John	7
Logan, Mathew	7
Lackey, Hugh L	7
Lewis, Morris	7
Lewis, Bill	8
Lot, Jack	10
Lane, Jack	13
Lee, Bill	13
Lewis, Joel	16
Lanford, A. M	20
Leonard, Wm	20
Ledbetter, Lewis	21
Lasier, Jack	22
Lamar, Raphael	23
Lunsford, Bud	24
Lambert, Miles	25
Lawrence, J	29
Lang, Joseph	29
Logan, Wm	31
Lewis, James	175, 32
Lavin, Manuel	32
Laman, Dan	22
Lindsey, Geo	23
Lilly, Richard	33
Lacy, Irvin	34
Langlois, P. L	34
Leakez, J. M	35
Lock, Adam	40
Lee, Isaac	41
Lawhon, P. A	41
Lee, John	44
Lehpard, Dave	45
Lane, R. P	45
Lester, Lovelace	45
Little, J. D	46
Longmire, Leroy	46
Land, Wm	46
Little, James	49

	PAGE
Little, Davis	49
Lindsey, Lewis	49
Lipscomb, O. C	50
Lee, Knox	51
Lamkin,Crump,alias Tecumseh	53
Leagan, Morris	54
Love, James	55
Lewis, Taylor	57
Langford, James	58
Lemuel, Eli	58
Lee, Kaufman	58
Lehew, Cicero	59
Lovejoy, Wm., alias Braden	60
Loomi , Warner	60
Lanley, Moses	61
Lovelace, Thos	62
Lusk, S. B	62
Langston, Herbert	63
Limestone County	63
Lea, Harris	65
Lamar County	65
Logan, David	67
Leir, Leteir	69
Lampasas County	70
Labarte, E. A	70
Lavaca County	71
Lee County	73
Lopez, Armstead	73
Linson, W. J	74
Lankford, Nathan	75
Llano County	77
Lee, George	77
Lamar, John	77
Larrimore Wm	77
Lott, David	78
Leapart, D P	78
Live Oak County	78
Longoria, Ruvinto	79
Liberty County	80
Lockhart Irvin	80
Lum, Pat	176, 81
Lockhart, Shade	81
Lockhart, David	81
Lewallen, Mrs. Wiley	83
Lenty, Bud	85
Lancaster, Alex	87
Lancaster, Frank	87
Lloyd, Frank	88
Linton, Wallace	88
Leon County	74
Lankford, Nathan	75
Lewis, W. H	79
Lasame, Robt	81

	PAGE		PAGE
Labaum, Bill	84	Lemmons, Poley	148
Looney, Isaac W	91	Lytle, Richard	149
Lovelace, J. C	95	Lyon, Thos	144
Little, Abe	95	Lava, Candelario	138
Longley, J. W., alias Patterson	95	Landry, Wesley	145
Lundy, John W	96	Lee, Chas., alias F. S. Garry	147
Lewis, Clint	178, 98	Lawrence, Primus	150
Lopez, Candelario	98	Lumley, John	153
Laurence, Sam	99	Luvo, Cypriano	153
Loupe, R. S	99	Lee, H. T	154
Lee, Jno	99	Love, Louis	155
Lisp, Robt	100	Lynn, Chas	157
Lanning, Tony	100	Lyon, W T	157
Lee, Sam	101	Lattimore, Henry	159
Lee, John	101	Levi, Washington	177, 164
Lewis, Thos	102	Lane, David	168
Lewis, Coney	102	Losson, Wm	168
Landy, J. O.	103	Leggett, Wells W	168
Lindsey, E. E	92	Larson, N. P	170
Langley, Stephen	105	Lazy, Jim	170
Lary, Lewis	107	Leach, ——	171
Lofton, Bud	112	Long, Wm	173
Loughery, B.	114	Lackey, John, or Jake	174
Lindsay, Joel	116	Lackey, Joel	174
Little, Wm	118, 116	Linson, Tom	174
Lynch, Joe	119	Lamaster, Billy	175
Land, Wm	119	Lockhart, J. W	176
Lowrie, Robt	121	Little, Aaron	176
Ludlow, Sidney	122	Long, John	178
Lindsay, ——	122		
Lewis, Phillip	123		
Lewis, E. M	124	**M**	
Lowe, Bob	124		
Loud, James	124	Mancho, Santiago	3
Lee, John	127	Miller, Alsey	4
Lucas, Gilbert	127	Martin, Gamboa	4
Landers, Wm	127	Martinez, Juan	4
Loftin, Aaron,	129	Murphy, Patrick	5
Lewis, Jas. L	129	Marshal, Gabriel	5
Liddell, Dan	129	Mason, Edward	5
Laves, John	130	McFarland, Scotty	5
Lugan, Tom	130	McCurry, Richard	7
Lindsey, Joel	174, 130	May, Taylor	7
Lockhart, A. P	132	Mitchell, Ben	7
Lacy, Chas	132	Morgan, ——	8
Lowe, Wm	133	Morgan, Thos	8
Lagrone, D. H	135	McCulloch, Green	8
Lopez, Pedro	136	McDowell, James	8
Lee, George	137	Miller, Chancy	8
Lee, Frank	139	McCoy, John	9
Lewis, Alex	139	Mitchell, Jack, alias Jack Matthews	10
Lewis, Neil	140		
Lea, Luke	146	Matthews, Jack, alias Mitchell	10

16

	PAGE
Malone, Geo	10
McGee, Robt	11
Montgomery, Lucinda	12
McKean, Jos	12
Moore, Coley	12
Magoffin, John	13
Meyer, Paul	14
Mackey, A. J	14
McAfee, Barney	14
Mayfield, Harry	15
May, S	15
McCallister, D. B	15
Momkin, Peter	16
McQuillen, C	16
Manning, Wm	16
Montgomery, R. M	16
May, Henry B.	16
Mackey, Jack	10
McGuire, Eli	15
Muckelroy, Ben	16
Murray, York	17
Marrow, Aleck	17
Milam, Chas	17
Mills, Jesse	17
McKinley, L. L	18
Morrison, ——	19
Mills, Milford	19
Morris, Wm	20
Middleton, John	31, 20
McClusky, N. T	21
Morrison, Geo	22
Majors, Riley	22
Maddox, James	22
Mayhor, Jno	22
Melton, Jno	22
Mitchell, Jack	24, 23
Moseley, W. J	23
McElroy, J. J	23
Miles, Thos	175, 23
McCollum, Thos	24
McDaniel, Jake	24
McCarty, Wm	24
Martin, Jno. H	24
Myers, Milton	25
Morales, Valentine	25
Moore, Columbus	26
Martin, D	26
Morris, A. J	26
McMeans, T. E	26
Monroe, James	26
Murphy, Tom	27
McKee, S. W	27
Morgan, A. C	27
McKissick, A. H	28
McInch, C. P	28
McKinney, Joe	28
McLain, C. P	29
Myers, D. T	29
McClendon, Z. A	30
Mills, Geo	30
Mahaffey, Henry	31
Mitchell, Wm	175, 31
Mathews, Joe	31
More, Benj	32
Morris, Bob	31
Miranda, Simon	33
Moore, John	33
Middleton, Austin	33
Murphy, E. M	33
Mathews, Alfred	33
McMahon, John	34
Moore, Wm	35
Myrick, Wm., Sr	35
Myrick, Wm., Jr	35
Mckeen, J. B	37
Moore, Buck	37
Mason, Jas. P	37
Myrick, Wm	38
Moore, Jake	39
Mayfield, Thos	40
Morris, Bob	40
Moore, Buck	42
McCarthey, Jeff	43
Moore, App	44
Meek, Lewis D	44
Mangle, ——	45
Mallard, E. W	46
Maroney, D. R. C	47
Martin, Smallard	47
McCrimmon, Lot	47
McCormick, Lum	37
Martin, Sell	49
Miller, Albert	49
McNab, John	49
McNab, Jasper	50
Mackey, Mace	50
McMarlin, Howard	50
McGreror, J. D	51
Mills, Thos	52
Miller, Lewis	52
McMickle, Columbus	53
Mathis, Peter	53
McCall, Sam, alias Kindrid	54
McCallum, Geo	54
Monroe, Geo	54
McKinnon, John	55

	PAGE		PAGE
McBride, A. Hillyard	55	Miller, A. R	77
McCarty, W. P	55	Moss, Mat	78
Montgomery, Robt., twice	55	Mosley, Geo	78
McCracken, Lycurgus	55	Mackey, Jiles	78
McLane, Silas	57	Mitchell, Ed	78
Miller, Henry	57	McAdams, L. L	78
Miller, John	58	Moore, J. P	80
Murphy, Bob	58	**Montague County**	81
Mitchell, Daniel	59	McConnell, A	82
May, Alexander	59	Masoner, James	82
Marion, Geo	59	Minnis, L. C	83
Mitchell, John	60	Masoner, Geo	83
Meyers, Shelton	60	Morehead, John	83
McDaniel, John	60	Mullin, —— 178,	84
Mitchell, C. R	60	McAllister, James	84
Martin, John	60	McKeever, John	84
McMillan, M., or McMullen ..178,	60	Medley, Frank	84
Morris, Jake	62	Marshall, John	84
Mullins, Z	62	Murray, Jack	85
Murray, John	62	McKey, Giles	85
McClure, James	63	**Matagorda County**	85
Mills, Tom	63	Mathews, Martin	86
Marshall, Ambrose	63	Monroe, Peyton	86
Medlock, Jerry	64	**Morris County**	86
McIntosh, Moses, alias Young	57	**Menard County**	87
McCarty, Joseph	65	Martin, John	87
Moseley, Isham	66	**Montgomery County**	88
McGinnis, Wm	67	May, J. Lew	88
McCoy, Monroe	67	Mass, Mack	73
McCarty, Clint	68	Mackey, Willis	89
Maxwell, Jackson	68	McRae, Dennis	89
McDaniel, Jack	68	Miller, Henry	90
Mason, Geo	68	McKee, L. S	90
McCarty, W. C	68	Moore, Thos	90
Morrisson, Geo	69	McRae, Alex'd	90
McElya, W. A	69	Moses, Elbert	90
Maness, James	69	**Marion County**	90
Mauldering, Berry	69	**McLennan County**	92
Mayfield, W. E. C 177,	69	Moore, B. T	93
May, W. C	70	Mare, A	93
Massie, J. W	70	Mullens, Jim	93
McNeal, James	70	Morris, Wm. H 173,	93
McKnight, Felix	71	Maclison, Chs., alias Temple	94
Mangum, Wm	71	McCloud, Ben	94
Mayo, Sallie	72	Martin, A. P	95
McMullen, Frank	72	Muse, Geo	95
Magee, James	72	Miller, James	96
Moore, Jas., alias Slim Jim	68	Meat, A	96
Middleton, Wm	73	**McCulloch County**	97
Morse, Dan L	73	McMahon, ——	97
Molette, Jim	73	**Madison County**	97
Mullins, Christopher	74	McMillen, Neil, Jr 174,	97
McWilliam, Wm	76	Mason, Jas. P	97

	PAGE		PAGE
McMillan, Theophlus	97	Mayfield, Frank	116
Mathis, Fred	98	Milton, Geo. W	116
McIver, John R. Killed	178, 98	Moore, Jas. A	116
McIver, Dr. Joseph	177, 98	Mimms, Chas	117
Mosly, Ransum	98	Murphy, John	117
Mattox, S. H	98	McDonald, Frank	118
Maverick County	98	Merchant, James	118
Martin, N. B	99	May, Chas	118
McDaniel, John	99	McDonald, Thos	118
Meader, Thos	99	Mayfield, Dudley	118
McMatt, Jesse	100	Mays, Martin	118
McWhorter, R. A	101	Moore, Chas	119
McRoberts, James	101	Mackey, Wm	119
McClender, J. C	101	Middleton, ——	106
McFarland, Henry	102	Maller, John	110
McGee, Richard	103	Mapps, David	121
McCorquodale, Ephraim	103	McDonald, John K	121
McLendon, Joseph	104	McDonald, Bailey	121
McGuffin, Frank, alias Jackson	89	Moody, G. W	121
McCloud, H. C	94	Mathews, L. L	122
Mixon, alias Glasco	96	Middleton, James	122
Moore, West	100	McCulloch, Horace	122
McLoud, August	105	Merriman, James	122
Millstead, Peter	105	Morrell, Zack	122
Morris, Edmond	106	Maddox, Joe	122
May, Lee	106	Metts, Marion	123
Morris, James	106	Morris, Chas	123
Munday, Orison	106	McCall, E. H	124
Moore, Wm	107	Mitchel, Rube	124
Miller, Jerry	108	McGown, Bob Ambrose	124
Moulton, Edward	108	McAdams, Jack	125
Martin, Frank	109	Mayers, Eph	125
McGinnis, Burt	109	McClelland, Isaac	126
Mann, Levi	109	McMullins, Jno., alias Dielard	126
Mann, Archie	109	Middleton, J. W	126
McMahon, John	110	Middleton, A. A. J	127
Mitchell, Dennis	110	Medlin, Wm	127
Moppin, G	111	More, Ed	128
Meeks, John	111	Moss, Richard	128
Marsh, M. D	112	Martin, E	128
McReynolds, Geo	175, 112	Moran, Pat	128
Milor, Volney V	175, 113	Mills, James	129
Mitchell, Jake	113	Miles, J. M	129
Mahalla, Rob't	113	Melvin, Hardy	129
Mooney, ——	114	Milburn, Moore	129
McCrary, John	114	Millege, Anderson	130
Murray, Joseph	114	Morman, Ben	131
McClane, Peyton	114	Moseley, B. F	132
McCord, Oliver	115	Miller, O. M	177, 132
McGraw, Wm	115	Morehead, Doc	132
McCord, Sarah	115	Meredith, Bud	133
McGlaughlin, Jno	115	Massey, H. C	133
Moss, Henry	116	Moran, Hugh	134

	PAGE
McGuffin, John	135
Mosley, James	136
Miller, John D	136
McKinney, Collin	136
Milton Brothers	122
Monroe, ——	126
McDaniel, Bill	137
Milam, Geo., alias Gibson	138
Marshall, Sam	138
Miller, J. P	139
Miller, Frank	139
McCarthy, Andrew	139
Moore, Joe	141
McAnally, Dick	141
McMillan, Taylor	141
Morris, Wm., alias Farris	141
Mintz, J. C	141
McDowell, Tink	143
Mitchell, Chas	144
McCambey, J. M	144
Martin, Floyd	144
Mayhan, Dick	145
Middleton, Geo	146
McCarroll, Sylvester	146
Moore, Jack	147
Mankins, Pete	148
Morris, John	148
Miller, Bud	149
Moffit, Austin	149
Moffit, Joseph	149
Mognus, Bill	178, 150
Montgomery, Sam	150
McGar, Moses	150
Moon, Austin	151
Murtos, Stephen	151
Marshall, Nero, alias Scott	138
McCants, Geo	151
Mason County	162
Martinez, Pancho	153
Munroe, J	154
McCowan, John	178, 154
Morris, Woods	155
Moore, S. M	155
Malone, T. J	155
Matthews, Ellison	156
Morrisson, Amos	157
Moore, Geo	157
Miller, Vic	157
Miller, John	157
May, Mallory	158
Miller, J. I	158
McMillan, Wm	159
McNeil, Wm	159
	PAGE
Mansker, P. C	159
Moore, Jessie	160
Moody, Geo	160
McKnight, A	160
McNeal, John T	161
Mann, John	161
McGlothlin, John	162
Mason, Jas. P	162
McFadden, J. N	163
Moss, Pinckney	163
McCullar, E	163
McDaniel, John	163
McGrew, Burrell	164
Morris, ——	164
Miller, Rob't H	164
Mintloe, Jourdan	177, 165
McDonald, John	165
Martin, Pedro	166
Montgomery, Cato	166
Moore, S	166
McKinney, R. B. E	167
Martin, W. A	167
Moore, Charley	168
Miller, ——	168
Mahoney, Jack, alias Geo	169
Martin, Rob't	169
Middleton, Sam	170
Morgan, Isaac	170
Matthewson, Frank	170
Matthews, E. C., alias Crist	171
Monroe, John	171
Mitchell, John	171
Mitchell, Mary	171
Martin, John	171
Murphy, Reuben	172
Mattison, M. J	172
McGinness, Bill	172
McLeary, Henry	172
McDonald, John	172
Montgomery, James	172
Milam, Geo	173
Madison courthouse burners	173
Mackey, Nat	174
Moore, Luke, murderers of	174
Miller, A. R	174
orrow, Mrs. Ratliff, murderers of	174
Musselwhite, Elzo	175
Mondragon, E	175
Manchaca, Cesario	175
Montgomery, Wm	175
McLeod, Norman	176
McCloud, Chas	176

PAGE

Moore, A., alias Munroe......... 176
Monroe, A., alias Moore......... 176
Miller, Geo. W...................... 178
Majanor, Simon J., murderer of 174
Mitchell, Wm...................... 175
Meek, Wm., alias Geo. Bates... 176
McGibben, ——. 178
Marksbury, Allen........ 178

N

Nichols, Geo........................ 5
Northcut, Wm...................... 14
Neal, Callaway..................... 17
Nichols, Dan....................... 26
Nelson, Geo........................ 31
Nelson, Fred....................... 33
Nanez, Damasio.................... 33
Norris, C........................... 33
Null, Thos......................... 43
Nolen, Wm......................... 44
Nichols, Sage...................... 45
Newson, W. H...................... 48
Nichols, James.................... 48
Nolen, Dallas...... 40
Nicholsson, Sam................... 44
Neill, H. K........................ 51
Noble, Dick........................ 53
Neal, L. M......................... 56
Norwood, Henry................... 57
Nash, John......................... 58
Nale, Richard...................... 59
Newells, Reuben................... 59
Neeley, Wm........................ 59
Neeley, Henry..................... 59
Nolan, J. J........................ 59
Nowell, Isaac.............. 60
Nichols, J. A...................... 60
Nix, Newton....................... 61
Neal, Wesley, alias Callaway... 55
Nichols, Geo....................... 67
Nelms, J. B........................ 68
Nowell, W. C....................... 69
Neal, Willis....................... 69
Neal, J. V......................... 70
North, Ed.......................... 72
Nichols, Geo., alias Baker, alias
   Burke........................... 68
Norton, John..................178, 84
Neal, Joe.......................... 84
Neaves, Walter J.................. 84
Nunn, Samuel..................176, 92
Nevils, Albert..................... 92

PAGE

Navarro County................... 99
Nacogdoches County............ 101
Newton County................... 102
Nelson, Geo., alias Williams... 107
Nichols, Ned...................... 107
Nelson, Jno. H...............178, 109
Nooner, A......................... 111
Nelson, Jno. W., Sr............... 117
Neal, Sarah........................ 118
Nevils, Paul....................... 120
Nelson, Richard................... 121
Newton, Aaron.................... 122
Neighbors, Wm.................... 126
Neal, Chs.......................... 126
Nichols, Knox..................... 126
Napoleon, Ed...................... 130
Nathan, Leopold................... 132
Norman, Bill...................... 123
Nichols, Wm....................... 126
Nunn, Wm......................... 141
Nance, Prior B.................... 141
Northington, Jno T 144
Norris, Jack....................... 150
Nanney, J. C....................... 155
Nelson, I. A....................... 158
New, Wm. J........................ 158
Newcome, Robert.................. 162
Nethery, Wm., or Netherly..177, 165
Nance, James...................... 167
Neal, J. M......................... 168
New York, John, alias Julius
   Van Welde...................... 170
Nunez, Calixto..................... 175
Nash, Richard..................... 177

O

Orosco, Ramon..................... 5
Overstreet, W. P.................. 6
Osteen, Ben....................... 8
Oliver, A. D....................... 15
Ogle, alias J. R. Elgo............ 4
Odom, Oliver...................... 17
O'Conner, Jno..................... 19
Oliver, Dun....................... 23
Olgin, E........................... 24
Orta, Antonio..................... 24
Oliver, Henry..................... 28
O'Neal, Wiley..................... 44
Olive, Robt........................ 44
Osburne, Rufus.................... 33
Owen, P. C........................ 35
Olney, Joseph (twice)............ 39

	PAGE
O'Conner, Arthur	40
Oliver, Tobe, alias Rector	43
Ormstead, Israel W	51
O'Neal, Jack	62
O'Neil, Reuben	64
O'Neil, James	64
O'Brien, Johnny	64
Orange, French	68
O'Neal, James	69
Olney, Joseph	77
Ohair, R. T	84
Owens, John	88
O'Neil, James R	88
Owens, Walter	176, 92
Owens, Cos	95
Odom, Syens	97
Ozuna, Serapio	99
O'Keef, John	99
O'Bannon, J. M.	100
Orange County	103
Osburn, James	105
Oglesby, Julius	105
Oliver, James	106
Oates, Jno. T	109
Odum, M. V	112
O'Conner, Jno.	120
Overstreet, Frank	123
Oliver, Malichia	124
Oliver, Chs	129
Owens, Oscar	129
Owens, Henry	130
Odom, James	130
Odum, Wm	132
Oliver, J	124
Oliver, John	143
Oliver, Robt	147
O'Conner, John	147
Oats, Willis	159
Olney, W. W	160
Oglesby, J. P	160
Orono, Albino	166
Orono, Marin	166
Owens, W	166
Oglesby, James	167
Owens, ——	167
O'Brien, D. J	172
Owens, Wm	172
Owensby, Gus	178
Owens, T. J., robbers of	177
Owens, Henry, alias Hoodle	177

P

	PAGE
Pope, Lem	6
Puckett, Richard T	8
Pucket, Bud	8
Perry, Alonzo	8
Powell, E. N.	9
Phule, H	9
Person, Rolan	10
Priest, Dock	11
Priest, M. W	11
Petty, Theodore	13
Patterson, James	16
Pruitt, James	16
Pope, Henry	16
Pinkston, Thos	16
Patrick, Andrew	10
Puffpower, Chas	17
Powers, L. M	18
Parker, Wesley	18
Phelp, T. T	18
Page, H. H	19
Page, W. H	19
Potts, Bill	19
Pew, Wade	20
Powers, Asa	21
Pierce, David	22
Pruitt, Geo	23
Pricel, J. H	23
Pettit, J. W	23
Pool, Ben	24
Perkins, Roder	24
Pinley, Jesse	27
Prichard, Wm	27
Parker, Pink	28, 27
Pain, Wm	28
Picard, Nathan	29
Powers, G. W	29
Powers, Thos	30
Patrick, E	30
Parker, Lafayette	30
Patton, J. R	31
Pitts, Lee	33
Paston, J. H	34
Parker, James	36
Perkins, Wm	36
Powell, Geo	40
Petty, Geo	40
Parason, Bill	40
Partilla, Elya	41
Pierson, Tom	42
Perkins, Chas	42
Priestly, Geo	43

	PAGE
Powers, Jas. H	43
Power, Wm. M	43
Potts, John	44
Peterson, Wm	44
Potts, Haywood	44
Phifer, Jack	46
Pitts, Robt	46
Parker, Keinchern T	46
Priestley, Wm	47
Penick, Taylor	49
Polk, Thos	51
Pressnal, A. R	51
Phillips, Gage	55
Peak, Wm	55
Paul, Wm	56
Pugh, Wm	57
Page, Geo	58
Pickett, Andrew	60
Parkhill, James	60
Parsons, Jeff	60
Pruitt, John	61
Pinson, Geo	62
Phillips, Gage	62
Phillips, Bill	62
Pevyhouse, A	64
Perry, B. M	64
Preston, Richard, alias Dick	64
Pelham, H. B	64
Peeples, Geo	64
Prewitt, Llewellyn	49
Pugio, Paschal, alias William Thompson	53
Potter, Ben	65
Pulley, W. L	65
Phillips, Jos	65
Parish, Leander	66
Phillips, R. E	67
Pozzine, Chas	68
Price, John	69
Pearce, Wesley	69
Parr, Frank	71
Pace, Dave	71
Porter, Isaiah	71
Pace, James	72
Philips, J.	72
Pitt, W. B	69
Perry, Olive (twice)	71
Peyton, Ed	78
Pritchard, Aaron	78
Phillips, Gage	79
Phillips, Ike	79
Perry, Wm	80
Perkins, Henry	179, 82
Page, Henry	86
Price, Wm A	86
Pink, Wilson	87
Province, P. P	177, 88
Purtle, Felix H	73
Phillips, Nep, alias Duncan	74
Phillips, Dan	74
Polk, R. T	77
Petty, John	78
Pinson, Sam	80
Parish, Wm	80
Peck, Wm	90
Pierce, Frank	91
Parker, Wade	92
Pretty, Joseph	93
Parsley, John	94
Prather, Mose	94
Pitts, Thos	95
Parker, Robt	95
Patterson, Sam	96
Pool, Elias S	96
Powers, Geo. W	96
Petit, J. W	97
Parks, John	97
Powlege, John N	97
Pigford, John	98
Polk, John	99
Poole, S. T	100
Parish, Abe	100
Payne, Sam	100
Parmaly, Jack	101
Panola County	104
Pitts, Martin, alias Geo Bell	95
Patterson, J.W., alias Longley	95
Purvis, John	173, 97
Parish, Wm	105
Pecos County	108
Presidio County	108
Polk County	109
Price, James H	109
Pickens, J., alias Burns	110
Parker County	110
Pate, James	110
Prince, Ike	110
Prince, Wesley	111
Phillips, James	111
Pitman, Geo	114
Payne, Ed. (twice)	114
Presnel, Jim	115
Pope, James	115
Pilcher, Jno. D	117
Prewitt, W. J	120
Porter, Winfield	111

	PAGE
Pugh, Chas	122
Putnam, ——	122
Porter, Ben	122
Perry, Richard	122
Pierce, Ben	123
Preston, Geo	123
Pope, Alfred	124
Pope, John	124
Payne, W. H	125
Parmer, David	125
Parker, John	125
Pormir, Bud	126
Patterson, Bill	126
Parker, John	127
Porter, Creed, alias Taylor	130
Payne, Doc	131
Parker, Monroe	131
Pitts, Obidah	133
Pinson, W. S	135
Powell, Bant	137
Pedro, ——	137
Patterson, James	139
Pierce, Frank	139
Philips, Dick	139
Prince, Heuse	141
Praylor, Jack	143
Pearce, John	146
Potts, John	146
Peyton, Wm	148
Porter, Harvey	148
Powell, A. J	150
Pettit, Millard	151
Palmer, Abe	151
Parks, James	152
Phoenix, Jim	144
Parker, E., alias Bowers	144
Pritchard, Wm., alias Wills, alias Hamilton	148
Phelps, J. A	154
Perez, Raman	154
Pruitt, Robt	155
Parker, Calvin	177, 156
Perkins, L. J	156
Price, Geo	157
Prasia, Martin	158
Pilet, Warren	159
Patton, Geo	161
Parsons, Z. L	161
Parker, Joe	163
Perkins, Edmond	165
Pratt, Joseph	165
Peralles, Silverio	166
Piper, Bill	169

	PAGE
Powers, Jno. B	171
Peter, Tie	172
Pease, Jim, alias Chepman	171
Pardue, Henry	174
Parsons, Wm., murderers of	177
Parker, W. C	177
Packwood, Jesse	175
Petty, John	176
Pearson, Jas. D	176
Parker, Joseph	173
Peterson, Bell	177
Pickett, Chas	177

Q

Quatlebum, Jas	12
Queen, Jenison	36
Queen, John	36
Quinihan, Cornelius	87

R

Rosas, Santiago	3
Rogers, Lewis	3
Raymon, ——	3
Reynolds, John	4
Rowland, Munroe	5
Ratliff, Wm	5
Ratliff, James	5
Ratliff, Geo	5
Ratliff, Joseph	5
Ruff, John	6
Richardson, Wm	8
Robinson, H. T	8
Rhodes, Ennis	9
Roly, James	9
Rola, James	9
Reed, Luke	9
Rivers, Harry	10
Reese, Sam	10
Reed, James	11
Ridout, Horace	12
Randle, Henry	12
Ramsey, Rave	14
Ramirez, Alexander	14
Raddatz, Frank	14
Roch, Ed	14
Redden, Wm	14
Raby, James R	15
Raby, Guy	15
Rooch, Daniel	15
Reeder, Ham	15
Riley, James	15

18

	PAGE
Ross, E. H.	16
Reyes, Damien	175, 16
Robinson, Witz	17
Roberts, Buck	17
Rodgers, Jno	20
Roan, Allen	23
Rice, Elias	24
Russell, Wm	24
Rector, Joseph	26
Richey, James	27
Rowell, Jno	28
Ross, S. P	28
Remson, Chs	32
Ramorez, Santiago	32
Riley, Bob	17
Roberts, John	31
Robinson, Winchester	31
Reuz, August	33
Reed, Oscar	35
Ridgeway, Wm. H	42
Ramsey, E	43
Rector, Tobe, alias Oliver	43
Race, Bloz	44
Robinson, Thos	44
Rawles, S. A	44
Robinson, Geo	44
Reddin, Thos	45
Romero, Louis	45
Richard, John	45
Roundtree, Ellen	47
Ridgeway, Bill, alias Wilder	38
Ross, alias Conroy	39
Rosanky, Herman	40
Rike, Henry	50
Robinson, Dick	51
Ross, Geo	51
Russell, Thos. (twice)	52
Rudder, Sam	53
Roberts, Jacob	53
Robinson, John	53
Roberts, James	53
Royalls, Shonae	53
Reid, Ruffian	55
Rogers, Wm	55
Robinson, T. C	55
Riley, James	56
Roco, Matilda	57
Raby, J. W	57
Robertson, Joseph	59
Rhodes, D. R	59
Rice, Worley	59
Riley, Elizabeth	60
Ruble, F. M	61

	PAGE
Robberson, Eugene	62
Rhodes, Henry	63
Reed, Andrew, alias Peter Alexander	58
Robinson, Alley	65
Roberts, James	66
Roberts, John	66
Russell, H. R	66
Rogers, Wm	66
Roberts, Jno. L	69, 67
Rice, S. A	68
Redding, Sam	69
Redding, Wm. Z	70
Roberts, James	71
Robert, Elbert	71
Roberts, Dan	71
Ryan, C	73
Redding, W. Z	77
Rodriguez, Marcos	78
Rogers, John	79
Rodgers, Chs	82
Rodgers, John	82
Reed, W. H	82
Redding, Shelton	87
Rogers, Lewis	90
Remington, Frank	90
Ragay, Philip	91
Rushing, W. J	93
Rable, Wm	94
Ruble, Gum	95
Rushing, Robt	95
Roseberry Wm	95
Russell, J P	96
Robinson, Jeff	96
Randolfe, Jno. P	96
Rushing, Alf	99
Ross, Dan	100
Robinson, Isaac	101
Roan, Henry	102
Roach, Edward	95
Robinson, Reuben, alias Thompson	96
Reed, Mary	106
Robertson, Ky	106
Roberts, Stephen	178, 106
Robertson, Wm	112
Rothschild, Absalom	112
Rockwall County	112
Red River County	112
Reed, Harrison	113
Retherford, Taul	113
Rice, Robt	113
Rusk County	114

	PAGE
Redwine, Isham	114
Robertson, Thos.	115
Runnels, Richard	115
Rhodes, Geo.	115
Roberts, Jesse	11, 116
Roquemere, Aaron	117
Roland, Willis	117
Rogers, Dock	118
Russell, T. J	119
Reed, Jos	120
Robinson, Frank	120
Robinson, Frank G	120
Rutherford, Frank	121
Robertson County	121
Roberts, Bill	121
Robertson, Henry	122
Richardson, S. C	122
Rains, ——	122
Robinson, Ike	123
Reed, Albert	123
Reynolds, Samuel	123
Rankin, Flax	125
Redding, W. L	126
Reaves, John	127
Robertson, J. T. M	128
Richardson, John	129
Robertson. Dick	130
Robinson, Sam	130
Rainbow, J. W	131
Reynolds, Stake	131
Rose, James	132
Ruff, Sam	133
Raspberry, Wm	133
Robertson, James	134
Reel, Wm	134
Reaves, Robert	134
Reel, Elisha	134
Reese, H. B.	134
Richards, T. J	135
Roque, Angel	136
Rimeras, Trinidad	136
Russum, John	123
Ritchets, ——	126
Rurton, ——	130
Reid, Phil, alias Thomas	139
Richards, John	139
Renfro, John	141
Rhine, Boon	141
Richardson, Jack	144
Roberts, John	146
Rolen, R. H	146
Roberts, Weldon	146
Rose, Mitchell	146
	PAGE
Roberts, James	147
Ratliff, James	147
Ratliff, Jack	147
Reed, James	148
Roach, Lucius	149
Richards, Wm., alias Wild Bill	149
Ridley, Solomon	151
Roe, Frank	151
Reid, Alex., alias Fry	139
Rowlet, Samuel	147
Raines County	162
Refugio County	164
Reina, Jacobo	153
Runnels, Ellis	156
Rose, ——	157
Rodgers, Josiah	157
Robinson, Lewis	157
Robertson, Thos	157
Robinson, Frank	158
Ross, Wm	158
Randle, W. H	158
Reeves, Joseph	159
Roberts, E. H	160
Roan, Frank	161
Richards, Trass	162
Richards, Wesley	162
Reynolds, Stark	162
Randolph, L. B	164
Ridgeway, Willis	164
Ridgeway, Matt	164
Rushing. James	165
Robbins, G. D	166
Reed, Chs	167
Rains, Tom	169
Robinson, Eugene	169
Ruble, Montgomery	170
Roberts, Buck	171
Rueger, Theodore	171
Ruby, Geo	178, 172
Robinson, Wm	172
Robbers of stage, Travis county	173
Rather, Jas	174
Rains, W. A	175
Robbers of stage between San Antonio and Kingsbury	175
Robbers of stage between Dallas and Fort Worth	175
Rosford, Thos	176
Renfro, G. B	176
Robbers of stage between Ft. Worth and Cleburne	177
Robinson, Tom	177
Rowley, J. F	177

	PAGE		PAGE
Rowley, Napoleon	177	Sisk, H	20
Rodriguez, Martin	178	Stockton, Porter	21
Rushing, Alfred	178	Summerville, M. W.	21
Rasco, Jesse	179	Salmon, Geo	21
Roach, James	177	Sagister, D. W	21
Ronley, Columbus	177	Shelby, J. J	21
Robbers of J. W. Hill	177	Smith, S. S	22
Robbers of T. J. Owens	177	Shelton, Jno	23
Robbers of —— Wheat	177	Steene, Phillips	23
Robbers of house of W. J.		Sanders, Lafayette	24
Deaton	177	Sanders, James	24
		Stinett, G. W	25
		St. Charles, Elbert	25
S		Shafercater, August	26
		Stephenson, Wm	26
Stidham, Wm., Jr	3	Scott, Samuel	27
Slaughter, John H	4	Stutts, Samuel	28
Schoonover, Frank	4	Smith, Thos. W	28
Scawts, August	4	Smith, R. T	28
Shafer, Henry	4	Scott, Samuel	29
Silvar, Antonio	4	Stevens, Miles	29
Spicer, C. C.	5	Smith, Wm	30
Stevenson, Albert	8	Sandy, Harrison	30
Scrofford, ——	8	Shadrick, R. M	30
Scott, Jack	8	Smith, Jack	31
Salter, Geo. W	8	Stephenson, Warren	32
Smith, Chs., alias Webb	8	Smith, Sam	32
Stewart, Edmond	8	Sovereign, P. C	32
Sanders, Alex'd	8	Sierra, Jose	32
Stockman, Chs	9	Smith, Thos., alias Ch. Ethel.	32
Shoemake, Calvin	9	Staggs, John	33
Smothers, Henry	9	Scurry, Polk	33
Schmidt, John	10	Sims, Isam	33
Strickland, Jos. W	10	Simpson, W. I	33
Sullivan, James M	12	Sherman, Cane	33
Schoonover, Isaac	12	Stevens, Wiley	33
Smith, Geo	13	Simpson, J. W	34
Stein, John	13	Sanders, Chas	34
Story, C. W	14	Shannon, F. M	34
Sharp, Richard	15	Stanford, John	34
Simms, Dick	15	Saunders, J. W	34
Swanner, Joel	16	Stokes, Z. P	35
Shaver, B. F	16	Stinnett, Clay	36
Slady, Sam	7	Shufler, John	36
Sanchez, Francisco	17	Stuart, John	37
Stratton, Chs	17	Smart, John, Sr	37
Steen, Peter	17	Sneed, Berry	37
Sherral, Joe	17	Sheffield, Wm	38
Smith, Thos	18	Stoors, Wm	38
Saunders, Chs	19	Shaver, Geo	39
Squires, Joseph	19	Smith, Wm	39
Sims, Dan	19	Spencer, Mat	40
Sneed, Elijah	20	Scull, Riley	40

	PAGE		PAGE
Stewart, Andrew	40	Simpson, Thos	61
Smith, Russell	41	Standefer, James	61
Stallings, Jeptha	41	Standefer, Calvin	61
Simpson, James	41	Sherman, Willard	61
Speed, W. W	42	Stover, W. E	61
Speed, G. W	42	Smith, Sidney	62
Smith, Jim	42	Sneed, Berry	63
Sears, Geo. W	42	Stevens, Ben, alias Smith	63
Shelton, M. L	43	Smith, Ben, alias Stevens	63
Sims, Dock	44	Smith, Preston	64
Squirrelhunter, Sam	44	Sherod, Nolly	64
Shelton, Freeman	44	Smith, Samuel	65
Spears, Everett	44	Smith, Charles W	65
Standifer, Lem	44	Staley, Thos	66
Shelley, Malley	45	Snow, James	66
Shelley, Stephen	45	Sarvis, James	66
Staton, Ned	46	Stamper, Judd	66
Simmons, Price	46	Seay, Thos	66
Slaughter, C. A	47	Smith, Wm	67
Sexton, Samuel	47	Suggs, Jno	66
Stevens, John	175, 48	Scott, ——	67
Standefer, Mack	48	Smith, Nathan, alias White	68
Snelling, Steve, alias Jno. Gage	33	Simmons, Stephen	68
Slim Jim, alias Jas. Wyrick	37	Slim Jim, alias James Moore	68
Shaver, G. W	178, 49	Sims, Campbell	68
Simmons, F. J	49	Scott, Isham	68
Sullivan, Dick, alias Hill	49	Smith, Chas	68
Setser, Sam	49	Scarborough, Wm	68
Smith, T. Y	49	Simmons, Robt	69
Sanders, B. F	49	Smith, D. W	69
Smith, August	49	Schenck, John C	69
Smoot, Hice	50	Shelling, Lindsey	69
Stokes, Lane	50	Scarborough, Middleton	69
Scott, W. M	50	Smith, D. D	69
Starks, W. J., alias Tescumbee	51	Short, G. W	70
Stewart, Wm	51	Shroyier, Robt	70
Sutton, Frank	53	Stedman, E. D	70
Smith, Cap	54	Strange, Wm	70
Smith, Bill	54	Smith, Wm	71
Spreggs, Daniel	54	Smith, Wm. E	71
Stewart, Allen	55	Scott, Wm	72
Stratton Richard	56	Samora, Joe	72
Seiter, Henriette	56	Samora, Green	72
Sapp, Wm	56	Sowery, John	72
Shannon, Isaac	57	Skipton, Geo	73
Sims, Sophia	58	Steward, John	73
St. Cloud, V. E	58	Stallings, Ben	73
Sally, Jerry	59	Sparks, Isaac	176, 74
Smith, Geo	59	Sanders, Richard M	74
Sneed, Nelson	59	Stockings, J. B	75
Strickland, Amos	60	Shelton, Ben	76
Swift, Pat H	60	Saunders, Wm	76
Sullivan, Bud	60	Sorrell, Tom	78

	PAGE
Stevenson, John, alias Edenfield	79
Shannon, David	79
Shanchez, Marcus	79
Shannon, Lou	79
Shannon, Alonzo	79
Sharp, Capt. Thos	79
Scott, Dan	81
Slaughter, Ben	81
Storey, John	82
Steel, John	82
Smith, Sam	83
Slack, Jacob	84
Skipworth, James	84
Smith, J	84
Staunton, Mike	84
Sheppard, Lee	85
Shire, Jacob	74
Sharp, John	78
Stripling, D	80
Stokes, Berry, alias Barry, N. S.	83
Sloan, Wm	89
Sands, J. B	89
Sands, R. C	89
Simonton, Madison	89
Spence, Page	91
Smith, W. B	91
Smith, Geo	91
Smith, Henry 176,	92
Sloan, Crockett	92
Saunders, Dr. W. H	93
Stephenson, Robert	93
Shelton, Nat	93
Smith, S. P	94
Shmidt, Jens	94
Stinson, Geo	94
Smith, John	94
Steel, Simon	95
Stokes, Gaines	95
Shepherd, J. D	95
Sims, A	95
Sweat, Green	96
Standifer, Burrell	96
Sims, Austin	97
Sanders, Lafayette	97
Surcey, W. P	97
Smith, Monroe	97
Scott, Elbert P 174,	98
Sandobal, Jesus	98
Sandobal, Antonio	98
Seamon, Jas., alias Hanseuno	98
Sheets, A. D	99
Stroud, Beaton	99

	PAGE
Stroud, J. B	99
Sims, Dan	100
Smith, Thos	100
Swink, Henry	100
Swann, J. C	101
Samuel, R. P	101
Shears, Vina	101
Sweatman, Green	103
Sweatman, Ben	103
Smith, Geo	103
Stewart, W. A	103
Spain, Emanuel	103
Seguin, Juan	98
Swink, James	100
Staggers, Mrs. E	105
Smith, Chs	106
Smalley, Robert	106
Self, Buck	106
Story, Joseph	107
Sullins, Bartholemew	107
Scoggins, Richard	107
Stephens, Chs	107
Spradley, John	107
Sheals, James	107
Standifer, Wm	107
Spencer, Wm	107
Sand Hill, Geo	108
Slade, Jerry	109
Snell, Frank	110
Stags, Tobe	110
Smith, Riley (twice)	112
Smith, John	114
Scales, J. H	114
Shelton, Adaline	115
Stokes, Wm	115
Stone, Enoch	116
Sanders, Zachary	116
Stanford, Adolphus	116
Smith, Thos	117
Stewball, James	117
Smith, Geo	117
Salmon, Henry	118
Salmon, Mary	118
Smith, Peter	119
Shadden, Wm 174,	119
Shadden, A. A 174,	119
Shadden, Jos 174,	119
Shadden, Hans 174,	119
Shankles, James 174,	120
Stutts, Frank	110
Smith, J. T	121
Smith, Calvin	121
Simmons, Wash	121

	PAGE
Smith, Taylor	122
Smith, Wm	122
Smith, Alf	122
Salter, Reuben	123
Steele, L. V	123
Shoats, Chris	123
San Jacinto County	123
Stewart, Jacob	124
Sprutt, Austin	124
Sprutt, J. D	124
Shelby County	124
Smith, W. B	125
Swindoll, Alex'd	125
Sanford John	126
Samples, John	126
San Saba County	126
Shaw, John	126
Spencer, George	125
Smith, James W	126
Stanfield, W. B	126
Smith County	127
Simpson, N. R	127
Scales, J. H	127
Sharpe, Geo	128
Scott, Archie	128
Standford, Peter	128
Simpkins, Ben	129
Simms, Thos	129
Swinney, Ransom	130
Strickland, John	130
Sharp, Geo	130
Shaw, M. V	131
Simpson, W. B	131
Scott, A. J	131
Sansom, Fletcher	131
Stockton, Sam	131
Snow, Wm	132
Sour, Ben	132
Spain, Joe	132
Smith, A. T	132
Shuler, Wm	132
Stanley, Aaron	132
Smith, Henry	133
Smith, Jeff	133
Strickland, Don	134
Scott, David	134
Stoddard, Thos	134
Sexton, Samuel	134
Smith, James	134
Scott, Alfred	135
Springs, Lucien	135
Smith, Geo	135
Samano, Felip	136
Spencer, Andrew J	136
Stapps, A. J	136
Stallcup, E. B	122
Spradley, J	126
Sheely, James	137
Sanchez, Marion	137
Scott, Nero, alias Marshall	138
Sterne, Geo., alias Elliott	138
Seymour, Godfrey	139
Smith, Alfred	141
Smith, R. H	141
Smith, Peter	141
Sharper, Wiley	141
Speck, Marshall	142
Smith, Jeff	142
Sanders, W. B	142
Sweeden, Lee	142
Smith, Byron	143
Smith, Bob	143
Stewart, J. H. D	143
Stifflemeyer, Wesley	144
Smith, Sam	145
Saunders, Fayette	145
Snow, Thomas	145
Smith, R. D	145
Smith, James A	145
Smith, Pulaski	145
Snyder, John, alias Childress	147
Sanders, Moses	147
Spoorland, Samuel	148
Stewart, John	148
Stephens, Henry	149
Stephens, John	149
Stephens, Ed	149
Simpson, Isaac	149
Shy, C. W	149
Sanders, Richard, Jr	150
Smith, Conrad	150
Stewart, W. H	150
Smith, Martin	151
Sewell, John	151
Stubblefield, Nelson	151
Shields, Reed	152
Solomon, W. E	146
San Augustine County	164
San Patricio County	165
Shackleford County	167
Schute, Irvan C. A	153
Sanchez, Droteo	153
Salero, Juan	154
Smith, Steve	155
Stanford, Jeff	156
Shields, Frank	157

	PAGE
Shields, John	157
Sasser, James	157
Stribling, Geo	157
Shaw, W. M	158
Scott, John	158
Stanley, Young	159
Smiley, Munroe	159
Straum, Thos	159
Shields, Wm	160
Sims, John	160
Short, Ed	175, 160
Stevens, Thos	161
Sloan, Doss	161
Saunders, Dick	162
Slatter, Fred	163
Saldanio, Elijio	165
Stanley, Marshall	165
Stanley, Adam	165
Saunders, G. W	165
Smith, P. H	165
Sutton, Frank	166
Statecap, Wesley	167
Southerland, J	153
Savage, Wm. A	161
Shoemake, Joe	163
Schubert, Wm., alias Byfield	169
Stone, Al	169
Stewart, B. K	170
Swipes, Jacob	170
Smith, Jim	170
Smith, Bill	172
Stroud, James	172
Scott, John	172
Sullivan, J. J	172
Seimers, F	172
Scroggins, Alf	172
Sneed, Bill	172
Stackman, John	173
Stokes, Joseph	173
Stokes, Wm	173
Stage robbers, Travis county	173
Scobee, J. B., murderers of	173
Shelton, Ed	174
Stone, John	174
South, Bester	174
Smith, Anthony, murderers of	175
Schoby, G. W., murderers of	175
Stage robbers, between San Antonio and Kingsbury	175
Stage robbers, between Dallas and Fort Worth	175
Stage robbers, between Fort Worth and Cleburne	177

	PAGE
Stephen, Alex. R., murderers of	176
Scruggs, Harde	178
Swofford, John B	178
Smith, Wm	175

T

	PAGE
Trevinio, Juan	3
Thompson, Wm. (Bill)	5
Tyner, Mart	6
Teaff, Jesse L	8
Tabor, Wm	8
Turney, Thos	8
Todd, John	9
Terrill, James	9
Turner, Sim	9
Townsend, Beth	9
Taylor, Balsch	10
Tomlinson, Wm	11
Thompson, Chs	14
Tyre, Neil	14
Taylor, Geo. W	15
Terry, James	15
Thompson, Thos	16
Taylor, John	16
Taylor, James	4
Tucker, Sim	173, 11
Tuton, Oliver	17
Turner, Isaiah	18
Turner, Dick	18
Tam, Silas	19
Tinsley, Homer	20
Thornton, Batty	20
Thompson, E. J	23
Tatum, Anderson	24
Tickereno, Evan	26
Tallent, F. M	27
Taylor, John	27
Trussell, J	30
Tores, Morgan	35
Turner, Mauly	36
Thompson, Bud	36
Tatum, Bud	38
Taylor, A. T	39
Tinker, Wm	39
Thompson, T. G	41
Trubey, Wm. M	43
Talley, Nathan	43
Tulkington, Henry	45
Thomas, Alfred	48
Thompson, Wm., alias Paschal Vagio	53
Trafton, Robert	55

	PAGE		PAGE
Thomas, W. S.	57	Tickle, James	101
Thaylor, C. H.	57	Truelock, Sam'l	104
Tabb, Jacob	57	Turner, W. A	104
Taylor, Gabe	58	Tatum, Thos.	104
Tubbs, John	58	Temple, Chas., alias Maclison.	94
Thomas, John	59	Thompson, Reuben, alias Rob-	
Thomas, Gilbert	59	inson	96
Taylor, Geo	60	Trevino, Benito	98
Taylor, Benj	60	True, John, alias Wm. Coyle...	104
Thayer, Wm. T	60	Thompson, John	105
Tatsch, August	63	Taylor, Henderson	106
Trammell, Wood	63	Thompson, Jack	107
Thompson, James M	63	Trowell, Jim	109
Taylor, Titus	63	Taylor, Zach	111
Thompson, Frank	64	Taylor, C. A	111
Thompson, Simon	64	Todd, Geo	115
Thrift, Wm	64	Talbert, Jno., alias Talaferro...	115
Tescubee, alias W. J. Starks...	51	Tipps, Blake	116
Trammel, Sim	65	Taylor, Henry	117
Tubbs, John	65	Thurmond, Jos	117
Terry, A. N	65	Thomas, Wm	117
Turner, John F	65	Thompson, J. S	117
Tinnin, Willis	67	Turner, W.	117
Thomas, Billie	68	Tutt, Ed	119
Taylor, Dick	69	Tatum, H. W	119
Thompson, Bill	69	Taylor, Rob't	119
Tanner, Samuel	71	Turner, Levi	120
Thomas, Philip H	75	Tyler, Willis	120
Taylor, Abe	77	Taylor, Geo	120
Travino, Manuel	79	Thompson, Alex'd	121
Taylor, J. W	80	Taylor, David M	122
Tubbs, William	80	Thomas, Geo	123
Taylor, Charley	81	Townsend, Louis	123
Turner, M. L	82	Townsend, Logan	123
Thompson, A. M	83	Turner, Frank	123
Tennon, John	83	Thurmen, Flem. (twice)	125
Taylor, Wm	83	Tines, James	125
Thompson, J. C	174, 84	Tucker, Tillman	125
Taylor, Thos	86	Tatum, Alex'd	125
Tipton, Bill	86	Thomason, D. B	125
Thomas, Chas	91	Truett, Jacob	126
Thomas, Wm	92	Thompson, Molly	127
Thomas, George	92	Thomas, Alfred	128
Tyer, Joseph	93	Taylor, W. L	129
Turner, Jack	94	Tate, James	129
Tront, John	94	Taylor, Frank	129
Thompson, Verge	95	Taylor, Rob't	131
Thomas, Major	95	Taylor, Creed, alias Porter	130
Thacher, Wm	96	**Tarrant County**	131
Tyler, Jobe F	97	Thomas, Joe R.	131
Tell, Wm	97	Trimble, Marion	131
Tickle, Geo	101, 100	**Trinity County**	132
Tickle, Robt	176, 101	Thompson, Alford	132

19

	PAGE
Tullas, Willowby	133
Thompson, Edmond	135
Thacker, Ezekiel	136
Thomas, Justus	138
Thomas, Phil., alias Reid	139
Townsend, Lee	139
Tisdale, J. W.	142
Tracy, Chas.	142
Thompson, James	142
Turner, Frank	142
Towles, Andy	142
Townsend, Beth	143
Taylor, Rob't	145
Taylor, B. F.	149
Tullis, James	150
Townley, Wm.	150
Tipton, J. W.	151
Taylor, Geo.	152
Thompson, Fountain	152
Thomas, Fountain.	152
Tucker, Albert J	152
Taylor, Wm.	152
Tibbet, Vigel	148
Tobias, Geo.	148
Travis County	168
Tunny, Alvin	154
Tisdale, Chs.	178, 154
Thelps, Joseph	156
Tompkins, Wash.	157
Thomas, Rodney	157
Taylor, Dave	159
Taylor, Major	159
Thomas, Isaiah	159
Turnan, Jack	159
Tanzey, Marion	159
Townsend, W. R.	159
Thompson, Henry	160
Thomson, James	161
Thompson, Richard	161
Thompson, Doc	161
Tate, Thos.	161
Terrill, Dave	162
Tollett, Sam	163
Tutt, Ben	163
Taylor, Floyd	163
Thomas, Henderson	166
Taylor, James	166
Taylor, Geo.	167
Tarnes, Angeil	153
Thomas. John	170
Townsley, Webb	171
Tague, ——	172
Terrell, G. A.	173

	PAGE
Thompson, ——	175
Teal, Eli	175
Thomas, Geo.	176
Tefire, Adam, alias Teefore	176
Theirber, Henry E.	176
Tetric, Geo. W., murderers of.	177
Tuttle, W. S	177
Talmage, C. H	178
Thompson, James	178
Turner, Sug.	178
Tate, Ed	179

U

	PAGE
Underwood, Nathan	25
Urban, Davis	69
Underwood, Nathan	87
Upshur County	133
Uvalde County	136
Ubanks, James	136
Uphalt, Lewis	158

V

	PAGE
Vasques, Polonio	3
Vice, F. M., alias Major Vice	4
Vager, Pedro	4
Vaughan, Wm.	11
Vosberg, Theodore	13
Vines, Wm.	15
Vanwinkle, Sam	25
Vanzant, Baxter	29
Villalores, Antonio	33
Verdry, Geo. P.	42
Vineyard, Joseph	39
Voyles, Oscar	59
Vaughn, Jesse	56
Vickers, ——	56
Venters, Thos.	57
Vines, Jackson	58
Vines, Washington	58
Vance, Joseph	174, 58
Von Cannon, Geo.	63
Vess, Louis	65
Valentine, Ed	73
Valreal, Ramajio	79
Vaums, P. B.	96
Villareal, Crescencio	98
Vawters, Dillard	102
Van Dyke, Jefferson	115
Van Dyke, Wilson	126

	PAGE
Vaughn, Gadrid	135
Victoria County	137
Verner, James	149
Vanu, Thos	150
Vowell, A. J	152
Vandever, Robt	153
Valdez, Filomino	153
Vaughn, Fed	158
Vanalstyne, J. T	160
Vaughn, John	162
Van Welde, Julius, alias New York John	170
Vance, Thos	173

W

	PAGE
Williams, Harry	3
Williams, Joe	4
Wittington, John	5
Weaver, Edward	5
Wood, L. E	6
Whittley, Jasper	6
White, Thos	8
Woodruff, Wm	8
Wood, Geo	8
Walter, Judge	8
Willett, N. F	8
Willett, E. T	8
Wilson, Jerry	8
Williams, D	8
Williams, Ervin	9
Williams, John, alias Gilmore	9
Wilson, Wm	10
West, Augustus	10
Whitley, Henderson	10
Washington, Frank	11
Whitington, John	12
Whitis, Rhodes	12
West, Richard	12
Wood, Wm	14
Ward, Harmon	14
Watkins, Joe	14
White, Shad	14
Williams, Marion	15
Westfall, Samuel	15
Watson, Dave R	15
Wilson, Geo. I	15
Williams, Frank	16
Williams, Robert	16
Woody, Wiley	16
Wilson, W. A	16
Waters, Wm	16

	PAGE
Webb, Chas., alias Smith	8
Williams, Barney, alias W. Barney	14
Williams, Scott	15
Williams, G. W	17
Wilkerson, Charles	18
Weldon, John	19
Wright, Thomas	174, 19
Wright, Wiley, Jr	174, 19
White, Thomas	20
Whitworth, E. R	21
Woods, A. J	21
Weston, John	21
Wilson, G. W	21
Wright, A. L	21
Wade, Howard	22
Watley, Wat	22
Weaver, Ezekiel	23
Weaver, Wesley	23
Williams, Spencer	23
Walker, Bailey	23
Williams, Henry	24
Waters, Pole	24
Winslow, Thos	24
Williams, Wm	24
Woods, Frank	25
Wise, P. H	26
Wilson, James	27
White, W. A	27
Wilson, Henry	27
Walters, Thos	28
Woods, Wm. E	29
Wilson, Henry	29
Wheeler, Fernande	29
Woods, Ella	29
Williams, James	29
Walters, Bell J	30
Walker, D. N	30
Walker, Nels	30
Watson, Shelt	31
Whitsitt, James	31
Welchell, Edward	31
Wise, Henry	31
White, W W	32
Warren, Morey	32
Wheat, J. C	32
Warmack, R. H	24
Wise, Henry	26
Watts, Thos	32
Weaver, Ed	33
Woesner, Henry	33
Warrior, Scott	33
Whatley, Ben	33

	PAGE		PAGE
Willis, Edward	33	White, T. D. O	53
Wallnetzek, Thos	33	Welch, Mike	53
Ward, Mason	34	Wasbburn, T. H., alias Frk.	
Willis, James	34	Warner	53
Willett, Nathan	34	Warner, Frank, alias T. H.	
Williams, Elbert	34	Washburne	53
Word, ——	37	Walker, Isaiah	53
Walker, ——	87	Wilson, Henry	54
Wyrick, James, alias Slim Jim	37	West, John C	54
Wilder, alias Bill Ridgeway	38	White, Bill	54
Wilcoxen, Hugh	38	White, Arch	54
Whittington, T. W	38	Wright, Wm	54
Williams, Alex'd	40	White, Miles	55
Weaver, James	40	Waldrip, James B	56
Walters, M. P	41	Waldrip, Ben	56
Whittington, John	41	Walker, James	56
Wilson, Joseph	42	Williams, Felix	56
White, Dan	42	Walker, Daniel	57
Williams, Bill	42	Williams, Charles	57
Williams, Bull, alias Dudley		Wilson, Mat	57
Hill	43	Wafford, Walter	58
Williams, Ish	43	Whitehead, O. C	58
Whittington, Park	43	Warren, James	58
Williams, Scott	43	Walter, Wm	59
White, Louis	43	Wortham, Thos	59
Waggoner, J. L	44	Williams, John	60
Waggoner, Wm	44	Wilkins, Isaac	60
Ward, Henry	44	Waldrup, Monroe	61
Williams, Sidney	45	Wilson, J. H	62
Williams, Wm	46	Wright, John S	62
Williams, Thos	46	Ward, John	62
Wood, Thompson	46	Wilcox, Henry	64
Whitesides, James	46	Walker, Bob, alias Anderson	53
Weaver, Geo	46	Wynn, Charley	44
Winters, John S	47	Wade, Nancy	65
Wiley, Albert	47	Widener, Mary J., alias Ander-	
Walker, Chs	47	son	65
Walters, Henry	48	Winfrey, Frank	65
Wilkins, John D	48	Wilkinson, Shepard	65
Whaley, W. H	48	West, Kinch	66
Wright, Bud	38	Winters, Nelson	66
Whiten, Louis, alias Clark	43	Ward, A	66
Wiley, Wm	49	Wisdem, Fred	67
Wash, David	49	Willis, Hampton	67
Wilson, Chas	49	Woodard, Chas	67
Warrenberg, Geo	49	Williams, Jno. M	68
Wilson, Isaac	50	Wallace, Wm	69
Williams, Thos	50	Williams, John	71
Washington, Jack	50	White, Ben	71
Weldon, T. A	51	Warren, John	71
Weldon, Joseph	51	Williams, Almstead	71
Woodley, Henry	52	Walton, Luther	71
Wyatt, Gus	52	Wright, Curtis	72

	PAGE
Webb, Pressly	72
White, Nathan, alias Smith	68
Wilkinson, John	74
Walton, Wm.	74
Walton, Thos.	74
Warren, Steve	75
Wiggins, Jno. H	75
Williams, James	77
Wagner, Peter	77
Worthing, Richard	77
Watts, Ben	78
Walk, Thos.	79
Woods, Henry	80
Walker, L. M.	80
Whaley, Isaac	82
Williams, W. H.	82
Wisdom, Joseph L.	82
Wilson, James	82
Waldrum, Wm	82
Willis, John	84
Waybourne, Rob't	84
West, Wm.	84
Waller, M. B. 177,	84
West, ——	84
White, Frank	84
Watson, Mat.	84
Wiggens, Rob't	86
Ward, W. A.	87
Wren, Otto, alias Bateman	88
Williams, Jackson	90
Wood, Alonzo	91
Wright, Chas.	92
Watson, Geo.	92
Wallace, S. W.	93
Williams, Thos. (three times)	93
Wilder, Vincent	93
Wortham, Henry	94
Williams, John	94
Warwick, Samuel	94
Weaver, Bud	94
Willis, Dock	94
Wallace, Andrew	94
Williams, Jack	94
Williams, J. F.	94
Williams, Moses	94
West, Geo.	95
Williams, Jack	95
Wilmer, Buck	95
Wilson, Chas.	95
Williams, Shep	95
Wilburn, Albert	96
Wright, Reuben	96
Wilburn, J. W.	96

	PAGE
Wright, Chas.	96
Wilburn, J. J.	96
Williams, Henry	96
Wilson, Jack	96
Witherspoon, J. F. (twice)	96
Ware, or Weir, Bill	97
White, Ras.	99
Walker, Amos	100
Williamson, Wm	100
Wattles, L. T.	101
White, W. L.	101
White, Steve	101
William, John	102
Wilson, D. W.	103
Winn, Thos.	104
Washington, Geo., alias Nick Bruce	89
Williamson, Joe., alias King	90
Walter, Harrell	90
Wright, James,	95
Whispering, Bob, alias Jackson	96
Wilson, Jno., alias Carry, alias Davis	96
Wicker, Bill	97
Wall, Chas.	105
Wilson, T. H.	105
Welch, James	105
Wynne, Wm.	105
Ware, Sigh	106
Womack, Lena	106
Washington, Irving	106
Warmington, Sylvester	106
Williams, Joe.	107
White, Josh.	107
Wallace, Geo.	108
Walteree, Till.	108
Wyley, Geo.	111
Whitesell, Eldridge	111
Whetstone, J.	111
Woods, Alex	113
Wilburn, Rachel	113
Wilson, John	113
Watts, Julius 178,	113
Williams, David	114
Williamson, Alex'd	114
Walton, Austin	118
Walker, Wm.	118
Whaley, Chas. E.	118
Whaley, Thos.	118
West, John	119
Wyche, Drew	119
Welch, Chas.	120
Williams, George, alias Nelson	107

Walters, Napoleon	110	Wilson, R. D	142
Washington, James	110	Williams, Martha	142
Wells, Mary.	112	Wilson, Mack	142
Wilson, James	122	Warmack, Hope	142
Wilson, W. H	122	Watson, Lee	142
Walker, Joel	122	**Wharton County**	143
Williams, Lum	122	Williams, Dave	143
Waddell, Wm	122	**Waller County**	144
Willis, ——	122	**Williamson County**	145
White, Robt	122	Weinort, E. H	145
Walker, Albert	122	Woolem, C. M	146
Wilson, Moses	122	Wilcox, E. S	146
Wilkerson, Allen	122	Williams, A. J	147
Wilson, Alex'd	122	Williams, Jack	147
Wilson, John	123	Wills, Wm., alias Hamilton,	
Wilburn, Borny, alias Bony		alias Pritchard	148
Wellbourn	123	**Wise County**	148
Wellbourn, B., alias B. Wilburn	123	Wiley, David	148
Williamson, Abe	123	Williams, T. J	175, 149
Woolam, James	125	**Walker County**	150
Wheeler, Cicero	125	Wood, Austin	152
Words, Ed	126	Williams, Harry	137
Williams, Samuel	126	Waller, Andrew	148
Weatherby, Richard	127	Wild Bill, alias Wm. Richards	149
Warren, Thos. F	127	**Washington County**	149
Walker, Jackson	127	Wiley, Anderson	151
Weeks, Tip	127	Warren, James	152
Walker, J. P	128	**Webb County**	153
Wayland, Timothy	128	**Wilson County**	165
Weaver, Henry	129	Whetstone, C. A	153
Wallace, Aaron	129	Wilson, Joseph	154
Whitman, E. G	129	Woods, David	155
White, James	129	Weaver, Louis	155
Williams, Joe	130	Woods, Tim	155
Weeks, Coley, alias Ferney	130	Whitefield, Wash	155
Williams, Green	174, 130	Weaver, Frank	156
Wooten, Edy	130	Wallace, Wm	156
Whatley, M	131	Walker, Geo	177, 156
Wingate, Ed. T	132	Wilson, C. C	156
Walker, Amos	132	Walker, Amos	157
Wingate, Frank	132	Walker, Andrew	157
Walker, Kirk	133	Walker, Thos	157
Wilkes, Peter	133	Williams, Frank	157
Woods, Chas	134	Williams, John	157
White, George, alias Johnson	134	Webber, Lewis	158
Williams, Elisha	135	Warren, James	158
Wallace, M. L	135	Williams, Chs	159
Wallick, J. E	135	Williams, Henry	159
Wilburn, Dan	135	Washington, Henry	159
Wall, Geo. W	136	Williams, Lum	159
Williams, C. M	138	Windling, ——	159
White, Henry	138	Watson, M	160
Wood County	140	Watkins, A	160

	PAGE
Ward, H. L.	161
Wallens, J. S.	161
Weeks, Fursen	162
Wallis, Frank P.	165
Williams, Jacob	166
Williams, Jake	166
White, James.	167
Walker, Nolan	167
Walker, James, alias Notton	167
Walker, Notton, alias James	167
Wallack, Julius	168
Wimberly, Ezekiel	168
Williams, Nat	162
Wilder, Chas	162
Wynn, P. W.	170
Woods, J. M.	170
Woods, S. W.	170
Walker, Geo	171
Wardlow, T. D.	171
Williams, Lewis	171
Whittington, Wm.	172
Wells, Bill.	172
Williams, Sam	172
Williams, John D.	172
White, Frank	173
Wild Harry, alias Bennis, Harry	169
Washington, Levi	164, 177
Wilkerson, Allen	173
White, Dr., murderer of	173
Wolf, Mrs., murderers of.	174
Washington, Alfred	174
Walters, A. W.	174
Woods, Alex	175
Wilson, John W.	175
Wells, Otho, murderers of	176
Williams, Sam	176
Wilson, Geo	176
Webb, Dr. J. S., murderers of	176
West, Solon	177
Wheat, ——, robbers of	177
Watkins, Clinton, murderer of	177
West, Robert	177

	PAGE
Walters, David	178
Williams, Thos. J	178
Woods, Jack, alias Gustine	173
Whitley, Nathan	175
Weekens, Tom, alias Adams	178

Y

	PAGE
Yeager, Frank	28
Young, Jno	32
Yerger, E. M.	35
Yoe, Gus	41
Young, James	49
Young, Moses, alias McIntosh	57
Young, Bob	60
Yates, Luke	67
Yates, Joseph	177, 69
Yarborough, E	69
Young, John	71
Yancey, Tom	94
Young, ——	94
York, Frank	97
Young, Wallace	90
Young, John	90
Young, Caleb	100
Yellow, Bill	103
Yarborough, Richard	107
Young, John	123
Yarbrough, Geo	130
Young, Frank	134
Yarbrough, Cela	142
Young County	153
Yeater, Henry	154
Yates, Joseph	161
Yarbrough, H. B.	176

Z

	PAGE
Zoozier, Ed	49
Zito, John	153
Zatopeck, Magdalen, murderers of	174

Solid gold suspension badge given to J.B. Gillett upon his
appointment as City Marshal of El Paso in June 1882.
Photo courtesy of the Texas Ranger Hall of Fame and Museum.

II.
Gillett's
Notebook

James B. Gillett, 1925. Photo from *Six Years with the Texas Rangers.*

Reward offered by Gov. Ark.

1873	Names	Crime	Where committed	Amt
"	Unknown	Murderers of Geo Herriott	Pope Co	$1.000
"	Jas E Murray	Horse Stealing	Grant "	200
"	Unknown	Attempted Murderers E.W. Dodson	Pope	$1.000
"	Jas Holland	Murder	Sebt "	200
"	Wm C Isbell	"	White "	200
"	Jno Armstrong	"	Sharp	200
"	Andrew Trellett	"	"	200
"	Gabriel Walker	"	Desha	200
"	Tom Armstrong	"	"	200
"	H. A. Timmons	Forgery	— —	200
"	Joseph Thompson	Murder	Sebt	200
"	O.C. Jones	Grand Larceny	Mississippi	200
"	Tom Morris	Murder	St. Francis	200
"	Unknown	assasinated Judge Mears	— —	500
"	Jno Richmond Jr			
"	Jack Richmond	Murder	Crawford	each 200
"	Lafayette Schultz			
"	Bud Morris			
"	C.C. Carlisle	"	Clark	200

Descriptions

Heighth	Age	Complexion	Eyes	Hair	Beard	Build	Wieght
5 ft 7		Dark	Black	Black	Scar on nose	Square	

1873	Names	Crime	Where Committed	Amt
"	Nick Baird	Murder	Hempstead	200
"	Geo McAntosh	"	Pulaski	200
"	A. J. Aiken	"	Sebastian	200
"	A. McClellan	"		200
"	Chas Bradley	"	Faulkner	200
"	Jno Arnold	"	Lawrence	200
"	Elias Williamson	"	Hempstead	200
"	E. O. Faghar	"	Drew	200
"	Jeff K. Jones	"	Faulkner	200
1874	Stokely D. Whaling	"	Arkansas	200 Each
"	Unknown	Robbing U.S. mail	Garland	500
"	J. B. Barnett	Rape	Hempstead	200
"	Barton D. Gillis	Murder	Hot Springs	200
"	W. H. Sauline	"	Jackson	200
"	Jno W. Fincher	attempting assassination	Nevada	200
"	Robt Robinson		Johnson	200
"	Wm Lewis	Murder	Lincoln	200
"	Jno Anderson	"	Faulkner	200
"	Jas H Scruggs	"	Izard	200

Hight	Age	Complex	Eyes	Hair	Beard	Build	Weight

1874	Names	Crime	Where Committed	Amt
1 "	Thos Williams	Murder	Faulkner	200
"	Cap Hammond	"	"	200
"	Tankersly	"	Clayton	200
"	E. D. Allison	accessary to	Montgomery	200
"	Henry Phillips	Murder	Pulaski	200
"	Jas Herschberger	Murder	— — —	200
"	Monroe Reeder	"	Desha	200
"	Steve Thetstone	"	Missississippi	200
"	Jno C Fair	"	"	200
"	Frank P Sanders	"	Ark	200
"	Leroy T. Davis	"	Phillips	200
"	Unknown	"	Scott	200
"	J. W. H. Daniels	"	Dorsey	200
"	Simeon Gill	"	Lincoln	200
"	Dan Austin	"	Pulaski	200
1875	Wood Miller	"	Crawford	200
"	Wm Sanders	"	Lonoke	200
"	Jas Crutcher	"	Jefferson	500
"	Geo Carlew	Grand Larceny	Woodruff	200

236

Hight	Age	Complex	Age	Eyes	Hair	Beard	Built	Wight
5 ft 6	25	Dark			Black			=17"
5 ft 6					Red			135

1875	Names	Crime	Where Committed	Amt
"	Jas Phillips	assault with intent to kill	Marion	200
"	Jno Anderson	Murder	Faulkner	300
"	Riley Thomas	"	Pike	300
"	Isaac Garner	Burglary	Calhoun	200
"	Geo. W. Lee	Murder	Pike	300
"	Elisha Blankenship	"	Izard	300
"	George Turpin	"	Ark	300
"	Andrew J Green	"	"	300
"	Wm King	"	"	300
"	Jas. T. Lyon			Each
"	Sam H Perkins	"	Sevier	500
"	Madison Vinson			
"	Wm Lewis	"	Lincoln	500
"	Jno McFadden	"	Johnson	200
"	Sam Osborne	"	Pope	300
"	Douglass Smith	"	Clark	300
"	Thos J Finch	"	Grant	300
"	Evans Moore	"	Pope	300
"	Alex Nelson Col xd	"	Woodruff	300

238

Height	Age	Complex	Eyes	Hair	Beard	Build	Weight
5 ft 3	25	Fair	Blue	Sandy			150
6 ft	32	Florid	Blue	Black		Erect	
5 ft 8	20 to 25	Dark	Dark	Dark		Stout	
5 ft 4	24		Black	Blues			
5 ft 7 or 8	18	Fair	Hazel	Light			130
5 ft 6	35		Gray	Dark Sandy		Heavy	160
5 ft 4	21	Dark	Large Black	Dark		Heavy	145
5 ft 8	22	Light	Blue				120
5 ft 8	25	Right eye out		Red	Red	Erect	145
5 ft 11	28		Large Gray	Dark Brown			150
5 ft 10	70	Florid				Heavy	170
5 ft 10	30	Dark	Dark	Dark	Dark		160
5 ft 8	25	Dark	Black	Black			140
5 ft 11	33	very Black					160

9 (1)

1875	Names	Crime	Where Committed	Amt
"	Thos. F. Galloway	Murder	Pope	300
"	J. R Snapp	accessary to murder	County	500
"	Jno Henry Sledge	Murder	"	500
"	Frank Hill			500
"	David Walls	Escaped Convict	State Penitentiary	500
"	Jas Walker	Murder	Miller	300
"	Jno Tate (cold)	Attempt to murder	Dorsey	500
"	Jno. Allen			
"	W. Allen	Releasing Prisoners	Washington	Each 500
"	Jarrett Trammell			
"	Juke Evans	Murder	Pulaski	500
"	Jas. M. Strader	"	St Francis	300
"	Bear Toter. Indian	"	Benton	200
"	Isaac H Jackson	"	St Francis	300
"	Unknown	"	Scott	500
	"	Desecrating Graves	Jefferson	500
1876	Pick en Benge (Indian)	Larceny	Crawford	300
"	Geo W Manes	Murder	Perry	500
"	Michael Ries (Dutch)	"	Miss	300

Height	Age	Complex	Eyes	Hair	Beard	Build	Weight
6 ft 1 in²	22		Dark	Dark		Slender	150 or 160
6 ft	25	Dark	Brown	Dark			170
5 ft 11	30	Light	Blue	Light			135
5 ft 7		Black					140
5 ft 10³	24	Dark	Black or Brown	Black		Slender	140
5 ft 7 or 8	20	Dark	Black	Black			
5 ft 11	25	Fair	Blue	Dark		Slender	
5 ft 10		Dark Brown					160
5 ft 6	25	Half Blood Cherokee					
5 ft 10	44	Sallow	Blue	Auburn	Red		150
6 ft	45	Red	Blue	Light	Red		170

"(1)

1876	Name	Crime	Where Committed	Amt
"	Chas. H. Britt (Negro)	Murder	Little River	300
"	Albert Trammell	"	Ouchita	100
"	Wm H. Pinckhard (Colored)	"	Dossey	300
"	Andrew Whitaker	"	Woodruff	300
"	J. K. Murphy	Horse Stealing	Lonoke	200
"	Virgis Nichols	Murder	Pope	300
"	Beaumont Brown	"	Carroll	300
"	Wm Henley	"	Sebastian	300
"	Pikens. T. Hill	"	Scott	300
"	Chill N Kerley	"	Stone	. 300
"	Jas. W. Martin	"	"	300
"	Newton Jones	"	Washington	500
"	Unknown	Firing upon Preachers	Pope	1000
"	"	murder Washington	Washington	500
"	Geo Green (cold)	Murder	Crawford	500
"	Chas E Ferry	"	Cross	500
"	Jesse Murphy	"	Little River	500
"	R. W. Holt	"	Jackson	300
1877	Henry Attebury	"	Boone	200

242

Height	Age	Compler	Eyes	Hair	Beard	Build	Weight
5 ft 7	21	Fair	Gray	Dark			130
5 ft 10	40	Dark Yellow				Compact Heavy	
5 ft 6	18		Blue	Dark			150
5 ft 10	30	Copper Color					
6 ft		Fair		Dark			175
5 ft 10	45	Dark		Black			150
5 ft 8	18		right eye out	Black Curly		Spare made	
5 ft 6	28					Square	130
5 ft 10	20			Light		Spare	
5 ft 8	33	Light		Light	Light		
5 ft 9	29	Fair	Gray	Sandy	Light Red		
5 ft 9	23	Fair	Blue	Light			140
5 ft 6	22	Dark Yellow					140
5 ft 6	22	Dark Yellow					155
5 ft 7		Dark		Black			130
5 ft 9	32	Light	Blue	Sandy	Sandy	Square	13"
5 ft 8	30		Blue	Light	Light		150

1877	Names	Crime	Where Committed	Amt
"	Wm Atterberry	Murder	Boone	200
"	Jno Cook	"	Jackson	500
"	Wm Kirk	"	St Francis	200
"	Chas McLain	Grand Larceny	Desha	100
"	John Skeen	Murder	Union	300
"	Wm "	"	"	300
"	Jake Riley	"	"	300
"	W W Lessens	"	"	300
"	Wm Dunkan	"	Green	200
"	Martin Vowell	"	"	200
"	Andrew Jackson	Robbery	Clay	200
"	Thos Purnell			
"	Frank Dill			
"	Jno Skeen	Murder	Union	Each 1000
"	Wm "			
"	Jake Kelley			
"	W W Lessens			
"	Unknown	Burning Court House	Crawford	500

Heighth	Age	Complexion	Eyes	Hair	Beard	Build	Wight
5 ft 10	26		Blue	Light		Heavy	170
5 ft 8	26	Fair	Gray	Light Sandy	Sandy	Spare	
5 ft 8	23	Dark	Brown	Black			140
6 ft 1		Dark	Dark Hazel	Black	Black		150
5 ft 5		Light	Light Blue	Light	Sandy	Heavy	144
5 ft 10			Blue	Light		Stout	170

1877	Names	Crime	Where Committed	Amt
"	Elias Langhorn			Each
"	L. E. Thomas	Murder	Ark	200
"	L. C. Thetford Jr			
"	Price Marshall (Noel)	"	Bradley	200
"	Riley Covington	"	Miss	25"
"	W. J. Armstrong	"	Lee	200
"	Dock Stein	Theft	Nevada	25"
"	Henry Edwards	Murder	White	200
"	Tarner Clark	"	Pope	200
"	Wm Kendricks	"	Phillips	15"
"	Robt Burton	"	Miss	200
"	Wm Johnson (Cold)	"	Chicot	2"
"	A W Lawson	Escaped Jail	Cross	200
"	Wm E Murray	"	Grant	2"
"	Jessie Harris	Murder	Sebb	2"
"	Dudley L Sloan	"	Miller	200
"	Jno Summers	"	Miss	200
1878	Joseph Davis	"	Randolph	200
"	Marcus Whitley	"	"	2"

Height	Age	Complexion	Eyes	Hair	Beard	Build	Weight &c.
6 ft	30	Dark	Dark	Dark			155
6 ft	21	Dark	Dark	Dark			140
5 ft 10	23	Black Negro	White				170
6 ft		Light					170
5 ft 6	30	Swarthy	Gray	Dark			135
5 ft 8	5'11		Dark	Black			
	25	Dark Brown				Chunky	
5 ft 6	26		Blue	Sandy		Square	130
6 ft	35	Fair	Blue	Auburn	Auburn		170

1878	Names	Crime	Where Committed	Amt
"	Joseph Kemp	Murder	Independence	15"
"	N. Milam (Cold)	Assts to Kill Escaped	Washington	150
"	Hardy Williams	Jail	Chicot	200
"	Geo. W. Jones	Murder	Scott	200
"	— Cochrane	"	"	200
"	Harper	"	"	200
"	Horse	"	"	200
"	Jas Collins	Neft Horse	Ark	15"
"	Jas Glenn	Attempt to Murder	Howard	15"
"	Jno Fitz Patrick	— — —	"	15"
"	Obe Chism	Rape	Conway	200

Descriptions

Height	Age	Complexion	Eyes	Hair	Beard	Build	Weight
5 ft 10	35	Dark	Sc.		Dark		
6 ft 3	30	Dark Brown	Scarred & weight	Heavy		Slender	160
5 ft 8		Florid		Brown	Sandy	Heavy	160
5 ft 10	28 to 30	Florid	Blue	Auburn			

Rewards from Kansas

James Coats comp light
Blue eyes light hair mustash
and Chin whiskers 5 ft 10 high
25 or 30 yers old. $300 Reward
Riley Co Nov 27. 1869
H. P.
H. P. Johnston Dark Complect
scar under right Eye dark
hair Brown mustash brown
whiskers. 6 ft high 35 or 40
yers old Reward $500 murder
Mitchell Co. aug 30th 1871

John S Vanepps fair comp
fair build Mediam gray Eyes
and hair 5 ft 11. 55 yers old
reward $300. Murder Cheroke
Co, July 21. 1893

John Scott alias Scotty
built strongly gray eyes
brown hair 5x8½. 28 years
old Reward $500 Murder
Ford Co. July 21. 1873

Willis Jackson dark comp
well built eyes and hair
black & higth 6ft 1 $500 Reward
on con. Murder Summer Co.
Aug 21. 1873

Hezekiar Williams dark
com. Slender built black
eyes and hair 6ft high
$500 on con Summer Co.
Murder aug 21. 1873

J. J. Elkins dark comp
darks eyes black hair
mustash dark no beard 5/19
$500 on con. Sumner Co.
murder aug 24, 1873

John Clayton jail braker
Washington Co. Reward $300
Dec 26, 1873

Thomas T. Rucker Slight
build small black eyes
light brown hair light brown must
5 ft 11. 25 years old $300 Reward on
con. murder Chorley Co. Feb 8th
1874

Boliver Ware alias J. A. Morgan
500 Reward Shawnee Co. con,
May 11th 1874

John Morrissey blue eyes
dark hair and mustash and
chin whiskers 5ft 9. 28 yers old
Reward $500 Murder Donleon
Co. Apr 7, 1875

Millard. F. Eaton. $500 Reward
Murder Lincoln Co. May 3rd, 1875

Jacob Meek $300 Jail braker
Ellis Co. Feb 8. 1876

Robspene Mills $300 Reward
Jail brakers Ellis Co. Feb 4th
1876
Bob Lancaster thick build
hair and mustash light 5ft ½
$500 reward att to kill Rusk Co
corn July 12, 1876

Sam Lappin Jail traker
Shanee Co. July 12, 1876. Reward
$500 dol

Dan Hensen alias Cherokee
$500 reward. Comanchie Co
Murder Nov 22, 1877

Fugitives from North Car

Patton Shape. Cherokee Co
Murder Reward $400. Aug 1871

William Haney Yancy Co
Murder Reward $400 Aug 1871

Luke Johnston. Nash County
Murder Sep 1871. $400 Reward
Eyes between brown and black
Large neck Small head ears
small high Forehead. 175 lbs

Adolphus. E. Stuart. Catawba Co
murder Reward $400. higth 5ft
Small Statue dark hair heavy
dark eyes brows dark beard
25 or 30 old. 140 lbs wide mouth
opens wide may 12 1873

Wm Bragg. Franklin Co murder
Reward $300 Carpenter and
wheelright 50 years old light
sandy hair scar on fore head
between eyes drunkard
com. July 25, 1873

R. A. Owens alias Jankins
Gaston Co murder Reward $400
25 years old 6ft high 165 lbs fair
com. dark hair blue eyes long
nose when he smiles a
wrinkle runs across twards
his ear Oct 1873

Henry Dickson
Green Co. murder $400 Reward
Ginger bread color 21 to 22
5ft 11 weight 160 lbs small mouth
Showes teeth when talking
Sep 23, 1873

$500 Reward
Charles E Ferry. murdered
David Redmond at White
burg Ark Dec 10th 1876
5ft 8 high 23 years old Smothe
hazle Eyes light hair slender
form Printer In Texas Driving
cattle

Reward from Mississippi
Horace Yates. Hinds Co $500

$5.000 Reward

Will be paid by the undersign
for the arrest and delivery of
Jackson. C. Bishop who
murdered Jacob Snider a banker
at Georgetown Colarado May
20th 1875 Discription. Bishop
is 39 years old 6 ft high weight
200 lbs raw boned well built
fair comp Considerbly tanned
from Exposure Sandy beard
generaly all over face heavy
brown mustash large light
blue eyes of a mild character
showing some white Roman
nose. large hands dark hair
walks stooped Shourldered thin
lips and compressed Smokes and
drinks when drinking is
Inclined to become bistrous
has full knolledge of mineing

operations has parents living
in Jackson County Mo near
Kansas Citty has a brother
living their and at George
Town Colarado and one in
Loneover County Calafornia
near Healsburg also relations
living near Carson City Nev
and Manhatten Kansas
Married a lady from Morris
town East Tenn near Knoxville
They are now temporally apart
She either living at Manhatten
or Morristown She has too
small children He will no
doutt try to carry on a ~~corre~~
Corispondance with some of the
above paries address ~~DJ~~

D. J. C

this reward stans good for 10
years

$500.00 Reward

The above Reward will be
given to any person who
will deliver to the Sheriff of
of Taylor County or confine
have him confined in any
in the State of Texas

Tom Walker

charged with assault to Kill
on the body of J W Carter

Discription — 24 or 26
years old About 5 ft 11 inches
high weighs 165 or 170 pounds
light complexion blue eyes
black hair (some gray in hair)
quick spoken but stammers
in spech clean shaved

W. A. Grounds
Buffalo Gap Tex
his farther Joe Walker lives in
Mc Mullin Co on Frio Creek

below Tildon Has a brother
William Walker alias ___ living in
same Co. He stands straight
steps firm is lightning
with a pistol

$1600 Reward
Curt Remington who assassinated
Chas Nachtrieb is twenty years old
about five feet ___ ___ in height
weighs about one hundred fifty
pounds, rather spare and smooth faced
and inclined to be red faced with
prominent cheek bones, and large
straight mouth and pretty even teeth
light short hair large ___ ___ a pleasant
boyish look has large hands and wears
number six boots, fond of ___
hot drinks very little does not use
tobaco when walking ___ ___ ___ ___ very
and carelessly with his head erect

is rather hard of hearing and always
has to the second time before under=
standing, has a low drawling way
of speaking, always smiles when
talking and is fond of company.
Has been in Colorado three years
is from Michigan.

The above reward is offered for
Goldberg & Pennington at Lead=
ville Colorado.

The sums for his apprehension are as
follows:

State of Colorado $510 Chaffee Co
$500, Mrs Nachtrieb $500, H. A. W.
Tabor $100, A. W. Weston $25. W. H.
Jones $25, Wood Bros. $25. Hiller
Hallock & Co. $20. P. F. Burr $20
and others $35.

   L. E. Tucker
   Sheriff Lake Co Colorado

Stetehens Co.

~~Bexar Co.~~ 1(4)

Jno A Hill. Murder.

78 yrs. old 5 ft 10 inches high Spare made
Sharp face. Dark hair Black whiskers
and mustache Scar on face near mouth
right side very dim. Blk eyes. wild look
about eyes. $100ᵒᵒ reward by friends of
Smith.

Bexar Co.

Jno Lanham. Murder.

21 yrs. old. 5 ft 7 inches high. 135 lbs.
fair complexion grey eyes light hair
large nose. smooth face. is an actor
in low negro character. talks somewhat
in that style. raised in Houston where
his mother now lives.

Fayette Co.

Jno. D. Hunt. Murder.

36 or 8 yrs old Grey eyes staring look
light hair. Turning bald headed
red mustache & Beard if not shaven
150 lbs 5 feet 8 inches high quick
spoken smokes a great deal florid
complexion

Milam Co.
Tom Walker. Murder.
20 years old 5 feet 4 or 5 inches
high. high cheek bones small
blue eyes Black hair smooth
face talks fast, very profane

Sam Bass
25 or 26 years old 5 feet 7 in high
black hair dark brown eyes brown
mustash large white teeth shows
them when talking. has very
little to say.

Henry Underwood
35 yes 5 ft 10 in weight 160 dark
hair brown whiskers dark complec
dark eyes pretty keen active
fellow

Frank Jackson
22 years old 6 ft high slender
spair maid keen and active
dark swarthy compx black curley hair
blue or gray eyes smoothe face

Jack Davis   3 (4)

28 or 9 years old 5 ft 11 in high
weight 185 lbs dark complextion
dark auburn curley hair heavy dark
mustache hazel eyes very thick
under lip walks slow generly goes
with his hands in his pockets
~ his real name is suppose
to be Ike Berry Brother to Jim
Berry one of the robbers that was
killed at Mexico Misouria Oct
1878,

JAMES F. COLLINS,

Twenty-eight years old, about 5 feet 11 inches high, dark hair, heavy eyebrows, which meet in center and extend downward on nose, slender build, weight about 140 lbs., good penman, rather ornamental.

Was Agent of this Company and of the Pittsburg, Cincinnati & St. Louis Railway Company, at Cadiz, Ohio, absconded in latter part of December. Stole a ticket to New Orleans, which may have been used or sold. Has a brother a railroad conductor, running from Tucson, Arizona.

Decamped with the funds of this Company and of the Railroad Company, and is also believed to have added forgery to his crimes.

It is our information that he also swindled his parents, and defrauded a sister of money sent for her support.

A liberal reward will be paid for his apprehension.

Communications may be addressed to any Agent of this Company, to be sent to the undersigned.

THE ADAMS EXPRESS COMPANY,

By L. C. WEIR, Manager.

Cincinnati, January 10, 1885.

SOUTHERN PACIFIC.

PASS *Mr. J. B. Gillette* *Sheriff*

Complimentary

On conditions, and between stations named, of lines specified on back until *Dec 31.* 1892, unless otherwise ordered.

No. *2202*   *J. Kruttschnitt*

GENERAL MANAGER.

This Ticket is good between *San Antonio* and *El Paso* on following lines :

Cal., Harrisburg & San Ant. Ry.   New York, Texas & Mexican Ry.
Gulf, Western Texas & Pacific Ry.

Is not transferable, and the person receiving and using it assumes all risk of accident, and especially agrees that the above Companies shall not be liable under any circumstances, whether by negligence of their agents, or otherwise, for any personal injury, or for any loss or injury to his property and in using this ticket, he will not hold any of the above Companies liable as common carriers.

Revocable at pleasure, and not good for passage unless signed in ink by person whose name appears on face. If presented by any other conductor must take up and collect fare.

(Sign here) *J. B. Gillett,*

S D CHILDS & CO

James B. Gillett

Marfa, Texas

Jas. B. Gillett

Alpine, Texas

$5o REWARD!

Will be paid for Jim Thompson, stage driver, for theft of $100 money, mule and other property. He has lived in Seguin, Austin and other places in this state; his occupation was usually stage and hack driver. About 30 years old, black hair and eyes—hair inclined to curl—small nose and features, dark complexion, weighs about 135 pounds. He was last seen at Pena Colorado, near Fort Davis. I will pay the above reward for his capture.

JOHN F. FOGG,
Brackett, Texas.

$100 REWARD FOR B. F. GILLETT.

He is about 5 feet 6 inches high; weighs about 160 pounds; is about 26 years old; has black hair, large black eyes, showing much of the white part of the eyes; has ruddy cheeks and small chin, a large nose, a little curved. His left arm has been broken, but it would not be noticed unless he holds it up straight; then shows deformed and crooked. Has broad, square shoulders, and, when walking, stoops forward a little and draws his shoulders up nearly to the tops of his ears. Worked for a lumber firm in Oregon for a year or two, and has selling lumber for the undersigned for the past year.

Arrest him for embezzlement, hold in jail and telegraph

ELLIOTT & ROE,
Fort Worth, Texas.

Fort Worth, Texas, January 12, 1883.

DESCRIPTION
OF
Hosey King
ALIAS

Taken _Nov 14th, 1889_
Residence: _Lincoln Co. Ark._
Legitimate occupation: _Tin Boy_
Criminal occupation: _Murder_
Nationality: _American_
Age: _33 yrs_; Height: _5 ft 11 in_
Weight: _145 lbs_; Build: _Stout_
Complexion: _Light_
Eyes: _Blue_
Color of hair: _Sandy_
Color of beard: _Blond but Dyed_
Style of beard: _Moustache_
Peculiarities of build or feature, scars,
marks, &c: _Index finger_
on one hand crooked and
perished to first joint
and very Red.

REMARKS:
Has an Uncle in Texas
by name of Hick King
said to be wealthy

(Signed:) _____

ED. 9—15—'81—1,000]

Wire W. W. Wills,
Ticket agent at Lincoln
Co. Ark. Nov 14th/89

Fifteen Hundred Dollars
reward offered for the
Arrest and Delivery to
Sheff of Lincoln Co. Ark.

Detectives traced him to
Texas and think he will
make his way to Mexico
by way of El Paso. They
are now looking for him
now.

J. M. Farmer
City Marshal
Fort Worth
Texas

_P.S._
Reward is for him
Dead or Alive.

$500 REWARD !

I will pay the above reward for the arrest and delivery to me, at Uvalde, of Pancho Rodrigues, the Mexican who murdered Koellmann and Stein on the west prong of Nueces, in Uvalde Co., Dec. 28, '84. He is described about as follows: Five feet, 10 inches high, weight 150 or 160 pounds, age 28, face full and slightly scarred by small pox, with small scar or mole on left jaw. He robbed the murdered men of a gray overcoat, with plaid lining, torn at bottom, a Mexican straw sombrero, with roll band and considerably worn, a pair congress gaiters, No. 6, both heels slightly turned outward, a dark coat and vest, with binding, small stripe lengthwise the cloth, both handmade, a pair of dark pants, slightly worn, worth about $6, a pair of light pants, worth about $5, a silver watch, open face, with large brass chain, a large plain gold ring, worth about $12, K. of H. badge, one octagon barrel Kennedy rifle.

H. W. BAYLOR,
Sheriff Uvalde Co.
Uvalde, Jan. 28, '85.

$100.00 REWARD!

I will pay, for the capture and delivery to me in any jail in the State of Texas, the above reward for one D. A., or Al Freeman and John Whaley who broke jail and escaped on the morning of the 27th of December 1882. Al Freeman is about 23 years old, about 5 feet 10 inches high, sallow complexion, has very little beard, keeps clean shaved, wore an old blue suit, a shopmade No. 6 boot, is a blacksmith; a painter and a gambler and will frequent gambling and assignation houses. Whaley is 23 or 24 years old, weighs about 150 lbs., 5 feet high, black mustache, no beard, wears a fine calf, shop-made, sewed boot with morocco tops. I will pay fifty dollars for either.

Addres JOHN T. INGRAM, Sheriff,
Seymour, Baylor county, Texas.

MURDER.

GEORGE DURHAM, charged with murder. Is about 6 feet high, weighs about 175 pounds, light complexion, blue eyes, sharp features, raw-boned, very high cheek bones, about 30 years of age, not talkative, but a close watcher and observer, one upper front tooth broken off, light mustache, no side whiskers, and chin clean shaven. Last seen riding an iron gray horse, having a red saddle and red saddle blanket. Durham has a loafing, easy, slouchy, sleepy gait.

A. J. BECK,
Deputy Sheriff, Terrell, Kaufman County.

ARREST JAMES BUCHANAN.

Twenty-seven years old, 135 pounds, slender built, black hair, small, thin black mustache, SMALL GRAY OR BLUE EYES, NO LASHES, EYE-LIDS RED, AS IF SORE. Has been shot in the right thigh. Gambles and frequents saloons. Is a desperate man. Dresses neatly. When last seen was riding bay horse, snip on nose, 14 or 15 hands high, branded V on left shoulder, has been cut with barbed wire under the throat latch. Address

W. T. HARRIS, Sheriff,
Waco, McLennan County, Texas.

$2000 REWARD

I will pay Two Thousand Dollars Reward for TOM BURGESS, dead or alive, who foully murdered J. C. McADA on the night of the 20th instant, in Karnes County, Texas. BURGESS is about 6 feet high, weighs about 180 pounds; thin whiskers, his finger next to his little finger on his right hand is the longest finger on his hand, he is a little inclined to be round shouldered, rough spoken.

D. A. T. WALTON,
Sheriff Bee Co. Texas.

BEEVILLE, TEXAS, May 21, 1884.

$1000. ONE THOUSAND DOLLARS REWARD! $1000.

GEORGE C. LEWIS, the absconding Treasurer of Palo Pinto County Texas, who left with some $6000.00 of County money, on July, 2nd, 1884; is about 5 feet 4 inches high, weighs about 130 pounds, 36 years old, light, but rather sallow complected, ha blue eyes, light hair, mustache and chin-whiskers; is slightly stoop shouldered, has a scrofulous scar under his right jaw and has a cupped scar on his temple; is of a restless and mercurial temperament, and as seldom still as a chained bear. He walks with a loose, swinging, but quick gait, head inclined forward and eyes downcast, often abruptly raising his head and looking around, but again quickly resuming his downcast atitude; is very talkative, and speaks rather loud, and frequently preludes his remarks with a dry, harsh, hacking laugh, and frequently strokes or pulls his beard, specially his chin-whiskers.

When he went away he wore black pants and a navy blue coat, and he habitually wears a gold or gold plated vest chain of the pattern of the brass chains used in Post Offices to fasten the mail-pouch keys to the desks.

He was last seen, July, 3rd, on the train about fifty miles from Ft. Worth, going in the direction of St. Louis; and as his mother resides at, or near Philadhlpeia, he may probably go there. Her name is Elizabeth A. Lewis.

The above reward, $500. by Palo Pinto County, and $500. by the sureties on his bonds as Treasurer, *and a commission of ten per cent on all money found in his possession,* and returned to us, will be paid for his delivery inside the jail door of Palo Pinto County Texas.

J. H. Baker,	D. L. Cunningham,
J. C. McQuerry,	C. C. Corbin,
F. J. White.	Joel McKee.
	Sureties on Bonds.

[Order of Commissioners' Court.]
Thursday, July 10th, 1884

It is ordered by the Court, that a reward of Five Hundred Dollars, be, and the same is herby offered for the arrest and delivery of GEO. C. LEWIS, Ex County Treasurer of Palo Pinto County, in the county jail of said Palo Pinto County; to be paid to the party making said arrest and delivery. To be paid out of the General Fund.

I hereby certify that the forogoing is a true copy of the original order on the minutes of the County Commissioners' Court.

J. H. Baker,
Clerk, Co. Court, P. P. Co.

NEWS Job Office Print, Palo Pinto, Texas.

Form No. 1.

THE WESTERN UNION TELEGRAPH COMPANY. 17

This Company TRANSMITS and DELIVERS messages only on conditions limiting its liability, which have been assented to by the sender of the following message. Errors can be guarded against only by repeating a message back to the sending station for comparison, and the company will not hold itself liable for errors or delays in transmission or delivery of Unrepeated Messages, beyond the amount of tolls paid thereon, nor in any case where the claim is not presented in writing within sixty days after sending the message.

This is an UNREPEATED MESSAGE, and is delivered by request of the sender, under the conditions named above.

THOS. T. ECKERT, General Manager. NORVIN GREEN, President.

NUMBER	SENT BY	REC'D BY	CHECK	

Received at El Paso Tex. 2.43 p May 9th 1883

Dated Eagle Pass Tex

To Jno Gillett City Marshel

Arrest Clay Dryer charged with murder bring
him here immediate at my expense if
not in El Paso get him if you
Can liberal reward will be paid for
him answer what your can do —   A Oglesby
Sheriff —

Index
to the James Gillett notebook

Aiken, A.J., 233
Allen, Jno., 239
Allen, W., 239
Allison, E.D., 235
Anderson, Jno., 237
Anderson, Jno. O., 233
Armstrong, Jno., 231
Armstrong, Tour, 231
Armstrong, W.J., 245
Arnold, Jno., 233
Arterberry, Henry, 241
Arterberry, Wm., 243
Austin, Dan, 245

Baird, Nick, 233
Barness, J.B., 233
Bass, Sam, 262
Bear Toter (Indian), 239
Berry, Ike, 263
Berry, Jim, 263
Bishop, Jackson C., 256
Blankenship, Elisha, 237
Bradley, Chas., 233
Bragg, Wm., 254
Britt, Chas. H., 241
Brown, Beaumont, 241
Buchanan, James, 270
Burgess, Tom, 270
Burton, Robert, 245

Carlisle, C.C., 231
Carter, J.W., 258
Chism, Obe, 247
Clark, Turner, 245
Clayton, John, 251
Coats, James, 249
Cochrane,___, 247
Collins, Jas., 247,264
Cook, Jno., 243

Covington, Riley, 245
Crutcher, Jas., 235
Curbun, Geo., 235

Daniels, J.W.H., 235
Davis, Jack, 263
Davis, Joseph, 245
Davis, Leroy T., 235
Dickson, Henry, 255
Dill, Frank, 243
Dunkan, Wm., 243
Durham, George, 270

Edwards, Henry, 245
Elkins, J.J., 251
Evans, Juke, 239

Faghar, E.Q., 233
Fair, Jno. C., 235
Ferry, Chas. E., 241, 255
Finch, Thos. J., 237
Fincher, Jno. W., 233
Fitzpatrick, Jno., 247
Fogg, John F., 267
Freeman, D.A. (Al), 269

Galloway, Thos. F., 239
Garner, Isaac, 237
Gill, Simeon, 235
Gillett, B.F., 267
Gillis, Barton D., 233
Glenn, Jas., 247
Green, Andrew J., 237
Green, George, 241
Grounds, W.A., 258

Hammond, Cap, 235
Haney, William, 253
Harper,___, 247

Harris, Jessie, 245
Henley, Wm., 241
Hensen, Dan, 253
Herschberger, Jas., 235
Hill, Frank, 239
Hill, Jno. A., 261
Hill, Pikens T., 241
Holland, Jas., 231
Holt, R.T., 241
Horse,___, 247
Hunt, Jno. D., 261

Isbell, Wm. C., 231

Jackson, Andrew, 243
Jackson, Frank, 262
Jackson, Willie, 250
Jankins,___, 254
Jenkins, Isaac H., 239
Johnson, Wm., 245
Johnston, H.P., 249
Johnston, Luke, 253
Jones, Geo. W., 247
Jones, Jeff K., 233
Jones, Newton, 241
Jones, O.C., 231

Kelley, Jake, 243
Kemp, Joseph, 247
Kendricks, Wm., 245
Kerley, Chill N., 241
King, Horsey, 268
King, Wm., 237
Kirk, Wm., 243

Lancaster, Bob, 252
Lanham, Jno., 261
Langhorn, Elias, 245
Lappin, Sam, 253

Lawson, A.W., 245
Lee, Geo. W., 237
Lesseur, W.W., 243
Lewis, George C., 271
Lewis, Wm., 233, 237
Lyon, Jas. T., 237

McClellan, A., 233
McFadden, Jno., 237
McIntosh, Geo., 233
McLain, Chas., 243
Manes, Geo. W., 239
Marshall, Price, 245
Martin, James W., 241
Meek, Jacob, 252
Milam, T.F., 247
Millard, F. Eaton, 252
Miller, Wood, 235
Mills, Robspiere, 252
Moore, Enaus, 237
Morgan, J.A., 251
Morris, Buck, 231
Morris, Tour, 231
Morrissey, John, 252
Murphy, J.K., 241
Murphy, Jesse, 241
Murray, James E., 231
Murray, Wm. E., 245

Nachtrieb, Chas., 259
Nelson, Alex, 237
Nichols, Virgis, 241

Osborne, Sam, 237
Owens, R.A., 254

Perkins, Sam H., 237
Phillips, Henry, 235

Phillips, James, 237
Picken Beuge (Indian),
    239
Pinckhard, Wm. H., 241
Purnell, Thos., 243

Redmond, David, 255
Reeder, Monroe, 235
Remington, B., 259
Richmond, Jack, 231
Richmond, Jr., Jno., 231
Ries, Michael, 239
Riley, Jake, 243
Robinson, Robt., 233
Rodriguez, Pancho, 269
Rucker, Thomas T., 251

Sanders, Frank P., 235
Sanders, Wm., 235
Sanline, W.W., 233
Shafe, Patton, 253
Skien, Jno., 243
Skien, Wm., 243
Schultz, Lafayette, 231
Scott, John "Scotty", 250
Skeen, John, 243
Skeen, Wm., 243
Skein, Dock, 245
Sledge, John Henry, 239
Sloan, Dudley L., 245
Smith, Douglas, 237
Snapp, J.R., 239
Snider, Jacob, 256
Staggs, Jas. H., 233
Strader, Jas. M., 239
Stuart, Adolphus E., 254
Summers, Jno., 245

Tankersly, 235
Tate, Jno., 239
Thetford, L.C., 245
Thetstone, Steve, 235
Thomas, L.E., 245
Thomas, Riley, 237
Thompson, Joseph, 231
Timmons, H.A., 231
Tramwell, Albert, 241
Tramwell, Jerry W., 239
Trellish, Andrew, 231
Tucker, L.R. (sheriff),
    260
Turpin, George, 237

Underwood, Henry, 262

Vanepps, John S., 249
Vinson, Madison, 237
Vowell, Martin, 243

Walker, Gabriel, 231
Walker, Jas., 239
Walker, Joe, 258
Walker, Tom, 258, 262
Walker, William, 259
Walls, David, 239
Ware, Bolivar, 251
Whaling, Stokely D., 233
Whitley, Marcus, 245
Whittaker, Andrew, 241
Williams, Hardy, 247
Williams, Hezekiah, 250
Williams, Thos., 235
Williamson, Elias, 233

Yates, Horace, 255